CAFE CHIMES COOKBOOK

To order, contact
CHASE PUBLISHING
A Division of A.C. Chase Associates LLC
P.O. Box 1200, Glen, NH 03838
Tel: 603-383-4166 Fax: 603-383-8162
e-mail: achase@chasepublishing.com
http://www.chasepublishing.com

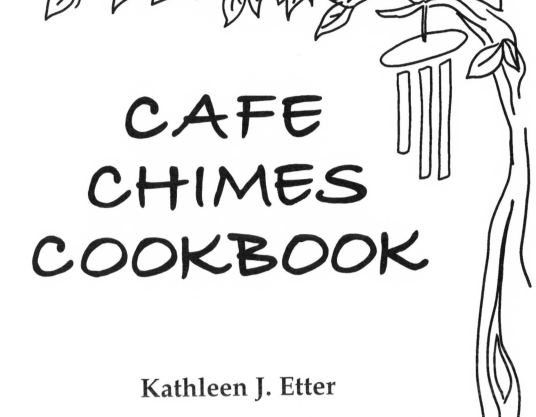

CAFE CHIMES COOKBOOK

Kathleen J. Etter

Illustrated by Shana Myers

CHASE PUBLISHING

CAFE CHIMES COOKBOOK

Copyright ©2000 by Anne C. Chase

Cover and Text Illustrations by Shana Myers
Book Design by Peg Grondin of Snow Pond

Library of Congress Catalog Card Number: 97-66909

ISBN: 0-9629651-2-X

First Edition
10 9 8 7 6 5 4 3 2 1

To order, contact
CHASE PUBLISHING
A Division of A.C. Chase Associates LLC
P.O. Box 1200, Glen, NH 03838
Tel: 603-383-4166 Fax: 603-383-8162
e-mail: achase@chasepublishing.com
http://www.chasepublishing.com

for Beau
for René
for Dane
with all my love forever

Foreword

*"So much has been given to me
I have no time to ponder over
That which has been denied."*

Helen Keller

This cookbook is a love story—love of food, love of community, and the love of its creator, Kathy Etter. Kathy died on April 19, 1998, at the age of 47, at the crown of a life lived with enthusiasm equaled by few people I know.

Kathy was a special friend, and we shared many mutual interests: healthy food, gardening, chocolate chip cookies, and a deep desire to nurture and support our community. Whether eating at the Cafe, taking one of Kathy's cooking classes, listening to her live radio spots, discussing her illness, reading her weekly newspaper columns, talking to her about this book, or collaborating with her on various community projects, I loved and admired the contagious energy and passion with which she approached her life.

Kathy accepted her health challenge with her characteristically positive attitude and a desire to learn and share from the experience. When hundreds of people gathered at a community benefit for Kathy and later at the community ceremony that followed her death, I was taken with the diversity and the number of people Kathy had touched in her far-too-short life. Truly the Power of One. I miss the companionship of that vibrant and energizing spirit.

The *Cafe Chimes Cookbook* is a natural evolution for Cafe Chimes, the vegetarian restaurant which Kathy Etter founded in 1990. Kathy believed that eating was one of life's great pleasures.

She also believed just as strongly in the process of creating and serving food—that in that passage lay an intrinsically important link of human connection to the source of food, the creation of food and the love and energy by which it was passed to the recipient. It is that spiritual connection that she wished to reflect in this cookbook. It is my hope that this book will provide an insight into Kathy's creative soul as well as a fun and inspiring culinary adventure.

David Brooks

Acknowledgments

This book began as a joyful collaboration between friends and colleagues. I was new to the community and eager to find a 'local' project for my small publishing company. Shana Myers, our illustrator, was fostering a burgeoning massage therapy practice, but yearned to practice her formidable artistic skills, and Kathy Etter had the dream of a cookbook that would truly express her love of wholesome food and the creative spirit of whole foods cooking.

In the midst of assembling the book, the unthinkable happened. Vibrant, sparkling Kathy was diagnosed with a virulent form of lung cancer. The community turned out to support her search for a healing path. Her friends surrounded her and her young sons with comfort and support. Her household ran, food appeared, Kathy was never alone. Surrounded by loving friends and family, Kathy died less than six months after her diagnosis.

During her illness, Kathy was unable to work on the cookbook. Shana and I continued the work and promised Kathy shortly before her death that the book would really happen. We saw the project as a way of keeping Kathy's indomitable spirit alive in this community and beyond its borders.

When Kathy died in April of 1998, we were left with a half-finished manuscript and our promise to Kathy. Then the true miracle began. Friends of Kathy, members of the community, employees of Cafe Chimes, former Cooking School attendees came forward to help. Kathy was a natural cook, not a recipe writer, so I moved from the role of editor and publisher to take on the considerable task of testing and formatting the recipes and writing the instructions. Kathy's recipes were designed for a crowd, not for an average family, so we found that every recipe needed scaling for home use.

When we first started the project, Kathy and I agreed that our goal was to present carefully-measured basic recipes that would work for the novice cook and still serve as a delightful springboard for the more adventurous, experienced cook. Kathy was an intuitive, creative cook who chafed at the idea of tight measurements for ingredients. She really wanted to foster creativity and individuality in cooking. Our challenge, after Kathy's death, was to preserve her free and spirited approach to cooking, while presenting clear and usable recipes for all cooks.

Without the generous gift of time and support from Kathy's many friends and colleagues, this book would never have reached completion. I have so many people to thank, not only for their practical assistance in testing recipes, but for their encouragement to continue the project which was quite daunting after Kathy's death. So many people helped! I owe a special debt of gratitude to my loving and patient husband, Ron Zager, who used his considerable skills as a bread baker to adapt Kathy's famous bread recipes for the home kitchen. In addition to baking endless loaves of bread, Ron chopped, sculled, and tolerated months of meals consisting solely of Cafe Chimes recipes. Elsa Steffanson, who served as Kathy's chef for many years, was an invaluable ally in testing recipes that we had in hand and in contributing additional recipes to those sections of the book that Kathy had left unfinished. In addition to Elsa, a group of Cafe Chimes employees, past and present, met regularly with me to assist with recipe selection and testing. This wonderful group of people included Ruth Malcolm, Kate Gavora and Bob Mantyla, Luci Gatchell, Patti Brown, and Laura Sorenson. Former Cafe Chimes Cooking Class students, Sara Jane Corson, my daughter-in-law Nancy Ritger, and Suzanne Felber tested many recipes and helped immensely because of their enthusiasm and past experience with Kathy's approach to cooking. Sara Jane Corson, also a skilled baker, collaborated with my husband in the difficult translation of the bread recipes for the home kitchen. A close personal friend of Kathy's, Cynthia Atkinson, devoted some of her very limited time to helping test and evaluate several recipes during the time that she was also helping care for Kathy.

During the long testing period, we met regularly with the Cafe Chimes group at Shalimar, a wonderful Indian restaurant in North Conway. The owners of Shalimar, Dhanwant Singh and Avtar Singh welcomed us graciously and allowed us to linger over many cups of tea while we discussed recipes. We are grateful for their hospitality and support.

Other members of the community stood by us during the entire process of completing the book. David Brooks, Director of the Children's Health Center in North Conway and a tireless leader in community projects, wrote the moving Foreword to the book and offered his help and encouragement for the duration of the project.

Elsa Steffanson, in addition to her role as recipe advisor and tester, wrote the Vegetarian Kitchen chapter of this book. The chapter contains information on how to set up a vegetarian kitchen and includes Elsa's memories of working with Kathy over the years.

At the time of Kathy's death, there was an outpouring of loving tribute from her friends, colleagues, and members of the community. We have included some poetry and reminiscences in the last chapter of this book, and we are grateful to those authors who have allowed us to use their work. Kathy's friend, Braden McKenzie, contributed several of his poems, as did Jay Rancourt and Rob Richardson. Alex Levin, who wrote a wonderful column in tribute to Kathy, allowed us to use his work in this book. Kathy's longtime friends, Anika Brand Hastings, Cynthia Atkinson, and Diane Johnson contributed their thoughts to this chapter in addition to providing missing background information on Kathy's early life in the Mount Washington Valley. Lastly, we thank Kathy's son, Beau for sharing memories of his mother.

I have been privileged to work with Shana Myers, our illustrator. Her free-spirited drawings adorn the cover and many pages of this book—capturing the essence of Kathy and her Cafe Chimes. We were also fortunate to have the talents of Peg Grondin in the design and production process. Her good eye, patience, and outstanding design skills have contributed enormously to the final appearance of the book. We thank Carolyn Brown, a local photographer, for taking several of the photographs that appear in this book. Her contribution is appreciated. We would also like to thank the many businesses in the Valley who supported our fund-raising activities for Kathy during the course of her illness.

This book indeed transcends the sum of its many parts. It is my hope that we collectively have succeeded in providing good reading and some recipes that will bring the pleasure of tasty, wholesome food. Most importantly, we hope that we have captured some small part of Kathy's spirited sense of fun, her zest for living each day to the fullest, and her dedication to the health and well-being of the community.

Anne C. Chase

Introduction

Kathy has asked me to speak for her.
If I were Kathy, I would say this:

> *There are many necessities beyond food that nourish our process of living. Two of these, ever present in my heart and soul, are seeing the infinite possibilities and dimensions in a single moment and the act of creating.*
>
> *Cafe Chimes has nourished my soul by challenging my creativity and my ability to make the most of each moment of my life. I will be forever grateful for this awesome opportunity.*
>
> *Through the years, the Cafe has attracted a colorful spectrum of people seeking sustenance on many levels. These welcome strangers and friends expressed concern for their health and well-being. I found delight in the task of responding to their need by creating the enclosed recipes. In various wonderful and magical ways, the collection of recipes grew.*
>
> *Thus the Cafe Chimes Cookbook was created. May it nourish your body and soul as the times we've spent together have nourished mine.*
>
> *Shana Myers*

Contents

Recipes by Chapter

Entrance to Kathy's Cafe Chimes
North Conway, New Hampshire

Shana Myers and Kathy Etter; Elsa Steffanson; Kathy Etter

Cooking Class at Cafe Chimes

In this food
I see the presence of the entire universe
supporting me

Thich Nhat Hanh

I WILL NOT DIE
AN UNLIVED LIFE

I will not die an unlived life.
I will not live in fear
Of falling or catching fire.
I choose to inhabit my days,
To allow my living to open me,
To make me less afraid,
More accessible,
To loosen my heart
Until it becomes a wing,
a torch, a promise.
I choose to risk my significance;
      To live
So that which came to me as seed
Goes to the next as blossom
and that which came
      To me as blossom,
Goes on as fruit.

                    Dawna Markova

BEGINNINGS

Beginnings

We decided to call this group of recipes "Beginnings" because the recipes did not fall readily into other categories. So here you will find a delicious potpourri of dishes that can serve as appetizers, sandwich fillings, side dishes, or condiments.

Baked Sunflower Sunshine Loaf

This recipe shows how versatile and creative vegetarian cooking can be. The Sunshine Loaf can be served as an appetizer before dinner. Just spread it on crackers. Or you can cut the loaf into thick slices and use as a sandwich filling. Rich in protein, the Sunshine Loaf can also be served as a dinner entrée.

SERVES 4-6

1 cup roasted sunflower seeds (see recipe for Roasted Nuts & Seeds on page 11)

1 small onion, chopped
2 cloves garlic, minced
½ cup warm water
½ cup olive oil
¼ cup tamari
½ cup whole-wheat flour
½ cup nutritional yeast
½ teaspoon dried basil
½ teaspoon red miso

Prepare the roasted sunflower seeds and set aside.

Place the onion, garlic, water, olive oil, tamari, flour, yeast, basil, and red miso in a food processor or blender and blend until smooth. Stir in the roasted sunflower seeds.

Pour the batter into an oiled 9x5x3-inch loaf pan. Bake at 350 degrees for 35 minutes. Cool slightly and turn onto a serving plate.

Whole-Wheat Miso Pâté

This recipe was often served as an appetizer the first night of the Cafe Chimes Vegetarian Cooking Classes. People are always intrigued by the ease of preparation and the delicious taste of this simple recipe.

MAKES ABOUT 2½ CUPS

2 cups dried whole-wheat bread crumbs

1 clove garlic, minced
1½ teaspoons red miso
¾ cup water
¼ cup tahini
pinch of dried thyme
pinch of dried rosemary
pinch of dried sage
1 teaspoon lemon juice

¼ cup fresh parsley, chopped

Place dried whole-wheat bread in a blender to create the bread crumbs. Place the crumbs in a mixing bowl and set aside.

In the same blender, blend all the remaining ingredients except the chopped parsley.

Pour this mixture into the mixing bowl with the bread crumbs and stir to blend. Stir in the chopped parsley. Place in a container with a cover and refrigerate overnight.

Place the chilled mixture in a serving bowl and garnish with chopped parsley. Serve with crackers or use as a sandwich spread.

Mexican Bean Dip

Because beans are so rich in protein, I love to use them often in simple recipes for my family and my customers. This one especially is a winner!

MAKES 1½ CUPS

1 15-ounce can of kidney beans, drained and rinsed
1 small onion, coarsely chopped
2 cloves garlic, chopped
1 tablespoon vinegar
2 teaspoons tamari
1 teaspoon chili powder
1 teaspoon cumin powder
½ teaspoon black pepper
½ cup prepared salsa (your choice of mild, medium, or hot)

1 cup fresh parsley, chopped

Combine all the ingredients except the fresh chopped parsley in a food processor or blender. Blend until smooth.

Pour into a small serving bowl. Stir in the parsley and chill for a few hours before serving. Serve with taco chips or raw carrots, celery, and green and red pepper strips.

Indian Peanut Dip

This recipe is a great treat served as a dip with crackers, cut carrots, or pita bread. If you add additional liquid such as water or honey, you can create an Indian Peanut Sauce which is delicious served with a grain casserole.

MAKES 1 CUP

½ cup smooth peanut butter
2 cloves garlic, chopped
1 small onion, coarsely chopped
1 tablespoon fresh ginger root, grated
¼ cup lemon juice
2 teaspoons tamari
2 tablespoons honey
1½ teaspoons coriander powder
1½ teaspoons cardamom
dash of cayenne pepper
½ cup water, if needed

½ cup fresh parsley, chopped

Combine all the ingredients except the chopped parsley in a blender or food processor. Blend until smooth. Add water as needed to reach the desired consistency.

Place in a small serving bowl. Stir in the chopped parsley and refrigerate, covered, until ready to serve.

Cafe Chimes Baba Ghanoush

From the first moment I sampled a friend's Baba Ghanoush, it became one of my favorite recipes. This delicious eggplant-tahini dip can be made hours ahead.

MAKES ABOUT 2 CUPS

1 large eggplant, unpeeled
2-3 cloves garlic, crushed
½ cup tahini
¼ cup lemon juice
2 teaspoons tamari
1 teaspoon red miso
1 teaspoon paprika
¼ teaspoon black pepper

1 cup fresh parsley, chopped fine

Preheat oven to 400 degrees. Prick the whole, unpeeled eggplant several times and place on a baking sheet. Bake for 30 minutes or until soft. Let cool on a rack.

Cut the cooled eggplant in half and scoop out the flesh into a bowl. Discard the skin.

Mash the eggplant with the garlic, tahini, lemon juice, tamari, miso, paprika, pepper, and most of the chopped parsley. Cover and refrigerate until chilled.

Garnish with the remaining chopped parsley. Serve with raw vegetables, toasted pita wedges, or crackers.

Tofu-Avocado Guacamole

From the moment we served this easy, yet elegant creation, it was an instant hit. Avocado is luscious and full of vitamin E, so go for it!

MAKES ABOUT 2 CUPS

2 ripe avocados, peeled, pitted, and cubed
1 pound firm tofu, crumbled
½ cup salsa, medium hot
¼ cup lemon juice
2 teaspoons tamari
½ teaspoon cumin powder
½ teaspoon cumin seeds
salt and pepper to taste
cayenne pepper (optional)

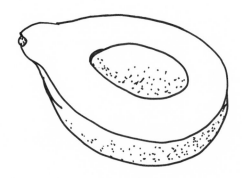

Place the avocado and tofu in a medium-sized bowl and mash with a fork until you reach the desired consistency.

Add the salsa, lemon juice, tamari, cumin powder, cumin seeds, and salt and pepper. Adjust seasonings to taste. If you prefer a spicier taste, add a little cayenne pepper.

Guacamole is wonderful served either as a dip or as a sandwich filler.

Baked Garlic & Red Peppers

SERVES 4-6 AS AN APPETIZER

1 *whole bulb elephant garlic*
3 *red peppers, seeded and quartered*
2 *tablespoons olive oil*

1 *15-ounce can white beans, drained and rinsed*
2 *teaspoons garlic powder*
2 *tablespoons tamari*
1 *teaspoon fresh rosemary, chopped*
¼ *cup fresh basil, chopped*
½ *teaspoon herb seasoning salt*
1 *teaspoon balsamic vinegar*
¼ *cup fresh parsley, chopped*
2 *teaspoons sesame seeds*

Remove the outer papery skins from the garlic, but do not break the cloves apart. Cut off the top of the garlic bulb. Place the garlic in an oiled baking dish surrounded by quartered red peppers. Drizzle olive oil on the garlic and red peppers. Bake at 350 degrees for 30 to 40 minutes or until the garlic is soft.

Remove the garlic from the baking dish and squeeze the baked cloves into a bowl. Add the beans, garlic powder, tamari, rosemary, basil, seasoning salt, and vinegar. Mash thoroughly with a potato masher. Fold in fresh parsley and baked red peppers. Put the mixture back into the baking dish. Bake uncovered at 350 degrees for 20 minutes. Sprinkle with sesame seeds.

Place in a serving dish and serve warm with crackers or chopped vegetables.

Gomashio

This Japanese condiment is very popular in the macrobiotic diet. In the Cafe, we usually make up a batch of this weekly and leave it on the counter for customers to sprinkle on their grain dishes. Sesame seeds are rich in iron, potassium, and phosphorus.

MAKES 1 CUP

1 cup sesame seeds
2 teaspoons sea salt

Wash the sesame seeds in a fine mesh strainer and dry. Place the sesame seeds and the sea salt in a cast-iron frying pan. Cook on medium heat for 7-10 minutes, stirring constantly for even pan-roasting. The sesame seeds may begin popping and will give off a nutty aroma when done.

Place the pan-roasted sesame seeds and sea salt in a suribachi (a Japanese grinding bowl which can be purchased at your local health food store) and grind until the sesame seeds are half-crushed. If you do not possess a suribachi, place the roasted sesame seeds and sea salt in a blender and quickly blend for 30 seconds or until half the seeds are ground.

Gomashio will keep fresh for several weeks in an air-tight container.

Roasted Nuts & Seeds

These roasted herbed nuts and seeds add wonderful flavor and texture to all kinds of recipes. Make up a batch in advance, so you'll have them ready to top off your dishes. Use this recipe to prepare roasted cashews, walnuts, sunflower seeds, pumpkin seeds, and sesame seeds.

MAKES 2 CUPS

2 cups dry, shelled, unsalted nuts or seeds
1 tablespoon tamari
1 teaspoon sesame oil
½ teaspoon herb seasoning salt
½ teaspoon ground coriander
½ teaspoon garlic powder
½ teaspoon ginger powder

Place the nuts or seeds on a cookie sheet and roast in a 350 degree oven for 5-10 minutes or until golden brown. The cooking time will vary depending on the kind of nuts or seeds you are roasting.

When the nuts or seeds are golden brown, remove from the oven and sprinkle on the tamari, sesame oil, and all the dry seasoning ingredients. Mix thoroughly and place in the oven again for 5 minutes. Let cool and place in a tightly covered jar.

11

Alice laughed. "There's no use trying," she said: "one can't believe impossible things."

"I daresay you haven't had much practice," said the Queen. "When I was your age, I always did it for half-an-hour a day. Why, sometimes I've believed as many as six impossible things before breakfast."

Lewis Carroll
From: Through the Looking Glass and What Alice Found There

BREAKFAST

Breakfast

There is something special about breakfast, yet it comes at a time of day when creativity and time are not exactly abundant. At Cafe Chimes, we offer a whole foods, continental-style breakfast. People seeking traditional eggs and bacon usually do an about-face and head to the nearest "regular" restaurant.

I urge you to participate in a morning meal that sustains your energy level easily until your next meal becomes a thought.

Cafe Chimes Morning Miso Soup

While visiting the Kushi Institute in Becket, Massachusetts (the primary group in America advocating a Macrobiotic Diet), I learned about the benefits of miso soup. A bowl of our Morning Miso Soup is a wonderful way to start the day. Once you allow yourself to feel the difference in your well-being, you may find yourself with a healthy habit.

MAKES 2 CUPS

1 dried shiitaki mushroom, sliced (soaked and drained)
2 cups water
½ medium onion, chopped
1 carrot, chopped
1 teaspoon wakame
1 heaping tablespoon red miso
drop of sesame oil
handful of roasted sunflower seeds (see recipe for Roasted Nuts & Seeds on page 11)

Pre-soak the dried shiitake mushroom in warm water and drain. In a medium saucepan, combine the shiitake mushroom, water, onion, carrot, and wakame. Bring to a boil and cook on medium heat for about 20 minutes, adding more water as needed. In a small measuring cup, combine the miso and a little of the cooked broth. Stir and blend. Remove the soup from the heat, thus stopping the boiling. Add the blended miso and broth and the sesame oil. Pour into a soup bowl and top with sunflower seeds.

Raspberry Seven-Grain Hot Cereal

I serve this hot breakfast cereal at least three times a week to the young people who chose me for their mother. Sometimes their complaints "get to me," but often they do concede that having a reserve of energy and wakefulness during the period before school lunch is worth it.

SERVES 4-5

1½ cups water
dash of sea salt
¾ cup seven-grain cereal (available at your local health food store)
¼ cup raisins
1 teaspoon cinnamon
½ cup soy milk
1 teaspoon vanilla extract
¼ cup frozen or fresh raspberries (or your choice of strawberries, blueberries, peaches, etc.)

In a heavy saucepan, bring the water and sea salt to a boil. Add the cereal and raisins, stirring right away to avoid lumps. Reduce heat to low and place the pan on a deflector to avoid burning. Add cinnamon, soy milk, and vanilla. Stir and cover. Simmer, covered, for 15-20 minutes, stirring occasionally. Add raspberries or your choice of fruit, stir, and simmer a few more minutes. Scoop into bowls and top with additional soy milk and/or sweetener.

You can start this cereal in minutes and then take your morning shower. Makes a wonderful breakfast when combined with Morning Miso Soup. WOW!

Breakfast Tofu Scramble

The Breakfast Tofu Scramble is usually the first to go on Sundays and every day. A popular offering during our Cafe Chimes Sunday Brunch, the Tofu Scramble resembles scrambled eggs with vegetables in texture and color. A healthy and delicious alternative to a traditional egg breakfast!

SERVES 4-6

2 tablespoons sesame oil
1 medium onion, chopped
1 celery stalk, chopped
½ red pepper, chopped
1 clove garlic, minced (optional)
1 pound firm tofu, crumbled
2 teaspoons tamari
½ teaspoon dried thyme
½ teaspoon turmeric
½ teaspoon herb seasoning salt

In a large skillet, sauté the onion and celery in sesame oil until the onion is translucent. Add the red pepper and the garlic, if desired, and cook until tender.

Add the crumbled tofu, tamari, thyme, turmeric, and seasoning salt. Stir to blend. Simmer 10 minutes without stirring. Adjust seasonings to taste and serve hot.

This is wonderful served with whole-wheat toast and organic strawberry jam with roasted potatoes on the side. What a way to go! For a lunch treat, serve the Scramble on a chapati with lettuce, salsa, and cheddar cheese.

Buckwheat Pancakes

MAKES 10-12 PANCAKES

½ cup buckwheat flour
½ cup white flour
¼ cup rolled oats
2 tablespoons turbinado sugar or brown sugar
3 tablespoons dough enhancer (see recipe on page 25)
1 teaspoon baking powder
½ teaspoon cinnamon

1¼ cups soy milk
4 tablespoons canola oil

In a large bowl, combine all the dry ingredients. Mix well. Add the soy milk and canola oil. Stir to blend just until the dry ingredients are moistened. If the mixture is too thick, add another ¼ cup soy milk.

Drop the batter by ¼ cupfuls onto a preheated oiled griddle or frying pan. When the pancake edges get dry, flip them over. Cook until the second side is golden brown.

Couscous with Raspberries & Mandarin Oranges

I've included this recipe because it is so easy, quick to prepare, and fun to eat. We serve this for breakfast, but it is also delicious as a simple dessert.

SERVES 4-6

1½ *cups couscous*
1½ *cups boiling water or apple or orange juice*
½ *cup maple syrup*
2 *teaspoons cinnamon*
½ *cup fresh raspberries*
½ *cup canned mandarin oranges, drained*

Place the couscous in a bowl and add boiling water or juice. Cover with aluminum foil and let sit for 15 minutes. Fluff gently with a fork and let cool. Add the maple syrup and cinnamon and toss gently. Mix in the fresh raspberries and mandarin oranges. Chill and serve.

Cafe Chimes Fresh Fruit Sauce

Every Sunday we offer a fresh fruit cup at our Cafe Chimes Brunch. I select fresh, ripe fruit which I chop and glaze with the following sauce. The almond butter adds a delicious dimension, but you can make the sauce without it.

MAKES ABOUT ½ CUP SAUCE (ENOUGH FOR 4-5 SERVINGS OF FRUIT)

1 tablespoon almond butter
2 tablespoon maple syrup
½ teaspoon vanilla
1 tablespoon lemon juice
2 tablespoons water

4 cups assorted cut fruit

Place the almond butter, maple syrup, vanilla, lemon juice, and water in a small bowl and whisk to blend. Cut the fruit into bite-sized pieces and place in a bowl. Glaze with the sauce and refrigerate until ready to serve.

Granola Fresh Fruit Cup in a Lemon Maple Glaze

This tangy glaze is delicious with a variety of fruit. You can use any combination of peaches, raspberries, melons, strawberries, blueberries, or pineapple. Let your taste and availability be the guide.

SERVES 4-6

¼ cup lemon juice
½ cup maple syrup

4 cups assorted cut fruit
1½ cups rain forest granola
fresh mint leaves for garnish

In a medium-sized bowl, stir together the lemon juice and the maple syrup. Cut the fruit of your choice into bite-sized pieces and toss in the bowl with the lemon and maple glaze.

Top with the granola and serve. Garnish with fresh mint, if available.

Frosty Fruit Smoothie

SERVES 2

1 banana
½ cup fresh or frozen strawberries
1¼ cups water
¼ cup orange juice concentrate
¾ cup soy milk
1 tablespoon vanilla extract
¼ teaspoon cinnamon

1 tablespoon honey (optional)
1 cup ice cubes

Place all the ingredients in a blender. For extra sweetness, add honey. Blend on medium/high until smooth and creamy. Add 1 cup of ice cubes. Blend and serve.

Smoothie Variations

Pineapple Banana Smoothie: Prepare the recipe above substituting ½ cup crushed fresh or canned pineapple for the strawberries. If using canned pineapple, drain before using.

Blueberry Banana Smoothie: Prepare the recipe above substituting ½ cup fresh or frozen blueberries for the strawberries.

Blueberry Strawberry Smoothie: Prepare the recipe above substituting ½ cup fresh or frozen blueberries for the banana.

BREADS & MUFFINS

Breads & Muffins

There is nothing more welcoming than the aroma of fresh baked bread! Bread is truly food for body and soul! At the Cafe Chimes, we have specialized in daily baking of our nutritious Whole-Wheat Mountain Bread. We use this bread for many of our hearty sandwiches and as a tasty accompaniment to our salads and other main course dishes.

The magic ingredient that makes our bread so light and delicious is our Dough Enhancer. I wonder if there would be a Cafe Chimes without the dough enhancer. We have become known for many reasons, but primarily because of our very special whole-wheat bread. The dough enhancer is an essential ingredient in our bread and muffin recipes. We developed this recipe through many trials, errors, and tribulations, and it is with thanks that I can share this recipe with all the future chefs with a "whole foods" heart.

Cafe Chimes Dough Enhancer

This is the magic ingredient that makes whole-wheat bread both light and delicious. It is also an essential part of our quick bread, biscuit, and muffin recipes. Make up a large batch and store it in your freezer, so it will be on hand when you feel like baking.

MAKES ABOUT 5⅔ CUPS

3 cups unbleached white flour
1 cup lecithin
½ cup gluten
¼ cup baking soda
¼ cup baking powder
¼ cup citric acid (available at your local health food store)
2 tablespoons sea salt
2 packages of E-mergen-C® (a powdered product available at your local health food store)

Combine all of the above ingredients in a large bowl and mix well. Store in an air-tight container in your freezer.

(Note: If you can't assemble the ingredients for the Dough Enhancer, you may substitute a packaged version. Follow package directions for determining the amount of dough enhancer to add to the bread recipes. Packaged dough enhancers are usually available at your local health food store, or in the baking section of your supermarket.)

Cafe Chimes Whole-Wheat Mountain Bread

The story of Cafe Chimes Whole-Wheat Mountain Bread is a joy to recount. Before I opened Cafe Chimes, I had only made bread twice in my life. My early attempts dismayed my family who nicknamed my breads "Door stoppers!" However, I didn't give up, and with the assistance of a machine with a dough hook and the Cafe Chimes Dough Enhancer recipe—suddenly we were baking awesome, light whole-wheat bread.

MAKES 2 LARGE LOAVES

3 cups warm water
½ cup turbinado sugar (or light brown sugar)
⅓ cup yeast

½ cup dough enhancer (see recipe on page 25)
2 teaspoons sea salt
⅓ cup canola oil

5½ cups whole-wheat flour
2 cups unbleached white flour

Use an electric mixer with a dough hook. Put warm water in the mixer bowl. Add turbinado sugar and yeast and stir. Let the yeast activate for a few minutes, making sure the yeast is fresh. (It will begin to move and bubble.) Add the dough enhancer, salt, and oil.

Start the mixer at low speed. While the mixer is on, add 2 cups whole-wheat flour, 2 cups white flour, then 2 more cups of whole-wheat flour. Mix for 4 minutes at low speed. Add 1 additional cup of whole-wheat flour. Mix for 4 more minutes. At this point, check the dough. The dough should form a big elastic ball which pulls all dough from the side of the bowl. If it is sticky, add ½ cup more whole-wheat flour. Continue mixing for 8-12 minutes.

Remove the dough from the mixer to a bread board or an oiled surface. Roll the dough around on the surface until the dough feels elastic. Form the dough into 2 loaves and set into oiled 9x5x3-inch bread pans. Cover loosely with waxed paper or parchment paper and place in a warm, draft-free spot to rise. This bread rises well in an oven that has been pre-warmed at the lowest possible setting for about 5 minutes. After pre-warming, turn off the oven. Place the bread dough in the oven for 30-35 minutes or until the dough doubles in size. Remove the dough from the oven. (This is a single-rising recipe.)

Preheat the oven to 350 degrees and bake the loaves for 30-35 minutes. The bread is done when the loaves sound hollow when tapped on top and bottom. Turn out on racks and cool before slicing.

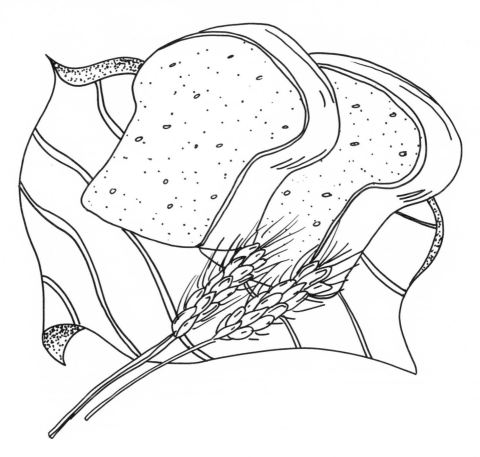

Bavarian Rye Bread

MAKES 2 LARGE LOAVES

1 large onion, finely chopped
2 tablespoons sesame oil

2¾ cups warm water
½ cup turbinado sugar (or light brown sugar)
⅓ cup yeast

½ cup dough enhancer (see recipe on page 25)
2 teaspoons sea salt
⅓ cup sesame oil
2 teaspoons caraway seeds

3½ cups whole-wheat flour
2 cups unbleached white flour
2 cups rye flour

In a skillet, sauté the onions in oil until translucent.

Use an electric mixer with a dough hook. Put the warm water in a mixer bowl. Add turbinado sugar and yeast and stir. Let the yeast activate for a few minutes, making sure the yeast is fresh. (It will begin to move and bubble.) Add the dough enhancer, salt, oil, caraway seeds, and sautéed onions.

Start the mixer at low speed. While the mixer is on, add 2 cups whole-wheat flour, 2 cups white flour, then 2 cups of rye flour. Mix for 4 minutes at low speed. Add 1 additional cup of whole-wheat flour. Mix for 4 more minutes. At this point, check the dough. The dough should form a big elastic ball which pulls all dough from the side of the bowl. If it is sticky, add ½ cup more whole-wheat flour. Continue mixing for 8 minutes.

Remove the dough from the mixer to bread board or an oiled surface. Roll the dough around on the surface until the dough feels elastic. Form the dough into 2 loaves and set into oiled 9x5x3-inch bread pans. Cover loosely with waxed paper or parchment paper and place in a warm, draft-free spot to rise. This bread rises well in an oven that has been pre-warmed at the lowest possible setting for about 5 minutes. After pre-warming, turn off the oven. Place the bread dough in the oven for 30-35 minutes or until the dough doubles in size. Remove the dough from the oven. (This is a single-rising recipe.)

Preheat the oven to 350 degrees and bake the loaves for 30-35 minutes. The bread is done when the loaves sound hollow when tapped on top and bottom. Turn out on racks and cool before slicing.

Tomato Basil Bread

MAKES 2 LARGE LOAVES

3 cups warm water
½ cup turbinado sugar (or light brown sugar)
⅓ cup yeast

½ cup dough enhancer (see recipe on page 25)
2 teaspoons sea salt
⅓ cup olive oil
1 cup sun-dried tomatoes, chopped
⅓ cup fresh basil, chopped (or 3 tablespoons dried)
2 teaspoons minced garlic (about 2 large cloves)

5½ cups whole-wheat flour
2 cups unbleached white flour

Use an electric mixer with a dough hook. Put the warm water in a mixer bowl. Add turbinado sugar and yeast and stir. Let the yeast activate for a few minutes, making sure the yeast is fresh. (It will begin to move and bubble.) Add the dough enhancer, salt, oil, tomatoes, basil, and garlic.

Start the mixer at low speed. While the mixer is on, add 2 cups whole-wheat flour, 2 cups white flour, then 2 more cups of whole-wheat flour. Mix for 4 minutes at low speed. Add 1 additional cup of whole-wheat flour. Mix for 4 more minutes. At this point, check the dough. The dough should form a big elastic ball which pulls all dough from the side of the bowl. If it is sticky, add ½ cup more whole-wheat flour. Continue mixing for 8-12 minutes.

Remove the dough from the mixer to a bread board or an oiled surface. Roll the dough around on the surface until the dough feels elastic. Form the dough into 2 loaves and set into oiled 9x5x3-inch bread pans. Cover loosely with waxed paper or parchment paper and place in a warm, draft-free spot to rise. This bread rises well in an oven that has been pre-warmed at the lowest possible setting for about 5 minutes. After pre-warming, turn off the oven. Place the bread dough in the oven for 30-35 minutes or until the dough doubles in size. Remove the dough from the oven. (This is a single-rising recipe.)

Preheat the oven to 350 degrees and bake the loaves for 30-35 minutes. The bread is done when the loaves sound hollow when tapped on top and bottom. Turn out on racks and cool before slicing.

Cafe Chimes Veggie Bread Bowls

Now this is where the fun begins. I am not sure how these Veggie Bowls were created, but they are definitely a gift from above. I am supplying you with a basic recipe. You add your own individual creative process.

MAKES 8 BOWLS

Make the Cafe Chimes Whole-Wheat Mountain Bread Dough (see recipe on page 26). Save one dough for the Veggie Bowls and bake the other into bread using a 9x5x3-inch bread pan.

Take a clean muffin tin, turn it upside-down, and spray the bottom with oil.

Divide the remaining bread dough into 8 equal pieces. Roll each into a ball in the palm of your hand. With precision and purpose, flatten each ball in your hands and form-fit each chunk of flattened dough onto the bottom of the muffin tin, thus structuring 8 upside-down bowls.

Bake the muffin tin upside-down at 350 degrees for about 20 minutes. Remove the whole-wheat bread bowls from the tin and let cool on a rack.

Fill with any combination that comes to mind. Here is one tasty approach:

1 tablespoon olive oil
2 medium onions, chopped
1 clove garlic, minced
2 stalks celery, chopped
1 green pepper, chopped
1 ripe tomato, chopped

1 teaspoon oregano
½ teaspoon herb seasoning salt
2 teaspoons tamari
2 tablespoons miso
2 cups cooked rice or any type of cooked
   grain or legume

Heat the oil in a large skillet and sauté the onions, garlic, celery, green pepper, tomato, and oregano until tender. Add the herb seasoning salt, tamari, and miso and stir to blend. Cook for 2-3 minutes. Add the rice or the legume and mix thoroughly. Let cool.

Spoon the cooled rice and vegetable mixture into the baked whole-wheat bread bowls and place on a cookie sheet. Bake for 15 minutes or until warm. Serve with a big bowl of soup or with a green salad. This is definitely a customer-pleaser!

31

Cinnamon Raisin Bread

MAKES 2 LARGE LOAVES

3 cups warm water
½ cup turbinado sugar (or light brown sugar)
⅓ cup yeast

½ cup dough enhancer (see recipe on page 25)
2 teaspoons sea salt
⅓ cup canola oil
2 tablespoons cinnamon
1 cup raisins
¾ cup chopped walnuts

5½ cups whole-wheat flour
2 cups unbleached white flour

Use an electric mixer with a dough hook. Put the warm water in a mixer bowl. Add turbinado sugar and yeast and stir. Let the yeast activate for a few minutes, making sure the yeast is fresh. (It will begin to move and bubble.) Add the dough enhancer, salt, oil, cinnamon, raisins, and walnuts.

Start the mixer at low speed. While the mixer is on, add 2 cups whole-wheat flour, 2 cups white flour, then 2 more cups of whole-wheat flour. Mix for 4 minutes at low speed. Add 1 additional cup of whole-wheat flour. Mix for 4 more minutes. At this point, check the dough. The dough should form a big elastic ball which pulls all dough from the side of the bowl. If it is sticky, add ½ cup more whole-wheat flour. Continue mixing for 8-12 minutes.

Remove the dough from the mixer to an oiled surface. Roll the dough around on the oiled surface until the dough feels elastic. Form the dough into 2 loaves and set into oiled 9x5x3-inch bread pans. Cover loosely with waxed paper or parchment paper and place in a warm, draft-free spot to rise. This bread rises well in an oven that has been pre-warmed at the lowest possible setting for about 5 minutes. After pre-warming, turn off the oven. Place the bread dough in the oven for 30-35 minutes or until the dough doubles in size. Remove the dough from the oven. (This is a single-rising recipe.)

Preheat the oven to 350 degrees and bake the loaves for 30-35 minutes. The bread is done when the loaves sound hollow when tapped on top and bottom. Turn out on racks and cool before slicing.

Cafe Chimes Cinnamon Swirls

The Cafe Chimes Cinnamon Swirls were a hit right from the beginning. They are called many unique names—sticky buns, those round things, crumpets, twirls—and we always know what the customer means when his pointed finger begins the circle movement in describing his need. These Swirls are moist, sweet, and abundant in complex carbohydrates—a perfect way to introduce a healthy breakfast for children and easy if you have a bread dough ready the day before.

MAKES 6 BIG SWIRLS

1 pound whole-wheat bread dough (see recipe on page 26 or use a prepared frozen
    or refrigerated loaf)
½ cup honey or maple syrup
1 teaspoon cinnamon
1 cup frozen or fresh fruit (you choose the combinations)
¼ cup nuts, poppy seeds, or granola

After making the bread dough recipe, save out one dough for your morning Cinnamon Swirl. If you are using frozen or refrigerated dough, bring the dough to room temperature. Roll out the whole-wheat dough on a lightly floured board to form an 11x17-inch rectangle. Spread the dough with honey or maple syrup using a rubber spatula. Sprinkle on the cinnamon. Pick a fruit or combination of fruit and place evenly over the rolled-out dough. Sprinkle on nuts, seeds, or granola.

Roll up the dough from the long (17-inch) side. Cut the long roll into 6 even-sized pieces. Space the rolls evenly on an oiled cookie sheet with the cut ends down. Bake at 350 degrees for 15-20 minutes.

Cinnamon Coffee Buns

Serve these tasty little buns for breakfast, teatime, or anytime.

MAKES 8 BUNS

1 pound whole-wheat bread dough (see recipe on page 26 or use a prepared frozen
   or refrigerated loaf)
½ cup turbinado sugar or light brown sugar
1 tablespoon cinnamon
½ cup chopped walnuts

After making bread dough, save out one dough for your morning
Cinnamon Coffee Buns. If you are using frozen or refrigerated dough, bring
the dough to room temperature. Roll out the whole-wheat dough on a lightly
floured board to form an 11x17-inch rectangle. Spread the sugar and
cinnamon evenly over the rolled-out dough. Sprinkle the chopped walnuts
over the dough.

Roll up the dough from the long (17-inch) side. Cut the long roll into 8
even-sized pieces. Space the rolls evenly on an oiled 11x17-inch cookie sheet
with the cut ends down. Bake at 350 degrees for 15-20 minutes.

Apple Raisin Quick Bread

Like the muffin recipes in this book, a quick bread is just that—quick and homemade. By using slightly different measurements and a bread pan instead of a muffin tin, you have a great addition to any meal.

MAKES 1 LOAF

1 egg
¼ cup corn oil or ½ cup applesauce
½ cup honey or maple syrup
1 cup soy milk
½ cup water

2 cups whole-wheat flour
½ cup rolled oats
1 tablespoon baking powder
1 tablespoon dough enhancer (see recipe on page 25)
1 teaspoon sea salt
1 teaspoon cinnamon
1 teaspoon allspice
½ cup roasted walnuts, chopped (see recipe for Roasted Nuts & Seeds on page 11)
½ cup dried apples, chopped
¼ cup raisins

In a large measuring cup, blend the egg, corn oil or applesauce, honey or maple syrup, soy milk, and water. In a large bowl, mix whole-wheat flour, rolled oats, baking powder, dough enhancer, sea salt, cinnamon, and allspice. Add the roasted walnuts, apples, and raisins.

Add the egg mixture to the blended dry ingredients and stir to mix. Bake in a lightly oiled 9x5x3-inch bread pan for 40-50 minutes at 350 degrees. The loaf is done when a toothpick inserted in the center of the bread comes out clean. Cool the bread in the pan for about 15 minutes, then turn it out on a rack to finish cooling.

Feel free to vary the combinations of nuts and dried fruits. I invite you to be creative!

Drop Biscuits

I frequently make these biscuits to serve with a cool summer salad. Somehow homemade biscuits make the whole meal taste better. See how easy it can be to make a smile!

MAKES 18 BISCUITS

1 cup whole-wheat flour
1 cup white flour
1 tablespoon baking powder
2 tablespoons dough enhancer (see recipe on page 25)
¼ cup applesauce
½ cup water
½ cup soy milk
2 chopped scallions (or 2 teaspoons of chopped fresh dill)

Combine the flour, baking powder, and dough enhancer in a bowl. Cream in the applesauce. Add water and soy milk and stir. Add the chopped scallions or fresh dill and stir to mix. Do not knead or overmix. Drop heaping tablespoons of the batter about an inch apart on a lightly oiled cookie sheet. Bake at 425 degrees for 15-20 minutes until golden. Serve immediately.

Quick & Easy Corn Bread

MAKES 9 SERVINGS

2 tablespoons canola oil
⅓ cup maple syrup
1½ cups soy milk

1 cup cornmeal
½ cup unbleached white flour
1 cup whole-wheat pastry flour
¼ cup corn grits
2 tablespoons dough enhancer (see recipe on page 25)
2 teaspoons baking powder
½ teaspoon sea salt.

In a large bowl, blend the oil, maple syrup, and soy milk. In a large measuring cup or bowl, blend the dry ingredients. Add the dry ingredients to the oil, syrup, and milk, and stir briefly with a whisk.

Pour the batter into a lightly oiled 8x8-inch baking pan. Spread the batter evenly and bake at 350 degrees for about 30-35 minutes or until golden. Cut into squares to serve.

There are many variations that add taste and texture to this easy bread. The following are just a few—add cranberries, nuts, and chopped apples. You can use apple juice instead of soy milk. Or try adding a finely chopped sweet red pepper along with one or two chopped jalapeno peppers.

Cafe Chimes Whole-Wheat Muffins

For over eight years, Cafe Chimes has offered warm muffins fresh from the oven. What a perfect way to start the day! These muffins are a delicious food choice—full of complex carbohydrates, protein-rich, and naturally sweetened. There's not much more that a body could ask for. The basic muffin recipe rarely varies. However, I'll bet I have duplicated the same muffin only a few times in eight years because I am always using different combinations of fruits, vegetables, nuts, and different grains and sweeteners. Check out the muffin variations which we've listed below. Experiment and above all, have fun!

MAKES 12 BIG MUFFINS

¾ cup honey or 1 cup turbinado sugar (light brown sugar)
1 cup soy milk
¼ cup water
1 cup applesauce
½ cup fresh or frozen fruit

1½ cups whole-wheat flour
1½ cups white flour
½ cup wheat bran
1 tablespoon dough enhancer
    (see recipe on page 25)
1 teaspoon baking powder
1 teaspoon baking soda
½ teaspoon sea salt
1 teaspoon arrowroot powder
1 teaspoon cinnamon
1 tablespoon vanilla or almond extract

In a large bowl, combine the honey or sugar, soy milk, water, applesauce, and fruit. Stir to blend. In another large bowl or measuring cup, combine the flour and other dry ingredients. Mix well. Combine the dry ingredients with the honey/milk mixture. Add the vanilla or almond extract. Stir and pour into greased muffin tins. Bake at 350 degrees for 20-25 minutes or until the muffins are firm to the touch.

This recipe makes a dozen muffins. Cool and freeze for the next day, and the next, and the next.

Muffin Variations

Almond Ginger Muffins: Prepare the basic muffin recipe. Add 1 teaspoon grated fresh ginger root to the honey/milk mixture. Instead of vanilla extract, use 1 tablespoon of almond extract.

Banana Walnut Muffins: Prepare the basic muffin recipe using 1 chopped banana for the fruit. Add ½ cup chopped walnuts to the final batter.

Blueberry Oat Bran Muffins: Prepare the basic muffin recipe using ½ cup fresh blueberries for the fruit. Top with ⅔ cup oat bran.

Carrot Coriander Muffins: Prepare the basic muffin recipe using ½ cup grated carrots instead of the fruit. Add 1 teaspoon ground coriander to the dry ingredients.

Chocolate Chip Muffins: Prepare the basic muffin recipe adding ½ cup chocolate chips instead of the fruit.

Cinnamon Apple Muffins: Prepare the basic muffin recipe using 1 apple, peeled, cored, and chopped for the fruit.

Maple Walnut Muffins: Prepare the basic muffin recipe substituting ⅔ cup maple syrup for the honey. Add ½ cup chopped walnuts to the final batter.

Orange Raisin Muffins: Prepare the basic muffin recipe substituting ⅓ cup frozen orange juice concentrate for the water. Use ½ cup raisins for the fruit. Add 1 teaspoon ground cardamom to the dry ingredients.

Pineapple Ginger Muffins: Prepare the basic muffin recipe using ½ cup fresh or canned pineapple chunks for the fruit. Add 1 teaspoon grated fresh ginger root to the honey/milk mixture.

Vanilla Raspberry Muffins: Prepare the basic muffin recipe using ½ cup fresh raspberries for the fruit. Use vanilla extract instead of almond extract.

If you get frustrated, angry,
sad or upset...
Cry over the onions
No one asks Questions

SALADS
DRESSINGS
& SAUCES

Salads, Dressings & Sauces

Creative cooking is all about transformation. If you mix the ingredients that are right in front of you together with a little faith, you can become an exceptional cook.

Over the years, usually by making mistakes, I have become confident in trusting my intuition in terms of what ingredients will combine well. The process never ceases to amaze me when I am considering a new recipe. It goes something like this: with my whisk in hand, I walk around the kitchen adding a little of this and a little of that.

On the following pages you will find some of the Cafe's creations. In the world of vegetarian cooking, salads are a main focus when meal planning is at task. Even on a cold winter's night, a hearty salad with a hot bowl of soup makes a nutritious and satisfying meal. We've included a wide choice of salads, and I'm sure you will find one that absolutely entices you to prepare it this instant!

The measurements for most of the sauces and dressings are meant as a starting point for creative cooking. I invite you to experiment and be outrageous. If you feel like adding a spice, then by all means do it. If you feel like omitting an ingredient, then do it.

The sauces can be used as dressings and the dressings as sauces. You can enjoy these creations on grains, vegetables, salads, as a dip, or whatever. The only thing that will hold you back is a lack of imagination.

Gold-Studded Arame Salad

Because arame is my personal favorite among sea vegetables, I tend to use it in all areas of cooking. This salad is especially colorful because of the black arame background laced with the golden corn kernels.

SERVES 4-6

For the Salad:

2 cups dry arame
2 cups warm water
2 cups fresh or frozen corn, blanched
1 medium cucumber, peeled and chopped
1 red pepper, finely diced
1 cup canned mandarin oranges, drained
6 leafy green lettuce leaves, washed

For the Curry & Tamari Dressing:

¼ cup water
2 tablespoons tamari
2 tablespoons olive oil
½ teaspoon curry powder
¼ teaspoon black pepper
¼ teaspoon herb seasoning salt

Soak the arame in 2 cups of warm water for 10 minutes. Discard the soaking water and let the arame drain on a clean, dry cloth.

Bring a medium saucepan of water to a boil over medium-high heat. Blanch the corn kernels by plunging them into the boiling water for about 1 minute. Scoop them out with a slotted spoon and hold under running cold water to stop the cooking. If you are using frozen corn, blanching is not necessary. Just thaw the frozen corn kernels briefly under cold running water.

Prepare the cucumber and red pepper. Place the arame, corn, cucumbers, red pepper, and mandarin oranges in a large bowl and toss gently. Refrigerate until ready to serve.

Place all the dressing ingredients in a small bowl and whisk thoroughly to mix. Pour over the chilled salad and toss gently. When ready to serve, arrange a bed of leafy green lettuce on a serving plate. Place the Arame Salad on the bed of lettuce and serve.

43

Cafe Chimes Tofu & Arame Salad

I view the following salad as one of the more hopeful signs for the future of good nutrition. Even though tofu wasn't universally popular and arame (seaweed) was largely unknown, I dared to combine the two in our Cafe Chimes salad bar. Much to my surprise, this recipe became a popular salad bar choice that needed refilling constantly—a positive sign that speaks to the changing attitudes towards tofu and sea vegetables!

SERVES 4

½ cup dry arame
1 cup warm water
1 pound extra-firm tofu, cubed
2 tablespoons roasted sesame oil
1 tablespoon tamari
1 teaspoon basil
¼ cup dried parsley (or ½ cup fresh)
1 teaspoon garlic powder
1 teaspoon paprika
½ teaspoon herb seasoning salt

Soak the arame in 1 cup of warm water for 10 minutes. Discard the soaking water and let the arame drain on a clean, dry cloth.

Towel dry the tofu, then cut into ½-inch cubes. In a skillet, heat the sesame oil and add the tofu.

Brown the tofu on medium heat, turning carefully with a spatula until brown on all sides. Add the tamari, basil, parsley, garlic powder, paprika, and seasoning salt. Mix gently with the tofu taking care not to break up the cubes.

Add the drained arame to the tofu mixture. Stir gently to blend and simmer for 3 minutes. Place in a serving bowl and chill in the refrigerator until ready to serve.

Bermuda Beet Salad

Because most of us don't consume beets on a regular basis, I always include this recipe in my first cooking class. I emphasize beets' nutritive value, vibrant color, and sweet flavor. This salad disappears!

SERVES 4-6

5 beets, cooked and sliced
1 medium Bermuda onion, thinly sliced and finely chopped
2 red apples, cored and thinly sliced
½ cup raisins
2 cups raw beet greens, finely chopped
½ teaspoon caraway seeds

¼ cup lemon juice
¼ cup cider vinegar
¼ cup honey
1 teaspoon tamari

2 tablespoons roasted sunflower seeds (see recipe for Roasted Nuts & Seeds on page 11)

Prepare the beets by cutting off the beet stems and greens, reserving greens. Gently scrub the surface of the beets to clean. Place the whole beets into boiling water, cover, lower the heat, and simmer until tender, about 40 minutes. Slide off the peels, cool, and slice.

Place the chopped onions, apples, raisins, sliced beets, beet greens, and caraway seeds in a bowl.

Mix together the lemon juice, vinegar, honey and tamari. Pour this mixture over the vegetables and fruits. Toss. Chill 4 hours. Toss again. Top with sunflower seeds and serve.

This salad makes a full meal when combined with quinoa or other grain dish.

Pressed Salad

A simple method for pressing a salad is to get out a big bowl, a small plate, and a big clean rock! Place the recipe ingredients in a bowl, cover, and press with a rock.

SERVES 4-6

3 cups green cabbage, cored and shredded (about ¼ medium head)
3 cups red cabbage, cored and shredded (about ¼ medium head)
2 medium carrots, shredded
1 teaspoon sea salt
3 tablespoons vinegar of your choice (cider, balsamic, or umeboshi)
1 teaspoon tamari (optional)

Cut all the vegetables and place in a large bowl. Add the sea salt and stir. Press down the ingredients with a plate that fits inside the diameter of the bowl. Weigh down the plate with a big rock. Press for at least 2-3 hours.

Drain the liquid from the salad and add the vinegar of your choice. Add tamari if desired and adjust seasonings to taste. Toss and refrigerate before serving.

The Purple Salad

My wonderful cookbook illustrator and dear friend, Shana Myers, brought purple to my life, and it has been a purposeful, purple life ever since! My clothes are predominately purple. I love lilacs and any purple food. That is why this simple, savvy salad is perfect for me.

SERVES 4-6

½ medium head of red cabbage,
  cored, thinly sliced, and blanched
½ cup raisins, soaked
½ cup roasted sunflower seeds
  (see recipe for Roasted Nuts & Seeds on page 11)
6 leafy green lettuce leaves, washed

Bring a large saucepan of water to a boil over medium-high heat. Blanch the sliced cabbage by plunging it into the boiling water for 1-2 minutes, or until you can just pierce it with the point of a sharp knife. Scoop out the blanched cabbage with a slotted spoon and hold it under cold running water to stop the cooking. Place the cabbage on a clean dry cloth and refrigerate for crisping and cooling.

When ready to serve, arrange a bed of leafy green lettuce on a serving plate. Top with the blanched purple cabbage, raisins, and roasted sunflower seeds. Serve with your favorite dressing or just sprinkle on a tablespoon of balsamic vinegar. An eye-pleaser for sure!

The Blizzard—Blanched Vegetable Salad

This salad works well with all kinds of vegetables. We suggest kale and bok choy as a good first choice. The daikon used in this recipe is a Japanese radish, so a little goes a long way. For a Japanese-style salad, try the Sesame-Tamari Dressing below, or you can simply top the salad with vinegar and tamari. This cold vegetable salad is a welcome addition to any warm summer night meal.

SERVES 4-6

For the Salad:

2 tablespoons hijiki
1 cup water
½ pound kale, washed, stemmed and
    coarsely chopped (about 3 cups packed)
½ head bok choy, coarsely chopped
3 carrots, cut in matchsticks
1 cup daikon, sliced in half-moons
1 medium onion, cut in half-moons
1 cup red cabbage, coarsely chopped
¼ cup toasted sesame seeds

For the Sesame-Tamari Dressing:

1 tablespoon canola oil
1 tablespoon sesame oil
2 tablespoons tamari
2 tablespoons rice or cider vinegar

In a small saucepan, combine the hijiki and water. Bring to a boil, reduce heat, and simmer for 10 minutes. Drain and set aside.

In large skillet, add 2 inches of water, and bring to a boil. Drop each vegetable separately into the boiling water and blanch 1-3 minutes each, so that the vegetables remain crisp and retain their color. Remove the blanched vegetables with a slotted spoon, hold briefly under cold water, and drain. End with the red cabbage. Chill the blanched vegetables. If you are short on time, it is possible to blanch the carrots, daikon, and onions at the same time for about 1-2 minutes, taking care to retain a crisp texture and bright color.

Arrange the chilled vegetables artfully on a platter and top with the drained hijiki.

In a bowl, blend the dressing ingredients with a whisk until well-mixed. Pour over the salad and top with toasted sesame seeds.

Endive & Watercress Salad

On the last evening of the Cafe Chimes Cooking Class, the students design the menu. We developed this salad recipe in response to a student's request for an endive dish. The sausage-shaped heads of Belgian endive are available at the grocery store. Usually served raw in a salad, endive is high in vitamin A, potassium, and iron.

Watercress is sold in bunches that resemble flat parsley. When preparing watercress, you should wash it thoroughly and pick the leaves off the stems. Watercress, which is rich in vitamins A and C, is a zesty addition to any salad.

SERVES 4-6

1 head of endive
6 romaine lettuce leaves
1 bunch of watercress
1 carrot, grated
2 scallions, chopped
½ cup alfalfa sprouts

Wash and gently tear up the endive and romaine lettuce leaves. Wash the watercress and remove the leaves from the stems.

Place the endive, romaine, and watercress in a salad bowl along with the grated carrot, chopped scallions, and sprouts.

Toss with your favorite dressing, or sprinkle on 3 tablespoons balsamic vinegar and fresh black pepper.

Mandarin Orange & Almond Salad

There is something elegant about serving a salad with mandarin oranges. This naturally sweet, juicy fruit compliments most meals. Try serving this salad with Cafe Chimes House Dressing on the side.

SERVES 4-6

For the Salad:

2 cups fresh spinach greens (about half a 10-ounce package)
3 cups leafy green lettuce, or your choice of lettuce
¼ cup alfalfa sprouts
½ medium cucumber, peeled and chopped
½ medium red pepper, cut in thin strips
1 cup canned mandarin oranges, drained
¼ cup slivered almonds

Wash and dry the spinach greens and lettuce. Place in a salad bowl. Arrange the sprouts around the edge of the bowl. Place the cucumbers, red pepper, mandarin oranges, and slivered almonds artistically on the salad greens.

Serve with Cafe Chimes House Dressing on the side (see recipe on page 61).

Pesto, Spinach & Avocado Salad

Just the name of this salad is good enough to eat. For convenience, I would recommend purchasing bottled pesto sauce in your local health food or grocery store.

SERVES 4-6

10-ounce package of fresh spinach greens
2 ripe avocados, pitted, peeled, and sliced
1 medium cucumber, peeled and chopped
2 carrots, grated
1 medium tomato, chopped
½ cup roasted walnuts (see recipe for
   Roasted Nuts & Seeds on page 11)

½ cup bottled pesto sauce (less for
   milder taste)
½ cup alfalfa sprouts
¼ teaspoon black pepper
¼ teaspoon herbed seasoning salt

Wash the spinach. Pit, peel, and slice the avocados. Place in a large bowl with the cucumber, carrots, tomato, and roasted walnuts. Add the pesto sauce and toss. When the pesto sauce is well-mixed with the salad, add the alfalfa sprouts and toss again. Add pepper and salt and adjust seasonings to taste. You can refrigerate this salad to marinate or serve immediately.

Pesto, Spinach & Avocado Salad with Tofu

For a delicious main-course salad, you can add cubed tofu which has been marinated in a pesto and wine mixture.

SERVES 4-6

8 ounces extra-firm tofu, cubed
¼ cup pesto sauce
1 clove garlic, minced

2 tablespoons red wine
2 tablespoons tamari

Cut the tofu in ½-inch cubes. In a medium-sized bowl, combine the pesto sauce, garlic, wine, and tamari. Add the tofu, stir to cover, and marinate in the refrigerator for about an hour. After marinating, add the tofu cubes to the salad along with the remaining marinade, if desired. Toss gently and serve.

Curried Kale & Avocado Salad

Kale is one of the most nutritious greens in the world. Filled with calcium, vitamins A and C, and potassium, it is a useful addition to many recipes. However, it is one of the few greens that cannot be served raw in a salad. Without steaming, it tends to be bitter, hard to chew and digest. So the following was an experiment that resulted in a wonderful braised salad. This recipe couples the crunch of the other vegetables with the softness of kale and onions. The quick extra step is worth the effort!

SERVES 4-6

For the Salad:

1 large onion, sliced in half-moons
1 cup of water
4 cups kale, stemmed and chopped (about 1 medium bunch)
1 medium ripe avocado, peeled, pitted, and cubed
1 medium tomato, chopped
1 medium cucumber, peeled and chopped
½ cup roasted sunflower seeds (see recipe for Roasted Nuts & Seeds on page 11)

For the Curry Vinaigrette Dressing:

¼ cup water
2 tablespoons tamari
2 tablespoons cider vinegar
2 tablespoons olive oil (optional)
½ teaspoon curry powder
¼ teaspoon black pepper
¼ teaspoon herb seasoning salt

Place the sliced onion in a large saucepan. Add water, cover, and steam for 3 minutes. Add the chopped kale, cover, and steam for 3-5 minutes until the kale is just tender. Drain the onions and kale, place on a clean, dry cloth, and put into the refrigerator to chill.

While the kale and onions are chilling, prepare the avocado, tomato, and cucumber. Place in a large bowl. Add the chilled kale and onions and top with the roasted sunflower seeds.

Combine all the dressing ingredients in a small bowl and whisk thoroughly to mix. Pour the dressing over the kale and avocado salad. Toss and chill before serving.

Almond Ginger Pasta & Tofu Salad

When my boys were young, this simple meal came about in my efforts to introduce the sea vegetable, arame. This mild tasting seaweed contains a bundle of minerals. This one-pot meal was an instant hit among children and in the cooking classes.

SERVES 4-6

For the Salad:

½ pound uncooked Jerusalem
   artichoke rigatoni or penne
½ pound extra-firm tofu, cubed
½ crown of broccoli, chopped
1 carrot, finely chopped
2 tablespoons arame
½ cup raisins
½ cup fresh parsley, chopped
½ cup slivered almonds

For the Almond Ginger Sauce:

½ cup almond butter
½ cup water
1 teaspoon tamari
1 tablespoon honey
1 tablespoon cider vinegar
1 tablespoon fresh ginger root, grated

Put a large pot of water on to boil over medium-high heat for the pasta. Cook the pasta until partially done, approximately 5 minutes. Do not drain.

Add the tofu, chopped broccoli, carrots, arame, and raisins to the partially cooked pasta and bring to a boil again. Simmer for about 3-5 minutes or until the pasta is done and the vegetables are just tender. Drain in a colander and place in a large bowl.

To prepare the Almond Ginger Sauce, place all the ingredients in a blender and blend at medium speed to mix. Add additional water if necessary and slowly blend to a creamy consistency.

Add the parsley and almonds to the vegetable and pasta mixture. Toss gently with the Almond Ginger Sauce. Chill and serve as a main dish salad. This recipe can also be served warm.

Tortellini & Chickpea Salad

The first time I consumed a cheese tortellini was in a pasta salad made by my dear friend, Andrea. My children were small and had seconds and thirds of this dish. I'm sure you will like this simple version of her delicious salad. If you don't have tortellini on hand, you can substitute penne or other short, chunky pasta. This salad can be served warm or cold.

SERVES 4-6

8-ounce package uncooked cheese tortellini or penne

1 tablespoon olive oil
4 cloves garlic, minced
2 cups cooked chickpeas, drained (or 1 19-ounce can, drained and rinsed)
½ tablespoons tamari
½ cup water
½ cup fresh tomatoes, chopped
1 medium red pepper, chopped
½ cup fresh parsley, finely chopped

Prepare the cheese tortellini or penne according to package instructions and drain.

In a large skillet, sauté the minced garlic in olive oil. Add cooked chickpeas and cooked tortellini or penne. Stir. Add tamari and water. Stir in the tomatoes and red pepper. Top with fresh parsley and serve warm as an entrée or cold as a summer salad.

Cafe Chimes Tabouli Salad

We have lots of requests for our Tabouli Salad. I think the secret to this salad's unique taste lies in the addition of the roasted sunflower seeds.

SERVES 4-6

For the Salad:

1 cup bulgur
1 cup boiling water
2 carrots, grated
1 medium cucumber, peeled and chopped
2 medium tomatoes, chopped
3 scallions, chopped
1 cup fresh parsley, chopped
½ cup fresh mint, chopped
½ cup roasted sunflower seeds (see recipe for Roasted Nuts & Seeds on page 11)

For the Lemon Tamari Dressing:

¼ cup cider vinegar
4 tablespoons lemon juice
½ cup olive oil
2 tablespoons tamari
3 cloves garlic, minced
pinch of sea salt
1 teaspoon black pepper

Rinse the bulgur a few times in a fine sieve. Place the bulgur in a large bowl, add boiling water, and cover with aluminum foil. Let sit for about one hour—peeking not allowed. Add the carrots, cucumber, tomatoes, scallions, parsley, mint, and roasted sunflower seeds. Toss gently.

In a bowl, blend the dressing ingredients with a whisk until creamy and well-mixed. Pour the dressing on the bulgur and vegetable mixture, toss gently, and refrigerate for a few hours before serving.

Bulgur & Lentil Salad with Tarragon & Walnuts

One day I was experimenting with ingredients, and somehow this salad came into existence. The combination of bulgur, lentils, and tarragon with the crunch of roasted walnuts is a perfect addition to any summer evening dinner. Great for lunch the next day too!!

SERVES 4-6

For the Salad:
1 cup bulgur
1 cup boiling water
1 cup dry brown lentils
4 cups water
1 cucumber, peeled and chopped
3 carrots, finely chopped
1 stalk celery, finely chopped
3 scallions, finely chopped
1 cup roasted walnuts (see recipe for Roasted Nuts & Seeds on page 11)
1 cup canned mandarin oranges, drained

For the Walnut Mint Dressing:
½ cup olive oil
¼ cup balsamic vinegar
1 tablespoon tamari
1 tablespoon fresh tarragon (or 1 teaspoon dried)
4 tablespoons dried mint
½ cup roasted walnuts (see recipe for Roasted Nuts & Seeds on page 11)
3 tablespoons orange juice concentrate
½ cup water
pinch of sea salt

Rinse the bulgur a few times in a fine sieve. Place the bulgur in a large bowl, add boiling water, and cover with aluminum foil. Let sit for about one hour—peeking not allowed. While the bulgur is sitting, wash the lentils. Combine the lentils with 4 cups of water in a large saucepan. Bring to a boil, reduce heat, and simmer, covered, for ½ hour or until tender. Drain and rinse with cold water.

While the lentils are cooking, chop the cucumbers, carrots, celery, and scallions. Place the vegetables and cooked lentils in the bowl with the bulgur and toss.

Place all of the dressing ingredients in a blender or food processor and blend at medium speed for about a minute until creamy and well-mixed. Pour the dressing on the bulgur salad. Toss and chill. When ready to serve, top the salad with the mandarin oranges and roasted walnuts.

Star Anise Tabouli with Maple Mustard Dressing

Up until this year, I had never even heard of star anise. I believe that Elsa introduced it to the Cafe by bringing some in for her tea. What a cooking discovery!!! You can purchase whole star anise from your health food store.

SERVES 6-8

For the Salad
1½ cups bulgur
1½ cups boiling water
2 whole star anise
3 carrots, grated
2 medium cucumbers, finely chopped
6 scallions, finely chopped
1 cup fresh parsley, finely chopped
½ cup roasted sunflower seeds (see recipe for Roasted Nuts & Seeds on page 11)

For the Maple Mustard Dressing:
½ cup olive oil
¼ cup lemon juice
1 teaspoon tamari
2 cloves garlic, minced
¼ cup maple syrup
1 teaspoon Dijon mustard
½ teaspoon miso
pinch of sea salt
pinch of black pepper

Rinse the bulgur a few times in a fine sieve. Place the bulgur in a large bowl, add boiling water and the whole star anise. Cover with aluminum foil and let sit for about one hour—peeking not allowed.

Discard the star anise from the cooked bulgur. Prepare the carrots, cucumbers, scallions, and parsley. Add the vegetables and sunflower seeds to the bulgur. Toss to mix.

Place all the dressing ingredients in a bowl. Whisk until well-mixed. Pour the dressing on the bulgur salad, toss, and refrigerate for at least one hour before serving.

Bountiful Bubble Berry Salad

My dear friend Anika named this salad perfectly. The first mouthful does taste like dancing bubbles. Full of protein and delicious, this salad will become a family favorite.

SERVES 4-6

For the Salad:

1½ cups wheat berries, soaked
1 cup wild rice
5 cups water
pinch of sea salt

1 red pepper, chopped
1 cup frozen peas, thawed
½ cup fresh parsley, finely chopped

For the Tahini Garlic Dressing:

1 small onion, coarsely chopped
2 cloves garlic, chopped
2 teaspoons tamari
1 tablespoon tahini
1 tablespoon sesame seed oil
¼ cup lemon juice
2 tablespoons cider vinegar
1 teaspoon dry mustard
½ cup water

The wheat berries must be soaked before cooking. Rinse the wheat berries thoroughly in a colander and place in a large saucepan. Add 4 cups of cold water and bring the water to a boil. Cook the wheat berries for 2 minutes. Cover the pot, remove from heat, and let stand for about 1 hour. Drain and add the soaked wheat berries to the wild rice for final cooking.

Wash the wild rice in a heavy saucepan and drain. Add the soaked wheat berries. Add fresh water and sea salt. Cover and bring to a boil. Reduce heat and steam, covered, for 45 minutes or until the wheat berries are tender. Place the cooked wheat berries and wild rice in a colander and rinse under cold water. Drain and cool.

Place the wheat berries and wild rice in large bowl and add the red pepper, thawed peas, and parsley. Toss gently to blend.

Place all the dressing ingredients in a blender or food processor. Blend at medium speed for a minute or until well-mixed. Adjust seasonings to taste. Pour over the wheat berry, rice, and vegetable mixture and toss gently. Chill at least one hour before serving.

59

Quantum Quinoa & Black Bean Salad

Quinoa is a protein-rich grain that has a couscous-like quality, but is superior nutritionally. I am so glad that someone is producing this old-new grain. It is now available in most health food stores. Don't be afraid of this largely unknown grain. It is very user-friendly and very tasty. I have not met a person yet who dislikes it upon first taste.

SERVES 4-6

For the Salad:

1 cup quinoa
2 cups water
pinch of sea salt

½ cup fresh or frozen peas, blanched
½ cup fresh or frozen corn, blanched
½ cup fresh parsley, chopped
1 15-ounce can black turtle beans,
   rinsed and drained
½ cup canned pineapple chunks,
   drained

For the Lemon Maple Dressing:

2 teaspoons tamari
¼ cup of lime or lemon juice
2 tablespoons maple syrup
1 teaspoon ground cumin
1 teaspoon ground coriander
⅓ cup olive oil
1 teaspoon red miso

Rinse the quinoa thoroughly in a fine sieve or colander. Place the quinoa, fresh water, and salt in a heavy saucepan. Bring to a boil, lower heat, and simmer, covered, for 20-25 minutes or until all the liquid is absorbed. Fluff with a fork and refrigerate to cool.

Bring a medium saucepan of water to a boil over medium-high heat. Blanch the peas and corn by plunging them into the boiling water for about one minute. Scoop them out with a slotted spoon and hold under cold running water to stop the cooking. If you are using frozen corn and peas, blanching is not necessary. Just thaw them briefly under cold running water.

Combine all the dressing ingredients in a small bowl and whisk thoroughly to mix.

In a large bowl, combine the cooled quinoa, blanched peas and corn, parsley, black beans, and pineapple chunks. Toss with the dressing and chill for a least an hour before serving.

Cafe Chimes House Dressing

Because I had no idea what I was getting myself into when I opened the Cafe, I tended to rely on friends for ideas and suggestions. This recipe came originally from my close friend, Cynthia. I don't recall how this particular dressing happened to end up as the main topping on all of the sandwiches we offered. However, I am very glad it turned out this way because this dressing has been by far the most popular offered at the Cafe. Enjoy!

MAKES 2 CUPS

½ onion, coarsely chopped
½ green pepper, seeded and coarsely chopped
1 clove garlic, minced
⅓ cup cider vinegar
½ cup tahini
¼ cup tamari
¼ cup canola oil
¼ cup water

1 tablespoon fresh dill weed, chopped (or 1 teaspoon dried)

Combine all the ingredients except for the dill weed in a blender and purée at low speed until smooth. Pour into a container with a lid (I prefer a glass jar), add the dill weed, cover and shake. Refrigerate before using.

For a delicious and simple cucumber salad, thinly slice a large European cucumber. Top with House Dressing and marinate for at least one hour before serving.

Diane's Dill Dressing

During the years I studied Whole Foods Cooking with my friend Diane Johnson, she created the following dressing and called it her house dressing. To this day, every time I prepare this recipe, I feel I am back in her kitchen on a hot summer's night tasting this wonderful dressing for the first time on a delicious cold boiled salad. YUM!!!

MAKES 1 CUP

¼ cup olive oil
⅓ cup white miso
1 tablespoon fresh ginger root, grated
½ cup fresh dill, chopped
½ cup scallions, chopped
½ cup water
2 tablespoons vinegar
1 tablespoon maple syrup

Combine all the ingredients in a blender. Blend on low speed until creamy. Refrigerate or use immediately.

Ruth's Tamari & Garlic Dressing

This is a very simple dressing—delicious on any green salad. A little tamari seems to "wake up" the lettuce.

MAKES ABOUT 1¼ CUPS

1 cup olive oil
2 tablespoons tamari
5 teaspoons lemon juice or white vinegar
1 tablespoon honey
1 large clove garlic, minced
1 teaspoon Dijon mustard (optional)

Combine all the ingredients in a small bowl and whisk until well-blended.

Raspberry Poppy Seed Dressing

Seems like everyone is watching their weight in the summer months. We developed the Raspberry Poppy Seed Dressing in response to requests for a healthy no-fat dressing. This dressing is perfect because it is filling, tasty, high in nutrients, and very low in fat. The combination came easily because I simply blended my favorite ingredients. The dressing is good on mixed greens and also combines well with a simple pasta salad. See the easy recipe below.

For the Raspberry Poppy Seed Dressing: Makes 1½ cups
½ cup frozen raspberries (or fresh)
½ cup water
½ onion, coarsely chopped
1 clove garlic
2 tablespoons cider vinegar
1 teaspoon tamari
2 tablespoons honey
2 tablespoons poppy seeds

Place the raspberries, water, onion, and garlic in a blender, and blend on low speed until smooth. Add the vinegar, tamari, honey, and poppy seeds. Blend briefly.

For the Pasta Salad: Serves 4-6
3 cups uncooked Jerusalem artichoke rigatoni or shells
3 scallions, chopped
2 carrots, grated
1 medium red pepper, chopped
½ cup fresh parsley, chopped
¼ cup roasted sunflower seeds (see recipe for Roasted Nuts & Seeds on page 11)

Put a large pot of water on to boil over medium-high heat for the pasta. Cook the rigatoni or shells in boiling water for approximately 8 minutes or until cooked al dente. Drain and chill.

Wash and chop the scallions, carrots, red peppers, and parsley. In a large bowl, combine the vegetables with the chilled pasta and the roasted sunflower seeds. Pour the Raspberry Poppyseed Dressing over the pasta and vegetable mixture and toss gently. Chill a few hours until serving time.

Almond Ginger Sauce

This is one of those sauces that "just happened." I first purchased almond butter years ago as a different choice for peanut butter and jelly sandwiches for my children. Years later I ordered a nine-pound tub of almond butter for the Cafe from the health food store, and a world of possibilities opened up. This sauce is wonderful on a pasta salad or garden salad.

MAKES 1 CUP

½ cup almond butter
½ cup warm water
1 teaspoon tamari
1 tablespoon honey
1 tablespoon fresh ginger root, coarsely chopped
1 tablespoon vinegar

Place all the ingredients in blender and purée at low speed. The sauce may be too thick because of the almond butter, so feel free to add more water slowly.

Teriyaki Ginger Sauce

There are many versions of Teriyaki Sweet and Sour Sauces in most recipe books. I seem to change my recipe each time I make it, so please be open to experimenting with measurements and ingredients. This sauce makes an incredible marinade for tofu or tempeh.

MAKES 1½ CUPS

½ cup water
¼ cup tamari
¼ cup lemon juice
1 clove garlic
1 teaspoon fresh ginger root, grated
¼ cup maple syrup
3 tablespoons roasted sesame seed oil

1 teaspoon white miso (optional)

Place all the ingredients in a blender and purée at low speed. The recipe should yield about 1½ cups, enough for any recipe. Feel free to use cider vinegar in place of the lemon juice. Add a dash of white miso for a nutritious full-bodied flavor.

Thai Peanut Sauce

With the popularity of international dishes on the rise in America, it was only a matter of time until we decided to offer a Thai Walker Sandwich at the Cafe. This Thai Peanut Sauce tops our delicious sandwich. It also blends well with grain casseroles and steamed vegetables.

MAKES 2¾ CUPS SAUCE

For the Sauce:
1 clove garlic, chopped
1 small onion, coarsely chopped
1 cup natural peanut butter
3 teaspoons tamari
¼ cup honey
¼ cup tomato sauce
½ teaspoon cayenne pepper
1 teaspoon ground coriander
½ teaspoon cinnamon
1 cup water
¼ cup lemon juice
3 tablespoons dried parsley

Place all the ingredients in a blender or food processor and blend for 2 minutes or until smooth and creamy. You may need to add more water because the peanut butter tends to thicken.

This sauce freezes well, so put the unused portion in small containers and freeze for a quick dinner choice.

Elsa's Traditional Marinara Sauce

MAKES ABOUT 1½ QUARTS SAUCE

2 tablespoons olive oil
1 large onion, chopped
3-4 cloves garlic, minced
4-5 white mushrooms, sliced
¼ cup fresh basil, chopped, or 1 tablespoon dried
2 teaspoons dried oregano
¼ cup fresh parsley, chopped, or 2 tablespoons dried
1 teaspoon fennel seeds
1 15-ounce can whole peeled tomatoes, drained
2 15-ounce cans plain tomato sauce
½ cup red wine
¼ cup fresh chopped parsley for topping

In a large saucepan or soup kettle, sauté the onion and garlic in oil until the onion is translucent. Add the mushrooms, basil, oregano, parsley, and fennel seed. (The fennel seeds will stay crunchy, so you may want to use a tea bell for the seeds.) Sauté until the mushrooms are tender.

Add the drained whole peeled tomatoes, breaking up the tomatoes as you put them in the pot. Add the tomato sauce and red wine. Allow to simmer for at least 2 hours on low heat, stirring occasionally to avoid scorching. The longer this cooks, the better the flavor.

Serve on the pasta of your choice or use as an ingredient in our pizza or calzone recipes. If you have any sauce left over, you can easily freeze it for a quick dish at any time.

Orange Scallion Sauce

Orange juice concentrate lends itself to a variety of culinary surprises. You may also experiment with other juice concentrates in place of the orange juice.

MAKES 2 CUPS

½ cup frozen orange juice concentrate
1 teaspoon white miso
2 teaspoons orange rind, grated
½ cup scallions, finely chopped
½ teaspoon tamari
½ teaspoon maple syrup
½ cup water

1 teaspoon arrowroot powder
1 cup cold water

Combine the orange juice concentrate, miso, orange rind, scallions, tamari, and maple syrup in a small saucepan on low heat. Add ½ cup water, stir, and simmer for 5 minutes. In a small bowl, add the arrowroot to one cup of cold water. Stir to mix, then add to the saucepan. Simmer, stirring, until the sauce is thick.

Serve with vegetables such as green beans, squash, or carrots. Also delicious on a grain casserole.

Fruited Black Bean & Carrot Sauce

This sauce could be titled "The I Can't Believe I Did This Sauce." I totally followed my intuition and below is the finished product of that path. I hope you enjoy the recipe, and I hope this opens up your own creative paths.

MAKES 2 CUPS

2 cups water
2 carrots, chopped

1 15-ounce can black beans, drained and rinsed
½ cup canned mandarin oranges, drained
¼ cup frozen orange juice concentrate
½ cup water
1 tablespoon tamari
1 teaspoon ground cumin

Bring water to a boil in a small saucepan and add the chopped carrots. Reduce heat and simmer for 5 minutes or until the carrots are tender. Drain the carrots.

Place the cooked carrots and all the remaining ingredients in the blender and blend on medium speed for a minute. This sauce can be served over herbed brown rice for a complete protein meal.

Miso Tahini Sauce

Tahini is a natural in dressings and sauces. Make an effort to always have some on hand because it is versatile and fun to use. This sauce is wonderful on croquettes and grain casseroles.

MAKES ABOUT 1 CUP

⅛ *cup water*
½ *medium onion, chopped*
1-2 *cloves garlic, minced*
½ *teaspoon fresh ginger root, grated*

¼ *cup tahini*
1 *tablespoon tamari*
3 *tablespoons vinegar*
½ *cup honey*
1 *teaspoon white miso*
1 *teaspoon Dijon mustard*

Place the water, onion, garlic, and ginger in a blender or food processor and purée. Add the remaining ingredients and blend one more minute. If the sauce is too thick, add water to reach the desired pourable consistency.

Tahini Sauce for Croquettes

Every time I make millet croquettes, I prepare this sauce. Simple, elegant, and easy are the passwords for this blend of ingredients.

MAKES 1½ CUPS

½ cup tahini
1 tablespoon umeboshi plum paste
¾ cup hot water
½ cup fresh parsley, finely chopped
½ cup fresh scallions, finely chopped

In a small bowl, mix the tahini and umeboshi paste. Slowly add hot water to bring the sauce to a creamy consistency. Add parsley and scallions and stir. This sauce will thicken as it sits due to the thickening properties of the tahini. If necessary, you may add more hot water.

Tahini Lemon Sauce

This is a great sauce for any vegetarian burger or as a topping for a grain casserole. It is easy to prepare. You may want to make a double batch and freeze some in small containers for later use.

MAKES 1¼ CUPS

½ cup tahini
4 teaspoons tamari
½ cup water
3 tablespoons lemon juice
½ medium onion, coarsely chopped
2 cloves garlic, chopped
¼ cup fresh parsley, chopped (or 1 tablespoon dried parsley)
dash of cayenne pepper
½ teaspoon paprika
½ teaspoon ground cumin

½ cup scallions, chopped

Place all the ingredients except the scallions in a blender and purée at low speed until creamy.

Because tahini tends to thicken, you may want to use more warm water to reach the desired consistency. Add chopped scallions after blending.

Outrageous Orange Tahini Sauce

MAKES 1¾ CUPS

1 small onion, coarsely chopped
1 clove garlic
1 teaspoon fresh oregano
2 tablespoons honey
½ cup frozen orange juice concentrate
½ cup tahini
2 tablespoons tamari
½ cup water

Place all the ingredients in a blender and blend on medium speed until creamy. You may need to add additional water because the tahini tends to thicken. This sauce is wonderful served with grain croquettes or as a marinade for tofu or tempeh. Combine with steamed greens and buttercup squash.

The Jack-O-Lantern's Grin Sauce

I invented this recipe on October 31. What fun I had imagining a pumpkin sauce!

MAKES 1¾ CUPS

1 cup canned pumpkin pulp
2 tablespoons almond butter
¼ cup honey or maple syrup
½ cup water

Place all the ingredients in a blender and blend at high speed for about a minute, or until smooth and light. You may need to add more water, since the almond butter thickens naturally.

This simple sauce should be made just before serving. Delicious served on warm gingerbread!

Food prepared with Love
Is nourishment for the Soul

SOUPS

Soups

A hearty bowl of soup on a winter afternoon comforts body and soul. Since we have many cold winter afternoons in the Mount Washington Valley, we always have tasty soups available at the Cafe and at home. Served with a green salad and a slice of whole grain bread, soup makes a satisfying and nutritious meal.

Most of the soups in this section can be put together in a couple of hours or less. They can be served immediately or refrigerated for a later meal. Most soups taste even better when the flavors have had a chance to mellow.

Brazilian Black Bean Soup

This soup is one of the Cafe Chimes' all-time favorites and is requested frequently. For a spicier soup, you can add a little more cayenne or use a hotter variety of salsa.

SERVES 4-6

1 cup dried black beans, soaked (or 2
   15-ounce cans, drained and rinsed)

2 tablespoons canola oil
1 large onion, chopped
2 cloves garlic, minced
2 stalks celery, chopped
1 carrot, sliced in half-moons
1 red pepper, chopped
1 green pepper, chopped
2 teaspoons ground cumin

½ teaspoon cayenne pepper
1 teaspoon chili powder
¼ cup dried parsley
6 cups fresh water
1 15-ounce can whole peeled tomatoes,
   chopped, liquid reserved
½ cup salsa (your choice of mild,
   medium, or hot)
½ cup red wine
2 tablespoons tamari
½ cup fresh cilantro, chopped

Pick over the dry beans and rinse thoroughly. Soak the beans overnight in 5 cups of water, or use the faster method: bring the beans and water to a boil, boil for 2 minutes, remove the beans from heat, and let stand for 1 hour. Drain and continue with the recipe.

In a large soup pot, sauté the onion, garlic, celery, and carrot in oil until the onion is translucent. Add the red and green pepper and sauté briefly. Add the cumin, cayenne, chili powder, and dried parsley, and stir to mix.

Add the drained beans and fresh water. Bring to a boil, reduce heat, and simmer for 1 to 1½ hours or until the beans are tender.

Add chopped tomatoes and reserved liquid, red wine, tamari, and cilantro, and simmer for 10-15 minutes. Adjust seasonings to taste and serve hot. Good served with tortilla chips.

79

White Bean & Garlic Soup

Serves 4-6

1½ *cups dry white pea or navy beans, soaked (or 3 15-ounce cans, drained and rinsed)*
2 *tablespoons canola oil*
1 *large onion, chopped*
4 *cloves garlic, minced*
2 *tablespoons fresh rosemary, chopped (or 1 tablespoon dried)*
1 *carrot, chopped*
2 *stalks celery, chopped*
8 *cups fresh water*
⅔ *cup white wine*
2-3 *tablespoons tamari*
¼ *cup dried parsley*
½ *teaspoon black pepper*
½ *teaspoon herb seasoning salt*
3 *scallions, chopped*
¼ *cup fresh parsley, chopped*

Pick over the dry beans and rinse thoroughly. Soak the beans overnight in 5 cups of water, or use the faster method: bring the beans and water to a boil, boil for 2 minutes, remove the beans from heat, and let stand for 1 hour. Drain and continue with the recipe.

In a large soup pot, sauté the onion, garlic, and rosemary in oil until the onion is translucent. Add the carrot and celery. Add the drained beans and fresh water. Bring to a boil, reduce heat, and simmer for 1 to 1½ hours or until the beans are tender.

Add the white wine, tamari, dried parsley, black pepper, and herb seasoning salt, and simmer for 5-10 minutes. Adjust seasonings to taste and serve hot in bowls topped with scallions and fresh parsley. This soup is especially good when refrigerated and reheated before serving.

Lentil & Spinach Soup

SERVES 4-6

For the Soup:

1½ cups dry brown or red lentils
2 tablespoons sesame oil
1 medium onion, chopped
2 cloves garlic, minced
3 carrots, chopped
½ teaspoon dried thyme
1 teaspoon dried basil
½ teaspoon black pepper
6 cups water
1x3-inch strip of kombu, rinsed
10-ounce package fresh spinach, coarsely chopped
1-2 tablespoons red miso
4 tablespoons tamari
2 tablespoons cider vinegar (optional)
3 scallions, chopped

Optional additions:

3 stalks celery, chopped
2 medium potatoes, diced
1 medium tomato, chopped

Pick over the lentils and rinse thoroughly. In a large soup pot, sauté the onion and garlic in oil until the onion is translucent. Add the carrots, thyme, basil, and pepper, and sauté 3 more minutes. If you are feeling creative, add other vegetables at this point and sauté.

Add the rinsed lentils to the soup pot along with the water and kombu. Bring to a boil. Reduce heat and simmer for 1 hour or until lentils are tender. Remove kombu strip, chop finely, and return to the soup pot. Wash the spinach, remove stems, and chop coarsely. Add to the lentil mixture in the soup pot and simmer for 3 minutes.

Just before serving, add miso and tamari and mix thoroughly. Add cider vinegar, if desired, and adjust seasonings to taste. Pour soup into bowls and top with chopped scallions.

81

Mediterranean Lentil Soup

SERVES 4-6

1½ *cups dry brown lentils, rinsed*
2 *tablespoons canola oil*
1 *large onion, chopped*
2 *cloves garlic, minced*
2 *stalks celery, chopped*
1 *large carrot, sliced in half-moons*
6 *cups water*
1 *15-ounce can whole peeled tomatoes, chopped, liquid reserved*
¼ *cup red wine*
3 *tablespoons tamari*

Pick over the lentils and rinse thoroughly. In a large soup pot, sauté the onion, garlic, celery, and carrots in oil until the onion is translucent. Add water and bring to a boil. Add the lentils, reduce heat, and simmer for 1 hour or until the lentils are tender.

Add the tomatoes and reserved liquid, wine, and tamari. Simmer 5 minutes. Adjust seasonings to taste and serve hot.

Curried Red Lentil Soup

Serves 4-6

1 cup dry red lentils, rinsed
2 tablespoons canola oil
1 large onion, chopped
2 cloves garlic, minced
2 stalks celery, chopped
1 tablespoon fresh ginger root, grated
2 tablespoons curry powder
6 cups water
¼ cup dried parsley
½ cup red wine
2-3 tablespoons tamari

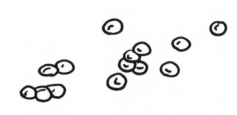

Pick over the lentils and rinse thoroughly. In a large soup pot, sauté the onion, garlic, and celery in oil until the onion is translucent. Add the ginger and curry powder and sauté briefly to mix. Add the water and lentils. Bring to a boil, reduce heat, and simmer for 45-50 minutes or until the lentils are tender.

Add the parsley, wine, and tamari, and simmer for 5-10 minutes. Adjust seasonings to taste and serve hot.

ginger root

Curried Split Pea Soup

SERVES 4-6

2 cups green or yellow split peas, rinsed
2 tablespoons olive oil
1 medium onion, chopped
1 clove garlic, minced
3 carrots, chopped
3 stalks celery, chopped
2 tablespoons curry powder
7 cups water
1x3-inch strip of kombu, rinsed
1 tablespoon tamari
2 tablespoons red miso
½ teaspoon herb seasoning salt
¼ teaspoon ground black pepper

½ cup roasted sunflower seeds (see recipe for Roasted Nuts & Seeds on page 11)

Pick over the green or yellow split peas and rinse thoroughly. In a large soup pot, sauté the onion, garlic, carrots, and celery in oil until the onion is translucent. Add curry powder and stir to blend with the sautéed vegetables.

Add the rinsed split peas, water, and kombu to the sautéed vegetables. Bring to a boil, reduce heat, and simmer for 1 to 1½ hours, or until the peas are soft. Add more water if necessary. Remove the kombu strip, chop finely, and return to the soup pot. Add tamari, miso, seasoning salt, and pepper. Adjust seasonings to taste. Pour into bowls and top with roasted sunflower seeds.

Split Pea Soup with Rosemary

Rosemary has a distinctive flavor that compliments this hearty soup nicely.

SERVES 4-6

2 cups green split peas, rinsed
2 tablespoons sesame oil
1 medium onion, chopped
2 cloves garlic, minced
1 stalk celery, chopped
1 carrot, sliced in half-moons
1 medium potato, cubed
2 tablespoons fresh rosemary, chopped (or 1 teaspoon dried)
6 cups water
1 15-ounce can whole peeled tomatoes, chopped, liquid reserved
2-3 tablespoons tamari
¼ cup red wine

Pick over the green split peas and rinse thoroughly. In a large soup pot, sauté the onion, garlic, and celery in oil until the onion is translucent. Add the carrot, potato, rosemary, and water. Bring to a rolling boil and add the rinsed split peas. Reduce heat and cook for 1 to 1½ hours, or until the split peas are soft. They will begin to break down and create a hearty broth. Add more water if necessary.

Add the chopped tomatoes and reserved liquid. Add the tamari and red wine. Simmer for 5 minutes, adjust seasonings to taste, and serve hot. Good with fresh bread and a green salad.

Creamy Millet & Corn Chowder

Becoming a vegetarian doesn't mean leaving all your favorite tastes behind. You are merely adapting them to a healthier version for a happier body and mind.

SERVES 4-6

2 tablespoons canola oil
1 large onion, chopped
2 cloves garlic, minced
2 stalks celery, chopped
2 large potatoes, cubed
5 cups water
¾ cup millet
2 cups extra soy milk
4 cups frozen corn
2-3 tablespoons tamari
½ cup fresh parsley, chopped (or 1 tablespoon dried)

In a large soup pot, sauté the onion, garlic, and celery in oil until the onion is translucent. Add the potatoes and water. Bring to a boil. Add the millet, reduce heat, and simmer 20 minutes or until the millet is soft.

Add the soy milk, frozen corn, and tamari. Simmer gently, stirring frequently until the corn is tender. Adjust seasonings to taste. Pour into bowls and top with chopped parsley. This chowder goes well with whole-wheat crackers from the health food store.

Healing Japanese Miso Soup

SERVES 4-6

6 cups water
1 tablespoon dried wakame
1 medium onion, sliced in half-moons
2 teaspoons fresh ginger root, grated
½ cup fresh shiitake mushrooms, chopped (or 3 dried, soaked and drained)
2 carrots, cut into matchsticks
1 cup chopped greens (watercress, collards, and kale are good choices)
4-6 teaspoons red miso
2 tablespoons tamari
3 scallions, chopped (optional)

In a large soup pot, bring the water and wakame to a boil. Add the onion, ginger, mushrooms, and carrots to the boiling water. Boil gently 4-6 minutes or until the vegetables are just tender. Add your choice of chopped greens and boil for 1-2 minutes.

Add 4-6 teaspoons of miso. A good guideline for miso is 1 teaspoon of miso to 1 cup of water. Go light with the miso at first, adding more if you wish. If you've added too much miso, you can always add more water. To finish the soup, add the tamari and adjust seasonings to taste. Simmer for 5 minutes to blend the flavors. Serve topped with chopped scallions, if desired.

Japanese Miso Soup with Daikon & Shiitake Mushrooms

SERVES 4-6

2 tablespoons sesame oil
1 medium onion, sliced in half-moons
2 cloves garlic, minced
1 cup fresh shiitake mushrooms, sliced (or 4-5 dried, soaked and drained)
1 teaspoon fresh ginger root, grated
1 carrot, cut in matchsticks
½ cup daikon, diced
1 cup Chinese cabbage, coarsely chopped
½ pound extra-firm tofu, cubed
6 cups water
1 tablespoon red miso
3-4 tablespoons tamari
cayenne pepper (optional)

1 8-ounce package udon noodles (optional)

In a large soup pot, sauté the onion and garlic in oil until the onion is translucent. Add the mushrooms, ginger, and carrots, and continue sautéing until the mushrooms are tender. Add the daikon, Chinese cabbage, and tofu, and sauté for 2 minutes. Add the water, bring to a boil, and simmer about 10 minutes until the daikon is tender. Add the miso and tamari and adjust seasonings to taste. Sprinkle sparingly with cayenne pepper, if desired.

If you are adding udon noodles, bring a separate large saucepan of water to a boil. Add the udon noodles to boiling water. Wait until the noodles rise to the surface. Reduce heat and simmer 10-15 minutes or until the noodles are tender. Drain and add to the soup pot before serving.

Carrot & Beet Soup

SERVES 4-6

3 whole beets, unpeeled and scrubbed
7 carrots, chopped
2 medium onions, chopped
6 cups water
1 bay leaf
1x3-inch strip of kombu, rinsed
½ teaspoon dried thyme
1 teaspoon herb seasoning salt
1 tablespoon sesame oil
1-2 tablespoons red miso
2 tablespoons tamari

1 teaspoon caraway seeds for topping hot soup
2 tablespoons chopped fresh dill for topping cold soup (or 1 teaspoon dried dill weed)

Cut off the beet stems and leaves and scrub gently. Place whole, unpeeled beets, 6 of the chopped carrots, and 1 chopped onion in a large soup pot. Add water, bay leaf, kombu, thyme, and seasoning salt, and bring to a boil. Reduce heat and simmer about 40-45 minutes or until the beets are tender. Discard the bay leaf. Remove the beets from the pot. Cool slightly, peel, and chop coarsely. Return to the soup pot.

While the beets are cooking, sauté 1 chopped onion and 1 chopped carrot in sesame oil in a skillet until the onion is translucent.

Purée the carrot-beet mixture in a blender or food processor until smooth and return to the soup pot. Add the sautéed carrots and onions. Add miso and tamari and adjust seasonings to taste.

This soup can be served hot or cold. The hot soup is good topped with caraway seeds. If serving cold, top with fresh or dried dill weed.

Red Russian Borscht

SERVES 4-6

3 medium beets, unpeeled and scrubbed
8 cups water
1x3-inch strip of kombu, rinsed
1 bay leaf
1 medium onion, chopped
½ head cabbage, cored and shredded
2 stalks celery, chopped
2 apples, peeled, cored, and chopped
1 tablespoon fresh dill weed, chopped (or 1 teaspoon dried)
1 tablespoon cider vinegar
2 tablespoons lemon juice
2 tablespoons tamari
1-2 tablespoons red miso

Cut off the beet stems and leaves and scrub gently. Place whole, unpeeled beets in a large soup pot. Add water, kombu, and bay leaf and bring to a boil. Reduce heat, and simmer about 40-45 minutes or until beets are tender. Discard the bay leaf. Remove the beets from the pot. Cool slightly, peel, and grate coarsely. Return to the soup pot. Remove kombu strip, chop finely, and return to the soup pot.

Add the chopped onion, shredded cabbage, celery, and apples to the soup pot. Cook 15 minutes at medium heat. Add dill, vinegar, lemon juice, tamari, and miso. Adjust seasonings to taste.

Callaloo Voodoo

This wonderful soup is a healthy adaptation of a traditional soup from Tobago.

SERVES 4-6

2 pounds silken tofu, drained, dried, and chopped
3 tablespoons peanut oil
3 scallions, minced
2 cloves garlic, minced
½ teaspoon dried thyme
1 10-ounce package fresh spinach, cleaned, stemmed, and coarsely chopped
 (In Tobago a local green called dasheen is used)
1 pound fresh or frozen okra, cut into rounds with tips and tails removed
7 cups water
½ teaspoon herb seasoning salt
¼ teaspoon ground black pepper
½ teaspoon crushed chili pepper (optional)
2 tablespoons tamari
2 tablespoons red miso
3 tablespoons fresh lime juice

Drain the tofu and gently press out extra moisture. In a large soup pot, heat the oil and stir in tofu. Add the scallions, garlic, and thyme and sauté for 2 minutes. Add the spinach, okra, water, seasoning salt, pepper, crushed chili pepper, and tamari. Bring to a boil, reduce heat, and simmer 30-35 minutes, stirring occasionally.

Remove the soup pot from heat and purée the tofu and vegetable mixture in a blender or food processor until smooth. Return to the soup pot and reheat gently. Add miso and blend thoroughly with a whisk. Add lime juice. Adjust seasonings to taste and serve hot.

Purée of Cauliflower Soup

SERVES 4-6

2 leeks, cleaned and finely chopped
2 tablespoons olive oil
1 teaspoon caraway seeds

1 head cauliflower, coarsely chopped
4 medium potatoes, peeled and chopped
6 cups water
1x3-inch strip of kombu, rinsed
1 bay leaf
2 tablespoons red miso
2 tablespoons tamari
½ teaspoon herb seasoning salt
¼ teaspoon black ground pepper

3 scallions, chopped

To clean the leeks, cut off the root ends at the very base. Cut off the top two inches of the leaves. Remove any bruised outside leaves. Split the leeks lengthwise. Turn the leeks about ¼-inch and make another lengthwise cut. This allows the leaves to be opened up and rinsed. Place in cold water and let stand until ready to use. Chop the leeks, retaining some of the tender green portions of the stalk. Heat the oil in a skillet and sauté the chopped leeks until tender. Add caraway seeds and set the sautéed leeks aside.

In a large soup pot, combine the cauliflower, potatoes, water, kombu, and bay leaf. Bring to a boil, reduce heat, and simmer 20-25 minutes or until the vegetables are tender. Discard the bay leaf. Remove the soup pot from the heat and purée the soup in a blender or food processor until smooth. Return to the soup pot and reheat gently.

Add the sautéed leek and caraway seed mixture to the soup pot. Add miso, tamari, seasoning salt, and pepper. Adjust seasonings to taste. Simmer for 10 minutes, stirring occasionally. Pour into bowls and top with chopped scallions.

Marvelous Minestrone

The ingredient list looks intimidating, but this soup really comes together in about 25 minutes—a truly delectable soup!

SERVES 6-8

2 tablespoons olive oil
1 large onion, chopped
2 cloves garlic, minced
2 stalks celery, chopped
1 carrot, sliced in half-moons
1 cup mushrooms, chopped
½ green pepper, chopped
½ red pepper, chopped
1 zucchini, sliced in half-moons
¾ cup broccoli florets, chopped
6 cups water
1 15-ounce can chickpeas, drained and rinsed
1 cup cooked rigatoni or rotini (½ cup uncooked)
1 15-ounce can whole peeled tomatoes, chopped, liquid reserved
½ cup red wine
¼ cup tamari
1 tablespoon dried basil
1 tablespoon dried oregano
¼ cup dried parsley

In a large soup pot, sauté the onion and garlic in oil until the onion is translucent. Add the celery, carrots, mushrooms, green and red pepper, zucchini, and broccoli. Sauté, stirring frequently, until the vegetables are just tender.

Add the water, chickpeas, cooked pasta, tomatoes and reserved liquid, wine, tamari, basil, oregano, and parsley. Bring to a boil, reduce heat, and simmer for 10-15 minutes. Adjust seasonings to taste and serve hot with fresh whole-grain bread.

93

Onion Soup

SERVES 4-6

1 tablespoon sesame oil
5 Spanish onions, thinly sliced
2 cloves garlic, minced
1 tablespoon fresh ginger root, grated
2 tablespoons ground mustard
4 teaspoons dried thyme
1 teaspoon dried rosemary
6 cups water
2 tablespoons tamari
2 tablespoons red miso
½ cup soy cheese grated (optional)
1 cup herbed bread croutons (optional)

In a large soup pot, sauté the onions in oil until translucent. Add the garlic, ginger, mustard, thyme, and rosemary. Sauté 2 minutes. Add water and bring to a boil. Reduce heat and simmer for 15 minutes.

Add tamari and miso and adjust seasonings to taste. Pour into bowls and top with grated soy cheese and herbed croutons, if desired.

Tangy Curried Parsnip Soup

SERVES 4-5

1 tablespoon canola oil
1 medium onion, chopped
2 cloves garlic, minced
1 tablespoon curry powder
1 tablespoon fresh ginger root, grated
2 cups parsnips, sliced (3-4 parsnips)
2 carrots, chopped
5 cups water
1 cup unsweetened apple juice
¼ teaspoon ground black pepper
2 tablespoons tamari
1-2 tablespoons red miso

3 scallions, chopped (or ½ cup cilantro, chopped)

In a large soup pot, sauté the onion and garlic in oil until the onion is translucent. Add ginger and curry powder and stir to blend.

Add the parsnips and carrots and sauté for 3 minutes. Add water, apple juice, black pepper, and tamari. Bring to a boil, reduce heat, and simmer covered 20 minutes, or until the vegetables are soft.

Remove the soup pot from heat. Purée the vegetable mixture in a blender or food processor. Return to the soup pot, reheat, and add miso. Adjust seasonings to taste.

Serve topped with chopped scallions or cilantro.

Barley Vegetable Soup

SERVES 4-6

2 tablespoons canola oil
1 medium onion, chopped
2 cloves garlic, minced
1 stalk celery, chopped
1 bay leaf
6 whole peppercorns
1 carrot, sliced in half-moons
1 potato, peeled and cubed
1 cup green cabbage, thinly sliced (optional)
7 cups water
1 cup barley, rinsed
1 15-ounce can whole peeled tomatoes, chopped, liquid reserved
¼ cup red wine (optional)
½ cup frozen peas
½ cup frozen corn
¼ cup dried parsley
2-3 tablespoons tamari

In a large soup pot, sauté the onion, garlic, and celery in oil until the onion is translucent. Add the bay leaf, peppercorns, carrot, potato, cabbage, if desired, and water. Bring the water to a rolling boil and add the barley. Reduce heat and cook 45-55 minutes or until the barley is soft.

Add the chopped tomatoes and the reserved liquid. Add red wine, if desired. Add the peas, corn, and parsley. Simmer for 5-10 minutes. Discard the bay leaf. Add tamari and adjust seasonings to taste.

Sweet Buttercup Squash Soup

Serves 4-6

2 tablespoons canola oil
2 medium onions, chopped
2 cloves garlic, minced
6 cups water
1 buttercup squash (about 1 pound), peeled, seeded, and cubed
1x3-inch strip of kombu, rinsed
1-2 tablespoons red miso
1 tablespoon tamari
3 scallions, chopped (or ½ cup parsley, chopped)
½ cup roasted sunflower seeds (see recipe for Roasted Nuts & Seeds on page 11)

In large soup pot, sauté the onions and garlic in oil until the onions are translucent. Add the water, squash, and kombu. Bring to a boil, reduce heat, and simmer until the squash is tender, about 20 to 25 minutes. Remove the soup pot from the heat and purée the soup in a blender or food processor until smooth. Return to the soup pot and reheat gently.

Add miso and tamari and adjust seasonings to taste. Top with chopped scallions or parsley and add a sprinkling of roasted sunflower seeds to each bowl.

Nasrudin was now an old man looking back on his life. He sat with his friends in the tea shop telling his story.

"When I was young I was fiery—I wanted to awaken everyone. I prayed to Allah to give me the strength to change the world.

"In mid-life I awoke one day and realized my life was half over and I had changed no one. So I prayed to Allah to give me the strength to change those close around me who so much needed it.

"Alas, now I am old and my prayer is simpler. 'Allah,' I ask, 'please give me the strength to at least change myself.'"

Sufi

SANDWICHES

Sandwiches

Cafe Chimes is best known for its hearty sandwiches. Originally we started out with just five different sandwiches. Then we expanded our vegetarian choices including the many "Walker" sandwiches served on a whole-wheat chapati (a round flat bread resembling a tortilla). These are especially popular with hikers who frequent the many trails and mountain peaks in the area.

A typical Cafe Chimes sandwich includes a large slice of bread, a bed of lettuce, the filling, a layer of carrots, sprouts, dressing, and another layer of lettuce. Topped with a second hearty slice of bread, these sandwiches are a complete meal in themselves. Serve them alone or with a bowl of homemade soup, and you'll have a satisfying and nutritious lunch or dinner.

Cafe Chimes Hummus

There is something special about this particular hummus. We receive daily compliments about this tasty filling. I believe the secret is to blend the hummus so that it is still chunky. At the Cafe we use our large Hobart mixer, but you can accomplish the same thing with a food processor. We omit the added olive oil that many recipes insist on and include toasted sesame seeds for crunch.

MAKES ABOUT 3½ CUPS

1 medium onion, chopped
2 cloves garlic, minced
2 tablespoons fresh lemon juice
2 tablespoons cider vinegar
1-2 tablespoons tamari
1 tablespoon curry powder (optional)
2 15-ounce cans chickpeas, drained and rinsed
¼ cup tahini
¼ cup toasted sesame seeds
½ cup fresh parsley, chopped (or ¼ cup dried)
salt and pepper, to taste

In a food processor, purée the onion, garlic, lemon juice, vinegar, tamari, and curry powder, if desired, until the mixture is smooth. Add half of the chickpeas and half of the tahini and blend until smooth. Add the remaining chickpeas and tahini and blend coarsely, so that the mixture is chunky.

Toast the sesame seeds in a heavy skillet over medium heat until they are golden. Shake the pan or stir constantly to avoid burning. Add the toasted sesame seeds and parsley to the hummus and stir to blend. Adjust seasonings to taste.

Serve as a sandwich filling. This is also delicious served as a dip with toasted pita wedges or fresh vegetables.

Curried Tofu à la Chimes

When the Cafe Chimes first opened, I didn't have much hope for success for a Curried Tofu Sandwich. Why? Because most people were not familiar with tofu, and curry is a strong flavor. Yet, our curried tofu was unique and extremely flavorful. Within a month, I knew I had nothing to worry about. Curried Tofu à la Chimes has remained one of the top three favorite sandwiches.

MAKES FILLING FOR 4 SANDWICHES

1 pound extra-firm tofu, frozen and thawed

For the Curry Sauce:
¼ cup canola oil
3 tablespoons tamari
2 tablespoons honey
1 medium onion, chopped
1 clove garlic, minced
1 tablespoon curry powder
½ teaspoon black pepper
½ cup water
2 tablespoons natural smooth peanut butter
2 tablespoons dried parsley

When tofu is frozen and thawed, it resembles a sponge in texture. Gently squeeze out excess water from the tofu and pat dry with a clean cloth.

Blend all the sauce ingredients in a blender or food processor until smooth.

Cut the tofu into 8 rectangular slices and place in a glass baking dish. Pour the Curry Sauce over the tofu and marinate several hours or overnight. Sprinkle parsley over the tofu slices and bake for 15-20 minutes at 350 degrees.

Serve hot or cold on Whole-Wheat Mountain Bread or on a chapati. The Curried Tofu is also good served hot with brown rice or couscous.

Tempeh à la Harlan Sandwich Filling

This sandwich is named after Harlan, a frequent customer and friend of Cafe Chimes. I remember him sitting at one of the tables saying, "I have a great recipe for a tempeh sandwich. If you made it, I would be here every day." He was right about it being a great recipe, and for years, he was at the Cafe every Monday, the only day we served the Tempeh à la Harlan Sandwich. Because of this sandwich, Monday was our busiest day of the week.

MAKES FILLING FOR 4 SANDWICHES

1 8-ounce package of 3-grain tempeh
2 cups water
2 tablespoons tamari

¼ cup mayonnaise or nayonnaise
1 stalk celery, chopped
1 carrot, grated
½ medium onion, finely chopped
¼ cup roasted walnuts, chopped (see recipe for Roasted Nuts & Seeds on page 11)
1 teaspoon cumin powder
½ teaspoon paprika
1 teaspoon garlic powder
¼ cup fresh parsley, chopped (or 2 tablespoons dried)

Place the block of tempeh in a large saucepan with water and tamari. Bring to a boil, reduce heat, and gently simmer for 15 minutes. Remove the tempeh, cool, and crumble with hands into a bowl.

Add the mayonnaise, celery, carrots, onion, walnuts, cumin, paprika, garlic powder, and parsley. Stir to mix. Adjust seasonings to taste and refrigerate.

Serve on a chapati or Whole-Wheat Mountain Bread with all your favorite fixings.

Tropical Tofu Spinach Sandwich Filling

This was another of those creations that just seemed to happen. You just can't go wrong with a combination of spinach, mushrooms, red pepper, and tofu.

MAKES FILLING FOR 4-6 SANDWICHES

1 tablespoon canola oil
1 medium onion, chopped
2 cloves garlic, minced
1 teaspoon oregano, fresh or dried
4-5 medium mushrooms, sliced
1 medium red pepper, chopped
¼ cup water
½ cup frozen orange juice concentrate
1 pound extra-firm tofu, cubed
1 tablespoon tamari
4 cups fresh spinach, stemmed and coarsely chopped

In a medium skillet, sauté the onion and garlic in oil until the onion is translucent. Add fresh or dried oregano. Stir and enjoy the aroma. Add the mushrooms and red peppers and sauté for 3-5 minutes. Add the water and orange juice concentrate. Stir and simmer for about 10 minutes.

Add the cubed tofu to the vegetable mixture. Add tamari and stir. Simmer for 10 minutes, stirring occasionally. Adjust seasonings to taste and cool slightly.

Wash and thoroughly dry the fresh spinach before chopping. Place the coarsely chopped and stemmed spinach in a bowl. Pour the sautéed vegetable and tofu mixture over the spinach. Stir to mix and refrigerate, covered.

Use as a sandwich filling. The mixture is delicious rolled in a warmed chapati!

Tofu, Cucumber & Avocado Sandwich Filling

MAKES FILLING FOR 4-6 SANDWICHES

1 pound extra-firm tofu, cubed
1 cup water
4 tablespoons tamari
1 medium European cucumber, sliced in half-moons
1 avocado, pitted, peeled, and chopped
1 medium red pepper, chopped
1 small onion, chopped
2 tablespoons fresh lemon juice
1 teaspoon garlic powder (or granulated garlic)
¼ teaspoon salt
½ teaspoon cumin powder
¼ teaspoon cayenne powder
¼ cup fresh parsley, chopped

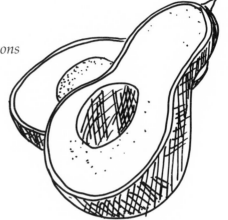

Place the cubed tofu, water, and tamari in a small saucepan. Bring to a boil, reduce heat, and cook over medium heat for 10 minutes. Drain and cool.

Combine the cucumber, avocado, red pepper, and onion in a medium bowl. Add lemon juice and stir. Combine the cooled tofu cubes with the chopped vegetables. Fold in the garlic powder, salt, cumin, cayenne, and fresh parsley. Chill.

Serve as a sandwich filling in chapatis. Also good as a salad served on leafy green lettuce or spinach leaves.

Italian Walker

The Italian Walker is simply a big Italian vegetable stir-fry in a chapati. We take all types of Italian vegetables, sauté them, and chill them for serving. We don't need a special sauce because sautéing the vegetables and herbs actually yields delicious natural juices.

MAKES FILLING FOR 4 SANDWICHES

1 tablespoon olive oil
1 medium onion, sliced
2 cloves garlic, minced
1 small eggplant, peeled and cubed
1 small zucchini, cubed
5 medium mushrooms, sliced

1 15-ounce can whole tomatoes in juice, chopped, liquid reserved
½ cup water
2 tablespoons tamari
½ teaspoon dried thyme
¼ cup fresh basil, chopped (or 1 tablespoon dried)
1 teaspoon dried oregano

Heat the olive oil in a large covered skillet and sauté the onions, garlic, eggplant, zucchini, and mushrooms until tender. Add the tomatoes with juice, water, and tamari. Cover and steam for about 3 minutes. Add the thyme, basil, and oregano. Simmer gently, covered, for 20 minutes.

This can be refrigerated and served cold. It is also delicious served warm on a chapati, or with noodles or rice.

Thai Walker

Once we developed a tasty Thai Peanut Sauce, and I realized that it would be a perfect sauce for a Walker Sandwich. This recipe uses quinoa as the sandwich filler, but you can easily substitute couscous or millet.

MAKES 4 SANDWICHES

½ cup quinoa, rinsed
¾ cup water
2 tablespoons dried parsley
½ teaspoon herb seasoning salt

4 chapatis
4 leafy lettuce leaves
1 cup broccoli, finely chopped
2 carrots, grated
1 cup alfalfa sprouts
½ cup Thai Peanut Sauce (see recipe on page 67)

Rinse the quinoa in a fine sieve. Place the quinoa in a medium saucepan and add the water. Bring to a boil, reduce heat, and simmer, covered, for about 10-15 minutes. Toss with a fork, add the parsley and herb seasoning salt, and stir to blend.

On each chapati, place a lettuce leaf, then about ½ cup of quinoa. Top with broccoli, carrots, sprouts, and the Thai Peanut Sauce. Roll up the chapatis and enjoy. You may want to have a fork handy, as the filling tries to escape!

Grain Walker

This is about the biggest, heartiest sandwich we offer at the Cafe Chimes. We take the Grain of the Day and build the sandwich from the bottom up. Consuming this sandwich satisfies the vegetable quota for the day!

MAKES 4 SANDWICHES

4 chapatis
4 leafy lettuce leaves
2 cups of cooked seasoned grains (your choice of brown rice, millet, quinoa, or couscous)
2 carrots, grated
½ cup alfalfa sprouts
½ cup Cafe Chimes House Dressing (optional—see recipe on page 61)
½ cup hummus (optional)

On each chapati, place a lettuce leaf, then about ½ cup of the cooked seasoned grains. Top with carrots, sprouts, and dressing, if desired. If you have hummus on hand, it adds a high-protein taste boost to this sandwich. Roll up the chapatis and serve.

Bulgur & Tofu Garden Burgers

Bulgur most closely resembles ground beef, so we use it for almost all of the garden burgers we create. The tofu in this recipe goes visually unnoticed, but provides a nutritional bonus in the form of protein. Serve on a whole-wheat bun with lettuce, tomato, and a dressing of your choice. WOW!!

MAKES 8 LARGE BURGERS

1 cup bulgur, rinsed
1¾ cups boiling water

1 tablespoon olive oil
1 clove garlic, minced
1 medium onion, finely chopped
3 stalks celery, finely chopped
1 teaspoon chili powder
1 teaspoon ground coriander
1 teaspoon garlic powder

1 pound firm tofu, drained and mashed
1 cup roasted sunflower seeds (see recipe for Roasted Nuts & Seeds on page 11)
2 carrots, grated
½ cup fresh parsley, chopped (or ¼ cup dried)
½ cup whole-wheat flour
½ cup rolled oats
¼ cup nutritional yeast
1 tablespoon tamari
1 teaspoon herb seasoning salt
¼ cup water, if needed

Rinse the bulgur in a fine sieve. Place in a large heatproof mixing bowl. Add boiling water. Cover and let sit for 20-25 minutes until all the water is absorbed.

Meanwhile, in a large skillet, sauté the garlic, onion, and celery in oil until the onion is translucent. Add chili powder, coriander, and garlic powder. Stir to blend.

When the bulgur is done, add the sautéed vegetables to the cooked bulgur in the bowl. Add the mashed tofu, sunflower seeds, grated carrots, and parsley. Add flour, oats, and nutritional yeast and stir to mix thoroughly. Add tamari and herb seasoning salt. Knead the mixture until it holds together, adding a little water if the mixture seems too dry.

With wet hands, form the mixture into 8 palm-sized patties. Bake on an oiled cookie sheet at 350 degrees for 25-30 minutes, or until lightly browned. Serve hot on a bun with the dressing of your choice.

Baked Falafels with Tahini Lemon Sauce

Falafels are spicy chickpea patties which are usually deep-fried. The first time I prepared Falafels at the Cafe, I nearly had to call the fire department. That was the first and only time I deep-fried anything. The smoke we created was scary! I quickly came up with a baked method to avoid frying.

SERVES 4-6

For the Falafels:
3 carrots, finely grated
½ cup fresh cilantro, chopped (optional)

1 medium onion, chopped
1 clove garlic, minced
2 cups cooked chickpeas, mashed (or 1 19-ounce can, drained and rinsed)
½ cup tahini
¼ cup whole-wheat flour
¼ cup nutritional yeast
½ cup water
¼ cup fresh parsley, chopped (or 2 tablespoons dried)
1 teaspoon ground cumin
½ teaspoon ground coriander
¼ teaspoon allspice
2 tablespoons tamari

For the Tahini-Lemon Sauce:
1 cup tahini
2 tablespoons tamari
½ cup water
2 tablespoons lemon juice
1 medium onion, finely chopped
1 tablespoon garlic powder
½ cup fresh parsley, chopped (or 2 tablespoons dried)
½ teaspoon cumin powder
pinch cayenne
pinch paprika

To prepare the Falafels, grate the carrots. Combine with chopped cilantro, if desired, and set aside.

Combine all the remaining Falafel ingredients in a food processor or blender. Mix thoroughly until creamy. Fold in the grated carrots and cilantro, if desired, and mix well.

Spread evenly in an oiled 10-inch glass pie dish and bake at 350 degrees for 20 minutes, or until lightly browned. (If you prefer, you can form into 6 palm-sized patties and bake on an oiled cookie sheet at 350 degrees for 20 minutes, or until lightly browned.)

Prepare the Tahini-Lemon Sauce while the Falafels are baking. Place all the sauce ingredients in a blender and blend until creamy. Add more water if necessary to maintain a creamy medium-thick consistency. Adjust seasonings to taste.

Cut the Falafels into wedges for sandwiches. Serve hot with Tahini-Lemon Sauce in warm pocket bread or a rolled chapati. You can also serve Falafels as an appetizer with vegetables and crackers.

Sunflower-Dill Vegetable Chimer

This recipe is one of those gifts that arise when the timing is right. While I was preparing the morning Cinnamon Swirls at the Cafe, someone commented on how interesting the Swirls would be as a type of sandwich. And from that conversation, the Cafe Chimes Chimers were born. You are only limited by your imagination. Anything goes in a Chimer, but this recipe gives you a way to start.

MAKES 6 CHIMERS

1 lb. whole-wheat bread dough (see recipe for Whole-Wheat Mountain Bread on
    page 26 or use a prepared frozen or refrigerated loaf)
1 medium onion, finely chopped
1 cup broccoli, finely chopped
1 cup cauliflower, finely chopped
1 cup summer squash, finely chopped
1 cup cheddar cheese, grated (optional)
1 cup roasted sunflower seeds (see recipe for Roasted Nuts & Seeds on page 11)
½ cup Cafe Chimes House Dressing (see recipe on page 61)
1 teaspoon fresh or dried dill, chopped

If you are using frozen or refrigerated dough, bring the dough to room temperature. Oil an 11x17-inch cookie sheet. Place the dough on a board and roll out into a large flat rectangle (approximately 12x16-inches).

Sprinkle the chopped onion, broccoli, cauliflower, and summer squash over the dough. Top with cheese, if desired.

Pour the House Dressing evenly over the cheese and vegetables. Sprinkle on most of the sunflower seeds (saving some). Starting at the short end, roll up the dough and filling. Using a serrated knife, cut the roll into 6 slices.

Place the slices flat on the oiled cookie sheet. Sprinkle with fresh dill and remaining sunflower seeds. Bake for 15 minutes at 350 degrees. Cool slightly before serving.

Greek Spinach & Feta Calzones

SERVES 4-6

1 lb. whole-wheat bread dough (see recipe for Whole-Wheat Mountain Bread on
*   page 26 or use a prepared frozen or refrigerated loaf)*
4 cups fresh spinach, stemmed, coarsely chopped, and dried
1 medium red onion, thinly sliced in half-moons
1 cup feta cheese, crumbled
½ cup black olives, sliced

If you are using frozen or refrigerated dough, bring the dough to room temperature. Oil an 11x17-inch cookie sheet. Roll out the dough with a rolling pin right on the cookie sheet, or if your rolling pin doesn't fit, place the dough on a board and roll out into an 11x17-inch flat rectangle. Fit the dough into the cookie sheet. Sometimes you have to hand-pull the dough to the corners of the cookie sheet.

Sprinkle the spinach, onion, feta cheese, and olives lengthwise down the middle third of the dough. Fold the left side of the dough across the filling lengthwise, then fold the other side across, so that the dough overlaps completely. Fold up the ends and pinch the dough to seal. Prick the dough here and there with a fork.

Bake at 350 degrees for 30-40 minutes. Remove from the oven, cool slightly, and cut into 4-6 serving pieces. Serve hot.

Italian Eggplant Calzones

SERVES 4-6

1 lb. whole-wheat bread dough (see recipe for Whole-Wheat Mountain Bread on
* page 26 or use a prepared frozen or refrigerated loaf)*
2 tablespoons olive oil
1 large onion, thinly sliced in half-moons
1 large green pepper, chopped
1 large red pepper, chopped
1 small eggplant, peeled and cut into small cubes
1 cup soy or mozzarella cheese, grated
¼ cup Parmesan cheese, grated
½ cup marinara sauce
¼ cup fresh basil, chopped (or 2 tablespoons dried)

If you are using frozen or refrigerated dough, bring the dough to room temperature. Oil an 11x17-inch cookie sheet. Roll out the dough with a rolling pin right on the cookie sheet, or if your rolling pin doesn't fit, place the dough on a board and roll out into an 11x17-inch flat rectangle. Fit the dough into the cookie sheet. Sometimes you have to hand-pull the dough to the corners of the cookie sheet.

In a large skillet, sauté the onion, green and red pepper, and the eggplant in oil about 5-7 minutes or until the eggplant is just tender. Remove from heat and pour off any accumulated liquid. The mixture should be dry. Stir in the mozzarella and Parmesan cheese and mix until well-blended.

Spread the vegetable and cheese mixture lengthwise down the middle third of the dough. Pour the marinara sauce over the vegetables and sprinkle with the fresh or dried basil. Fold the left side of the dough across the filling lengthwise, then fold the other side across, so that the dough overlaps completely. Fold up the ends and pinch the dough to seal. Prick the dough here and there with a fork.

Bake at 350 degrees for 30-40 minutes. Remove from the oven, cool slightly, and cut into 4-6 serving pieces. Serve hot.

Rice & Vegetable Sushi Nori Rolls

There are several types of sushi, among them the traditional raw tuna and sushi rice rolled in a sheet of nori seaweed and served with wasabi added to a soy sauce dip. I happen to prefer the vegetable sushi nori rolls with lots of different vegetables and nuts added for a crunch. The preparation of this particular recipe is far from traditional. However, it is delicious!

MAKES 4 ROLLS

1 cup uncooked sweet brown rice
1½ cup water
3 tablespoons rice vinegar
4 sheets of nori seaweed
1 tablespoon umeboshi plum paste
2 carrots, cut in matchsticks
6 scallions, chopped
½ cup roasted sunflower seeds (see recipe
    for Roasted Nuts & Seeds on page 11)

wasabi (available prepared in most
    grocery stores or Asian markets)
tamari sauce (optional)
sliced pickled ginger (available in most
    grocery stores or Asian markets)

Wash the rice and drain. In a heavy saucepan, combine water and sweet brown rice. Bring to a boil, cover, reduce heat, and simmer for 40-50 minutes or until all the liquid is absorbed. Cool slightly. In a bowl, blend the cooked sweet brown rice and the rice vinegar.

Place a sheet of nori on a sushi mat (available at most health food stores or Asian markets). If you don't have a mat, you can simply roll up the nori and filling by hand. Using a knife or wet finger tips, spread the rice and vinegar mixture evenly on the sheet of nori leaving an inch on the top and bottom. You are making 4 rolls, so use a quarter of each ingredient on each roll. With a knife, spread the umeboshi paste thinly over the top of the rice. Place the carrots and scallions evenly over the rice mixture. Top with sunflower seeds.

Roll the nori and filling in the mat, keeping it firm, even, and smooth. Using your finger tips, wet the top end of the nori with water so that it will stick together as you finish rolling.

Use a very sharp knife to slice each roll across into bite-size pieces about ¾-inch wide. Serve with wasabi and sliced pickled ginger. If you wish, you can blend the wasabi with tamari sauce. This makes a very spicy dipping sauce for the nori rolls. The recipe may sound complicated, but with a few attempts it will be easy. Promise!

"Who are you?" said the Caterpillar.

This was not an encouraging opening for a conversation. Alice replied, rather shyly, "I—I hardly know, Sir, just at present—at least I know who I was when I got up this morning, but I think I must have been changed several times since then."

Lewis Carroll
From: Alice's Adventures in Wonderland

QUICHES

Quiches

During Cafe Chimes' first month of operation, I was having a desperate time attempting to perfect a whole-wheat quiche crust that would stay firm during refrigeration. I wasn't having much luck. One night, near tears because the flour crust wouldn't cooperate, I turned around and saw the word, RICE, written on a big bin. Then the idea was launched—make a crust out of something I could do! A brown rice quiche crust is simple, unique, and nutritious. We use organic, free-range eggs when possible. For many people making the transition to a whole foods selection, this choice is just what they are looking for.

Cafe Chimes Basic Quiche

Like many selections at Cafe Chimes, we use a basic quiche recipe and elaborate from the base of that recipe. We have never served quite the same quiche twice. By using different combinations of vegetables, herbs, nuts, garnishes, and seasonings, we have managed to create thousands of different quiches. By preparing the following recipes, you will be on your way to creating an innovative and unique style of your own.

SERVES 6-8

1 cup uncooked short-grain brown rice
1⅔ cups water
1 cup cheddar cheese, grated
1 tablespoon sesame or canola oil
1 medium onion, chopped
2 cloves garlic, minced

2 cups vegetables of your choice,
    chopped (see Quiche Variations for
    suggested combinations)
4 eggs
1½ cups whole milk
1-2 tablespoons tamari
½ teaspoon black pepper

Wash rice and drain. In a heavy saucepan, combine water and brown rice. Bring to a boil, cover, reduce heat, and simmer for 40-50 minutes, or until all liquid is absorbed. Do not allow to cool.

Set out an oiled 10-inch pie plate. With wet hands, firmly pat the warm brown rice into the pie plate, bringing the rice to the top rim of the plate. Cover the rice crust with ¾ cup of the grated cheddar cheese.

In a skillet, sauté the onion and garlic in oil until the onion is translucent. Add the vegetable and spice combinations of your choice. Sauté until the vegetables are just crisp tender. For vegetables that require a longer cooking time, add ¼ cup of water, cover, and steam for 3-5 minutes until the vegetables are just tender. Add the vegetable mixture to the pie plate over the grated cheese.

In a bowl, whisk together the eggs, milk, tamari, and seasonings until well-mixed. Pour this mixture over the vegetables in the pie plate. Top with the remaining ¼ cup cheddar cheese. Cover the pie plate with a raised "tent" of aluminum foil, so the foil doesn't touch the surface of the quiche filling. Bake covered at 350 degrees for 50 minutes. Remove the foil and bake uncovered for 10-15 minutes. A knife inserted in the center of the quiche should come out clean. Let stand for about 10 minutes before serving.

If serving later, refrigerate, then cover with aluminum foil and reheat at 350 degrees for 35-40 minutes.

Quiche Variations

Following are some vegetable combinations that we have used successfully at the Cafe. Feel free to make up your own concoctions of vegetables and spices. In addition to the endless variety of vegetables that you can use for the quiches, you can substitute other cooked grains such as millet or couscous for the brown rice crust.

Broccoli & Squash Quiche: Prepare the basic quiche recipe using 1 cup chopped broccoli and 1 cup chopped winter squash for the vegetable combination.

Curried Cauliflower Quiche: Prepare the basic quiche recipe using 2 cups chopped cauliflower, 2 stalks chopped celery, and 1 teaspoon curry powder for the vegetable combination.

Eggplant & Pepper Quiche: Prepare the basic quiche recipe using 2 cups chopped eggplant, 1 small chopped green or red pepper, and ½ cup chopped tomato for the vegetable combination.

Kale & Celery Quiche: Prepare the basic quiche recipe using 2½ cups chopped kale and 2 stalks chopped celery for the vegetable combination.

Mexican Black Bean Quiche: Prepare the basic quiche recipe using 1 15-ounce can of black beans (drained and rinsed), 2 large chopped carrots, 1 teaspoon ground cumin, and ¼ cup salsa for the vegetable combination. Top with ½ cup crumbled corn chips during the last 10 minutes of baking.

Parsnip Quiche: Prepare the basic quiche recipe using 2 cups chopped parsnips, 1 teaspoon ground ginger, and ½ teaspoon cinnamon for the vegetable combination.

Potato Dill Quiche: Prepare the basic quiche recipe using 2 cups cubed potatoes and 1 teaspoon dried dill weed for the vegetable combination.

Spinach Mushroom Quiche: Prepare the basic quiche recipe using 2 cups chopped fresh spinach, ¼ cup chopped fresh basil, and 4-5 sliced mushrooms for the vegetable combination.

Sweet Potato & Walnut Quiche: Prepare the basic quiche recipe using 2 cups peeled and cubed sweet potatoes and ¼ cup roasted walnuts for the vegetable combination.

Zucchini Quiche: Prepare the basic quiche recipe using 1 cup sliced zucchini, 2 chopped carrots, 2 stalks chopped celery, ½ cup chopped tomato, and ½ teaspoon fennel seed for the vegetable combination.

Add any of the vegetable and spice combinations above to the sautéed onions and garlic in the basic recipe. Sauté until crisp tender, or add ½ cup of water, cover, and steam for 3-5 minutes until the vegetables are just tender. Add the vegetable mixture to the pie plate over the grated cheese, as in the basic recipe.

If all else fails...
Add Red Peppers
and call it "Gourmet"

PIZZA

Pizza

The whole-wheat Sicilian deep-dish vegetable pizza is almost the first thing to disappear at the Cafe. It just looks so good, it sells itself. And every day for the past eight years, we have produced wonderful variations on our basic pizza recipe. My approach in this section will be to share with you our basic vegetable deep-dish pizza, then elaborate on the more unique types.

Refer to the bread section to obtain the recipe for the Cafe Chimes Whole-Wheat Mountain Bread. My suggestion would be to make this up in batches of two doughs. Use one dough for pizza and make the other into bread. Or you can freeze the remaining dough and use it later for pizza crusts or cinnamon swirls. If all else fails, you can usually go to the frozen or refrigerated section of your grocery store and purchase a one-pound loaf of whole-wheat dough. Thaw and you are ready to create!

Cafe Chimes Vegetable Deep-Dish Pizza (Basic)

SERVES 4-6

*1 lb. whole-wheat dough (see recipe for Whole-Wheat Mountain Bread on page 26 or
    use a prepared frozen or refrigerated loaf)*
1 cup spaghetti or pizza sauce
2 cups vegetables of your choice, chopped (see suggested combinations below)
2 cups soy cheese or mozzarella, grated
2 teaspoons Italian spices

If you are using frozen or refrigerated dough, bring the dough to room
temperature. Oil an 11x17-inch cookie sheet. Roll out the dough with a rolling
pin right on the cookie sheet, or if your rolling pin doesn't fit, place the dough
on a board and roll out into a flat rectangle. Fit the dough into the cookie
sheet. Sometimes you have to hand-pull the dough to the corners of
the cookie sheet.

With a rubber spatula, spread the spaghetti sauce over the dough. Sprinkle
on a thin layer of cheese, then the vegetables, more cheese, lastly the spices.

Place in a hot oven at 400 degrees for 15-20 minutes. Cool slightly before
cutting.

Suggested Vegetable Combinations for Pizza

- *1½ cups fresh spinach, chopped
  1 medium red pepper, sliced
  2 cloves garlic, minced
  1 small onion, sliced in half-moons*

- *1½ cups broccoli, chopped
  4-6 mushrooms, sliced
  1 small onion, sliced in half-moons*

- *3 cloves garlic, minced
  1 small onion, sliced in half-moons
  ½ cup black olives, sliced*

- *½ small eggplant, peeled and thinly
    sliced
  1 large tomato, thinly sliced
  ¼ cup fresh basil, chopped
  2 cloves garlic, minced*

- *1 cup zucchini, sliced
  1 large tomato, thinly sliced
  1 small onion, sliced in half-moons*

125

Presto Pesto Red Pepper Feta Cheese Pizza

We started serving Pesto Pizza several years ago, and it was an instant hit. If you don't have the time or the ingredients handy to make your own pesto sauce, I would suggest purchasing bottled prepared pesto sauce from the grocery store.

SERVES 4-6

1 lb. whole-wheat dough (see recipe for Whole-Wheat Mountain Bread on page 26 or
  use a prepared frozen or refrigerated loaf)
½ cup spaghetti or pizza sauce
½ cup pesto sauce
1½ cups soy cheese or mozzarella, grated
½ cup feta cheese, crumbled
1 medium red pepper, thinly sliced
2 teaspoons Italian spices
½ cup fresh parsley, chopped

If you are using frozen or refrigerated dough, bring the dough to room temperature. Oil an 11x17-inch cookie sheet. Roll out the dough with a rolling pin right on the cookie sheet, or if your rolling pin doesn't fit, place the dough on a board and roll out into a flat rectangle. Fit the dough into the cookie sheet. Sometimes you have to hand-pull the dough to the corners of the cookie sheet.

With a rubber spatula, spread the spaghetti sauce over the dough. Spread the pesto sauce on top of the red pizza sauce and swirl the two sauces together. Sprinkle the mozzarella, feta cheese, and red pepper over the dough. Top with Italian spices.

Bake at 400 degrees for 15-20 minutes. Cool slightly before cutting. Top with fresh chopped parsley before serving.

The Chimes Mexican Pizza

The Mexican Pizza is a Saturday must. Elsa makes this pizza to perfection. Her secret—she tops the crust with salsa and crispy nachos.

SERVES 4-6

1 lb. whole-wheat dough (see recipe for Whole-Wheat
   Mountain Bread on page 26 or use a prepared
   frozen or refrigerated loaf)
1 cup mild or medium salsa (your choice)
1 small green pepper, thinly sliced
1 small red pepper, thinly sliced
½ medium onion, thinly sliced in half-moons
½ cup pitted black olives, sliced
2 cups soy or mozzarella cheese, grated
2 teaspoons Italian spices
½ teaspoon ground cumin or cumin seed
1 cup crumbled nachos or any corn chips

If you are using frozen or refrigerated dough, bring the dough to room temperature. Oil an 11x17-inch cookie sheet. Roll out the dough with a rolling pin right on the cookie sheet, or if your rolling pin doesn't fit, place the dough on a board and roll out into a flat rectangle. Fit the dough into the cookie sheet. Sometimes you have to hand-pull the dough to the corners of the cookie sheet.

With a rubber spatula, spread the salsa over the dough. Sprinkle the sliced vegetables, olives, cheese, Italian spices, and cumin over the crust. Top with crumbled corn chips.

Bake at 400 degrees for 15-20 minutes. Cool slightly before cutting.

The Sunday Triple-Cheese Pizza

Many of our international pizzas are a hit because they are unique and tend to please the adult palate. However children tend to prefer simple flavors, and this recipe is a popular choice for them. Even those who have never had a whole-wheat crust before like this pizza. The Cafe serves this pizza every Sunday, because we tend to attract families with children at this time.

SERVES 4-6

1 lb. whole-wheat dough (see recipe for Whole-Wheat Mountain Bread on page 26 or use a prepared frozen or refrigerated loaf)
1 cup spaghetti or pizza sauce
1 cup mozzarella cheese, grated
1 cup cheddar cheese, grated
½ cup Parmesan cheese, grated
2 teaspoons Italian spices

If you are using frozen or refrigerated dough, bring the dough to room temperature. Oil an 11x17-inch cookie sheet. Roll out the dough with a rolling pin right on the cookie sheet, or if your rolling pin doesn't fit, place the dough on a board and roll out into a flat rectangle. Fit the dough into the cookie sheet. Sometimes you have to hand-pull the dough to the corners of the cookie sheet.

With a rubber spatula, spread the spaghetti sauce over the dough. Sprinkle on an even layer of each of the cheeses. Top with the Italian spices.

Place in a hot oven at 400 degrees for 15-20 minutes. Cool slightly before cutting.

Red, White & Green Pizza

SERVES 4-6

*1 lb. whole-wheat dough (see recipe for Whole-Wheat Mountain Bread on page 26 or
use a prepared frozen or refrigerated loaf)*
1 cup pesto sauce
½ cup sun-dried tomatoes, soaked
2 cups hot water
1 cup mozzarella cheese, grated
1 cup cheddar cheese, grated

If you are using frozen or refrigerated dough, bring the dough to room temperature. Oil an 11x17-inch cookie sheet. Roll out the dough with a rolling pin right on the cookie sheet, or if your rolling pin doesn't fit, place the dough on a board and roll out into a flat rectangle. Fit the dough into the cookie sheet. Sometimes you have to hand-pull the dough to the corners of the cookie sheet.

Soak the sun-dried tomatoes in hot water for 15 minutes. Drain and slice tomatoes in half.

Spread the pesto sauce over the pizza dough. Add a thin layer of the mozzarella and cheddar cheese. Top with a layer of sun-dried tomatoes. Add the remaining cheese.

Place in a hot oven at 400 degrees for 15-20 minutes. Cool slightly before cutting.

The Chimes Hawaiian Pizza

*1 lb. whole-wheat dough (see recipe for Whole-Wheat Mountain Bread on page 26 or
    use a prepared frozen or refrigerated loaf)*
¾ cup spaghetti or pizza sauce
¾ cup canned crushed pineapple, drained
1 small red pepper, chopped
1½ cups mozzarella cheese, grated
½ cup cheddar cheese, grated
1 teaspoon dried oregano

If you are using frozen or refrigerated
dough, bring the dough to room temperature.
Oil an 11x17-inch cookie sheet. Roll out the
dough with a rolling pin right on the cookie
sheet, or if your rolling pin doesn't fit,
place the dough on a board and roll out
into a flat rectangle. Fit the dough into
the cookie sheet. Sometimes you have
to hand-pull the dough to the corners
of the cookie sheet.

With a rubber spatula, spread the
spaghetti sauce over the dough. Spread
on an even layer of the pineapple and
red pepper. Add a layer of mozzarella and cheddar cheese. Top with oregano.

Place in a hot oven at 400 degrees for 15-20 minutes. Cool slightly before
cutting.

Sweet Brown Rice Crusted Pizza

This pizza is one that we use for a daily special. The crust is made from sweet brown rice which has a naturally sticky consistency and will stay together.

SERVES 4-6

2 cups uncooked sweet brown rice
3 cups water
1 cup cornmeal
1 cup spaghetti or pizza sauce
1½ cups fresh spinach, chopped
½ medium onion, thinly sliced
4-5 mushrooms, sliced
2 cups mozzarella cheese, grated
2 teaspoons Italian spices

Wash the rice and drain. In a heavy saucepan, combine the water and sweet brown rice. Bring to a boil, cover, reduce heat, and simmer for 40-50 minutes or until all liquid is absorbed. Do not allow to cool.

Lightly oil an 11x17-inch cookie sheet and sprinkle with cornmeal. With wet hands, firmly pat the warm brown rice into the cookie sheet, forming a full-size rice crust with edges reaching the top rim of the cookie sheet. The warm rice is much easier to spread.

With a rubber spatula, spread the spaghetti sauce over the rice crust. Top with spinach, onion, and mushrooms. Sprinkle on the cheese and Italian spices. Bake in a hot oven at 400 degrees for 15-20 minutes. Cool slightly before cutting to let the rice crust set up.

CHICKPEA TO COOK

A chickpea leaps almost over the rim of the pot
where it's being boiled.

"Why are you doing this to me?"

The cook knocks him down with the ladle.

"Don't you try to jump out.
You think I'm torturing you.
I'm giving you flavor,
so you can mix with spices and rice
and be the lovely vitality of a human being.

Remember when you drank rain in the garden.
That was for this."

Grace first. Sexual pleasure,
then a boiling new life begins,
and the Friend has something good to eat.

Eventually the chickpea
will say to the cook,
                    "Boil me some more.
Hit me with the skimming spoon.
I can't do this by myself.

I'm like an elephant that dreams of gardens
back in Hindustan and doesn't pay attention
to his driver. You're my cook, my driver,
my way into existence. I love your cooking."

The cook says,
            "I was once like you,
fresh from the ground. Then I boiled in time,
and boiled in the body, two fierce boilings.

My animal soul grew powerful.
I controlled it with practices,
and boiled some more, and boiled
once beyond that,
                    and became your teacher."

                    Jelaluddin Rumi

132

GRAINS

Grains

The word "grain" doesn't do justice to the wisdom and grace of this wonderful food source. For it is grain that feeds the world population; and it is grain that supplies our bodies with fuel as it radiates in the form of complex carbohydrates.

As you experiment with the many different types of grains, you will become more confident in engineering your own style of creating wholesome grain dishes. It took years of developing recipes at the Cafe before I began combining different grains with different grains, and different grains with different bean combinations. And, wow, what doors opened into majestic ballrooms of possibilities! Be crazy, be alive, be daring, and create your own dancing creations!

Since day one at Cafe Chimes, we have offered a new and different grain casserole each day. This means that we have made over 2,550 one-of-a-kind grain dishes since we opened our restaurant. We do not use recipes—we simply create according to our whim of that day and according to whatever ingredients are available in the refrigerator. So, the following is a sampling of some of our favorites along with some general advice on the preparation of rice and other grains.

The following recipes give instructions for cooking rice and other grains in a heavy saucepan using the traditional steamed rice method. You can also use a pressure cooker for steaming grains—we use this method at the Cafe. I recommend purchasing a heat deflector to avoid scorching of the grains on the bottom of the saucepan or pressure cooker, particularly if you're cooking on a gas range.

Always wash your grains before using them. Put dry grains in the saucepan and add water to clean out the debris that will usually float to the surface. The dirty water can then be drained off. I usually repeat this process two or three times. For smaller grains such as millet and quinoa, you may want to use a fine sieve or colander.

Many of the recipes in this section call for roasted nuts or seeds as a topping or ingredient. I like to make up a batch of these tasty nuts in advance and store them in a jar. You will find the recipe for Roasted Nuts & Seeds on page 11.

Sure Brown Rice—Step One

Brown rice tastes wonderful simply steamed and served. However, our Cafe Chimes customers are looking for interesting, complex, and unusual dishes. To meet this need, we have developed a basic recipe for creating appetizing brown rice that is sure to please all. Our recipe for Sure Brown Rice is the basis for many of the recipes you will find in this section on grains.

SERVES 4-6

1½ cups long- or short-grain brown rice
3 cups water (or 2¾ cups for drier rice)
pinch of sea salt
1x3-inch strip of kombu, rinsed

½ teaspoon herb seasoning salt
½ teaspoon black pepper
½ teaspoon garlic powder
½ cup dried parsley
1 tablespoon tamari
1 tablespoon canola oil

Wash the rice in a heavy saucepan and drain. Add fresh water, sea salt, and kombu. Cover and bring to a boil. (Or pressure cook according to the directions on the pressure cooker.) Lower the heat and simmer, covered, for approximately 45-50 minutes, or until all the liquid is absorbed. Remove the kombu strip and chop finely.

Place the cooked brown rice in large bowl. Add the chopped kombu. Sprinkle on the herb seasoning salt (I like to use Herbamere®), black pepper, garlic powder, and dried parsley. Add the tamari and canola oil and toss gently.

Now you have 'Step One' to creating a huge variety of wonderful grain recipes.

Brilliant Greens & Rice with Arame

As you move more into the practice of vegetarian cooking, you will become familiar with the wonderful world of greens. The term includes all types of leafy green vegetables such as collards, kale, bok choy, beet tops, dandelion greens, broccoli rabe, Swiss chard, spinach, etc. Greens are high in chlorophyll, complex carbohydrates, calcium, and vitamins. We really do believe that a green a day will keep the doctor away!

SERVES 4-6

For the Rice:
1½ cups short-grain brown rice
3 cups water (or 2¾ cups for drier rice)
pinch of sea salt
1x3-inch strip of kombu, rinsed

½ teaspoon herb seasoning salt
½ teaspoon black pepper
½ teaspoon garlic powder
½ cup dried parsley
1 tablespoon tamari
1 tablespoon canola oil

For the Greens:
4 cups raw collards or kale, chopped
1 medium onion, chopped
1 clove garlic, minced
2 tablespoons sesame oil
1 teaspoon tamari
1 teaspoon cider vinegar
¼ cup dried arame, soaked in ½ cup hot
  water and drained

Wash the rice in a heavy saucepan and drain. Add fresh water, sea salt, and kombu. Cover and bring to a boil. Lower the heat and simmer, covered, for 45-50 minutes, or until all the liquid is absorbed. Remove the kombu strip and chop finely.

Add the chopped kombu to the cooked brown rice. Sprinkle on the herb seasoning salt, black pepper, garlic powder, and dried parsley. Add the tamari and canola oil and toss gently.

Wash the collards or kale, then chop diagonally. In a large skillet, sauté the onion and garlic in the sesame oil. When the onion is translucent, add the collards or kale. Stir to blend. Reduce heat, cover, and steam for about 4-6 minutes. Add the tamari, vinegar, and drained arame. Toss, cover, and steam for about 1 more minute. The greens should be just tender and retain a bright green color. Place the colorful greens on top of the herbed rice and serve immediately.

Chinese Brown Rice

SERVES 4-5

1½ cups short-grain brown rice
3 cups water (or 2¾ cups for drier rice)
pinch of sea salt

½ teaspoon herb seasoning salt
½ teaspoon black pepper
½ teaspoon garlic powder
¼ cup dried parsley
1 tablespoon tamari

2 tablespoons sesame oil
1 large onion, chopped
2 stalks celery, sliced at an angle
1 clove garlic, minced
1 tablespoon fresh ginger root, grated
½ pound extra-firm tofu, cubed
  (optional)
1 8-ounce can sliced water chestnuts,
  drained
1 cup Chinese cabbage, shredded
1 cup bok choy, shredded
1 tablespoon tamari
½ teaspoon hot chili oil (optional)

(Note: you may be able to find a packaged mix of fresh oriental vegetables at your supermarket.)

Wash the rice in heavy saucepan and drain. Add fresh water and sea salt. Cover and bring to a boil. Lower the heat and simmer, covered, for 45-50 minutes, or until all the liquid is absorbed.

When the rice is cooked, sprinkle on the herb seasoning salt, black pepper, garlic powder, and dried parsley. Add the tamari and toss gently.

In large skillet, sauté the onion, celery, garlic, and ginger in oil until the onion is translucent. If desired, add the cubed tofu and sauté briefly to brown. Add the drained water chestnuts, Chinese cabbage, and bok choy. Cook for 5 minutes, stirring occasionally, or until the Chinese cabbage and bok choy are just tender.

Combine the vegetable mixture and rice. Stir in tamari and chili oil, if desired, and adjust seasonings to taste. Top with additional grated fresh ginger for a flavorful finish.

Taj Mahal Brown Rice Casserole

It has been only recently that I have begun to enjoy the flavor of curry. I believed that all Indian spices had to be hot. But now, much to my surprise, I find I love the enticing smells and taste of the Indian cooking seasonings without a fiery level of spiciness. If you add the curry powder directly to the rice while cooking, the rice will absorb the flavor, thus creating a richer tasting rice.

SERVES 4-6

1½ cups long-grain brown rice
½ cup brown lentils
3½ cups water
1x3-inch strip kombu, rinsed
1 tablespoon curry powder

½ teaspoon herb seasoning salt
½ teaspoon black pepper
½ teaspoon garlic powder
½ cup dried parsley
1 tablespoon tamari
1 tablespoon canola oil

1 15-ounce can whole peeled tomatoes, chopped, liquid reserved
2 tablespoons sesame oil
1 teaspoon curry powder
1 teaspoon ground coriander
1 teaspoon cumin seed
2 medium onions, chopped
2 stalks celery, chopped
1 clove garlic, minced
½ cup water
1 tablespoon tamari
½ cup fresh cilantro, chopped

Wash the rice and lentils in a heavy saucepan and drain. Add fresh water, kombu, and 1 tablespoon curry powder. Cover and bring to a boil. Lower the heat and simmer, covered, for 45-50 minutes, or until all the liquid is absorbed. Remove the kombu strip and chop finely.

Return the chopped kombu to the cooked rice and lentils. Sprinkle on the herb seasoning salt, black pepper, garlic powder, and dried parsley. Add the tamari and canola oil and toss gently.

Remove the whole tomatoes from the can and chop, reserving the liquid. In a large saucepan or covered skillet, warm the oil and add 1 teaspoon each of curry powder, coriander, and cumin seed. Add the onions, celery, and garlic and sauté for 2 minutes. Add the chopped tomatoes and reserved liquid. Bring to a boil, reduce heat, and simmer, covered, for 15 minutes. Add water and tamari to create a tasty broth and heat gently to blend flavors.

Combine the vegetable mixture with the cooked rice and lentils and stir gently. Serve topped with chopped cilantro.

Brilliant Star Anise Apple Rice Delight

Something told me one day to add the whole spice of star anise to the rice and trust in the results. I am thankful I chose to listen that day because it led me to a multitude of seasoning experiments and the best rice dishes ever! Instead of star anise, you can use whole cardamom, coriander, cloves, and cinnamon sticks. Be outrageous!!!

SERVES 4-6

1½ cups long-grain brown rice
3 cups water (or 2¾ cups for drier rice)
pinch of sea salt
3 whole star anise
1x3-inch strip of kombu, rinsed

½ teaspoon herb seasoning salt
½ teaspoon black pepper
½ teaspoon garlic powder
½ cup dried parsley
1 tablespoon tamari
1 tablespoon canola oil

1 tablespoon sesame seed oil
1 medium onion, chopped
2 tablespoons ground coriander
1 teaspoon allspice
1 teaspoon cinnamon
1 stalk celery, chopped
3 carrots, chopped
2 apples, cored and chopped
½ cup raisins
⅓ cup water

3 scallions, chopped
1 apple, cored and sliced

Wash the rice in a heavy saucepan and drain. Add fresh water, sea salt, whole star anise, and kombu. Cover and bring to a boil. Lower the heat and simmer, covered, for 45-50 minutes, or until all the liquid is absorbed. Remove the kombu strip and chop finely. Discard the star anise.

Return the chopped kombu to the cooked brown rice. Sprinkle on the herb seasoning salt, black pepper, garlic powder, and dried parsley. Add the tamari and canola oil and toss gently.

Heat the oil in a heavy skillet with a cover and sauté the onion until translucent. Add the coriander, allspice, and cinnamon and stir. Add the celery, carrots, apples, and raisins. Stir. Add water and steam, covered, for about 10 minutes.

Add the sautéed vegetables and fruit to the seasoned rice and stir. Garnish with scallions and apple pieces. Reheat, if necessary, in a large covered casserole in a 350 degree oven for about 20 minutes.

139

Brown Rice with Tangy Fruit & Vegetables

I know some good cooks out there who hesitate to combine fruits and vegetables. However, I find I have incredible luck in finding irresistible combinations. As soon as this delicious fruit and vegetable casserole is written on our Specials Board, it is almost gone.

SERVES 4-6

1½ cups long-grain brown rice
3 cups water (or 2¾ cups for drier rice)
1x3-inch strip kombu, rinsed
pinch of sea salt

½ teaspoon herb seasoning salt
½ teaspoon black pepper
½ teaspoon garlic powder
½ cup dried parsley
1 tablespoon tamari
1 tablespoon canola oil

2 tablespoons olive oil
1 medium onion, chopped
1 teaspoon dried basil
1 teaspoon cinnamon
3 stalks celery, chopped
2 carrots, peeled and chopped
1 clove garlic, minced
½ cup water
1 cup canned mandarin oranges, drained
½ cup frozen raspberries, thawed
¼ cup lemon juice
¼ cup maple syrup
¼ cup tamari
2 tablespoons bottled or deli pesto sauce

⅓ cup bottled or deli pesto sauce
½ cup fresh cilantro, chopped

Wash the brown rice in a heavy saucepan and drain. Add fresh water, kombu, and sea salt. Cover and bring to a boil. Lower the heat and simmer, covered, for 45-50 minutes, or until all the liquid is absorbed. Remove the kombu strip and chop finely.

Return the chopped kombu to the cooked brown rice. Sprinkle on the herb seasoning salt, black pepper, garlic powder, and dried parsley. Add the tamari and canola oil and toss gently.

While the rice is cooking, heat the oil in a large skillet and sauté the onion until translucent. Add the basil and cinnamon. Add the celery, carrots, and garlic. Stir and add water. Cook over low heat about 10 minutes, or until vegetables are just tender. Add the mandarin oranges and raspberries. Stir gently. Add lemon juice, maple syrup, and tamari. Add 2 tablespoons of the pesto sauce and simmer for about 5 more minutes.

Add the sautéed vegetable and fruit mixture to the seasoned rice. Add the remaining ⅓ cup pesto and stir. Top with fresh chopped cilantro.

For a delicious variation, sauté 6 sliced mushrooms along with the onion and add to the celery, carrots, and garlic. Slivered almonds also make a nice addition to this dish.

Golden Curried Apple Brown Rice Casserole

Here is another recipe that uses both fresh vegetables and fruits. This dish will win you praise for your individuality and imagination in preparing such an interesting casserole.

SERVES 4-6

1½ cups long-grain brown rice
3 cups water (or 2¾ cups for drier rice)
pinch of sea salt
1x3-inch strip kombu, rinsed

½ teaspoon herb seasoning salt
½ teaspoon black pepper
½ teaspoon garlic powder
¼ cup dried parsley
1 tablespoon tamari
1 tablespoon canola oil

1 tablespoon canola oil
1 medium onion, chopped
1 apple, cored and chopped (or ⅔ cup dried apples)
2 carrots, chopped
½ medium buttercup squash, peeled and cubed
½ teaspoon cinnamon
½ teaspoon allspice
2 teaspoons curry powder
½ cup water
½ cup chopped walnuts
½ cup raisins
2 tablespoons tamari
¼ cup honey

½ cup canned crushed pineapple, undrained (optional)
½ cup canned mandarin oranges, drained (optional)

Wash the brown rice in a heavy saucepan and drain. Add fresh water, sea salt, and kombu. Cover and bring to a boil. Lower the heat and simmer, covered, for 45-50 minutes, or until all the liquid is absorbed. Remove the kombu strip and chop finely.

142

When the rice is done, place in a large bowl and sprinkle on the herb seasoning salt, black pepper, garlic powder, and dried parsley. Add the chopped kombu. Add tamari and canola oil and toss gently.

In a skillet, sauté the chopped onion in the oil until translucent. Add the apple, carrots, and squash. Stir in the cinnamon, allspice, and curry powder. Add the water, walnuts, and raisins, and simmer for 10-15 minutes, or until the squash is tender. Mix in the tamari and honey.

Add the sautéed vegetable mixture to the seasoned rice and stir. Adjust seasonings to taste. You may want to add some more herb seasoning salt at this point. Top with the pineapple and mandarin oranges, if desired.

Simple Sweet Brown Rice Balls

Sweet brown rice is a glutenous and sticky rice which can be used for rice balls and as an ingredient in veggie burgers. Children love to help make rice balls.

MAKES 8-10 RICE BALLS

1½ *cups sweet brown rice*
1¾ *cups water*
pinch of sea salt

¼ *cup sesame seeds (or 1 cup scallions, finely chopped)*

Wash the rice in a heavy saucepan and drain. Add fresh water and salt. Cover and bring to a boil. Lower the heat and simmer, covered, for approximately 45-50 minutes, or until all liquid is absorbed.

When the rice is cool enough to handle, form rice balls with wet hands using about ¼ cup of rice for each rice ball. Roll the rice balls in sesame seeds or chopped scallions. Serve with steamed greens.

Crescent Moon Sweet Brown Rice Croquettes

This unique manner of serving a grain selection never goes unnoticed. Sweet brown rice has a naturally sticky consistency that lends itself easily to the formation of any shape. We like to present these croquettes shaped like crescent moons. Serve with collards or any bright greens.

This is a basic recipe, but is open to all types of experimentation by the adventurous cook. For a special occasion, try wrapping the croquettes in steamed collard greens.

SERVES 4-6

2 cups sweet brown rice
3 cups water
pinch of sea salt
1x3-inch strip of kombu, rinsed

2 tablespoons canola oil
1 medium onion, chopped
2 stalks celery, chopped
2 cloves garlic, minced

½ teaspoon herb seasoning salt
½ teaspoon black pepper
½ teaspoon garlic powder
½ cup dried parsley
1 tablespoon tamari
1 tablespoon canola oil
½ cup roasted sunflower seeds
    (see recipe for Roasted Nuts & Seeds
    on page 11)

Wash the sweet brown rice in a heavy saucepan and drain. Add fresh water, sea salt, and kombu. Cover and bring to a boil. Lower the heat and simmer, covered, for 45-50 minutes, or until all the liquid is absorbed. Remove the kombu strip, chop finely, and return to the cooked rice.

Meanwhile, heat the oil in a skillet and sauté the onion, celery, and garlic until the onion is translucent.

Mix the sautéed vegetables with cooked rice in a large bowl. Sprinkle on the herb seasoning salt, black pepper, garlic powder, and dried parsley. Add the tamari, canola oil, and roasted sunflower seeds. Mix well.

With wet palms, form the rice and vegetable mixture into 8 crescent moons. Place on an oiled cookie sheet and bake at 350 degrees for 15-20 minutes, or until slightly browned. If you prefer crisper croquettes, place them under the broiler for 3-5 minutes just before serving. Serve with any bright greens.

145

Basmati Rice & Roasted Cashews

If you have never had the chance or inclination to cook with basmati rice, you are in for a treat, not to mention a sensory titillation from the unique aroma. I always use brown basmati rice because it is not refined. But families who are still making the transition to a whole foods diet might want to start with the bleached white basmati rice. The wonderful flavor of this simple rice is enriched to perfection by the small amount of oil in the recipe.

SERVES 4-6

2 cups white or brown basmati rice
3 cups water
pinch of sea salt
1x3-inch strip of kombu, rinsed
1 tablespoon corn oil (or roasted sesame oil)

½ teaspoon herb seasoning salt
½ teaspoon black pepper
½ teaspoon garlic powder
½ cup dried parsley
1 tablespoon tamari
1 tablespoon canola oil

¼ cup fresh parsley, chopped
½ cup roasted cashew pieces (see recipe for Roasted Nuts & Seeds on page 11)

Wash the rice in a heavy saucepan and drain. Add fresh water, sea salt, kombu, and oil. Cover and bring to a boil. Lower the heat and simmer, covered, for 35 minutes, or until all the liquid is absorbed. Remove the kombu strip and chop finely.

Place the cooked basmati rice in large bowl. Add the chopped kombu. Sprinkle on the herb seasoning salt, black pepper, garlic powder, and dried parsley. Add the tamari and canola oil and toss gently. Top with fresh parsley and roasted cashews. Serve with a green salad.

Brown Basmati Rice with Glazed Candied Carrot Rounds

We use about twenty-five pounds of basmati rice every week in Cafe Chimes because our customers enjoy the nutty flavor of this nutritious grain.

SERVES 4-6

2 cups brown basmati rice
3 cups water
1x3-inch strip of kombu, rinsed
pinch of sea salt

1 teaspoon herb seasoning salt
½ teaspoon black pepper
½ teaspoon garlic powder
½ cup dried parsley
1 tablespoon tamari
1 tablespoon canola oil

5 carrots, washed and chopped into rounds
1 cup water for steaming

For the Glaze:

⅓ cup maple syrup
⅛ cup lemon juice
1 teaspoon fresh ginger root, grated
2 tablespoons tamari
1 teaspoon arrowroot powder
¼ cup water

Wash the brown basmati rice in a heavy saucepan and drain. Add fresh water, kombu, and sea salt. Cover and bring to a boil. Lower the heat and simmer, covered, for 35 minutes, or until all the liquid is absorbed. Remove the kombu strip and chop finely.

Add the kombu to the cooked basmati rice and sprinkle on the herb seasoning salt, black pepper, garlic powder, and dried parsley. Add the tamari and canola oil and toss gently.

Wash the carrots and cut into rounds. Place in a covered saucepan, add water, and steam about 5-8 minutes, or until carrots are just tender.

Prepare the glaze by combining the maple syrup, lemon juice, ginger, tamari, and arrowroot with water in a small saucepan. Stir over medium heat until the glaze is clear and slightly thickened. Add the steamed carrots and stir gently until the carrots are coated with glaze.

Place the seasoned rice in a serving dish and top with the glazed carrot rounds. A spectacular presentation!

Indian Vegetable Stew on Basmati Rice

The length of this recipe may discourage you at first reading. However, I implore you to make every attempt to prepare this incredible mouth-watering gourmet dish! The level of spiciness is on the mild side, but you can increase the intensity by adding cayenne pepper.

SERVES 4-6

For the Rice:

2 cups brown basmati rice
3 cups water
pinch of sea salt
1x3-inch strip of kombu, rinsed

½ teaspoon herb seasoning salt
½ teaspoon black pepper
1 teaspoon garlic powder
½ cup dried parsley
1 tablespoon tamari
1 tablespoon sesame oil

For the Indian Vegetable Stew:

2 teaspoons cumin seed
¼ teaspoon ground cloves
½ teaspoon ground cardamom
½ teaspoon ground mustard
½ teaspoon ground turmeric
½ teaspoon cinnamon
1 teaspoon ground coriander

2 tablespoons canola oil
2 cloves garlic, minced
2 tablespoons fresh ginger root, grated
4 teaspoons red barley miso in 3 cups water
2 tablespoons lemon juice
3 tablespoons honey or maple syrup
1 medium onion, chopped
4 carrots, chopped
8-10 button mushrooms, washed and quartered
1 medium head of cauliflower, broken into florets
3 medium potatoes, diced
1 medium red pepper, chopped
2 tablespoons tamari
2 tablespoons garlic powder
¼ teaspoon cayenne pepper (optional)
¾ cup soy milk
½ cup roasted cashew pieces (see recipe for Roasted Nuts & Seeds on page 11)

Wash the rice in a heavy saucepan and drain. Add fresh water, sea salt, and kombu. Cover and bring to a boil. Lower the heat and simmer, covered, for 35 minutes, or until all the liquid is absorbed. Remove the kombu strip and chop finely. Add the chopped kombu to the cooked rice. Sprinkle on the herb seasoning salt, black pepper, garlic powder, and dried parsley. Toss to blend the seasonings. Add the sesame oil and tamari and toss again gently.

In a small bowl, combine the cumin seed, ground cloves, cardamom, mustard, turmeric, cinnamon, and coriander. Set aside.

148

In large soup kettle or Dutch oven, heat the oil and add garlic and ginger. Sauté for 1 minute, letting the garlic and ginger fill your kitchen with delightful aromas. Add the mixed spices, stir, and cook 1 minute. Add the miso broth, lemon juice, and honey or maple syrup. Add the onion, carrots, mushrooms, cauliflower tops, potatoes, and red pepper. Cook, covered, until tender, about 10-15 minutes. Add tamari, garlic powder, cayenne pepper, if desired, and soy milk. Stir to blend and heat gently. Adjust the seasonings to taste, adding more tamari if desired.

Serve the vegetable and spice mixture in bowls over the cooked and herbed basmati rice and top with the roasted cashews.

Once all the ingredients are chopped and the rice is prepared, this recipe only takes about 20 minutes to prepare. It is an attractive dish with a delicious aroma!

Temptation Turkish Pilaf

This is a different and easy way to prepare a rice casserole. First you sauté the vegetables, then add the uncooked rice and steam all the ingredients together. The wonderful aroma from this dish will create enthusiastic requests for a repeat of this recipe soon.

SERVES 6

1 medium onion, chopped
1 clove garlic, minced
2 tablespoons olive oil
4 stalks celery, chopped
2 carrots, sliced
½ teaspoon allspice
½ teaspoon ground coriander
½ teaspoon cinnamon
½ teaspoon fennel seeds
1 tablespoon water

2 cups white or brown basmati rice
3 cups water
pinch of sea salt
1 cup currants or raisins

2 tablespoons tamari
½ cup slivered almonds

Sauté the onion and garlic in oil in a heavy saucepan until the onion is translucent. Add celery, carrots, allspice, coriander, cinnamon, fennel seeds, and 1 tablespoon water. Sauté 3 more minutes.

Wash the rice and add to the sautéed vegetables and spices in the saucepan along with water, sea salt, and currants. Bring to a boil. Lower the heat and simmer, covered, for 35 minutes or until all the liquid is absorbed. Do not peek.

When the rice is cooked, season with tamari. Let the rice sit for a few minutes, fluff with a fork, and top with slivered almonds. This recipe is great with simple steamed vegetables and a tofu and arame salad.

One-Stop Rice & Bean Dish

Because of my busy lifestyle, I really appreciate a fast and easy method of cooking. This one-pot meal, served with a salad, provides good nutritional balance. This dish is perfect topped with gomashio.

SERVES 4-6

1½ cups short-grain brown rice
1 15-ounce can of black beans, drained and rinsed
3 cups water
2 carrots, chopped
1x3-inch strip of kombu, rinsed.

½ teaspoon herb seasoning salt
½ teaspoon black pepper
½ teaspoon garlic powder
½ cup dried parsley
1 tablespoon tamari
1 tablespoon canola oil

gomashio (see recipe for Gomashio on page 10)

Wash the brown rice in a heavy saucepan and drain. Add the drained and rinsed black beans. Add fresh water, carrots, and kombu. Bring to a boil. Lower the heat and simmer, covered, for 45-50 minutes. Remove the kombu strip and chop finely.

Place the cooked brown rice and beans in large bowl. Add the chopped kombu. Sprinkle on the herb seasoning salt, black pepper, garlic powder, and dried parsley. Add the tamari and canola oil and toss gently. Top with gomashio or roasted sunflower seeds, if desired.

Brazilian Black Bean & Rice Casserole

This complete protein meal is a sure crowd-pleaser because of its exotic background, spicy flavors, and rich dark color.

SERVES 4-6

1½ cups short-grain brown rice
1 15-ounce can of black beans, drained
   and rinsed
3 cups water
1x3-inch strip of kombu, rinsed

½ teaspoon herb seasoning salt
½ teaspoon black pepper
½ teaspoon garlic powder
½ cup dried parsley
1 tablespoon tamari
1 tablespoon canola oil

2 tablespoons olive oil
1 medium onion, chopped
2 cloves garlic, minced
1 medium green pepper, chopped
1 medium red pepper, chopped
3 carrots, chopped
1 cup bottled salsa (medium or hot, your
   choice)
1 tablespoon tamari

1 cup tortilla chips

Wash the brown rice in a heavy saucepan and drain. Add the drained and rinsed black beans. Add fresh water and kombu. Cover and bring to a boil. Lower the heat and simmer, covered, for 45-50 minutes, or until all the liquid is absorbed. Remove the kombu strip and chop finely.

Place the cooked rice and beans in a large bowl and sprinkle on the herb seasoning salt, black pepper, garlic powder, and dried parsley. Add the chopped kombu. Add tamari and canola oil and toss gently.

In a skillet, sauté the onion and garlic in the olive oil until the onion is translucent. Add the green and red peppers and carrots and sauté for approximately 5 minutes or until just tender. Add the salsa and stir. Mix in the tamari.

Add the sautéed vegetables to the seasoned rice and beans and stir. Adjust the seasonings to taste. Serve topped with tortilla chips.

Ginger Wild Rice with Water Chestnuts

Wild rice is not a rice, but the seed of an aquatic grass that is native to America. It tends to be expensive depending on the grade, so we limit its use at the Cafe and usually combine it with long-grain brown rice. Wild rice is never refined and is rich in fiber, protein, B vitamins, and minerals.

Serves 4-6

2 cups wild rice (or 1 cup wild rice and 1 cup long-grain brown rice)
2½ cups water
pinch of sea salt

2 tablespoons olive oil
1 medium onion, chopped
2 cloves garlic, minced
1 8-ounce can of sliced water chestnuts, drained and chopped
1 teaspoon fresh ginger root, finely grated

1 tablespoon sesame oil
1 tablespoon tamari
½ teaspoon herb seasoning salt

½ cup fresh chives, chopped
½ cup roasted sunflower seeds (see recipe for Roasted Nuts & Seeds on page 11)

Wash the wild rice and brown rice in a heavy saucepan and drain. Add fresh water and sea salt. Bring to a boil on high. Lower the heat and simmer, covered, for approximately 45-50 minutes.

While the rice is cooking, heat the oil in a skillet and sauté the onion, garlic, and water chestnuts. When the onion is translucent, add the ginger and sauté briefly to retain the ginger's fresh flavor.

Mix the cooked rice and sautéed vegetables in a large bowl. Season with sesame oil, tamari and herb seasoning salt.

Top with fresh chives and roasted sunflower seeds for an attractive presentation.

For a delicious variation, sauté other vegetables such as chopped broccoli or sliced daikon along with the onion, garlic, and ginger.

153

Chickpea, Rice & Millet Delight

SERVES 4-6

1 cup short-grain brown rice
½ cup millet
1 15-ounce can chickpeas, drained and rinsed
3 cups water
1x3-inch strip of kombu, rinsed

½ teaspoon herb seasoning salt
½ teaspoon black pepper
½ teaspoon garlic powder
½ cup dried parsley
1 tablespoon tamari
1 tablespoon canola oil
¼ cup parsley, chopped
gomashio for topping (see recipe for Gomashio on page 10)

Wash the brown rice and millet in a fine sieve or colander and drain. Add fresh water and kombu, cover, and bring to a boil on high. Lower the heat and simmer, covered, for 50 minutes. Do not peek!!! Stir in the chickpeas. Remove the kombu strip and chop finely.

With a large wooden spoon, scoop the chickpeas, rice, and millet into a large bowl. Add the chopped kombu. Sprinkle on the herb seasoning salt, black pepper, garlic powder, and dried parsley. Add the tamari and canola oil and toss gently. Top with chopped parsley and gomashio if desired.

This is a complete protein meal, simple and delicious. For a tasty variation, make quick veggie burgers. Allow the grains to cool. With wet hands, form the grain mixture into 6 patties. Place the patties on an oiled cookie sheet and bake at 350 degrees for 15-20 minutes, or until slightly browned. If you prefer crisper patties, place them under the broiler for 3-5 minutes just before serving.

Nutty Millet & Garlic

This unusually easy dish is very tasty due to the flavorful nature of the simple ingredients. If you prepare this dish once, I guarantee it will be a regular at your dinner table.

SERVES 4-6

2 tablespoons sesame oil
2 cloves garlic, minced
1 cup roasted cashew pieces (see recipe for Roasted Nuts & Seeds on page 11)

1½ cups millet
3 cups water
pinch of sea salt

¼ cup fresh parsley, chopped

In a deep heavy skillet, sauté the garlic and nuts in oil for about 3 minutes, or until lightly browned.

Wash and drain the millet in a fine sieve or colander and add to the sautéed nuts and garlic in the skillet. Pan roast over medium heat for about 5-7 minutes, stirring constantly, until the millet is golden brown and gives off a nutty aroma. Add water and salt, cover, and bring to a boil. Reduce heat and simmer, covered, for 25-30 minutes. Remove the pan from the heat and fluff the millet with a fork. Mix in the chopped parsley. Place the millet in a serving bowl and serve warm. This dish is excellent when accompanied by a garden salad and a loaf of homemade bread.

For a delicious variation, combine ½ cup roasted sunflower seeds with ½ cup roasted cashew pieces.

Magic Millet Croquettes with Star Anise

If millet is cooked alone, it tends to be somewhat bland in a croquette or patty. However, I have discovered that by using extra cooking water with seasonings, you can create a moist, flavorful croquette.

SERVES 4-6

2 cups millet
4 cups water
3 whole star anise
1 teaspoon ground coriander
pinch of sea salt

2 tablespoons olive oil
1 medium onion, chopped
2 cloves garlic, minced
2 stalks celery, chopped
2 tablespoons tamari
½ cup fresh parsley, finely chopped
1 teaspoon herb seasoning salt

Wash the millet in a fine sieve or colander and drain. Add fresh water, star anise, coriander, and sea salt. Cover and bring to a boil. Lower the heat and steam, covered, for approximately 25-30 minutes.

While the millet is steaming, sauté the onion, garlic, and celery in oil in a skillet until the onion is translucent.

When the millet is cooked, remove and discard the star anise and place the millet in a large bowl. Add the sautéed onion, garlic, and celery. Toss and season with tamari, parsley, and herb seasoning salt. Mix thoroughly and adjust seasonings to taste.

Allow the millet to cool until it can be handled. With wet hands, form the millet into 8-10 croquettes or patties. Place the patties on an oiled cookie sheet and bake at 350 degrees for 15-20 minutes or until lightly browned. If you prefer crisper patties, place them under the broiler for 3-5 minutes just before serving. Serve as the main course at dinner or as burgers at lunch topped with your favorite sauce or dressing.

Quinoa & Brown Rice

Quinoa was totally unknown to me five years ago. Now that I've been introduced to this wonderful grain, we use it regularly in the Cafe because of its unique nutty taste, high protein content, versatility, and fast cooking process. This dish is a simple mixture of quinoa and brown rice which can be easily dressed up with colorful vegetables such as chopped carrots, steamed greens, or buttercup squash for a nutritional bonus. Once you've mastered the art of combining grains, try substituting millet or pearl barley for the quinoa. Or add a half cup of wild rice and a half cup of soaked wheat berries for an interesting texture.

SERVES 4-6

1 cup short-grain brown rice
1 cup quinoa
3¼ cups water (or 3 cups for drier grains)
pinch of sea salt
1x3-inch strip of kombu, rinsed

½ teaspoon herb seasoning salt
½ teaspoon black pepper
½ teaspoon garlic powder
½ cup dried parsley
1 tablespoon tamari
1 tablespoon canola oil

½ cup roasted sunflower seeds
   (see recipe for Roasted Nuts & Seeds
   on page 11)

Wash the rice and quinoa in a fine sieve and drain. In a heavy saucepan, combine the rice and quinoa, water, sea salt, and kombu. Cover and bring to a boil. Lower the heat and simmer, covered, for 45-50 minutes. Remove the kombu strip and chop finely.

Place the cooked brown rice and quinoa in large bowl. Add the chopped kombu. Sprinkle on the herb seasoning salt, black pepper, garlic powder, and dried parsley. Add the tamari and canola oil and toss gently. Top with roasted sunflower seeds.

(Note: If you are using wheat berries, they should be soaked before cooking. Place them in a saucepan and add 4 cups of cold water. Bring the water to a boil and cook the wheat berries for 2 minutes. Cover the pot, remove from heat, and let stand for about 1 hour. Drain and add to the other grains for final cooking.)

157

Barley & Brown Rice Vegetable Casserole

This barley and brown rice casserole differs from the others because I use miso as the main seasoning. Miso aids in digestion, and the rich flavor is a plus. This is a wonderful mid-winter evening meal that is best served with a green vegetable salad.

SERVES 4-6

1 cup short-grain brown rice
1 cup barley
3½ cups water
pinch of sea salt
2 tablespoons red barley miso

2 tablespoons canola oil
1 medium onion, chopped
2 cloves garlic, minced
2 stalks celery, chopped
1 teaspoon dried basil
1 teaspoon ground coriander
1 medium winter squash, peeled and cubed
¾ cup water
2 cups broccoli, broken into florets
2 tablespoons maple syrup
2 tablespoons tamari
¼ cup water

½ teaspoon herb seasoning salt
½ cup roasted sunflower seeds
     (see recipe for Roasted Nuts & Seeds
     on page 11)

Wash the rice and barley together in a heavy saucepan and drain. Add fresh water, sea salt, and miso. Stir to dissolve the miso. Cover and bring to a boil. Lower heat and simmer, covered, for 50 minutes.

Meanwhile, heat the oil in a large skillet with a cover and sauté the onion, garlic, and celery until the onion is translucent. Add the basil, coriander, and the squash. Add ¾ cup water. Bring to a boil. Reduce heat, cover, and steam for about 10 minutes until squash is just tender. Add the broccoli florets. Steam for 2 minutes, covered. Combine the maple syrup and tamari with ¼ cup water and add to the vegetables. Toss and warm for one more minute.

In a large bowl, combine the rice, barley, and sautéed vegetables. Toss and season with herb seasoning salt. Top with roasted sunflower seeds.

Simple Couscous

Couscous is a finely cracked wheat that cooks quickly and makes a tasty side dish. I don't recommend washing couscous before cooking because it becomes mushy.

SERVES 4-6

1¾ cups water
1½ cups couscous
2 tablespoons dried parsley
½ teaspoon garlic powder

Bring water to a boil. In a heatproof bowl, combine the boiling water, couscous, parsley, and garlic powder. Cover tightly and let sit for 10 minutes. Fluff with a fork and serve immediately.

Couscous Almond Croquettes

SERVES 4-6

2 cups couscous
2½ cups boiling water

2 tablespoons sesame oil
2 medium onions, chopped
1 clove garlic, minced
4 carrots, grated
½ cup slivered almonds

1 teaspoon almond extract
1 teaspoon herb seasoning salt
¼ cup fresh parsley, chopped

Put the couscous in a large heatproof bowl. Add boiling water. Cover and let sit 20 minutes.

Meanwhile, in a skillet, sauté the onions, garlic, carrots, and almonds in oil until the onions are translucent. Add almond extract, seasoning salt, and parsley to the vegetable mixture and stir.

When the couscous is ready, mix it with the sautéed vegetables. With wet hands, form the vegetable and couscous mixture into 6-8 croquettes or patties. Press the mixture firmly when forming the croquettes. Place on oiled cookie sheet and bake at 350 degrees for 25 minutes or until lightly browned.

Serve in a whole-wheat bun with a bowl of hot homemade soup or as a main course at dinner with steamed greens and tofu.

Baked Rigatoni & Wheat Balls

Because I enjoy *easy*, I included this recipe in the cookbook. We prepare it frequently at the Cafe and in our cooking classes. Most people love the 'no-meat' balls and are surprised by the tastiness of these little gems.

SERVES 4-6

½ of an 8.5-ounce package of wheat ball mix
3 cups uncooked Jerusalem artichoke rigatoni or penne
1½ cups chopped broccoli (optional)
3 cups marinara sauce
1 cup mozzarella, grated (optional)
¼ cup fresh parsley, chopped

Start this recipe about 1½ hours before serving time, as the wheat balls take some time to prepare and cook. Prepare 12 1-inch wheat balls according to the directions on the package. The secret to wheat balls is to make them very small as they double in size while they cook. Be sure to drain the wheat balls when they are cooked. If you like, you can bake the boiled, drained wheat balls briefly as recommended on the package for added crispness.

In a large pot, cook the rigatoni until just al dente. If you are using the broccoli, add it to the rigatoni during the last 3 minutes of cooking. Drain and set aside.

In a 9x13x2-inch glass casserole, combine the wheat balls, rigatoni, broccoli, and marinara sauce. Top with grated mozzarella, if desired, and bake, uncovered, at 350 degrees for 25 minutes. Top with fresh parsley and serve.

"But I should be bigger. Look at all those other big, brilliant mountains!" Cranmore blurted out.

"As long as you are comparing yourself to others, you are unable to grow," said Washington.

In a weak, weary voice Cranmore asked, "I have tried so hard—I stretch each morning till my tippity-top is sore. How can I be BIG and IMPORTANT?"

"Keep stretching Cranmore, and you will only grow your outsides. To really grow, you must grow your insides. Everyday look at your reflection in the pond and say:

'I AM IMPORTANT
    I LOVE AND VALUE MYSELF.'"

Kathy Etter
From: Cranmore's Adventure

162

TOFU & TEMPEH

Tofu and Tempeh Dishes

Tofu and tempeh, like most ingredients in vegetarian cuisine, are versatile and fun to play with. They may be used as a meat substitute in any of your favorite recipes. They can also be substituted for each other.

Tofu comes in many different forms ranging from silken to extra-firm. We recommend extra-firm for any recipe that calls for cubes or rectangles, firm for any recipe that requires crumbling the tofu, and soft or silken for making sauces and creamy textures.

Tempeh also comes in different varieties. They are all cooked the same way—what variety you choose is simply a matter of personal preference. Tempeh is easiest to work with and more aesthetically pleasing when cut into thin triangles. It's a little more work, but worth the effort. To create triangles, stand the block of tempeh on its side and slice in half lengthwise into two thin rectangles. Lay the tempeh flat and cut each rectangle in half lengthwise. You should now have four strips of tempeh. Pile them one on top of the other and cut the tempeh diagonally, corner to corner, in bite-sized triangles. Children especially enjoy watching the triangles appear.

Tofu & Green Pea Curry

The wonderful aroma from this dish will bring everyone for dinner on time. I always enjoy serving this and other curry dishes with fragrant basmati rice.

SERVES 4

1 cup frozen peas
1 tablespoon sesame oil
1 medium onion, chopped
1 clove garlic, minced
1 tablespoon curry powder
½ teaspoon garam masala powder
1 pound extra-firm tofu, cut in 1-inch cubes
1 tablespoon tamari

Thaw the frozen peas and set aside. Heat the sesame oil in a large skillet and add the onion and garlic. Sauté briefly and add the curry powder and garam masala. Stir to blend. Add the cubed tofu and sauté, stirring gently, until the tofu is browned and the onion is translucent.

Add the thawed peas and the tamari. Cover and cook briefly for 2-3 minutes until the peas are done. Adjust the seasonings to taste and serve hot over basmati rice.

Tofu & Vegetable Kebabs

MAKES 4 KEBABS

For the Marinade:
2 tablespoons sesame oil
¼ cup tahini
¼ cup fresh lemon juice
3 tablespoons tamari
1 medium onion, coarsely chopped
2 cloves garlic
¼ cup dried parsley

For the Kebabs:
3 carrots, cut on the diagonal in 1-inch slices
8 small new potatoes, cut in large chunks
1 cup water
1 8-ounce package mushrooms, whole
2 large red peppers, cut in broad slices
2 large green peppers, cut in broad slices
1 pound extra-firm tofu, cut into 8 cubes

Combine all the marinade ingredients and blend in a food processor or blender until smooth.

Prepare the vegetables and tofu for the kebabs. Steam the carrots and new potatoes in water until crisp tender, about 3-5 minutes.

Place the vegetables and the tofu on skewers, alternating ingredients. Use 2 cubes of tofu per skewer. Place kebabs in a baking pan and brush with marinade. Let marinate for 15-30 minutes.

Bake at 350 degrees for 20 minutes. Brush again with marinade and broil for an additional 5 minutes or until the kebabs are lightly browned. Serve over rice and spoon on any leftover marinade.

Simple Tofu Squares with Arame

This is a quick and easy side dish that will add protein to any meal. The recipe calls for arame which is a sea vegetable. Arame will contribute calcium and trace minerals to your dish as well as adding color and texture.

MAKES 4 SIDE DISH SERVINGS

2 tablespoons dried arame, soaked and drained
1 cup hot water

2 tablespoons sesame oil
1 pound extra-firm tofu, cut in ½-inch cubes
2 tablespoons tamari
½ teaspoon herb seasoning salt
½ teaspoon garlic powder
¼ teaspoon paprika
¼ cup fresh parsley, chopped

Soak the arame in a cup of hot water for 5 minutes. Drain in a colander and set aside.

Heat the sesame oil in a large skillet and add the cubed tofu. Brown the tofu cubes, stirring frequently.

To the browned tofu, add the tamari, seasoning salt, garlic powder, paprika, and parsley. Stir to blend and sauté gently for a few minutes. Add the drained arame and stir. Serve hot.

167

Tofu & Udon Lo Mein

SERVES 4-6

1 tablespoon sesame oil
1 pound extra-firm tofu, cut in 1-inch cubes
2 tablespoons fresh ginger root, grated
2 cloves garlic, minced
4-5 fresh or dried shiitaki mushrooms, sliced (soak dried mushrooms before slicing)
1 medium onion, cut in half-moons
4 cups water
1 tablespoon red barley miso
1 8-ounce package uncooked udon noodles
2 carrots, sliced on the diagonal
1 cup broccoli florets, coarsely chopped
2 tablespoons tamari

Heat the sesame oil at a low temperature in a large soup pot and add the cubed tofu. Brown the tofu cubes, stirring frequently. Add the ginger, garlic, mushrooms, and onion. Sauté until the onion is translucent.

Combine the water and miso. Add to the soup pot and simmer for 5 minutes. Add the udon, carrots, and broccoli. Cook over medium heat for 10-15 minutes or until the udon noodles are done. Add tamari. Adjust seasonings to taste and serve hot.

Savory Tofu Dream

In this easy recipe, the tofu is marinated overnight in savory Almond Ginger Sauce and baked. This dish is delicious served with herbed millet or short-grain brown rice.

SERVES 4-5

1 pound extra-firm tofu, cut in rectangles

For the Almond Ginger Sauce:
½ cup almond butter
½ cup water
1 teaspoon tamari
3 teaspoons honey
1 teaspoon vinegar
1 tablespoon fresh ginger root, grated

Cut the tofu into small rectangles, approximately 1x2-inches, and place in a nonreactive baking dish.

To prepare the Almond Ginger Sauce, place all ingredients in a blender and blend at medium speed to mix. Add additional water if necessary and slowly blend to a creamy consistency.

Pour Almond Ginger Sauce over the tofu rectangles, cover, and marinate in the refrigerator overnight.

When ready to serve, bake the marinated tofu for 15-20 minutes at 350 degrees. Serve hot with your choice of grain dish.

169

Honey Mustard Tofu

This is a simple recipe that can be easily transformed into an elegant party dish. Wrap the tofu squares inside steamed spinach or collard leaves, using a toothpick to hold things together. A sure hit! For everyday, serve the tofu squares warm in a sandwich or on rice or couscous.

SERVES 4-6

For the Honey Mustard Sauce:
1 tablespoon fresh ginger root, grated
2 cloves garlic, chopped
⅓ cup honey
⅓ cup Dijon mustard
¼ cup tamari
¼ cup white wine
¾ cup cashews

For the Tofu:
2 tablespoons canola oil
1 large onion, chopped
2 teaspoons fresh ginger root, grated
1 pound extra-firm tofu, cut in bite-sized squares
3 scallions, chopped

To prepare the Honey Mustard Sauce, combine the ginger, garlic, honey, mustard, tamari, white wine, and cashews in a food processor or blender. Blend until smooth and set the sauce aside.

Heat the canola oil at a low temperature in a large skillet and add the onion, ginger, and tofu squares. Sauté the mixture until the tofu squares are browned and the onion is translucent. Add the Honey Mustard Sauce and stir gently to blend. Top with chopped scallions.

Wrap in steamed spinach or collard leaves for a party dish, or serve warm over rice or in a sandwich.

Tofu-Mushroom Stroganoff Sauce

At Cafe Chimes, we are committed to low-fat dishes that retain a rich and tasty texture and flavor. In this recipe, the tofu-tahini sauce replaces the traditional high-fat, high-cholesterol sour cream sauce. This easy dish is perfect for a special occasion or a simple family dinner. The sauce freezes well for later use.

SERVES 4-6

½ pound soft or silken tofu, crumbled
juice from ½ lemon
2 tablespoons canola oil
½ cup tahini
¼ cup tamari
up to ½ cup warm water if needed to thin sauce

1 tablespoon sesame oil
1 medium onion, chopped
2 cloves garlic, minced
½ pound button mushrooms, quartered
5-7 fresh or dried shiitaki mushrooms, sliced (soak dried mushrooms before slicing)
1 teaspoon paprika
½ teaspoon dried thyme
1 teaspoon dried dill weed
up to ½ cup water if needed to thin sauce
2 tablespoons fresh parsley, chopped

In a blender or food processor, combine the tofu, lemon juice, oil, tahini, and tamari. Blend until smooth. If the sauce is too thick, you may add warm water to thin the mixture to a smooth, creamy consistency. Set the sauce aside.

Heat the sesame oil in a large skillet. Add the onion and garlic and sauté until the onion is translucent. Add the button and shiitaki mushrooms, paprika, thyme, and dill weed. Sauté until the mushrooms are tender, stirring frequently.

Add the tofu sauce from the blender to the mushroom mixture and cook briefly over low heat until heated and slightly thickened. Add more water if necessary and stir to blend to desired consistency. Serve hot over pasta and top with fresh parsley. We recommend fettuccine or udon noodles.

Baked Tofu with 'The Sauce'

Sometimes I am surprised at what we can create if we don't let fear hold us back. 'The Sauce' is a tangy concoction that was born because I had some leftover crushed pineapple. It is delicious poured over tofu and baked for an easy main course, as in this recipe. It can also be served on a grain casserole or as a dressing for a summer salad treat.

SERVES 4-6

For 'The Sauce':

½ cup water
1 tablespoon white miso
½ cup canned crushed pineapple
2 tablespoons lemon juice
¼ cup maple syrup
1 clove garlic, minced
1 teaspoon tamari
½ teaspoon cinnamon
½ teaspoon coriander powder

For the Tofu:

1 pound extra-firm tofu, frozen and thawed
1 medium onion, sliced

Place all the sauce ingredients in a blender or food processor and purée until creamy.

Thaw the tofu and squeeze out all the liquid. Slice into 8 pieces. Place the sliced tofu and onion in a 9-inch square baking dish. Pour the sauce over the tofu, cover, and bake at 350 degrees for 20-25 minutes. Remove cover and bake an additional 5 minutes.

Thelma's Tempeh Dish

Opening a package of tempeh can be a labor of love, but having a sharp pair of scissors handy will be helpful. This savory dish is worth the effort.

SERVES 4-6

1 8-ounce package of tempeh
2 cups water
2 tablespoons tamari
2 tablespoons sesame oil
2 onions, chopped
½ teaspoon curry powder
4 tablespoons tahini
1 tablespoon honey
½ cup raisins
½ cup peanuts
1 tablespoon arrowroot powder if needed to thicken sauce
½ cup water if using arrowroot powder

Place the block of tempeh in a large saucepan with 2 cups water and 2 tablespoons tamari. Bring to boil and cook for 15-20 minutes or until most of the liquid is absorbed. Reserve any leftover broth.

While the tempeh is cooking, heat the sesame oil in a large skillet and add the onions and curry powder. Sauté until the onions are translucent.

In a small bowl, combine the tahini and honey and stir until blended.

See the instructions for cutting tempeh on the first page of this section. Cut the cooked tempeh into triangles and combine with the sautéed onions. Add the peanuts and raisins and sauté gently. Add the tahini and honey mixture and stir to blend. Add the leftover broth from cooking the tempeh. When the tahini is heated, it should thicken the sauce. If you prefer a thicker sauce, dissolve 1 tablespoon of arrowroot in a half-cup of water and add to the skillet. Cook gently, stirring constantly, until the sauce has thickened.

Serve warm over noodles or fettuccine. For extra flavor, you may want to add a little sesame oil and minced garlic to the cooked noodles.

Mexican Tempeh & Avocado

SERVES 4-6

1 8-ounce package of tempeh
2 cups water
2 tablespoons tamari
1 clove garlic, minced
1 medium avocado, pitted, peeled, and cubed
¼ cup fresh parsley, chopped
⅓ cup scallions, chopped

¼ cup prepared salsa (your choice of mild, medium, or hot)
2 teaspoons ground cumin
1 tablespoon tamari
¼ teaspoon cayenne (optional)
¼ cup roasted sunflower seeds (see recipe for Roasted Nuts & Seeds on page 11)

Place the block of tempeh in a large saucepan with 2 cups water and 2 tablespoons tamari. Bring to a boil and cook for 15-20 minutes or until most of the liquid is absorbed. Cool slightly.

While the tempeh is cooking, combine the garlic, avocado, parsley, and scallions in a large bowl.

See the instructions for cutting tempeh on the first page of this section. Cut the cooked tempeh into bite-sized squares or triangles and add to the vegetables along with the salsa, cumin, and tamari. If spicy food is to your liking, add ¼ teaspoon cayenne, keeping in mind that a little goes a long way. Top with roasted sunflower seeds.

Serve immediately on warmed tortillas, or cold for lunch the next day.

Sizzlin' Tempeh Fajitas

SERVES 4-6

1 8-ounce package of tempeh
2 cups water
2 tablespoons tamari
2 tablespoons canola oil
1 large onion, cut in half-moons
2 cloves garlic, minced
1 medium green pepper, cut in strips
1 medium red pepper, cut in strips
4-5 medium mushrooms, sliced
1 teaspoon chili powder
1 teaspoon cumin powder
$\frac{1}{8}$ teaspoon cayenne
$\frac{1}{4}$ teaspoon black pepper
$\frac{1}{2}$ teaspoon paprika
2 tablespoons dried parsley
1 tablespoon tamari
$\frac{1}{4}$ cup tomato juice or red wine (optional)

Place the block of tempeh in a large saucepan with 2 cups water and 2 tablespoons tamari. Bring to a boil and cook for 15-20 minutes or until most of the liquid is absorbed.

While the tempeh is cooking, heat the canola oil in a large skillet and add the onion, garlic, green and red peppers, and mushrooms. Add the chili powder, cumin, cayenne, pepper, paprika, and dried parsley. Sauté the vegetables and spices until the onion is translucent, stirring frequently. Add the tamari and tomato juice or red wine, if desired.

See the instructions for cutting tempeh on the first page of this section. Cut the cooked tempeh into triangles and combine with the cooked vegetables. Stir gently and adjust seasonings to taste. Serve warm over rice or in warm tortillas.

Pizza Tempeh

We call this dish "Pizza Tempeh" because it smells just like pizza when it's cooking. Begin this recipe a few hours ahead, as it needs to marinate for several hours—the longer the better. This recipe can be served as a side dish, with noodles as a main course, or in a sandwich for a meal on the go.

SERVES 4-6

For the Marinade:

¼ cup canola oil
juice from 1 lemon
2 tablespoons tamari
2 tablespoons paprika
1 teaspoon dried thyme
½ teaspoon dried rosemary
2 cloves garlic, minced (or 2 teaspoons garlic powder)
¼ cup red wine (optional)

1 8-ounce package of tempeh, cut in bite-sized triangles

To prepare the marinade, combine the oil, lemon juice, tamari, paprika, thyme, rosemary, garlic, and wine in a medium bowl and whisk until well-blended. If you prefer, you can use a blender.

See the instructions for cutting tempeh on the first page of this section. Cut the tempeh into bite-sized triangles. Place the tempeh triangles in a nonreactive dish and pour the marinade over them. Let marinate for at least 3 hours.

Transfer the tempeh and marinade to a 9x13-inch baking pan. Broil the tempeh for 10 minutes or until it is lightly browned. Serve hot.

Tempeh with Leeks & Tomato

The secret for success with this tangy recipe is to thoroughly clean the leeks. Leeks are usually very sandy, and if they're not squeaky clean, they will add a nasty crunch to your tempeh. To clean the leeks, cut off the root ends at the very base. Cut off the top two inches of the leaves. Remove any bruised outside leaves. Split the leek lengthwise. Turn the leek about ¼-inch and make another lengthwise cut. This allows the leaves to be opened up and rinsed. Place in cold water and let stand until ready to use.

SERVES 4-5

1 8-ounce package of tempeh
2 cups water
2 tablespoons tamari
1 medium leek, cut in ½-inch diagonal slices
2 tablespoons olive oil
8-10 cherry tomatoes, halved or whole (or 1 medium tomato, chopped)
2 cloves garlic, minced
½ cup red wine
¼ teaspoon black pepper

Place the block of tempeh in a large saucepan with 2 cups water and 2 tablespoons tamari. Bring to a boil and cook for 15-20 minutes or until most of the liquid is absorbed. Cool slightly. See the instructions for cutting tempeh on the first page of this section. Cut the tempeh into bite-sized triangles.

Heat the oil in a large skillet and sauté the sliced leek until tender, stirring frequently. Add the tempeh triangles and garlic. Sauté gently to lightly brown the tempeh. Add the tomatoes and sauté for 2-3 minutes. Add the red wine and pepper and simmer for 5 minutes. Adjust seasonings to taste and serve hot over your favorite pasta. Penne is a good choice for this dish.

177

Tempeh with Pesto & Red Pepper

Serve this delightful concoction with the pasta of your choice. My family enjoys rigatoni or rainbow rotini.

SERVES 4-6

1 8-ounce package of tempeh
2 cups water
2 tablespoons tamari

2 tablespoons olive oil
3 cloves garlic, minced
1 medium onion, chopped
1 large red pepper, cut in strips
1 cup prepared pesto sauce
2 tablespoons tamari
¼ cup red wine
2 tablespoons nutritional yeast
¼ cup chopped walnuts (optional)
½ cup water if needed to thin sauce

Place the block of tempeh in a large saucepan with 2 cups water and 2 tablespoons tamari. Bring to a boil and cook for 15-20 minutes or until most of the liquid is absorbed. Cool slightly and reserve any leftover cooking liquid. See the instructions for cutting tempeh on the first page of this section. Cut the tempeh into bite-sized triangles.

Heat the oil in a large skillet and sauté the garlic, onion, and red pepper until the onion is translucent. Add the pesto sauce, tamari, red wine, and nutritional yeast, along with any leftover cooking liquid from the tempeh. Stir to blend. Add the tempeh triangles and walnuts, if desired. Stir to blend and heat gently for about 5 minutes. Add additional water if the sauce is too thick. Adjust seasonings to taste and serve hot over your choice of pasta.

VEGETABLE MAINSTAYS

Vegetable Mainstays

In this section, you'll find a tempting array of main dish recipes and vegetable side dishes which can be combined to make a full meal.

Be adventurous in your combinations. Combining the huge variety of plant foods is a creative, never-ending sensation in vegetarian cooking. I only suggest guidelines to get you started. However, there are no limits. Go beyond what you think you know!

Sesame Gingered Carrots & Leeks

Serves 4-6

1 tablespoon sesame oil
1 large leek, cleaned and sliced diagonally
2 teaspoons fresh ginger root, grated
1 tablespoon tamari
½ cup water
5-6 carrots, cut in matchsticks
1 tablespoon roasted sesame seeds (see recipe for Roasted Nuts & Seeds on page 11)

Clean the leek by cutting off the root end at the very base. Cut off the top two inches of the leaves and remove any bruised outside leaves. Split the leek lengthwise. Turn the leek about ¼-inch and make another lengthwise cut. This allows the leaves to be opened up and rinsed. Place in cold water and let stand until ready to use. Slice the leek diagonally before cooking.

In large skillet with a cover, heat the oil and sauté the sliced leek until just tender. Add the grated ginger and tamari and stir. Add the water and carrots. Cover and steam quickly until the carrots are still slightly crisp, approximately 2-3 minutes. Serve topped with sesame seeds.

Indian Eggplant

SERVES 4-6

2 tablespoons canola oil
2-3 cloves garlic, minced
1 medium onion, chopped
4-5 mushrooms, sliced
1 medium eggplant, peeled and cubed
4 teaspoons curry powder
1 teaspoon ground coriander
1 teaspoon garam masala
½ to 1 cup water, if needed
¼ cup tahini
1 medium tomato, chopped
¼ cup fresh parsley, chopped (or 2 tablespoons dried)
1 cup frozen peas, thawed
2 tablespoons tamari

In a large skillet, sauté the garlic, onions, mushrooms, and eggplant in oil on medium heat, stirring frequently, until the mushrooms are tender and the eggplant has collapsed. Add curry powder, coriander, and garam masala, and sauté briefly to blend the spices. Add water if needed. Add tahini, tomato, parsley, peas, and tamari. Simmer gently for 5 minutes. Adjust seasonings to taste.

This dish is delicious served hot over basmati rice with cashews. It also makes a tasty topping for pita bread—serve hot or cold.

Emerald Steamed Greens

Although children still have reservations about cooked green vegetables, we find that adults seem to really enjoy the freshness and flavor of lightly steamed greens. And your body just says thank you a million times over!

SERVES 4-6

1 bunch collards, stemmed and coarsely chopped
1 bunch kale, stemmed and coarsely chopped
1 tablespoon tamari
1 tablespoon vinegar or lemon juice

In a large skillet, place the cleaned and chopped greens in a couple of inches of boiling water. Cover and steam for 4-6 minutes until the greens are just tender, but still bright green. Sprinkle on tamari and vinegar or lemon juice and serve immediately.

This simple method of preparation works for any one of several green leafy vegetables: collard greens, kale, mustard greens, spinach, escarole, as well as bok choy, broccoli, and Chinese cabbage. Adjust the steaming time so that the greens are just tender. You may need a little more time for the broccoli and cabbages.

My Favorite 'Greens' Dish

<small>SERVES 4-6</small>

1 tablespoon canola oil
2 onions, cut in half-moons
1 clove garlic, minced
5 shiitake or regular mushrooms, chopped
1 bunch of your favorite greens, stemmed and coarsely chopped (good choices include
  kale, collards, mustard greens, escarole, or spinach)
½ cup water
1 tablespoon tamari
1 tablespoon brown rice vinegar or cider vinegar

In a large skillet with a cover, sauté the onions and garlic in oil until the onions are translucent. Add the mushrooms and sauté until tender. Add your choice of chopped greens and water. Cover and steam for 4-6 minutes until the greens are just tender and bright green. Add tamari and vinegar and serve immediately.

Cabbage & Kale Casserole with Caraway Seeds

SERVES 4-6

1 tablespoon canola oil
2 cloves garlic, minced
1 medium onion, sliced in half-moons

½ medium green cabbage, shredded
½ pound kale, stemmed and coarsely chopped (about 3 cups packed)
1 teaspoon caraway seeds
¾ cup water
2 tablespoons vinegar
2 tablespoons tamari
¼ teaspoon black pepper

In a large skillet with a cover, sauté the garlic and onion in oil until the onion is translucent. Add the cabbage and kale and stir to mix. Top with caraway seeds.

Add water, cover, and steam for 8-10 minutes until the cabbage is just tender. Sprinkle with vinegar, tamari, and black pepper, and stir to mix. Adjust seasonings to taste.

Serve with a grain casserole or a simple brown rice for a hearty main course.

Cabbage Rolls with Teriyaki Sauce

MAKES 8 CABBAGE ROLLS

For the Teriyaki Sauce:
2 cloves garlic, minced
1 small onion, coarsely chopped
¼ cup honey or brown sugar
2 tablespoons cider vinegar
2 tablespoons lemon juice
⅓ cup tamari
2 tablespoons sesame oil
½ cup water

For the Cabbage Rolls:
8 large green cabbage leaves, steamed
½ cup water
3 cups cooked and seasoned Sure Brown Rice (see recipe on page 135)
1 cup green cabbage, finely shredded
½ cup carrots, grated
½ cup scallions, diced
½ cup broccoli crowns, finely chopped
½ cup fresh parsley, chopped

Place all the Teriyaki Sauce ingredients in a blender or food processor and blend until smooth. Set aside.

In a large skillet with a cover, steam the cabbage leaves in water for 15 seconds. Place immediately in cold water. Drain and pat dry on a towel.

In a large bowl, mix the cooked Sure Brown Rice with the shredded cabbage, carrots, scallions, broccoli, and parsley. Add 1 cup of Teriyaki Sauce and stir to mix. Reserve the remaining sauce. Spread a layer of the rice and vegetable mixture on each cabbage leaf. Roll up each stuffed cabbage leaf and secure the roll with a toothpick.

Place the cabbage rolls in a large 9x13-inch baking dish. Pour the remaining Teriyaki Sauce over the cabbage rolls, cover with foil, and bake at 350 degrees for 20-25 minutes.

The cabbage rolls are delicious as a dinner main course with a Mandarin Orange Salad.

Red Cabbage, Collards & Shiitake Mushrooms

Those who follow a macrobiotic diet believe that shiitake mushrooms have powerful healing properties. Conventional nutritionists regard shiitake mushrooms as a valuable source of potassium. I just think that they are very tasty and add a gourmet touch to any dish.

SERVES 4-6

1 tablespoon sesame oil
1 medium onion, cut in half-moons
2 cloves garlic, minced
4-5 fresh or dried shiitake mushrooms, sliced (soak dried mushrooms before slicing)
3 cups red cabbage, coarsely shredded (about ½ medium head of cabbage)
1 bunch collards, stemmed and coarsely chopped
½ cup water
2 tablespoons tamari
1 tablespoon cider vinegar

In a large skillet with a cover, sauté the onion and garlic in oil until the onion is translucent. Add the mushrooms and sauté until tender. Add the shredded cabbage and collards. Add water, cover, and steam for 4-6 minutes or until the collards are bright green and just tender. Add tamari and vinegar and serve.

Sesame noodles topped with parsley compliment this colorful vegetable dish.

Sweet & Sour Collards with Wakame

SERVES 4-6

½ cup wakame, soaked and drained
1 cup water
1 tablespoon sesame oil
1 medium onion, chopped
1 bunch collards, stemmed and coarsely chopped on the diagonal
¼ cup vinegar
2 tablespoons honey
1 tablespoon tamari
1 teaspoon miso mustard
½ cup water

Soak the wakame in boiling water for 5 minutes and drain.

In a large covered skillet, sauté the onion in oil until translucent. Add the collards and drained wakame.

In a measuring cup, combine the vinegar, honey, tamari, and miso mustard. Add to the onions, collards, and wakame in the skillet. Add water, cover, and steam 5-7 minutes or until collards are just tender.

This recipe makes a light and delicious vegetable side dish. Serve with quinoa, an ancient and nutritious cultivated grain, to round out the meal.

Onions & Ginger with Arame

Sea vegetables such as arame and hijiki need to be soaked and drained before they are combined with other ingredients in a recipe. Arame is the lightest in flavor among the sea vegetables and is an excellent introduction to this new flavor experience. This attractive recipe is good served with sweet brown rice balls.

SERVES 4-6

1 cup arame
1 cup warm water
1 tablespoon sesame oil
2 cloves garlic, minced
2 medium onions, sliced
1 tablespoon fresh ginger root, grated
1 red pepper, cut in strips
½ teaspoon herb seasoning salt
¼ cup fresh parsley or cilantro, chopped

Soak the arame in warm water for 5 minutes and drain.

In a skillet, sauté the garlic, onions, and ginger in oil until the onions are translucent. Add the red pepper strips and sauté until just tender. Add the drained arame and stir to blend. Simmer for 3-5 minutes. Add seasoning salt and adjust seasonings to taste. Serve topped with fresh parsley or cilantro.

Sweet Moroccan Onions

SERVES 4-6

2 tablespoons canola oil
2 cloves garlic, minced
3 large Spanish onions, sliced in half-moons
1 teaspoon allspice
2 teaspoons cinnamon
1 tablespoon garam masala
¼ cup honey
¼ cup raisins
¼ cup cashews
½ cup water, as needed
¼ cup fresh parsley, chopped

In a large saucepan, heat the oil and add the garlic and onions. Sauté for 3 minutes, then simmer covered for 10 minutes, stirring occasionally.

Add allspice, cinnamon, garam masala, and honey. Stir in the raisins and cashews. Simmer 15 minutes covered, stirring occasionally. Add water if needed to prevent burning.

Serve over basmati rice and garnish with fresh parsley.

Caramelized Fennel & Leek Pasta Delight

If you have never used fennel bulbs or don't even know what they are, you are in for a treat. Also sold as anise, the fennel bulb has a mild unique flavor that is delightful in this pasta dish. Go for it!!!

SERVES 4-6

2 tablespoons olive oil
2 large white fennel bulbs, halved and thinly sliced
2 leeks, thinly sliced
3 onions, thinly sliced
2 tablespoons maple syrup
⅓ cup water
1-2 tablespoons tamari
1 pound Jerusalem artichoke pasta twists or rotini

Trim the greens away from the fennel bulbs, wash, and slice in half. Then slice halves into ¼-inch slices. Cut the leeks in half lengthwise and wash thoroughly by submerging in cold water. Drain and slice thinly in a crosswise direction. Slice the onions.

Heat the olive oil in a large skillet and sauté the sliced fennel, leeks, and onions on low heat for about 20 minutes, stirring often, until translucent and golden brown. Slowly add the maple syrup, water, and tamari. Stir and continue cooking for about 5 minutes.

Cook the pasta in a large pot of boiling water according to package directions, but keep it firm. Drain in a colander and place in a large bowl. Add the sautéed vegetables, toss, and serve.

Sweet Red Peppers with Leeks & Daikon

SERVES 4-6 AS A SIDE DISH

1 tablespoon dry hijiki
1 cup water
2 medium leeks, cleaned and coarsely sliced
   on the diagonal
2 tablespoons sesame oil
2 cloves garlic, minced
1 sweet red pepper, cut in strips
3 cups daikon, halved and cut in half-moons
½ cup water
¼ teaspoon herb seasoning salt
1 tablespoon tamari
¼ cup fresh parsley, chopped

In a small saucepan, combine the hijiki and water. Bring to a boil, reduce heat, and simmer 10 minutes. Drain and set aside.

Clean the leeks by cutting off the root ends at the very base. Cut off the top two inches of the leaves and remove any bruised outside leaves. Split the leeks lengthwise. Turn the leeks about ¼-inch and make another lengthwise cut. This allows the leaves to be opened up and rinsed. Place in cold water and let stand until ready to use. Slice the leeks diagonally before cooking.

In a large skillet, sauté the garlic and leeks in oil until the leeks are tender. Add the red pepper and daikon and sauté briefly. Add ½ cup water, bring to boil, cover, and steam for 3 minutes. Add the drained hijiki, seasoning salt, and tamari. Adjust seasonings to taste. Serve topped with fresh chopped parsley.

This dish is a good accompaniment to sweet brown rice or croquettes.

Baked Stuffed Red Peppers with Feta Cheese

This recipe takes some time to prepare, but makes a festive and colorful party dish.

SERVES 4-6

4 large red peppers, cut in half lengthwise
¼ cup water
1½ pounds feta cheese, crumbled
2 cloves garlic, minced
1 10-ounce package fresh spinach, finely chopped
¼ cup fresh mint, chopped (or 1 teaspoon dried mint leaves)
¼ cup fresh parsley, chopped
2 tablespoons lemon juice
¼ cup water

In a large skillet with a cover, steam the red pepper halves in water until tender, approximately 3-5 minutes. Drain and remove from heat. Allow to cool.

In a bowl, mix the feta cheese, garlic, spinach, mint, parsley, and lemon juice. Stuff the cheese and spinach mixture into the cooled pepper halves.

Place the stuffed red peppers in a shallow baking dish, add water, and bake uncovered at 350 degrees for 15-20 minutes. Add more water if necessary. Serve warm or at room temperature.

Red Peppers & Greens

Serves 4-6

1 tablespoon canola oil
2 cloves garlic, minced
1 medium onion, cut in half-moons
1 red pepper, cut in strips
½ cup water
1 bunch kale, stemmed and coarsely chopped
1 tablespoon tamari
1 tablespoon balsamic or cider vinegar

In a large skillet with a cover, sauté the garlic and onion in oil until the onion is translucent. Add the red pepper strips and sauté for 2 minutes. Add water and kale. Cover and steam for 5-7 minutes, or until the kale is bright green and just tender. Add tamari and vinegar. Stir to mix and serve immediately.

Chickpea Vegetable Stew

SERVES 6

2 tablespoons sesame oil
2 stalks celery, chopped
2 cloves garlic, minced
1 medium onion, chopped

4 cups water
1x3-inch strip of kombu, rinsed
3 small potatoes, peeled and chopped
1 small sweet potato, peeled and chopped
1 small winter squash, peeled, seeded, and chopped

1 15-ounce can whole tomatoes, chopped, liquid reserved
1 15-ounce can chickpeas, drained and rinsed
2 cups fresh spinach or Swiss chard, chopped
1 teaspoon dried thyme
½ teaspoon dried oregano
½ teaspoon paprika
½ teaspoon black pepper
1-2 tablespoons red miso
1 tablespoon tamari

In a large soup pot, sauté the celery, garlic, and onion in oil until the onion is translucent.

Add water and kombu to the soup pot and bring to a boil. Add the potatoes, sweet potato, and squash. Reduce heat and simmer, covered, until the vegetables are tender, approximately 25 minutes. Remove the kombu strip, chop finely, and return to the soup pot.

Add the chopped tomatoes and reserved liquid, chickpeas, and spinach or Swiss chard. Simmer over a medium-low heat until the spinach or chard is bright green and just tender, about 3 minutes. Add thyme, oregano, paprika, and black pepper. Add miso and tamari and adjust seasonings to taste.

Potatoes, Green Beans & Chickpeas with Rosemary

SERVES 4-6

2 tablespoons canola or olive oil
2 cloves garlic, minced
1 medium onion, chopped
1 teaspoon dried rosemary
4-5 button mushrooms, sliced
1½ cup fresh green beans, tips removed
1 15-ounce can whole peeled tomatoes, liquid
    reserved
4-5 medium potatoes, cubed
1 15-ounce can chickpeas, drained and rinsed
¼ cup red wine
¼ teaspoon black pepper
1 tablespoon tamari
½ cup fresh parsley, chopped
¼ cup roasted sunflower seeds (see recipe for Roasted Nuts & Seeds on page 11)

In a large skillet, sauté the garlic, onion, and rosemary in oil until the onion is translucent. Add the mushrooms and green beans and sauté 3-5 minutes until the mushrooms are tender. Chop the tomatoes and add to the skillet along with the reserved liquid. Add the potatoes and simmer gently 15-20 minutes until the potatoes are tender. Add the drained chickpeas. Add red wine, black pepper, and tamari and stir to blend.

Adjust seasonings to taste and serve topped with chopped parsley and roasted sunflower seeds.

Cafe Chimes Twice-Baked Potatoes

Almost anything goes in this recipe! Just take a peek in the fridge and see what comes to mind. A basic recipe follows, but we've also added some tasty variations.

SERVES 4

4 large baking potatoes
2 tablespoons canola oil
2 cloves garlic, minced
1 medium onion, chopped
1 cup green cabbage, shredded
½ teaspoon dried rosemary
½ teaspoon thyme
¼ cup red wine

1 15-ounce can small white beans, rinsed and drained
¼ cup scallions, chopped
¼ cup fresh parsley, chopped
1 tablespoon nutritional yeast
¼ teaspoon black pepper
2 tablespoons tamari

Scrub the potatoes, pierce with a fork, and bake at 350 degrees for 45-50 minutes. Remove from oven and make a lengthwise slit in the top of each potato. Scoop out the potato pulp and place in a bowl.

In a large skillet, sauté the garlic and onion in oil until the onion is translucent. Add the cabbage, rosemary, and thyme and sauté until the cabbage is just tender. Add the red wine and beans. Stir to mix and cook for 2-3 minutes. Add to the potato pulp in bowl. Add the scallions, parsley, nutritional yeast, black pepper, and tamari. Mix all together and restuff into the potato shells. Place the stuffed potatoes in a baking dish. Cover and bake at 350 degrees for 15 minutes or until warm.

For other delicious variations:

- Add ½ cup salsa and substitute a 15-ounce can of black beans for the white beans.

- Add 1 cup chopped and sautéed broccoli florets.

- Add 2 chopped green peppers sautéed with 1 chopped tomato and 1 tablespoon fresh chopped basil.

- Top potatoes with 2 tablespoons soy or cheddar cheese before the final baking.

Sweet Potato, Parsnip & Kale Casserole

I had a dream one night and visualized a round casserole topped with colorful spiraling vegetables creating a rainbow circle. I did not go into the deeper meaning (if there was one), but I received the message to create what I saw. Make rainbows every day!

SERVES 4-6

1 medium onion, thinly sliced into half-moons
3 sweet potatoes, peeled and thinly sliced into half-moons
6 parsnips, washed and thinly sliced into half-moons
2 cloves garlic, minced
½ pound kale, stemmed and coarsely chopped (about 3 cups packed)
½ cup water
2 tablespoons tamari
½ cup roasted walnuts or sesame seeds (see recipe for Roasted Nuts & Seeds on
    page 11)

In an oiled, round casserole dish, arrange the onions, sweet potatoes, and parsnips in alternating layers in a circle. Sprinkle minced garlic over the vegetables. Cover and bake at 350 degrees for 40-45 minutes, or until the vegetables are tender.

When the vegetables are baked, combine the chopped kale and water in a large skillet and steam covered for 5-7 minutes, retaining the vibrant green color and nutrients of this wonderful green.

Arrange the steamed kale in a circular pattern over the baked vegetables. Sprinkle with tamari and top with roasted walnuts or sesame seeds.

This goes well with sweet brown rice or a mixed green salad on the side.

198

Baked Squash & Hummus

This simple dish was always a favorite at our cooking classes. Serve with couscous and steamed collards for a colorful and nutritious meal.

SERVES 4-6

1 medium buttercup squash, peeled and cut in chunks
1 cup Cafe Chimes Hummus (see recipe on page 101)
2 tablespoons tamari
½ teaspoon garlic powder
¼ teaspoon herb seasoning salt
¼ cup fresh parsley, chopped

Place chunks of squash in a large saucepan, cover with water, and boil 10-12 minutes or until tender. Drain, reserving water for soup stock, and cool.

In a large bowl, mash the squash and add the hummus, tamari, garlic powder, seasoning salt, and parsley. Mix thoroughly.

Place the squash and hummus mixture in an oiled 8x8-inch baking dish and bake at 350 degrees for 15 minutes. If desired, top with your favorite chopped nuts.

Baked Buttercup Squash with Molasses-Raisin Sauce

This baked squash is topped with a delicious Molasses-Raisin Sauce. Sauces are the most creative outlet for a cook. I had some molasses left over from a gingerbread recipe and happened upon it one morning. I created the following sauce in my mind and transformed it into a real thing to be enjoyed.

SERVES 6-8

For the Sauce:

2 tablespoons molasses
2 tablespoons maple syrup
½ teaspoon dry mustard
1 tablespoon cider vinegar
1 tablespoon lemon juice
¼ cup water
¼ cup raisins
3 tablespoons tahini
½ teaspoon rosemary

For the Squash:

1 medium to large buttercup or kobocha squash
1 medium onion, thinly sliced
¼ cup frozen cranberries (or ¼ cup chopped dried apricots)
½ cup chopped walnuts (optional)
½ cup water

Place the molasses, maple syrup, mustard, vinegar, lemon juice, water, raisins, tahini, and rosemary in a small bowl and whisk to blend.

Scrub, but do not peel the squash. Cut off the top and scoop out the seeds.

Fill the squash with the sliced onion, cranberries or apricots, and chopped walnuts, if desired. Pour in the molasses-raisin sauce. Retain any leftover sauce for serving. Place the stuffed squash in a Dutch oven or a baking dish with a cover and add ½ cup water. Bake, covered, at 350 degrees for an hour or until the squash is tender.

To serve, cut the squash into 6-8 pie-shaped wedges. Serve any leftover sauce on the side. This recipe is great served with a grain casserole or steamed broccoli.

Festive Fall Casserole

SERVES 4-6

*1 medium buttercup squash, peeled and
    cut in 1-inch cubes*
*2 medium sweet potatoes, peeled and cut
    in 1-inch cubes*
½ cup honey
2 tablespoons tamari
1 teaspoon cinnamon
1 teaspoon nutmeg
½ teaspoon ground cardamom
½ teaspoon herb seasoning salt
1 tablespoon dried parsley
½ cup chopped walnuts or slivered almonds

Peel and cube the squash and sweet potatoes. Place in a medium saucepan, cover with water, and boil 20-30 minutes or until soft. Remove from the pan and reserve the liquid for making soup stock.

In a large bowl, mash the squash and sweet potatoes. Add the honey, tamari, cinnamon, nutmeg, cardamom, seasoning salt, and parsley. Mix well to blend. Place in an oiled 9-inch casserole dish and bake uncovered at 350 degrees for 20 minutes. Top with walnuts or slivered almonds.

This tasty casserole goes well with long-grain brown and wild rice and a green salad.

Vegetables Nashimi

Nashimi simply means waterless cooking, but I find a little water necessary. We use a large Dutch oven for this stove-top dish. We usually start with onions on the bottom because the flavor permeates the dish. After the onion, the secret to success is layering the vegetables with the longest cooking time closer to the heat.

SERVES 6-8

1 medium onion, quartered
1 small rutabaga, peeled and cut in large 3-inch cubes
1 medium buttercup squash, peeled and cut in large 3-inch cubes
6 inches of Daikon radish, cut in large 2-inch chunks
4 carrots, cut in 1-inch diagonal chunks
½-1 cup water, as necessary
2 tablespoons tamari
¼ cup fresh parsley, chopped

Prepare the vegetables. In a large Dutch oven or heavy soup pot with a cover, layer the vegetables, starting with the onion. Add the rutabaga, squash, daikon, and carrots.

Add ½ cup water and bring to a boil. Reduce heat, cover, and simmer for 40-45 minutes, checking occasionally to see if additional water is needed. When the vegetables are tender, sprinkle on the tamari. Top with fresh chopped parsley.

These vegetables are delicious served with a simple brown rice topped with sunflower seeds and chopped scallions.

POTLUCK

Potluck

These days, people are returning to the joys of potluck gatherings. It's always easier to get together with friends when the meal doesn't involve days of work and planning. In this section, we've included a few recipes that feed a lot of people and are easy to tote.

If you're bringing an appetizer, we suggest the Mexican Bean Dip or the Cafe Chimes Baba Ghanoush which can be found in the Beginnings section of the book. For desserts, you can't go wrong with the Cafe Chimes Chocolate Cake or Elsa's Peanut Butter Cookies, both in the Desserts chapter.

So, set the time and place, call up your friends, relax, and enjoy the great food and company.

Greek Goddess Pasta Salad

When we first decided to offer a salad bar at the Cafe, we had fun creating the salads that would be offered on a regular basis. The following salad became an instant favorite.

SERVES 8-10

For the Salad:
1 pound uncooked Jerusalem artichoke rigatoni
¼ pound feta cheese, crumbled (about 1 cup)
3 scallions, chopped
½ cup parsley, chopped
2 carrots, grated
1 red pepper, chopped
½ cup medium-size pitted black olives, drained and sliced
4 large bottled or canned pepperoncini peppers, drained and chopped

For the Greek Goddess Dressing:
½ cup olive oil
3 tablespoons cider vinegar
3 tablespoons lemon juice
1 teaspoon honey
2 teaspoons tamari
1 teaspoon black pepper

1 tablespoon dried parsley

Put a large pot of water on to boil over medium-high heat for the pasta. Cook the rigatoni in boiling water for approximately 8 minutes, or until cooked al dente. Drain and chill.

Place all the dressing ingredients except the parsley in a small bowl and whisk until well-blended. Add the dried parsley and whisk to blend. Refrigerate while preparing the salad.

Combine the feta cheese, chopped scallions, parsley, grated carrots, red pepper, olives, and pepperoncini peppers with the chilled pasta in a large bowl. Add the Greek Goddess Dressing. Chill at least one hour before serving.

205

The Positive Thinker Salad

Years before I opened the Cafe, I attended a potluck gathering where a friend brought this delicious salad. I experimented and came up with the following version which has since become a leading entrée on our salad bar. One can't help but have positive thoughts while eating this salad!

SERVES 8-10

For the Salad:
1 cup soybeans, soaked
1 cup wheat berries, soaked
6 cups water

3 scallions, chopped
3 carrots, grated
1 medium cucumber, peeled and chopped
½ medium red onion, finely chopped
1 medium red pepper, chopped
1 medium green pepper, chopped
1 stalk celery, finely chopped

For the Lemon Garlic Dressing:
2 cloves garlic, crushed
½ teaspoon sea salt
½ teaspoon black pepper
1 tablespoon tamari
2 teaspoons dill weed, fresh or dried
1 teaspoon dry mustard
¼ cup cider vinegar
½ cup mayonnaise or alternative
juice from one lemon
½ cup parsley, chopped

Pick over the dry soybeans and wheat berries and rinse thoroughly. Both the soybeans and the wheat berries need to be soaked before cooking. Place them in a large saucepan and add 5-6 cups of water to cover. Bring to a boil, boil for 2 minutes, and remove from heat. Let the soybeans and wheat berries stand for 1 hour. Drain and continue with the recipe.

Place the soaked soybeans and wheat berries in a large saucepan, add fresh water, cover, and bring to a boil. Reduce heat and simmer for 2-3 hours, or until the soybeans and wheat berries are tender. Add more water if needed.

While the soybeans and wheat berries are cooking, chop all the vegetables and place them in a big bowl.

In a small bowl, blend all the dressing ingredients with a whisk until well-blended and creamy.

When the soybeans and wheat berries are tender, pour off the cooking water and cool. Toss with the vegetables in the bowl. Pour on the dressing, toss gently, and chill for a couple of hours until ready to serve.

Bountiful Brown Rice with Wheat Berries & Wild Rice

This elegant grain dish with its nutty taste and crunchy texture is always a welcome addition to a potluck supper. It can serve as a main course casserole or as a delicious side dish.

SERVES 8-10

½ cup wheat berries, soaked
½ cup wild rice
1 cup long-grain brown rice
1 cup short-grain brown rice
5 cups water
1x3-inch strip of kombu, rinsed

2 tablespoons sesame oil
1 large onion, diced
2 cloves garlic, minced
2 stalks celery, diced

½ teaspoon herb seasoning salt
½ teaspoon garlic powder
½ teaspoon black pepper
½ cup dried parsley
2 tablespoons canola oil
2 tablespoons tamari
1 cup roasted sunflower seeds (see recipe
   for Roasted Nuts & Seeds on page 11)
2 tablespoons chives, chopped

The wheat berries must be soaked before cooking. Rinse the wheat berries thoroughly in a colander and place in a large saucepan. Add 4 cups of cold water and bring the water to a boil. Cook the wheat berries for 2 minutes. Cover the pot, remove from heat, and let stand for about 1 hour. Drain and add the soaked wheat berries to the other grains for final cooking.

Wash the wild rice and brown rice in a large heavy saucepan and drain. Add the soaked wheat berries, fresh water, and the kombu. Cover and bring to a boil. Lower the heat and simmer, covered, for 50 minutes or until the wheat berries are tender. Remove the kombu strip and chop finely.

While the grains are cooking, sauté the onion, garlic, and celery in sesame oil in a large skillet until the onion is just translucent.

Place the cooked rice and wheat berries in large serving bowl. Add the chopped kombu and the sautéed vegetable mixture. Sprinkle on the herb seasoning salt, garlic powder, black pepper, and dried parsley. Add the tamari and canola oil and toss gently. Top with roasted sunflower seeds and chopped fresh chives. A protein-rich dish!

207

Easy Rigatoni, Veggie & Tofu One-Pot Meal

This is the ultimate in one-pot meals. Boil water, add the ingredients, strain, season, serve, and savor. The end!

SERVES 8-10

1 pound uncooked Jerusalem artichoke rigatoni
3 tablespoons arame, soaked in 1 cup hot water
1 cup carrots, chopped
1 cup snow peas, whole or halved
2 cups broccoli, coarsely chopped
1 pound extra-firm tofu, cubed
½ cup raisins
3 tablespoons tamari
2 tablespoons roasted sesame oil
1 teaspoon herb seasoning salt
½ teaspoon garlic powder
½ teaspoon paprika
½ cup roasted sunflower seeds (see recipe for Roasted Nuts & Seeds on page 11)

Put a large pot of water on to boil over medium-high heat for the pasta.

Meanwhile, soak the arame in hot water and set aside. Wash and chop the carrots, snow peas, and broccoli. Cut the tofu into cubes.

Cook the rigatoni in boiling water for approximately 3 minutes. Do not drain.

Add the chopped vegetables, tofu cubes, and raisins to the rigatoni and boiling water. The vegetables will cool the cooking water to a simmer. Simmer for about 5 minutes until vegetables are just tender and the pasta is done al dente. Drain in a colander and place in a large bowl.

Drain the arame and add to the drained pasta and vegetable mixture. Stir to combine. Add the tamari, sesame oil, herb seasoning salt, garlic powder, and paprika. Toss to blend the seasonings. Top with roasted sunflower seeds and serve.

Vegetarian Chili—The Easy Way

During the long winter months, we have constant requests for this Vegetarian Chili. Because we like to be creative with our recipes, the chili is never prepared the same way twice. Elsa likes it spicy. I prefer mild. You can adjust your spices to accommodate your style very easily. One variation that is an instant winner calls for using cooked black beans instead of kidney beans. Or you can use both!

SERVES 8-10

2 tablespoons olive oil
1 medium onion, chopped
2 cloves garlic, minced
2 large carrots, chopped
2 stalks celery, chopped
2 tablespoons ground cumin
1 teaspoon cumin seed
2 tablespoon chili powder
½ teaspoon cayenne
2 15-ounce cans red kidney beans, drained and rinsed
2 cups bulgur, washed
4-5 cups water

2 cups of mild to hot salsa (your choice)
3 tablespoons tamari
1 tablespoon miso

In a large soup kettle, sauté the onion and garlic in olive oil until the onion is translucent. Add the chopped carrots and celery and stir. Add the ground cumin, cumin seed, chili powder, and cayenne and stir to blend. Add the bulgur and kidney beans with about 4 cups water. Bring to a boil, reduce heat, and simmer, covered, until tender, approximately 50 minutes. Check after 30 minutes of cooking and add the remaining cup of water if necessary.

Add the salsa and stir. If you prefer a spicier version, you can add more chili powder and cayenne at this point. Mix in tamari and miso just before serving.

This recipe can be prepared a day ahead and reheated. It is delicious served in warmed bread bowls (see recipe on page 31).

ON EATING AND DRINKING

And when you crush an apple with your
teeth, say to it in your heart,
"Your seeds shall live in my body,
And the buds of your tomorrow shall
blossom in my heart,
And your fragrance shall be my breath,
And together we shall rejoice through all
the seasons."

Kahlil Gibran

DESSERTS

Desserts

I love desserts, and I have enjoyed developing many different desserts over the years for the Cafe Chimes Vegetarian and Nutrition Cooking Classes.

Once you develop a taste for natural sweeteners and whole-grain flours, the following desserts will be sufficiently satisfying. As you commit to wean yourself from high-fat, high-sugar desserts, you may celebrate the day when the following desserts are preferable to the traditional variety!

Fruit Medley Cobbler

SERVES 4-6

1 pear, sliced
1 apple, sliced
1 cup strawberries, sliced
1 banana, sliced
½ cup raisins
2 tablespoons honey
½ teaspoon vanilla
¼ cup walnuts, chopped

¼ cup applesauce
½ cup turbinado sugar or light brown sugar
½ cup whole-wheat flour
1 cup rolled oats
1 teaspoon cinnamon
1 teaspoon allspice

In a mixing bowl, combine the pear, apple, strawberries, banana, raisins, honey, and vanilla. Toss gently. Lay evenly in an oiled 8x8-inch baking dish. Sprinkle chopped nuts over the fruit.

In a medium bowl, cream together the applesauce and the sugar. Add the flour, oats, cinnamon, and allspice. Mix with a fork to create crumbs. Sprinkle on the fruit mixture in the baking dish. Bake 30-40 minutes at 325 degrees. Serve warm.

Extraordinary Baked Apples

SERVES 4

4 large apples, cored
1⅓ cup granola
½ teaspoon cinnamon
½ teaspoon ground coriander
¼ cup warm water
1 teaspoon orange rind, grated
½ cup honey
½ cup apple juice
2 tablespoons lemon juice
½ cup water

Scrub and core the apples.

In a bowl, combine the granola, cinnamon, and coriander. In a measuring cup, combine the water, grated orange rind, and honey. Add to the granola and spices in the bowl and stir. Fill the cored apples with this mixture. Place the apples in a 9x9-inch baking dish. Mix together the apple juice and lemon juice and pour over the stuffed apples. Pierce the apples with a fork. Add water. Cover and bake at 350 for 15 minutes. Remove the cover and bake an additional 20-25 minutes or until fork tender.

Cafe Chimes Chocolate Cake

On the very first night of Cafe Chimes Cooking Class, I serve this chocolate cake with the tofu whipped cream. Believe it or not, people always leave smiling!

SERVES 6-8

For the Cake:
½ cup applesauce
½ cup maple syrup
1 teaspoon vanilla
½ cup water
½ cup soy milk
2 squares melted unsweetened chocolate
2 tablespoons cider vinegar

1 cup white flour
1½ cups whole-wheat flour
1½ tablespoons baking powder
1 tablespoon baking soda
1 tablespoon arrowroot powder
½ teaspoon sea salt

For the Raspberry Tofu Whipped Cream:
1 pound tofu, soft or silken
juice from one lemon
1 teaspoon vanilla extract
1 teaspoon almond extract
½ cup maple syrup
1 cup raspberries (thawed if using frozen)

¼ cup slivered almonds for topping

In a large bowl, combine the applesauce, maple syrup, vanilla, water, soy milk, chocolate, and vinegar. In a large measuring cup, combine the dry ingredients and add to the applesauce mixture. Mix until well-blended and pour into a lightly greased and floured 9x9-inch cake pan. Bake at 350 degrees for 30 minutes. Test middle for firmness.

Combine all the Tofu Whipped Cream ingredients in a blender or food processor and blend until smooth. Spoon over cake slices and sprinkle with slivered almonds.

215

Couscous Cake with Currants & Tahini-Maple Topping

The unusual ingredients and topping lend themselves to a most interesting dessert. Naturally sweetened and a good source of calcium, this is a nutrient-rich dessert.

SERVES 4-6

For the Couscous Cake:

1 cup couscous
2 cups apple juice

In a small saucepan, bring the apple juice to a boil. Add the couscous and stir. Pour into a small deep bowl. Cover and place in refrigerator to chill.

For the Tahini Maple Topping:

⅔ cup tahini
⅓ cup warm water
½ cup maple syrup
1 teaspoon vanilla extract
½ teaspoon almond extract
1 teaspoon lemon juice
1 teaspoon cinnamon
⅓ cup currants (or raisins)
fresh raspberries and mint leaves for garnish

In a small bowl, combine the tahini and warm water. Stir until blended. Add the maple syrup, vanilla, lemon juice, and cinnamon. If mixture is too thick, add a little more warm water until the sauce reaches a smooth pourable consistency.

Invert the chilled couscous cake onto a serving platter. It should maintain the contour of the bowl. Drizzle the tahini topping over the couscous cake and sprinkle with currants. Garnish with fresh raspberries and mint leaves.

216

Gingerbread

Serves 4-6

1 cup dark brown sugar
1 cup white flour
1½ cups whole-wheat flour
½ cup wheat bran
1 tablespoon baking powder
1 teaspoon baking soda
1 tablespoon arrowroot powder
1 teaspoon cinnamon
1 teaspoon allspice
1 teaspoon ground ginger
½ teaspoon salt

2 tablespoons canola oil
⅓ cup maple syrup
½ cup soy milk
½ cup applesauce
½ cup water
1 tablespoon lemon juice
½ cup raisins (optional)

In a large bowl, combine the brown sugar, white and whole-wheat flour, wheat bran, baking powder, baking soda, arrowroot, cinnamon, allspice, ginger, and salt.

To the dry ingredients, add the canola oil, maple syrup, soy milk, applesauce, water, lemon juice, and raisins, if desired. Stir to blend.

Pour the batter into an oiled 9x9-inch baking dish and bake at 350 degrees for 35 minutes, or until a toothpick inserted in the cake comes out clean.

This gingerbread is delicious plain or served warm with The Jack-O-Lantern's Grin Sauce on page 75. Make the sauce just before serving.

Lemon Sundae Cake

This cake can be made for a festive celebration such as a birthday. It is light and moist, and the glaze adds the perfect touch.

SERVES 4-6

For the Cake:

⅔ cup soy milk
¼ cup lemon juice
⅓ cup canola oil
¾ cup maple syrup
⅓ cup water
1 teaspoon vanilla extract
2 teaspoons lemon extract

2 cups whole-wheat flour
1 teaspoon baking powder
1 teaspoon baking soda
½ teaspoon sea salt
rind from one lemon, grated
2 teaspoons poppyseeds

For the Glaze:

6 tablespoons maple syrup
6 tablespoons water
2 teaspoons lemon juice
1 teaspoon arrowroot powder or
    cornstarch
½ cup confectioners sugar

In a large bowl, combine the soy milk, lemon juice, canola oil, maple syrup, water, vanilla extract, and lemon extract. In a large measuring cup, combine whole-wheat flour, baking powder, baking soda, and sea salt. Add to the wet ingredients in bowl. Blend thoroughly and fold in the grated lemon rind and poppyseeds.

Pour into an oiled 7x11-inch cake pan or baking dish and bake for 30-40 minutes at 350 degrees. Cool in the pan.

Prepare the glaze by combining the maple syrup, water, lemon juice, arrowroot, and confectioners sugar in a small saucepan. Heat to almost boiling, stirring constantly. Cool and pour over the cooled cake just before serving.

218

Angelic Raspberry Lemon Cake

SERVES 4-6

½ cup maple syrup
¼ cup corn oil
½ cup water
1 egg, beaten
1 teaspoon grated lemon peel
juice from one lemon
1 cup raspberries (thawed if using frozen)

1½ cups whole-wheat flour
½ teaspoon baking soda
½ teaspoon sea salt
½ teaspoon baking powder
1 tablespoon dough enhancer (see recipe on page 25)
confectioners sugar

In a large bowl, combine the maple syrup, corn oil, water, egg, lemon peel, lemon juice, and raspberries.

In a large bowl or measuring cup, combine the flour, baking soda, sea salt, baking powder, and dough enhancer. Pour into the wet ingredients and fold in gently to mix. Pour into an oiled 9x9-inch baking dish or cake pan. Bake at 350 degrees for 30 minutes. Check the middle for firmness. Cool and dust the cake with confectioners sugar before serving.

Puff Pastries

MAKES 8 PASTRIES

For the Filling:

1 cup turbinado sugar or light brown sugar
¼ cup cream cheese
1 teaspoon almond extract
¼ cup chopped walnuts
½ cup fresh or frozen fruit (raspberries, blueberries, peaches are good choices)

For the Pastries:

1 pound whole-wheat bread dough (see recipe on page 26 or use a prepared frozen
    or refrigerated loaf)
1 cup rolled oats

In a bowl, cream together the sugar and cream cheese. Add the almond extract and stir to blend. Add the walnuts and fruit and mix gently with the creamed sugar and cream cheese.

Roll out the bread dough into a 12x24-inch rectangle. Cut into 8 square pieces.

In the center of each dough square, place 2 tablespoons rolled oats and ¼ cup filling mixture. To make puffs, fold opposite corners of the dough across the filling and pinch to seal. Let sit for 20 minutes before baking.

Place the pastries on an oiled cookie sheet and bake at 350 degrees for 20 minutes.

Almond Bars

These Almond Bars are among the most delicious treats you may ever have the pleasure of experiencing. They can be served as a warm dessert or as granola bars for a snack the next day.

MAKES 10-12 BARS

2 cups whole almonds, ground
1½ cups whole-wheat flour
½ cup rolled oats
1 teaspoon baking powder
1 teaspoon cinnamon
1 teaspoon cocoa powder
1 teaspoon ground coriander
1 tablespoon dough enhancer (see recipe on page 25)

½ cup tahini
½ cup honey
¾ cup warm water
1 tablespoon vanilla extract
1 teaspoon almond extract

In a blender or food processor, grind the almonds with the whole-wheat flour at high speed for 20-30 seconds or until the mixture reaches a crumb-like consistency.

In a large bowl, combine the ground almonds and flour with the oats, baking powder, cinnamon, cocoa powder, coriander, and dough enhancer. In a large measuring cup combine the tahini, honey, water, vanilla, and almond extract. Mix with the dry ingredients in bowl. Stir briefly to blend, then press the batter into an oiled 9x13-inch baking dish. Bake at 350 degrees for 25-35 minutes. Cut into bars or squares with a sharp knife once the pan has cooled slightly.

Cafe Chimes Granola Bars

Because we are surrounded by the White Mountains, we usually are frequented by lots of outdoor enthusiasts. These granola bars were the result of many requests for a tasty hiking snack.

MAKES 10-12 BARS

2 cups turbinado or light brown sugar
1 cup applesauce
2 tablespoons vanilla extract
2 tablespoons almond extract
½ cup raisins
½ cup walnuts, chopped
½ cup dried apples
½ cup chocolate chips (optional)

3 cups rolled oats
2 cups whole-wheat flour
2 tablespoons arrowroot powder
2 teaspoons baking soda
2 teaspoons baking powder
1 tablespoon cinnamon
2 tablespoons dough enhancer (see recipe
   on page 25)

In a big bowl, combine the brown sugar, applesauce, vanilla and almond extract, raisins, walnuts, dried apples, and chocolate chips, if desired. In a large bowl, combine the rolled oats and other dry ingredients. Whisk the dry ingredients into the brown sugar/applesauce mixture. Spread the batter evenly on an oiled 11x17-inch cookie sheet. Bake 35 minutes at 350 degrees. Check for firmness. Cool and cut into rectangular pieces.

These granola bars definitely can be frozen and thawed quickly. A great high-energy, high-carbohydrate hiking treat!

Chocolate Chip Squares

These delicious Chocolate Chip Squares freeze well to have on hand for a quick snack.

MAKES 10-12 BARS

1 cup applesauce
½ cup maple syrup
½ cup honey
1 teaspoon vanilla
1 teaspoon almond extract
½ cup soy milk
½ cup water

1 cup white flour
1½ cups whole-wheat flour
1 cup rolled oats
1 teaspoon baking soda
1 teaspoon baking powder
1 teaspoon cinnamon
1 teaspoon sea salt
1 tablespoon arrowroot powder
1 tablespoon dough enhancer (see recipe on page 25)

½ cup slivered almonds
1 cup chocolate chips

In a big bowl, cream the applesauce, maple syrup, honey, vanilla and almond extract, soy milk, and water. In a large bowl or measuring cup, combine the flour and other dry ingredients. Combine the wet and dry ingredients, except for the almonds and chocolate chips, and mix together well with a whisk.

Pour the mixture into an oiled 9x13-inch baking dish. Top with chocolate chips and almonds. Bake at 350 degrees for 25 minutes. Test the middle for firmness. Cool and cut into squares.

Simply Elegant Almond Cookies

MAKES ABOUT 3 DOZEN COOKIES

1 cup rolled oats
1 cup whole roasted almonds
1 cup whole-wheat flour
½ teaspoon baking soda
pinch of sea salt
1 tablespoon dough enhancer (see recipe on page 25)

½ cup maple syrup
½ cup corn oil
1 teaspoon vanilla extract
1 teaspoon almond extract
½ cup slivered almonds

Combine the oats and whole almonds in a blender or food processor. Pulse until the mixture resembles corn meal. Place in a large bowl and add the flour, baking soda, sea salt, and dough enhancer. In a large measuring cup, combine the maple syrup, corn oil, vanilla extract and almond extract. Add to the dry mixture and stir, adding slivered almonds.

Shape the cookie dough by hand into small crescents and press onto an oiled cookie sheet. Bake at 375 degrees for 12 minutes.

Apple & Almond Whole-Wheat Cookies

Every once in a while I will choose to use real butter in cookies. However, you can eliminate much of the fat in these cookies by substituting natural applesauce.

¼ *pound butter (or 1 cup applesauce)*
1 cup honey
1 egg, beaten
1 tablespoon almond extract
1 cup dried apples

1½ cups whole-wheat flour
½ *cup rolled oats*
1 teaspoon baking soda
1 teaspoon sea salt
1 tablespoon cinnamon
1 tablespoon nutmeg
1 tablespoon dough enhancer (see recipe on page 25)

½ *cup slivered almonds*

In a large bowl, cream the butter or applesauce and honey. Add a beaten egg, almond extract, and apples. In a large bowl or measuring cup, combine the whole-wheat flour and other dry ingredients. Add to the wet mixture and mix well. Spoon the batter onto an oiled cookie sheet and flatten with the wet palm of your hand. Top each flattened round with slivered almonds. Bake at 350 degrees for 8 minutes.

Maple Peanut Butter Chocolate Chip Cookies

MAKES ABOUT 4 DOZEN COOKIES

½ *cup maple syrup*
½ *cup honey*
½ *cup applesauce*
¼ *cup canola oil*
1 *tablespoon vanilla*
½ *cup peanut butter*

2½ *cups whole-wheat flour*
¾ *cup rolled oats*
1 *teaspoon baking soda*
½ *teaspoon sea salt*
1 *tablespoon arrowroot powder*
2 *tablespoons dough enhancer (see recipe on page 25)*

½ *cup chocolate chips*

In a large bowl, combine the maple syrup, honey, applesauce, canola oil, vanilla, and peanut butter. In a large bowl or measuring cup, combine the flour and other dry ingredients and add to the wet mixture. Stir briefly to mix and add chocolate chips. Refrigerate the dough for several hours or overnight.

When the dough is chilled, use a small ice cream scoop or a tablespoon to drop the batter onto an oiled or non-stick cookie sheet. Flatten each cookie using the wet palm of your hand. Bake 12-15 minutes at 350 degrees.

Grain-Sweetened Chocolate Chip Cookies

When we first opened the Cafe, I made regular delicious Toll House Chocolate Chip Cookies. As customers began asking for an alternative, I made up this low-fat, wholesome cookie. Enjoy warm from the oven!

MAKES ABOUT 4 DOZEN COOKIES

1 cup turbinado sugar or light brown sugar
½ cup applesauce
2 tablespoons vanilla extract
2 teaspoons almond extract
2 tablespoons vinegar

1½ cups whole-wheat flour
½ cup white flour
¾ cup rolled oats
1 teaspoon baking soda
1 teaspoon sea salt
1 tablespoon arrowroot powder
1 tablespoon dough enhancer (see recipe on page 25)

¾ cup grain-sweetened chocolate chips, carob chips, or regular chocolate chips

In a large bowl, combine the sugar, applesauce, vanilla and almond extracts, and vinegar. In another large bowl or measuring cup, combine the flour and other dry ingredients and whisk into the sugar/applesauce mixture. Add your choice of chocolate chips. Refrigerate for several hours or overnight.

When the dough is chilled, use a small ice cream scoop or a tablespoon to drop the batter onto an oiled or non-stick cookie sheet. Flatten each cookie using the wet palm of your hand. Bake 12-15 minutes at 350 degrees.

Raspberry-Almond Cookies

We developed these delicious cookies in response to requests for a taste-good cookie using all natural ingredients.

MAKES ABOUT 2 DOZEN SMALL COOKIES

1 cup whole almonds, ground
1 cup rolled oats, ground
1 cup whole-wheat flour
1½ cups light brown sugar
¼ teaspoon cinnamon
½ cup dough enhancer (see recipe on page 25)
pinch of sea salt

¼ cup corn oil
3 tablespoons vanilla extract
1 tablespoon almond extract
1 tablespoon lemon juice
½ cup water
¼ cup raspberry jam

In a food processor or blender, grind the whole almonds and rolled oats to a crumb-like consistency.

In a bowl, combine the ground almonds and oats with the flour, brown sugar, cinnamon, dough enhancer, and sea salt. In a large measuring cup, combine the corn oil, vanilla extract, almond extract, lemon juice, and water. Mix into the dry ingredients with a spoon until well-blended.

With hands, shape the dough into balls. Place 2 inches apart on an oiled or non-stick cookie sheet. Press thumb or a thimble into the center of each cookie and fill with ½ teaspoon raspberry jam. Bake for 15 minutes at 350 degrees.

Walnut Macaroons

I usually introduce the unusual at the Cafe Chimes Cooking Class, and these cookies are no exception. After scanning the ingredients, you may wonder how these macaroons can taste good, but they really do, especially warm.

MAKES ABOUT 2 DOZEN COOKIES

3½ cups shredded unsweetened coconut
1 cup whole-wheat flour
¼ teaspoon sea salt
1 teaspoon dough enhancer (see recipe on page 25)
½ cup roasted walnuts, chopped

½ cup maple syrup or ¾ cup brown sugar
1⅓ cups water
2 tablespoons almond extract
1 tablespoon vanilla extract

In a large bowl or measuring cup, combine the coconut, flour, salt, dough enhancer, and walnuts. In another large bowl, combine the maple syrup or brown sugar, water, and almond and vanilla extracts. Stir to mix. Combine with the coconut and flour mixture and stir to blend.

Use a small ice cream scoop or a tablespoon to drop the batter in rounded mounds onto an oiled or non-stick cookie sheet. Bake at 350 degrees for 25 minutes.

Elsa's Peanut Butter Cookies

These tasty cookies require a bit of effort, but they are well worth it!

MAKES ABOUT 3 DOZEN COOKIES

1 cup peanut butter
2 cups turbinado sugar or light brown sugar

¼ cup dough enhancer (see recipe on page 25)
1 tablespoon arrowroot powder
1½ teaspoons baking powder
½ teaspoon baking soda
2 cups whole-wheat flour
1 cup white flour
½ cup oat bran
½ teaspoon salt

¾ cup applesauce
⅔ cup water
⅓ cup canola oil
1 tablespoon vanilla extract

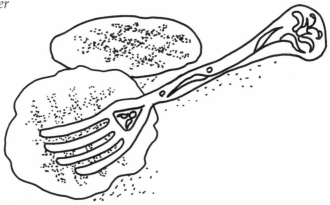

In a large bowl, cream together the peanut butter and the sugar.

In another bowl, mix together the dough enhancer and the other dry ingredients. Add the creamed peanut butter and sugar mixture to the dry ingredients and mix together until the mixture has a fine, crumbly consistency.

In a large bowl, mix together the applesauce, water, canola oil, and vanilla extract. Add to the peanut butter and dry ingredient mixture and blend thoroughly.

Using a small ice cream scoop or a heaping tablespoon, drop batter onto an oiled cookie sheet and bake at 350 degrees for 12-15 minutes.

INGREDIENTS

Ingredients

In this section, we've assembled a list of many of the recipe ingredients that you will find in this book. We have tried to include the most important ingredients and those foods, spices, and condiments that may be new to you.

Ingredients

Arame: Arame is a fine, black seaweed that is usually sold dried in small packets in natural food stores and in Asian markets. Arame has a delicate flavor and is used as an ingredient in salads and main course dishes. Arame, like other seaweeds, should be soaked before using.

Arrowroot Powder: Arrowroot powder is made from a tuber usually grown in the West Indies. It is used as a thickener in sauces, soups, and desserts. Arrowroot powder is available in the spice or baking sections of most supermarkets and in Asian and health food stores.

Barley: Barley is a hearty whole-grain that has been cultivated for centuries in the Middle East. It has a chewy texture and a sweet, nutty flavor. Barley is available as brown, whole hulled barley or as white, pearled barley. Pearled barley has been processed and is less nutritious than the brown variety. Pearled barley is available in boxes in supermarkets. Brown whole hulled barley can often be found in natural food stores.

Bulgur (cracked wheat): Bulgur is wheat that has been cracked, parboiled, and dried. It is a mainstay of Middle Eastern, Greek, and Turkish cooking. Bulgur is fast to cook and easy to digest. It is a primary ingredient in tabouli and can be used as a meat substitute in vegetarian burgers. Bulgur is available in bulk in both fine and coarse textures at natural food stores and is often sold in boxes in supermarkets.

Cardamom: Cardamom is an aromatic spice that is frequently used in South and East Asian and Middle Eastern cooking. Whole or ground cardamom is available in the international or spice sections of local supermarkets.

233

Carob (St. John's Bread): Carob powder and carob chips are derived from the carob bean or pod of a Mediterranean evergreen tree. It is said that John the Baptist survived on the carob pod during his days in the wilderness. Carob is similar in taste to chocolate and can be used in beverages, bread doughs, or in cookies when in chip form. Carob powder and chips are available at health food stores, or at your local supermarket.

Cayenne: Cayenne powder is made from ground, red chili peppers. It is used to add "heat" to spicy recipes and is an ingredient of curry powder. If you are adding cayenne powder to a recipe at the end of the cooking process, you can avoid a harsh taste by sautéing the powder briefly in a little oil before adding it to the cooked food. Cayenne powder is available in the spice section of supermarkets and in natural food stores.

Chapati: Chapati is a flat unleavened bread, much like a tortilla. Packaged chapatis are available in health food stores or supermarkets.

Cilantro: The fresh green leaves of coriander are called cilantro (or Spanish or Chinese parsley). The greens are pungent and aromatic. Cilantro is frequently used as an ingredient or as a garnish in Asian, East Asian, Central and South American dishes. Cilantro can be found in the produce section of local supermarkets.

Coriander: Coriander refers to the dried seeds of a spice. Ground coriander is the most frequently used form of the spice. It is a common ingredient in curry powders. Coriander is available in the spice section of supermarkets and at health and specialty food stores.

Couscous: Couscous is finely cracked wheat or millet that has been partly refined to produce a quick cooking grain. It can be served alone or used as an ingredient in recipes. It is available in bulk and in boxes at health food stores or at your local supermarket.

Croquettes: In this book, the term croquettes refers to cooked grains which are formed into patties or other shapes for baking or frying.

Curry Powder: Curry powder is a combination of ground spices which includes cumin, turmeric, cardamom, coriander, cayenne, and cinnamon. Some curry powder mixes also include nutmeg, cloves, fennel, and black pepper. You can buy prepared curry powders at your local supermarket or mix your own according to your taste preferences and tolerance for spiciness and heat.

Daikon: Daikon is a long, white Japanese radish. It is used as an ingredient in salads and in vegetable and grain dishes. Daikon can be found in the produce section of many supermarkets and in natural food stores and Asian markets.

Dough Enhancer: Dough Enhancer is a blend of ingredients designed to improve the rising and texture of breads and other baked goods. Ingredients for the Cafe Chimes Dough Enhancer can be found at natural food stores. There are also commercial Dough Enhancers on the market which are available in supermarkets and specialty food stores.

Fennel Bulbs: Often labeled in supermarket produce sections as "anise," the fennel bulb has a mild licorice flavor. Fennel bulbs can be used raw in salads or cooked in stews and vegetable dishes.

Feta Cheese: Feta cheese is a white, soft cheese usually made from goat's or sheep's milk. Feta cheese is commonly produced in Greece, the Balkans, and the Middle East. It is usually sold in blocks and can be salty because it is stored in brine. Feta can be served sliced, grated as a topping, or as a recipe ingredient. It is available in most supermarkets as well as in Middle Eastern groceries and specialty cheese shops.

Garam Masala: Garam Masala is a ground spice mixture that includes a combination of cardamom, cinnamon, cloves, coriander, cumin, and black peppercorns. Prepared Garam Masala powders are available in the spice sections of some supermarkets and in Asian or international food markets. You can also mix your own blend of spices according to your taste preferences.

Ginger Root: Fresh ginger is a knobby, light brown root. It is known for its fresh, pungent flavor. When cut, the flesh of the ginger root should be firm, juicy, and golden. It is often used finely grated. Ginger root is available in the produce sections of most supermarkets and in Asian food stores. It can be stored in a plastic bag and refrigerated or frozen for several weeks.

Gomashio: Gomashio is a Japanese condiment that is a combination of ground sesame seeds and sea salt. It is frequently used as a seasoning in place of salt at the table.

Hijiki: Hijiki is a black, thick form of seaweed that is dried and sold in packets at natural food stores and Asian markets. Hijiki must be soaked before cooking.

Kombu (Konbu): Kombu is a form of seaweed that is dried and packaged in thick strips. Dried kombu should be rinsed before cooking. In this book, kombu is a frequent ingredient in grain and soup recipes. After cooking, the strips of kombu can be removed, then chopped and added back to the other recipe ingredients. Kombu is available in natural food stores and in Asian markets.

235

Leeks: Leeks are a member of the onion family. They have a milder and less pungent flavor than regular onions. They have been described as "overgrown scallions." Leeks are delicious in soups, sauces, and vegetable dishes. Fresh leeks are often gritty and dirty when sold and must be carefully cleaned before cooking. To clean the leeks, cut off the root end at the very base. Cut off the top two inches of the leaves and remove any bruised outside leaves. Split the leek lengthwise. Turn the leek about ¼-inch and make another lengthwise cut. This allows the leaves to be opened up and rinsed. Place in cold water and let stand until ready to use. Slice the leek diagonally before cooking. Leeks are available in the produce section of supermarkets and at natural food stores.

Lentils: Lentils are small, quick-cooking legumes which do not have to be soaked before cooking. They are used in soups, salads, and entrées. Brown lentils, which are the most common, are available in supermarkets and natural food stores. Red lentils, which are golden when cooked, are sold in the international departments of supermarkets and in natural food stores.

Millet: The millet produced in the United States has tiny, round, yellow grains and is commonly sold as bird food. The millet sold for people-consumption has been hulled and is a nutritious, high-protein food. Millet can be cooked like rice and used with other grains in main course dishes, soups, casseroles, and side dishes. Millet is available in bulk at natural food stores and in some supermarkets.

Miso: Miso is a fermented soybean paste that comes in a variety of forms, each with its own flavor, texture and color. In this book, we have used red barley miso which has a hearty flavor and white miso (rice miso) which has a sweeter, more delicate flavor. All misos are somewhat salty and have the consistency of peanut butter. Miso should always be added at the end of a recipe and never boiled. Boiling destroys the digestive and antibacterial enzymes which make miso such a healthful addition to vegetarian recipes. Miso is available at some supermarkets and in Asian and natural food stores.

Nori: Nori is a variety of seaweed that is dried and sold in dark green sheets. It is most frequently used as the wrapper for sushi rolls. Nori is available in Asian food markets and in natural food stores.

Nutritional Yeast (sometimes called Brewer's or Torula Yeast): Nutritional yeast is a form of food yeast that is grown on a molasses solution. Nutritional yeast is not a live yeast and cannot be used as a leavening agent in baked goods. It comes in powder or flake form and can be used directly on vegetables, baked potatoes, and other foods as a condiment. It can also be used as a cooking ingredient. Nutritional yeast is available at natural food stores and some supermarkets.

Pepperoncini: Pepperoncini are small, hot, pickled peppers that are available in jars or cans. They are frequently used in Italian cooking and can be found in supermarkets or specialty food stores.

Pesto Sauce: Pesto sauce is made from basil or cilantro, olive oil, and pine nuts. It also can contain Parmesan cheese. It is frequently used as a topping for pasta and as an ingredient in soups and vegetable dishes. Bottled pesto sauce is available at supermarkets, specialty food markets, and natural food stores.

Quinoa: Quinoa is a wheat-free grain which is indigenous to South America. It was used hundreds of years ago by the Incas, but was largely forgotten until recently. It is highly nutritious, rich in vitamins and minerals. Quinoa has a mild, nutty aroma and is slightly crunchy. It cooks quickly and can be used as a plain side dish or as an ingredient in soups, stews, and mixed grain dishes. Quinoa is sold in natural food stores and in some supermarkets.

Rice: Rice has been the mainstay of many Asian diets for over 3,000 years. It is now widely grown in warm humid climates around the world. Rice comes in many varieties from the bland "milled" white rice that Americans favor to the many forms of brown and aromatic basmati rices that are gaining in popularity. In this book, we use short and long-grain brown rice, sweet brown rice, brown and white basmati rice, and wild rice. Many varieties of rice are available at natural food stores, Asian markets, and in supermarkets.

> *Brown rice* is the whole unpolished rice grain, with the outer hull and a portion of the bran removed. It has a chewier texture than white rice and a nutty flavor.

> *Short-grain brown rice* has small grains and is somewhat sticky when cooked.

> *Long-grain brown rice* is lighter in texture with grains that remain separate after cooking.

> *Sweet brown rice* is a glutenous short-grain variety that contains an opaque starch.

> *Basmati rice* is an aromatic long-grain rice that is grown in India or Pakistan. Both brown and white basmati rice are light and fluffy when cooked.

> *Wild rice* is not really rice, but the seed of an aquatic grass which is related to the rice plant. Wild rice has a distinctive, nutty flavor. Because it is costly, it can be mixed with other kinds of rice to add an interesting texture and flavor.

Salsa: Salsa is usually a cooked Mexican or Southwestern-style spicy tomato-chile sauce. Prepared salsas are often sold in mild, medium, and hot varieties and are readily available in supermarkets and natural food stores. Many stores also carry uncooked or "cruda" versions of the sauce. In this book, we use prepared salsas often as a recipe ingredient—you choose the level of spiciness.

Sesame Oil: Light sesame oil is pressed from unroasted sesame seeds. Roasted dark sesame oil is extracted from roasted seeds. Light sesame oil can be used for cooking, while the dark roasted oil is usually reserved as a flavoring for recipes. Sesame oil is available at natural food stores and in the international section of some supermarkets.

Shiitake Mushrooms: These flavorful mushrooms are sold both dried and fresh in many supermarkets, Asian markets, and natural food stores. They are a common ingredient in Japanese, Chinese, and Korean cooking. Shiitake mushrooms have a distinctive flavor and a smooth, chewy texture. To reconstitute the dried variety, pour boiling water over the mushrooms, cover, and soak for about an hour. When the mushrooms are soaked, remove the stems and thinly slice the caps. Shiitake mushrooms must be cooked before eating.

Soy Milk: Soy milk is made from cooked soybeans, water, and salt. Some varieties are sweetened with barley malt or rice syrup. Soy milk can be used in place of dairy milk in soups, sauces, desserts, and on cereal. Soy milk is useful for people who are lactose intolerant or who want to avoid dairy products. Many varieties of soy milk are now available in supermarkets and in natural food stores.

Star Anise: Star anise is an aromatic spice which is commonly used in Chinese and Southeast Asian cooking. The spice is star-shaped with eight points. In this book, the star anise is added whole during the cooking process in grain recipes and removed after cooking. Star anise is available in the spice section of some supermarkets and in natural food stores and Asian markets.

Tahini: Tahini is a smooth paste that is usually made from unroasted, hulled sesame seeds. It is an ingredient in appetizers and spreads such as hummus and in salad dressings, sauces, and entrées. Tahini is sold in most supermarkets, natural food stores, and in Middle Eastern food stores.

Tamari: Tamari sauce was traditionally a wheat-free byproduct of the miso-making process. It was made from the liquid that rises to the top of the wooden vats during the fermentation of miso. The Tamari sauce that is now widely available is a Japanese-style natural soy sauce. Some brands remain wheat-free, but not all. Tamari is a dark, rich sauce that is an excellent seasoning for cooking. It is a regular ingredient in many of the recipes in this book. Tamari sauces are available in Asian markets, natural food stores, and in the Asian sections of some supermarkets.

Tempeh: Tempeh is usually made from cultured soybeans which are pressed into squares. Most tempeh is available frozen in natural food stores and in Asian sections of supermarkets. Some varieties of tempeh are made from grains, beans, and other seeds. Tempeh absorbs the flavors of other recipe ingredients and has a meaty texture. It is an important food staple in Indonesia.

Tofu: Tofu is a bean curd that is made from soybeans. It is sold in rectangular cakes and comes in varying degrees of firmness—ranging from soft or silken to extra-firm. Tofu has little flavor of its own, but absorbs seasonings well. It is an important source of protein in Asian diets and a good meat substitute in many types of recipes. Tofu is available in the refrigerated sections of supermarkets, Asian markets, and natural food stores.

Turmeric: Turmeric is a ground spice that is widely used in Indian and Middle Eastern cooking. It is a member of the ginger family. Turmeric has a yellow-orange color and is a common ingredient in curry powder. Turmeric is available in the spice section of supermarkets and in Middle Eastern and Indian food markets.

Udon: Udon are thick Japanese-style noodles that are made from whole-wheat flour, but do not contain eggs. Udon noodles are sold in Asian sections of some supermarkets and in Asian markets and natural food stores.

Umeboshi Paste: Umeboshi paste is made from small, purple, pickled plums. It has a strong, sour/salty taste and should be used sparingly in cooking. Packaged Umeboshi is usually available in Asian markets and in some natural food stores. It will keep indefinitely when refrigerated.

Wakame: Wakame is a mild-tasting seaweed that is usually sold dried in small packets. It must be soaked before use. Wakame is used to flavor soups, beans, and grain dishes. Wakame can be purchased at Asian markets and natural food stores.

Wasabi: Wasabi is a very hot Japanese horseradish that is usually available in powdered form in Asian markets and some supermarkets. The powder is mixed with water to form a paste. The paste is served on the side with sushi and is sometimes used to flavor soy sauce and dipping sauces.

Wheat Berries: Wheat berries are the whole grains of wheat that can be milled into flour or processed for cereals or cracked wheat. In this book, wheat berries are cooked whole and combined with other grains in a variety of recipes. They have a delicious nutty flavor and a chewy texture. Wheat berries take a long time to cook and need to be soaked before the final cooking process. They can usually be found in bulk in natural food stores and in some supermarkets.

A VEGETARIAN KITCHEN

A Vegetarian Kitchen

For many of us, the exploration of Vegetarian cooking is the opening of a new chapter in our lives. We may find that our kitchens need to be revamped for this great adventure. In this section, Elsa Steffanson, who was the primary cook at Cafe Chimes for many years, shares her memories of working with Kathy Etter along with her advice for setting up a vegetarian kitchen.

A Vegetarian Kitchen

by Elsa Steffanson

The kitchen is the heart of a house. We gather in the kitchen to laugh, cry, share sorrows and joys. We celebrate and mourn in the kitchen. The food that comes from our kitchen is both a necessity and a pleasure. We need it to survive, and most of our lives—from daily routine to special events—flow around food. Often we find comfort in a warm kitchen with an especially pleasurable sweet, a cup of tea, and a good friend.

The kitchen can also be a place of great creative flow. Here, you are limited only by your imagination and schedule. Because we do live in a busy time, we cannot always give as much energy as we would like to being creative. A little planning can help if your goal is to set up a kitchen that lends itself to creativity and delicious vegetarian cooking.

I had the wonderful experience of working with Kathy Etter in running Cafe Chimes and the Cooking Classes. I joined her when the Cafe was about a year old, and for many years I was the primary cook. I also helped Kathy preside over the many sessions of the Cafe Chimes Cooking Classes. Over the years we worked together, we had the opportunity to discover and develop an efficient working system. Mind you, this was often through trial and error. Kathy would have rearranging attacks when I was not there, and the next day I would have to call and ask where things could possibly be hiding.

Kathy's approach to cooking and to helping others embark on the adventure of vegetarian cooking was to encourage creativity and experimentation. At the beginning of every Cooking Class, and at almost all of her public talks and programs, Kathy would tell her "Daisy Ham" story. It went something like this:

"Daisy Ham"

Once there was a young couple, recently married and still very much wanting to be in each other's space. One particular evening as they were preparing dinner together, the young husband observed his wife cutting off the ends of the daisy ham. Interested in a phenomenon he had never observed before, he asked, "Why do you cut off the ends?"

She replied, "Because, you goose, you're supposed to do it that way."

"But, why?" he asked again, sweetly.

"I don't know why," she replied. "My mother taught me to do it this way."

Well, her husband was a gentleman of inquisitive nature. The next time they visited her mother, he asked his mother-in-law about the daisy ham.

"Well dear," she said, "that's just the way it's done. No two ways about it. It's the way my mother prepared daisy ham, and it's the way I've done it ever since I can remember."

Not wanting to upset his mother-in-law, and having pushed the subject far enough with his young wife, he let it drop for a while. But around the holidays, they all went to see Grandma in the nursing home. Our fellow, young and full of life's questions, hadn't really forgotten about the daisy ham. He had just let it slide quietly to the back of his mind for later research. Now its time had come.

"Gram," he suggested, "let's go for a spin down the hallway." Halfway down the hall, he asked the burning question. "Why do you cut off the ends of the daisy ham?" Grandma thought this a curious question from a young fella, but she just smiled up at him.

"Why, sonny," she replied, "when we first came to this country, we weren't rich and had only one baking pan. To fit the ham in the pan and not waste any of the middle, we had to cut a little off both ends."

244

Kathy related this story to our eating habits and recipes. Because we've always done something doesn't mean it's written in stone, and we need to keep an open mind to other possibilities.

Cooking Classes hold some of my fondest memories. For years, customers at the Cafe would ask, "When are you going to teach a class, so we can cook tasty vegetarian food too?"

Finally Kathy and I gave in, looked at each other and said, "Okay, when?"

"Thursday nights?"

Done, and a new adventure began. Neither of us had a clue about what format to apply to a cooking class, but we shared from the heart all that we knew.

Our first class was lots of fun and educational for all of us, even though we were more than a little disorganized. But we persevered, and eventually a six-week series evolved that covered basic nutrition, most of the grains and legumes, and a number of interesting lectures.

Each week would bring a similar routine. Kathy would prepare for the class during the day, while I held down the fort at the Cafe. Then both of us would greet the students and review the evening's menu. Together we shared beliefs and myths about food, shortcuts, and our different styles in the kitchen. The real magic began when Kathy gathered the class in the dining room and began a short lecture, leaving me behind to add and create as the kitchen gods willed. Through this process, Kathy and I were able to introduce a large number of our friends and neighbors to the joys of creative whole foods cooking.

When you are first setting up a vegetarian kitchen, experiment with your own space. Ideally, everything you need should be within two steps and well-organized. Remember, a journey of a thousand miles begins with one step. This applies to your whole foods journey as well. Add to your supplies of spices and foods a little at a time. Keep it simple and fun. Try storing dry grains, beans, and spices in glass jars; they add a nice decorative accent and allow you to know what is on hand at a glance.

We had a young man working at the Cafe one summer. He was interested in continuing to work with whole foods and spices at home. Wanting to encourage that spirit and enthusiasm, I purchased small glass canning jars, found my way to the health food store, and chose twelve of my favorite spices. I then filled the jars and didn't label them, as we had been following intuition in our training sessions at the Cafe. By simply smelling different spices and deciding if they were what we wanted to use to complete any scrumptious dish, we sharpened our creative talents. (Our most delicious dishes have been created this way.) I did help our young friend out a little and put the labels in the bottom of the jars. This method may sound intimidating, but it's not. Listen to your own inner voice, but try to have at least a dozen different spices on hand for creating your own delectable dishes.

You don't have to rush out and purchase all these, but here are some of my favorites: Basil, Cayenne, Chili Powder, Cinnamon, Ground Coriander, Curry Powder, Ground Ginger (I usually grate fresh ginger root), Nutmeg, Rosemary, Sage, Thyme, and Turmeric.

For years after I took over cooking full-time at the Cafe, Kathy would still make the muffins every morning. She felt it was her daily connection with me and the Cafe, and it helped us stay in tune. She would come bounding down the stairs with her baseball cap and pigtails flying and ask if there was anything we needed. At that time I would check the basics we absolutely had to have:

Brown rice *(short or long-grain)*
Tamari
Sesame Oil or Canola Oil
Garlic *(fresh and powdered)*
Herb Seasoning Salt *(we used Herbamare®)*

One or more of these is used in almost all the recipes. Keep them close to your work area.

Whenever possible, you will want to take advantage of fresh local produce. For the times when availability and time may limit your selection, it is handy to have canned beans, tomatoes, frozen orange juice concentrate, etc., on hand. Of course, fresh is always better, because some of these processed products contain preservatives and may have less nutritive value.

If you have ever torn through a tomato or onion with a dull knife, you must know true kitchen frustration. A sharp knife is an excellent investment to save both time and energy. At the Cafe, we used Japanese flat knives. They were the right size and weight for us and generally saw many years of use before being retired. A major bone of contention between Kathy and me was her habit of leaving knives in the sink. Of course she saw the wisdom of not putting a knife in a sink full of soapy suds, but in a rush the best of us forget things. Many a time I would draw a sharp blade from its bubbly bath and display it to my partner in crime. In return, her sparkling blue eyes and beautiful smile would say to me, "Sorry Elsa." After Kathy died, her son Dane came to work with us, and history repeated itself. There were the same eyes and the same smile which evoked a few tears from yours truly. Today, house policy still dictates that one must never put knives in the sink—although I'm not such a grump about it anymore.

We have discussed foods and spices and other such stuff. Now let us consider the utensils that you might be cooking in. I try to avoid using aluminum cookware. According to some studies, aluminum is unhealthy for you. It also does not distribute heat evenly and may make cooking more of a chore than necessary. Obviously, we can't all go out and purchase new cookware, but, if possible, a good 2- or 3-quart saucepan and one large skillet should serve the purpose. You will also need a large soup pot or Dutch oven, a muffin tin, and a cookie sheet. If you will be baking bread, you will want to have a bread pan or two. We have found that stainless steel works well at the Cafe. At home, I like to use a cast iron set passed to me by my Mum, who received it from her mother. For me, using cast iron reinforces the connection with not only generations of my family, but the history of mankind through the ages. Pottery evokes the same kind of thought.

If ever you have time to visit a working museum, stop and see the kitchen. We are blessed with being able to create a meal in an hour versus the several hours and many hands required in the kitchens of just 150 to 200 years ago. You will find that whole foods cooking will take a little longer than popping something in the microwave, but the fresh taste and nutrition are worth the effort. Like any new task or challenge, the beginning is a learning process. It will require time and patience on your part (and perhaps on the part of your family as well) while you master this new technique. Once you have the basics, that information is yours forever. Run with it.

Make any recipe yours, and have fun playing in the kitchen.

KATHY, GONE IN APRIL

Moving swiftly away
through the new trees,
booted feet stride up the green gold path,
littered with catkin,
and crisscrossed with the unseen trails
of salamander and toad.

Braids swinging,
her cap rakish on her head,
she tosses a saucy grin over her shoulder
and moves on.

Crossing open ground
wet in places,
she jumps the tussocks,
her arms flung wide
like fledgling wings.
Birdsong and laughter
ripple over the base
amphibian
bluster and croak.

She steps over
the still form upon the bed,
and springs away,

going on ahead.

                    Jay Rancourt
                    4/21/98

MEMORIES

OF

KATHY

Memories of Kathy

Our cookbook author, Kathy Etter, was a vital and cherished member of the community. She shared her warm and generous spirit with everyone she encountered during her years in the Mount Washington Valley, and her positive impact has endured. After Kathy's untimely death in 1998, her friend David Brooks wrote of her, "Kathy embraced life with passionate and positive energy. She was always a mother first, hiking with her sons, taking them on trips to the ocean, and constantly involving them in her life. Whether volunteering in her sons' schools, hiking on her beloved Cranmore Mountain with family and friends, eating chocolate chip cookies, or creating culinary delights at her vegetarian restaurant, Cafe Chimes, Kathy loved her life and the people who surrounded her."

When Kathy became ill, the community rallied to support her and her family. When she died at the age of 47, there was an outpouring of appreciation and love for this extraordinary woman. The tributes to Kathy came in many forms from many sources, and we have included a sampling of these moving reminiscences in this section.

We have also included biographical information and some of the many newspaper columns that Kathy wrote for *The Conway Daily Sun* over the course of several years. The columns covered a myriad of subjects—nutrition, wellness, vegetarianism, meditation, fasting, concern for a healthy environment, etc. We've chosen a few that reflect Kathy's intense focus on living a healthy and productive life, fostering change, learning, and sharing.

It is impossible to remember Kathy without thinking of her smile, her blue eyes, her sense of fun, her love for her family and friends, and her irrepressible and joyful approach to living. She touched all who knew her with a sense that life was a good thing, that each day was meant to be lived to the fullest. It was a privilege for me to work with Kathy and to help fulfill her dream of writing a cookbook that would reflect her exuberant and creative approach to cooking healthy food. It is my hope that this book will take its place as a small part of the legacy that Kathy has left for all those of us who were fortunate to know her.

Anne C. Chase

250

About the Author

Kathleen J. Etter was born December 3, 1950 in Swamscott, Massachusetts. She attended grammar and high school there and went on to receive an Associates Degree in Early Childhood Education from North Shore Community College in Beverly, Massachusetts. Although Kathy grew up in Massachusetts, she spent many of her weekends and holidays skiing and hiking in New Hampshire's Mount Washington Valley. Her grandfather was one of the principals of Cranmore Mountain, a ski area located in North Conway, New Hampshire. Kathy's regular family visits to the area were the beginning of a strong, life-long connection to the Conway community.

After college, Kathy moved north, first to Fryeburg, Maine, a nearby community, and subsequently to North Conway. Using her training in early childhood education, Kathy worked initially as a teacher in day-care centers in both Fryeburg and North Conway.

The mother of three sons, Kathy entered whole-heartedly into the life of the community. She was active in many community activities, but is especially remembered for her instrumental role in establishing and leading a Keystone

Club for pre-teens and young teenagers. Kathy facilitated weekly group meetings designed to foster the young members' self-esteem and assist them through the difficulties of growing up. The Club provided an environment of trust in which the youngsters could share their feelings, problems, and experiences. Based on International Personal Development's "Yes Course" for adults, the Keystone Club postulated techniques for personal growth through self-esteem, positive living, and taking responsibility for one's own actions.

As her own children were growing up, Kathy developed a strong desire to focus her energy into something new in her life. With her family in mind, she decided to learn more about nutrition and the foods we eat. She took a vegetarian cooking course for the purpose of preparing healthy and nutritious food for her family. These classes were the beginning of a life-long commitment to vegetarianism and healthy eating.

In early 1990, Kathy was approached by a friend who had a turn-key business that he thought she might be interested in. The business turned out to be a popcorn, nuts and candy shop located in a below-ground level of a building in the center of the village of North Conway. Kathy wrote that,

> *"The birth of the Cafe is still somewhat of a mystery to me. As I recall, it all started with a longing to be part of something in which I would develop my creativity that had been stagnant while having and raising children...When I realized that (the business) was to sell candied popcorn and candy, the idea was not acceptable to me as it interfered with many of my basic beliefs. However, a spark was ignited, and I pondered the idea of a health food cafe, which would be in line with what I believed in."*

The offer came just at the same time that Kathy was pursuing her interests in healthy and nutritional foods.

Kathy opened the door to Cafe Chimes on June 23rd, 1990. She envisioned a small shop that would create and serve healthy and nutritious foods that everyone would enjoy. At the time, there were no vegetarian restaurants in the Mount Washington Valley. Kathy's concept was a success, and the Cafe Chimes soon attracted a loyal following. After getting the Cafe off the ground, Kathy offered a regular series of Vegetarian Cooking and Nutrition Classes that became a popular community mainstay.

During the years that Kathy ran Cafe Chimes, she pursued her interest in vegetarianism and nutrition, receiving Certification in Vegetarian Nutrition in

1995 from the Association of Vegetarian Dietitian and Nutrition Educators. In addition she received Certification in Holistic Health Counseling and attended the WAY TO HEALTH Seminar at the Kushi Institute. She served as a member of the Nutritional Committee at the local high school and gave countless presentations for community groups, offering her energies to improve the health and well-being of her fellow community members.

In addition to all this, Kathy wrote magazine articles and a regular column for *The Conway Daily Sun*, a local newspaper serving the Mount Washington Valley. Several of her columns are excerpted in this chapter. In 1991, she wrote a children's book entitled *Cranmore's Adventure*. The story of a little mountain that wanted to grow larger, the book is a charming allegory that stresses the power and importance of self-respect and affirmation for children and adults alike. It reflects Kathy's profound belief in the power of positive thoughts and in the beauty and dignity of each living creature. The book was illustrated by Elizabeth Irwin and published locally by Express Graphics.

It was a long-standing goal of Kathy's to write a cookbook. In Spring of 1997, after this cookbook project was begun, she wrote in her newspaper column that she would be submitting reprints of past favorite articles for publication for a while:

> *"The reason for this is that I will be joyfully consumed with the immense project of writing the Cafe Chimes Cookbook. I have been pregnant and full with this book for about three years; and now the time is right for its birth. I will be in labor for the entire ten weeks, but it will be a labor of love. My best effort will be not less than everything. After mentally embracing this project, physically I will be found in front of my computer for days on end. It will be quite a change of pace for me, and a sense of panic sometimes gets hold of my best intentions. Commitment brings a full range of expectations and goal setting...So, the goal for completion of this project is the availability of this book by late Autumn. Imagine and Believe."*

Unfortunately, Kathy was overtaken by illness in the Autumn of 1997 and was unable to complete her cookbook. Kathy's colleagues and friends continued work on the cookbook during her illness starting with the recipes, commentaries, and quotations that she had been able to gather together. Although Kathy was soon unable to do any further work on the book, she knew that the project was ongoing and that a Cafe Chimes Cookbook would

253

eventually appear. She wanted the book to reflect her joyful and creative approach to cooking as well as her strong commitment to healthy and nutritious food. She regarded the cookbook as her gift to the community that had given her so much during her lifetime.

Kathy Etter died at the age of 47 on April 19, 1998, surrounded by the love of her community, friends, and family.

Kathy Etter

Positive Thinking for Healthy Living

Autobiography in Five Short Chapters

by Portia Nelson

CHAPTER ONE

I walk down the street.
   There is a deep hole in the sidewalk.
   I fall in.
   I am lost....I am helpless.
    It isn't my fault.
It takes forever to find a way out.

CHAPTER TWO

I walk down the same street.
   There is a deep hole in the sidewalk.
   I pretend I don't see it.
   I fall in again.
I can't believe I am in the same place.
    But, it isn't my fault.
It still takes a long time to get out.

CHAPTER THREE

I walk down the same street.
   There is a deep hole in the sidewalk.
   I see it is there.
   I still fall in ... it's a habit ... but,
    my eyes are open.
    I know where I am.
It is *my* fault.
I get out immediately.

CHAPTER FOUR

I walk down the same street.
   There is a deep hole in the sidewalk.
   I walk around it.

CHAPTER FIVE

I walk down another street.

I use this poem to end all presentations or talks I am invited to do.

In regards to lifestyle decisions and attitude, in which chapter did you place yourself? In order to develop my thoughts more fully in an area like this, I tend to reach for the book *Living with Joy* by Sanaya Roman. She states, "Your attitude determines how you experience the world. An attitude that creates joy is one in which you interpret what happens to you through the filter of joy. Your attitude and outlook act like a filter. When you have a positive, optimistic outlook, it filters out the negative and denser experiences. Your attitude is the words you use when you talk to yourself."

It would seem that an attitude then can be altered by changing the way one carries on discussions within the subconscious and conscious levels of our being. Simple? YES! Easy? Well, it can be.

To further develop this idea, I think we need a specific area to elaborate on. Since my field is food choices, I believe this is as good a starting place as any. You learn many attitudes about food as you grow. Probably you eat whatever you have been given on your breakfast, lunch, and dinner plate. As you mature, it may be important to develop your own set of realities regarding food—more specifically, healthy, nutritious choices. When you allow yourself time to think about the continuing habits of unhealthy food choices, you may begin to see a pattern of self-destruction because the future consequences loom as a real possibility. This is an attitude, and by changing the way you think about certain foods, you can take the chance to change what you eat.

An attitude of balance can be achieved almost as simply as desiring the process to begin. By wanting to eat more wholesome foods, you are halfway there, or perhaps in Chapter Three of the poem. I believe attitude is the one thing on which our future together depends. I would like to end by suggesting a Chapter Six in the above selection. How about, "I believe, imagine, and create my own highway."

(Kathy Etter's column appeared in *The Conway Daily Sun* on June 14, 1996)

Kathy Etter

Healthy Lifestyle Is Everybody's Responsibility

This a story about four people named Everybody, Somebody, Anybody, and Nobody.

There was an important job to be done and Everybody was sure that Somebody would do it. Anybody could have done it, but Nobody did it. Somebody got angry about that, because it was Everybody's job. Everybody thought Anybody could do it, but Nobody realized that Everybody wouldn't do it.

It ended up that Everybody blamed Somebody when Nobody did what Anybody could have done.

Author Unknown

To me this is a story about shirking responsibility. The author has cleverly played with words bringing a knowing smile to the reader's face. We all can admit to avoiding certain responsibilities once in a while depending on the situation and personal circumstances. We all can admit to consuming certain foods that are known to result in poor health, i.e., foods high in fats, foods high in refined sugars, alcohol, coffee. But who will take the responsibility for these inferior food choices? Nobody, Anybody, Somebody, Everybody??

My guess is that it is Everybody's job to be fully responsible for his own health. People often feel terribly guilty about their dietary indiscretions. The resistance to making dietary changes often is a major obstacle, yet may need to be rewarded. Psychiatrists know that when patients begin to express their resistance to new ideas, the process of resolving the resistance can begin. Everybody choosing a diet out of unbalanced, refined, high fat and high sugar foods are like smokers in the 1950's. They may not have stopped yet, but they know they cannot keep it up forever. That knowledge is half the battle. A quote by Dean Ornish, M.D., Founder and President of the Preventive Medicine Research Institute, brings out an interesting perspective. "One of the surprising findings in our study is that, for many people, it is easier to make big changes in diet and lifestyle than to make only moderate ones. Although this goes against conventional wisdom, we found it to be true.

"When people make only moderate changes in diet and lifestyle, they have the worst of both worlds. They have the sense of deprivation because they're not able to eat and do every-thing that they want, but they're not making changes big enough to make them feel much better or to have much effect on their weight, their choles-terol, or their health. On the other hand, when people make comprehen-sive changes in their diet and lifestyle, they begin to feel so much better so quickly that the choices become clear and, for many people, worth making."

This is the end of the story about four people named Everybody, Somebody, Anybody, and Nobody. They all agreed that each has an important job to do. They each have a body, and if they don't take care of that body, where would they live???

(Kathy Etter's column appeared in *The Conway Daily Sun* on June 1, 1996)

257

Kathy Etter

Positive Healing

"When we are born and take our first steps, we are on an unknown journey. As our footprints are left behind, we may look ahead and bump into roadblocks, obstacles, dilemmas that provide us with the challenge to handle each in a way that serves us. Most times we do not know or have the answer why these challenges are given to us, yet deep down we have a knowing that it is essential to our life, our truth, and our growth."

This was how I began the conversation last night with my three sons informing them that I have developed lung cancer. As we held hands, there was much sadness balanced with a unifying laughter that caught us by surprise and lightened our hearts. The questions were asked, yet the answers were not always available. To explain the unexplainable is a difficult task. As one friend said, "This isn't only your lesson. Your children and friends are souls who agreed to be with you this lifetime, so we are all prepared to do whatever is asked." And then she said, which made me laugh, "I always knew you weren't going to live your life like everyone else. I never know what you were going to do next!"

So, to the members of my community, I write you this letter from the parts of my heart that I have been given the opportunity to be in touch with. I want you to know that I greet this as one event in my life that will lead me to a deeper truth of understanding. I look at this as a spiritual opportunity, and one that I feel grateful for having been chosen to receive. Are these mere new-age words, an attempt to motivate a positive view? There may be some truth to that, but I can honestly share with you that I am in touch with "something" that brings me a profound sense of peace knowing that I have developed cancer. This "something" has no definition and is just making its way into my life; and I trust this is occurring for my highest good and vision.

The big question seems to be for everyone and myself included is, "How did this occur? It doesn't make sense!" I know that I have come to be regarded as a person who advocates a healthy lifestyle for a healthful life. Eating the "right" types of food, exercising, enjoying a positive outlook on life are qualities that I live everyday. All that I have to offer you is that it is not for us to know right now.

There are a couple of things you can do for me and my family as a community. I hold a unique belief in the power of the collective consciousness. I have a great sense of joy knowing that I am not alone, that there is guidance and assistance just for the asking. My first request is for you to view this news with a warm and loving heart by sending healing thoughts instead of anxiety or dread. It's easy to do: When a thought enters your consciousness that makes you aware of fear-based thinking, just say, "I now change that thought and send Kathy healing thoughts of love and light."

If everyone develops this, I believe the universe will give assistance, love, healing, and support. If a community is centered on a vision of

258

the highest purpose, doors open. (This works in all circumstances.) ...

And my last request is that when you see me at the Cafe or around town, please feel free to offer a hug which I believe is one of the most priceless gifts we can give or receive.

I will leave you with a quote. "Look at events from a higher perspective and realize that everything happening to you can be seen as a good thing. This is the wisdom of your soul, for your soul is always trying to help you see your life in a higher way."

(excerpted from Kathy Etter's column in *The Conway Daily Sun*, November 14, 1997)

ANNIVERSARY (FOR KATHY)

We stepped off on Easter, knowing well we could not stay,
But only to explore, looking out and in and at one another.
A test, you might say, of gear and goals
and all those things that point the way
and testing each the other.

Rushing first, then slowing, then arriving at a pace that suited
both our separate styles.
Forward moving, feeling, acknowledging each step,
we spoke of easy smiles,
Of comfort with life, with both its pain and pleasure,
Of approaching every curve, preparing for each treasure
as yet unseen.

The path smoothed out, yet never smooth.
We guided, stepped, and helped each other through,
Sometimes looking back at paths wondering what we'd do
should we cross that path again.

You spoke to me of travel,
and said before your Earthbound days were done,
You would take your five senses, (excuse me six),
out into the world and set them free.
Gathering every sight and smell and taste
and breathe them in as one.

But I speak to you of travel now,
and know that not every one's on path or road
or some expanse of sea.
And some require not the slightest move,
for it is travel just to be.

260

And when all your fellow travelers speak
of all their journeys done,
Tell them that we traveled once,
You and I,
Once around the sun.

Braden McKenzie

Kathy Etter

Kathy Etter influenced my life a great deal. She taught me all her views on life. She introduced me to a better way of thinking through the Keystone classes which she created and taught. Her ideas about vegetarianism changed my eating habits. Kathy influenced my life like no one else could. She was my mother.

"Kathy," I would say because that is how I addressed her. People say that it is odd for a child to call his or her parent by their first name. They say that it is a sign of disrespect. I thought that it was the greatest thing in the world. I can remember that day when my mother would no longer be "mom" but "Kathy."

We were going to school, my mother, my two brothers, and I. The car was filled with the wails of three young boys screaming "mom" this and "mom" that. Finally, as we neared our elementary school, my mother stopped the car in the middle of the road and turned in her seat. She looked at us and said that from now on we were to call her Kathy because she sick of hearing the word "mom." And from that day on, we called her Kathy. She was no longer just my mother, but a person as well.

When I was about ten years old, Kathy started a course called Keystone. It was based on a class she had taken called the "YES Course." The YES Course taught adults a better way of thinking. It helped them express their emotions and deal with things of their past. Keystone taught these same ideas, but to a younger audience. Kathy thought that these ideas would be a great thing for kids and young adults. She was right. The groups met once a week for periods during the school year. It was open to anyone at no cost, but donations were accepted and usually given. Most of the time, there were from twenty to thirty kids there. These young adults walked away from Keystone more aware of their surroundings and with a better sense of who they were. I know I did. I attended every gathering. Keystone lasted about four years until Kathy found another way to give back to the community.

Kathy had been taking macrobiotic cooking classes and learning about healthy eating. She now wanted to open a vegetarian restaurant. Her idea

262

would eventually become Cafe Chimes. It was a truly unique place serving everything from humus sandwiches to fresh carrot juice. Kathy wanted it to be her journey for about three years, but three rapidly turned into eight.

I associated the Cafe and Kathy as one. She worked five days a week from 6:30 in the morning until 4:00 in the afternoon. That's how we lived. We all pitched in to make the Cafe grow. Whether it was picking up the produce at the local health food store or working for two dollars an hour, my brothers and I helped. I think I'll always remember her at Cafe Chimes—Kathy's smiling face behind that ugly yellow counter.

In the Fall of 1997, Kathy was diagnosed with cancer. I was told that it was a rare form of lung cancer particular to non-smoking, middle-aged women. I was shocked to find that a woman with Kathy's lifestyle could have cancer. She ate extremely well, exercised, and her positive outlook on life could not have been greater. I looked at it as no big deal, just a little obstacle in Kathy's life that she was sure to overcome. I had read about people with cancer who had cured themselves by eating right. I figured this was going to be no problem for Kathy with all her knowledge about healthy eating and her great support group of friends. To my surprise, it became a struggle.

The cancer had been growing for over a year, and the doctors could not remove it surgically because it was too widespread. Kathy tried everything, but to no avail. I could not comprehend the notion that nothing was working. It had to work, we'll find something, I kept telling myself. In the Spring I remember sitting down with my mother.

"Beau, I'm dying," she said. It hit me so hard that I didn't know what to say.

"I know."

My mother left me with the knowledge of who I was. She had taught me to find myself. Along with her understanding of healthy eating, she blessed me with her always-positive attitude. Her outlook on life was to accomplish as much as you can and to give to everything you see. She befriended everyone, and I find I do the same. She left me knowledge that I could never have gotten anywhere else, and for that I thank my mother, Kathy Etter.

Beau Etter-Garrette

Alex Levin

The Smile of One Woman

Often times, a smile is what a person uses to cover his or her fear, or insecurity, or wanting. But if you look closely, you can see that such smiles begin and end with the mouth. Real smiles—smiles that offer an honest open heart—are born of some inner lifespring and spill out in places that the lips alone can't completely express. They make the eyes sparkle and the creases around cheeks and eyebrows dance. Kathy Etter had that kind of smile.

I did not know Kathy well; our paths crossed on occasion, but when we did connect, I felt a genuine appreciation for her attitude and her work. I sensed it was mutual, and it probably was... Kathy seemed to appreciate everyone.

When I was running a GED class for a group of low-income single moms, Kathy came in one day as an invited guest to talk about nutrition to the women, most of whom were out of shape and didn't give a whole lot of thought about what they ate, beyond what they craved and thought they could afford. And though Kathy gave them information they had heard a dozen times before, when she spoke, they listened to her intently because she seemed to understand that most of what they ate and fed their children was based on the belief that because of money and circumstance, they hadn't many choices.

Kathy didn't talk at them; she talked with them—no matter how obese, no matter how many Little Debbie's they snacked on as they sat and listened, she didn't judge them. Nor was Kathy worried about them accepting her. Instead she seemed to recognize that her most important work was to accept them. And more so than with any words of wisdom, she succeeded at this with her smile.

Kathy had made up some kind of tabouli-rice creation and some sort of bean thing for the women to try. When she brought in the big bowls at the beginning of the session, they looked at her askance. "You really think we're going to eat that stuff?" was the general response. But much to my surprise, by the time the brief discussion was over, the women were more than ready to sample what she offered.

I can't say that Kathy changed their lives right then and there like the passing of some magical shakti, but even a couple of years later, the women still remembered that nice lady with the weird but really good food and the things she had said, the alternatives she offered. In the end I think she nudged them a little bit in a healthier direction, got them thinking a little bit about what it was they were putting in their bodies and the bodies of their children.

A story I've written of before, *The Hundredth Monkey*, seems particularly appropriate when talking about Kathy. In brief, that story is about a group of scientists who introduced sweet potatoes to an island of monkeys. Right from the start, the monkeys enjoyed the potatoes, eating them right off the ground, dirt and all. Then one day a young female monkey known as Imo took her potato down to a stream, washed it off, and discovered just how much better a clean potato tasted. Over time, a few more monkeys tried Imo's trick, but the whole of the tribe was certainly not sold on the idea. Gradually however, more and more monkeys started washing their potatoes, until one day that hundredth monkey washed a potato and suddenly a radical change occurred...all the monkeys began to wash their potatoes.

The two lessons that I culled from that story are first, that change creeps along slowly—often infuriatingly slowly—until a critical mass is reached at which point the change becomes explosive. The second lesson is, in essence, just how important it is for each of us to keep washing our potatoes, despite how odd it might seem to the world around us.

Of course when I speak of potato-washing and Kathy, it's about much more than food. Living consciously, expressing love fully, are forms of potato-washing as well. Last Friday, Kathy's memorial service, essentially designed by her, was all about that. More than one person mentioned to me in the days following the service,

how reflecting on Kathy's life really made them look at what they were doing with their own lives. Were they really enjoying each day as if it were their last on this earth—fully awake, fully conscious? I know that for myself, looking around and seeing so many other people giving consideration to the quality of their own consciousness and experience was incredibly strengthening.

Experiencing so many kindred spirits makes one wonder just how soon that hundredth monkey is going to come along and shift the balance that transforms our world from a place where greed rules, where insecurities rob us of precious moments, to a place ruled instead by attitudes of consciousness and kindness—a place where smiling eyes of light, love, and wakefulness are as common and as glorious as the flowers of the fields.

(Alex Levin's column appeared in *The Conway Daily Sun* on April 30, 1998.)

STOPPING TO SEE AN OLD FRIEND
(for Kathy Etter)

This old screen door I've seen before.
The squealing hinge, the tiny bell that rings,
the inviting smells of cooking from the heart.

I pause outside and see you through the hazy screen.
Flying braids propelled by haste,
then giving today's soup a taste.
"Ellie, the soup is awesome!" you say.
Then from somewhere out of view, "Thanks, I added more garlic."
Your smile reveals your pleasure.

Your smile,
I could hardly wait to see it.
I know the greeting well.
If ever there was a smile,
let's say a smile to define a smile,
it is yours.

Oh, that smile,
not just mouth or eyes, but from somewhere deep.
Your soul smiles.

I reach out and touch the screen,
all I need do is give a push
and the tiny bell will announce my visit,
and you will look up
and beam.

But I only stand,
my hand still against the fading screen.
You pause for just a moment
as if perhaps
you feel my presence,
but only for a moment.
You could never stop for long.

I find myself back up on the street.
Eric pours a double Americano and says something
about the Crash Test Dummies.
Then another voice,
"Follow your heart," it says, "follow your heart."
And I know why
I stopped to see an old friend.

Braden McKenzie

KATHY, CYNTHIA & DIANE

Three women gather together
often, by candle, moonlight,
with music, dance.
They are free together.
Through the years,
telling their sacred stories,
weaving a tighter and tighter
fabric of friendship.
The essence of what
they gave to each other
is presence.
What began with a meal
evolved into a celebration
of the three souls.
Today heaven's grace continues
to nurture the two women.
When they are pure and open
she finds them.
Just as she said,
"All you have to do is ask
and I will come to you."

Cynthia Atkinson
& Diane Johnson

Remembering Kathy

When I think of Kathy, the first words that come to my mind are *imagine* and *believe*, two of Kathy's favorite words. Imagine and believe are exactly what I did, and Kathy came to me. I was working and needed a very special care giver for my nine-month-old son, Darren. Kathy and her young son, Beau, came into my Natural Food Store in 1981, and I watched how she interacted with him for some time. Before Kathy left that day, I asked her if she would be willing to care for my baby while I worked. She was a woman whom I had never met before. I connected with and trusted in her essence immediately.

What I experienced for the seventeen years of friendship was a truly supportive, committed, adventurous, sensitive friend with whom I had a spiritual bond. We grew together with our families and friends. Her character expressed a celebration of life and friendship to all. What she did and believed were always ritualized in some way and then practiced forever. That was one of her secrets. I remember how she would wrap up the children's school clothes, make a special dinner, have dessert first, and make a special event of that back-to-school time. She had rituals for holidays, birthdays, and anything that needed to be honored. Our Friday hikes were one of the most endearing of our times together. Several of our rituals became meaningful to a larger community of friends.

Cafe Chimes was really born out of the macrobiotic cooking classes and Monday night dinners that I held at my home. For seven years, I taught cooking classes and served dinners to the community on a weekly basis. Kathy attended every one. She said the only thing that would stop us was a birth. We didn't have death on our minds then. Children, husbands, friends, anyone who wanted to come attended the dinners. It was not long after I stopped cooking for the public that Kathy had another idea—to open a Cafe where she could use her knowledge of healthy whole foods and provide a gathering place for her beloved community.

Cafe Chimes was a beautiful dream come true for Kathy—a wonderful celebration of food, friendship, service to the community, education, reverence

269

for life and good health. Her entire family worked in the Cafe. Kathy was a true servant to the community. She gave her heart and soul to it. And in the end, that community of precious souls that Kathy touched, touched her back. A tremendous outpouring of love came during her passing. I am blessed to have walked the path and shared life with Kathy for seventeen precious years.

Diane Johnson
8/2/00

Kathy

Kathy was inspiring. Yet she had no idea just how much she inspired those around her. We were the best of friends for over seventeen years. We met when our boys were babies. At first, I put her on a pedestal because I had never been witness to anyone with such incredible mothering skills. When I confessed this to her, she shared her shortcomings, her doubts, her fears, her tests and trials. Her open, vulnerable heart kindled our deepening friendship, and we had a hearty laugh about the notion of being a "perfect" Mom. We shared so many years of confiding, encouraging, tears, and laughter over our dear sweet boys.

Kathy was strong. She decided to open a health food cafe, and she had very few resources. How would that work? She had incredible faith and trust in the Universe. She knew once she got her vision clear, this Universe would provide, and she expected it would. I was absolutely awestruck as I watched the Cafe unfold—a cooler landed in driveway, a bread mixer on its way. Doubts were few, support was unanimous, success was assured.

Kathy was generous. She always remembered everyone's birthdays and special days. And she loved pouring her heart into finding and presenting each precious gift. Nothing last minute, everything with forethought. She cherished her friends and family and delighted in being generous.

Kathy was creative. She was a master of combinations, whether it was her wild purple outfit for the day or the "special of the day" on the menu at Cafe Chimes. She had a unique way of being in the world that was often huge and sometimes even a bit outrageous.

Kathy was spiritual. Sometimes wondering if she fit into the framework of any given religion, yet welcoming pieces of different belief systems, different faiths, she developed her own spiritual nature by devouring inspirational books, tapes, and courses. She was always questioning and connecting to nature.

Kathy is ever present for me. I will always remember her spirit, her smile, her generosity, her courage, her honesty, her vulnerability, and her never-ending sense of humor. In her last months, Kathy, Diane, and I joked how she would go ahead to the spiritual world and set the table for us to follow—a glorious feast...a glorious reunion.

Cynthia Atkinson

Summer 2000

Dear Kathy,

It has been just over two years since you left us here on earth. I hope that wherever you are now is all that you imagined and believed it to be. Sometimes I imagine you up in the heavens with other loved ones, cooking a delicious feast for everyone to enjoy. You nourished so many of us for so many years—both with your nutritious, wholesome foods and, just as nourishing, with your warm eyes and immense, welcoming smile. You made each of us who walked into Cafe Chimes feel as though we were the most special person in the whole world.

You continue to fill me with hope. That has been one of your greatest gifts. You welcomed your illness as a teacher and taught those of us surrounding you about hope and love and joy and laughter. You have taught me about the amazing ability that one person has to make a difference in this world. I am frequently stopped by people who want to share a favorite "Kathy Story." Their stories are lessons about love and goodness and hope. Your passion touched and enriched countless people's lives. You brought sunshine and happiness wherever you went and shared it with the world.

Your boys are growing into incredibly outstanding young men. You would be so proud of all three. I am honored to continue to be a part of their lives, and love that they want to be a part of mine. You live on through so many of us, but directly through them. They are doing you proud.

And I have a little baby girl, Kathy! I feel your presence so often and know that you are not only my guardian angel, but also little Ani Sky's. Every night as she drifts off to sleep, I look at your picture in her room and say to her, "May all the angels protect you and watch over you and keep you safe until the morning." Your joy-full spirit continues, dear Kathy. I miss you. *Imagine* and *Believe*.

Anika Brand Hastings

BLUE EYES SHINING (for Kathy)

Your blue eyes shining with the light of creation,
delighting in service and deep celebration
of living and loving and cooking and sharing,
and in receiving the compassionate caring
from those who have marveled at your
capacity to give,
enriching, enhancing so many who've lived,
privileged to know you, blessed with your presence.
Thank you so much for sharing your essence!

from Rob Richardson

APPENDIX

About the Illustrator

In early 1997, when the *Cafe Chimes Cookbook* project was getting underway, artist Shana Myers, a close friend of Kathy Etter, agreed to create the cookbook cover and illustrate the text. Her lively drawings are found throughout the book and are a special tribute to her friend, Kathy.

Shana is indeed a woman of many talents. In addition to her artistic endeavors, she is a licensed practitioner of therapeutic massage with offices in North Conway and Jackson, New Hampshire. She established her practice in the Valley eight years ago when she stepped off the Appalachian Trail, settled in Jackson, and opened Ahh Moondance Massage Therapy in North Conway. After the North Conway office celebrated its fifth year of operation, Shana opened a second office in Jackson where she also teaches yoga. At the time this book is going to press, Shana is relocating her Jackson office to her new building, also in Jackson. This new wellness center, Balance W.O.R.K.S.

(standing for Wellness, Opportunities, Relaxation, Knowledge, and Spirituality) will house her massage practice, yoga and other wellness classes, and a small shop. In addition, the yoga studio will also be available for other community activities.

Shana has been a licensed therapeutic massage practitioner for twelve years. She trained at the Esalen Institute in Big Sur, California, and the Boston Shiatsu School. Prior to pursuing her career in massage therapy, Shana acquired an MA in Drawing and Painting and an MS in Experiential Education. She explored several professions including those of scenic technician, renaissance body painter, freelance muralist, graphic artist, medical photographer, and industrial arts/math/art teacher. She also served as a ropes course builder and instructor, working with corporate groups, teachers, and physically and mentally challenged teens throughout the lower United States and Alaska.

Shana continues to expand her knowledge of any modality which facilitates health! She is passionate about heightening peoples' awareness about their health and about preventative measures which promote health and well-being.

When Shana is not nurturing the community through massage or volunteering in local events such as school and hospital presentations, she's mountaineering in any weather with her Labs, Ocha and Ecru. They love massage too!

When Shana is asked, "If you could do one thing in this lifetime, what would it be?" she smiles and simply replies, "Make a difference...with compassion."

Permissions & Acknowledgments

Page xxi
Reprinted from *Present Moment Wonderful Moment: Mindfulness Verses for Daily Living* (1990) by Thich Nhat Hanh with permission of Parallax Press, Berkeley, California

Page xxii
"I Will Not Die An Unlived Life" from *The Art of the Possible* by Dawna Markova, Copyright ©1991 by Dawna Markova, used by permission from Conari Press.

Page 12
From *Through the Looking Glass and What Alice Found There* by Lewis Carroll, 1872

Page 98
Sufi Passage from SOUL FOOD: STORIES TO NOURISH THE SPIRIT AND THE HEART by JACK KORNFELD and CHRISTINA FELDMAN
Copyright ©1996 by Jack Kornfield and Christina Feldman.
Reprinted by permission of HarperCollins Publishers, Inc.

Page 116
From *Alice's Adventures in Wonderland* by Lewis Carroll, 1865

Page 132
From *The Essential Rumi*, Translated by Coleman Barks, HarperSanFrancisco, 1995.
Copyright ©1995 by Coleman Barks.
Reprinted by permission of Coleman Barks.

Page 162
From *Cranmore's Adventure* by Kathleen J. Etter
Text Copyright ©1991 by Kathleen J. Etter. Illustrations Copyright ©1991 by Elizabeth Jane Irwin. Reprinted by permission of Kathleen J. Etter

Page 210
From *The Prophet* by Kahlil Gibran
Copyright ©1923 by Kahlil Gibran and renewed 1951 by
Administrators C T A of Kahlil Gibran Estate and Mary G. Gibran.
Reprinted by permission of Alfred A. Knopf Inc.
and by permission of Gibran National Committee, P.O. Box 116-5487,
Beirut, Lebanon; Fax (+961-1) 396916;
E-mail: k.gibran@cyberia.net.lb.

279

Page 255
"Autobiography In Five Short Chapters" from the book, *There's A Hole In My Sidewalk*, Copyright ©1993 by Portia Nelson.
Beyond Words Publishing, Hillsboro, Oregon.
Reprinted with permission.

Page 255
From *Living With Joy* by Sanaya Roman ©1986.
Reprinted with the permission of HJ Kramer/New World Library, 14 Pamaron Way, Novato, CA 94949

Page 257
Quotation by Dean Ornish, M.D.
Reprinted by permission of Dean Ornish, M.D., Founder and President, Preventive Medicine Research Institute, Clinical Professor of Medicine, School of Medicine, University of California, San Francisco

Pages 255-259
Newspaper columns by Kathy Etter appeared originally in *The Conway Daily Sun*, Conway, New Hampshire.
Reprinted by permission of Kathleen J. Etter.

Page 264
Newspaper column by Alex Levin appeared originally in *The Conway Daily Sun*, Conway, New Hampshire.
Reprinted by permission of Alex Levin.

Index

281

285

Notes

Notes

Notes

DATE DUE

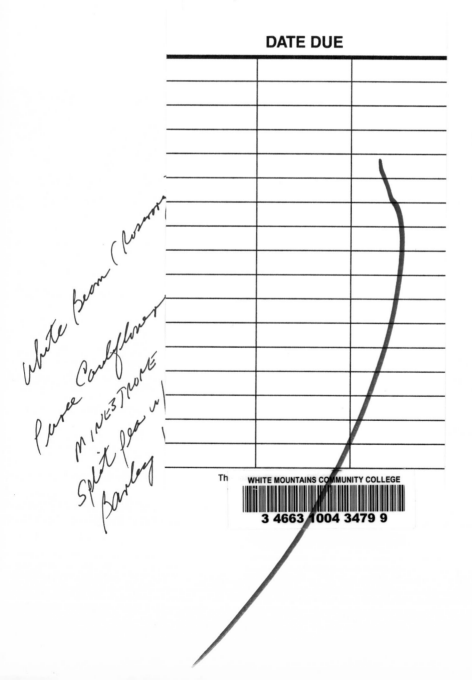

White Bean (Rosmy
Puree Cauliflower
MINESTRONE
Split pea w/
Barley

Peter Brereton's

Touring Guide
to English Villages

Mitchell Beazley

Acknowledgements
The author and publishers are grateful to
those listed below for their kind permission
to reprint the following extracts: Methuen
London for the quotation from *In Search of
England* by H. V. Morton (p. 14); Gerald
Duckworth & Co Ltd for the quotations
from *Complete Verse* by Hilaire Belloc
(pp. 52 and 61); George Sassoon for the
quotation from 'Blighters' by Siegfried
Sassoon (p. 72).

Few travel books are without errors, and no
guidebook can ever be completely up to
date, for telephone numbers change
without warning, and hotels and pubs
come under new management, which can
affect standards. While every effort has
been made to ensure that all information is
accurate at the time of going to press, the
publishers will be glad to receive any
corrections and suggestions for
improvements, which can be incorporated
in the next edition.

Editor Leonie Hamilton
Researcher Catherine Jackson
Editorial assistant Alison Hancock
Picture researcher Brigitte Arora

Edited by
Mitchell Beazley International Limited
87–89 Shaftesbury Avenue
London W1V 7AD

Designed by Grub Street Design, London

© Mitchell Beazley Publishers 1984
© Text: Peter Brereton 1984
© Maps and illustrations:
Mitchell Beazley Publishers 1984

ISBN 0 85533 460 6

Maps by Hussein Hussein.
Illustrations by Bill Le Fever.
Typeset by Bookform, Formby.
Printed and bound in Italy by
New Interlitho, Milan

The Village

A townsman's lament

The Church, the Inn, the Hall between,
The cob-built dwellings round the green,
The village school where once it seems
Summer was constant. Are they dreams
That conjure up those far-gone days
Of village life and village ways?

Beyond the village lay the weir,
And there with homemade fishing gear
We'd spend the lengthy daylight hours,
Returning home to flick'ring fires
That filled the cottage with a glow
And warmed those nights of long ago.

A townsman now, all that's long past,
A golden age that couldn't last;
Hard to resist the City's claim,
The spur of all the wealth and fame,
The various posts on City Boards,
The pent-house flat quite close to Lords.

The Church, the Inn, the Hall between,
The cob-built dwellings round the green;
Have they much changed? Each woodland track
Was my preserve. Oh years roll back;
Give me the peace I knew before,
Far from the distant traffic's roar.

INTRODUCTION

The villages described in this guide are scattered throughout the length and breadth of England. They have been grouped into 12 distinct areas. The descriptions of the villages in each area are preceded by a brief introduction, describing the nature of the countryside and peculiarities of the area, as well as the types of building material to be found there. Within each area, a number of villages have been grouped together. The maps will show that these groups of villages lie within a few miles of a pleasant country town, where a variety of hotel accommodation is available. This enables the motorist, based at one of these towns, to visit the surrounding villages within the course of a day or two.
Mileages are given for each tour, but they can only be approximate.

Touring centres
The name, address and telephone number of one or two hotels have been given. After the telephone number, there is a symbol, which gives a rough price band as shown below. Prices should, however, always be checked before booking.

It is emphasized that *A Touring Guide to English Villages* makes no claim to being a hotel guide. However, a selection of hotels has been included to allow the reader quick reference to available accommodation across a broad price range.

Hotel price bands
Charge for single room; bed and breakfast
❶ up to £10
❷ £10–15
❸ £15–20
❹ £20–30
❺ £30–40

Typefaces
Bold type is used throughout the guide for emphasis, to draw attention to something of special interest or importance. ***Bold italic*** is used for cross-references within the description of one village, or area introduction, to other villages in the guide.

Village pubs
These have been indicated beneath the text relating to the villages. Telephone numbers have only been given where accommodation is available.

Symbols
Against the names of villages and the pubs within the villages there is a variety of symbols, which are explained below.

Village symbols
❖ Tends to be crowded in high season
△ Feature of historic or architectural interest
★ Museum
† Church of interest
◇● Literary associations

Pub symbols
A Accommodation
R Restaurant
Bs Bar snacks
Ra Real ale

CONTENTS

PREFACE

The structure and development of the villages of England represent, I suggest, the stable and enduring factor that, more than any other, illuminates the history of England and the way of life of her people. When did it all begin? Centuries before the Norman invasion, as early as the 5thC, little groups of hutted settlements were developing. Vast forests were cleared to make way for farmsteads, around which communities were established providing the workforce to till the land and care for the livestock. Cultivation took place in long, narrow strips, known as selions, which spread in almost geometric pattern across great unhedged fields, each selion or series of selions being the responsibility of individual farmers. This open-field system of farming that had begun in Anglo Saxon times continued, unchanged, until about the 14thC which marked the beginning of the gradual development of an enclosed-field system. Even today, however, in meadows that surround the village it is possible to detect the parallel ridges and furrows that once formed the basis of land tenure. These primitive Anglo Saxon village communities were bound together, gradually, by the imposition of a manorial feudal system, whereby the land around the village became incorporated into the estate of a 'lord' to whom the peasant, or serf as he had now become, was legally bound. This meant he could not leave his lord's estate or sell his own land, the time to cultivate it being conditional upon his provision of free labour for his lord on certain days of the week. This system of serf-dom continued to be the basis of agricultural life until several centuries after the Norman Conquest.

Although the system remained unchanged, the arrival of the Normans did at least herald the start of a more structured way of life. The census carried out in 1086 and recorded in the Domesday Book sprang from William the Conqueror's belief in an ordered society, enabling him to discover the wealth and power of the noblemen to whom he had allocated land as well as the numbers of their vassals. The Domesday Book proved that most numerous in the English population were the villeins who provided the labour for the manors; and although the life of servitude of these villagers continued much as it had always done, the arrival of these new lords of the manor did at least provide some form of stability. The word manor, although today used when describing the pre-Norman scene, in fact only became part of the vocabulary with the arrival of the Norman lord who built his new 'manoir' in the village, a solid structure in the midst of what were little more than hovels. Thus, many of the older English villages as seen today grew and developed around the manor house, the name of the village often deriving from that of the family who occupied the manor for generation after generation.

A question that needs to be answered by the compiler of a guide, who for reasons of space must be selective is why have these particular villages been chosen? It would be foolhardy to claim that the selected villages stand alone — a unique list of beautiful villages, superior to hundreds of others scattered throughout the length and breadth of the country. All that can be said is that each village has been chosen for its picturesque quality, the charm and historic interest of the buildings it embraces, and the beauty of the rural scenery that surrounds it. The types of village vary enormously. They range from those that lie placidly in pastoral inland areas, to others found in the more rugged scenery of the moors and the coastline.

What distinguishes a village from a town? This is a further problem that I had to resolve in my selection. A few of the listed villages are places which some might consider to be small towns. *Burford*, Oxfordshire, and *Lavenham*, Suffolk, are two examples, both wool towns of importance at one time, but with the decline of that trade perhaps now better described as villages. In any case it would have been a pity to leave either out. At the other end of the scale are tiny villages comprising only a handful of houses such as *Llanyblodwel*, Shropshire, *Combe*, Berkshire, and the estate village of *Etal*, Northumberland.

The description of each village is of necessity brief. It is hoped, however, that the limited information provided will serve as a useful introduction, prompting the visitor to delve more deeply into the structure, history and traditions of a particular village. In this respect obvious sources of information are church guides — booklets that can be purchased inside the church — in which details of village history are often given; the village shop, where pamphlets about the area are normally available; and finally the word of mouth of the villagers themselves. This verbal information is likely to be twofold. First is the factual information, the pinpointing of buildings of particular interest that, if tucked away, could easily be missed by the stranger. Second, often of equal interest, is the folklore of the village, strange superstitions and customs passed from one generation to the next over centuries, possibly by now more fiction than fact but none the less interesting for that.

There is no such thing as a typical English village. But despite considerable variations there are some features common to many villages. Listed below are notes on the buildings, landscape and traditions which to some degree form the framework of the villages described within the pages of this guide.

MANOR HOUSE, CHURCH AND PARSONAGE

Reference has already been made to the manor, perhaps built originally by the Normans and rebuilt or extended by their descendants over the centuries. These lords of the manor, while building their houses, often constructed the church next door from the same building materials. Sometimes the church was newly built; sometimes it was constructed on the site of an earlier Saxon church or became an extension of it. Many of these churches contain a side chapel, named after the manor family and containing their dead and memorials to them. The erection of the parsonage, near the church, was often also the work of the lord of the manor who appointed the priest for the Living. Sometimes this close knit group of buildings is found at the heart of the village as in *Stanton Harcourt*, Oxfordshire, and *North Cadbury*, Somerset.

In other cases such as that at *Minster Lovell*, Oxfordshire, the hall, now a glorious ruin, stands by the church outside the village, adjacent to the former manorial farm and manorial dovecot. At *Sudbury*, Derbyshire, hall and church occupy grounds set apart from the village buildings, the result of the removal of the entire village by the 17thC lord of the manor. The estate villages of *Milton Abbas*, Dorset, and *Edensor*, Derbyshire, are further examples of villages built by the owners of the estate and then re-sited so as not to impair the view from the hall.

VILLAGE INN

Although not all the villages in the guide boast a manor house, at least one inn is likely to be seen in all but the smallest of them. The pub represents the focal point of village life, a social institution unknown outside these shores where gossip is exchanged and where traditional recreation such as darts and shove halfpenny takes place. Often the inn is one of the older buildings. Sometimes it stands by the church, perhaps once a medieval church house where the churchwardens brewed ale for feast days. Indeed many of the older inns were not purpose built, developing from buildings of a different kind such as the Crown Inn at *Chiddingfold*, Surrey, first built as a rest house for Cistercian monks in 1285, or the White Horse at *Shere*, Surrey, which began life in 1475 as a farmhouse.

VILLAGE BUILDINGS
All the villages in the guide contain a wealth of older buildings, houses and cottages that vary in style of architecture and building material according to their age and locality. But it needs to be appreciated that few of these older buildings date from much before the 16thC, the period that marked the beginning of the half-timbered cottages and farmhouses seen today. Before then the home of the villager was little more than a hovel, built of wattle and daub or mud and straw and roofed with thatch or turf. The stone cottages of the Cotswolds came even later, originating from the 17thC and 18thC.

TITHE BARN
In medieval times the maintainance of the church and its incumbent depended on the receipt of one tenth of the produce of the land that lay within the parish. This payment in kind was stored in the tithe barn, examples of which can be seen at *Stanway*, Gloucestershire, and *Selworthy*, Somerset.

VILLAGE SCHOOL
Although once an integral part of most villages the school-house is becoming rarer. Declining populations and the requirements of a broader form of education mean that many of the old school buildings in the smaller villages no longer exist, or have been put to other uses. Among many examples is the school at *Tissington,* Derbyshire, now a tea-shop; that at *Ilmington*, Warwickshire, converted into a chapel; and the school in the model village of *Ford*, Northumberland which now houses an art gallery.

VILLAGE SHOP
The single composite village store, the place where everything from bootlaces to bananas can be bought, still survives. Unhappily this survival is now threatened by competition from the supermarkets of the neighbouring towns and the increased mobility of the villagers that enables them to get there. The numbers of village shops, like those of the schools, are decreasing and leaving a gap in what was once an essential part of village life.

PRESERVED PROPERTIES
Mention is made in the guide of the many preserved properties found in or around the villages. Some of these are in the keeping of the National Trust. The care of others usually rests either with statutory bodies such as the Department of the Environment and the Local Authority or with voluntary societies and individuals. Thus, preserved for all time, are parts of our heritage that include castles, stately homes, ancient cottages, museums, monuments, forests, lakes, gardens, huge tracts of land, and many miles of coastline.

VILLAGE GREENS
The green, variable in size and shape, often dates from medieval times and continues to serve as the hub of social and recreational activity. In

some parts, Cornwall in particular, village greens are a rarity. Elsewhere, however, the green is much in evidence and the character of the village devolves from it. Some greens are vast expanses like those in the very different villages of *Long Melford*, Suffolk, and *Frampton-on-Severn*, Gloucestershire. Others are small, providing room for little more than perhaps a prominent tree or the war memorial.

The shape of the green, like the size, varies from one village to the next although a surprising number are triangular in shape. The provisions of the various village greens are widespread. Ducks and geese wander around the ponds that grace many of them. Often the green is the venue for May Day dancing, and sometimes greens such as that at *Welford on Avon*, Warwickshire, surround a permanent maypole. Grimmer reminders of the past are seen where the lock-ups (known as roundhouses or blindhouses) have been preserved, or the stocks such as those to be found at *Aldbury*, Hertfordshire, and *Abinger*, Surrey.

The village green conjures up thoughts of cricket, a sport now more than 200yrs old and often played on greens central to the village like that in *Tilford*, Surrey. Proof that cricket continues to be a popular pastime is the size of the entry for the National Inter Village Competition of 1982, a total of 650 villages competing. Ironically the winners of this competition for the past 3yrs came from Wales, a country more associated with rugby than cricket.

CUSTOMS AND TRADITIONS

Many villages preserve customs of great age, some of them believed to date from pagan times. One of the most common traditions still in force is the Beating the Bounds Ceremony. This takes place, normally, on Holy Thursday when the clergyman and boys of the village perambulate the bounds of the village, beating the perimeter with peeled willow wands. The May Day ceremonies, also widely practised, originate from pre-Christian times and often incorporate maypole and Morris dancing. Well Dressing, common to many Derbyshire villages, is not confined to Derbyshire for it also takes place at villages such as *Bisley*, Gloucestershire. Some villages practice traditional ceremonies unique to themselves, such as that of the Horn Dance in *Abbots Bromley*, Staffordshire or the quaint bottle-kicking ceremony at *Hallaton*, Leicestershire.

DISTINCTIVE FEATURES

Among the thousands of English villages there are those that claim possession of a distinctive feature, something that no other village can match. Among those that figure in this guide is *Porlock*, Somerset, where Culbone Church is said to be the smallest medieval church in England. The lovely school building attached to the almshouses at *Ewelme*, Oxfordshire, is claimed to be the oldest of its kind to function, continuously, as a school. The timber-framed town hall at *Fordwich*, Kent, is believed to be the smallest town hall in England. At *Alfriston*, Sussex, the thatched oak-framed 14thC clergy house is unique.

Geddington, Northamptonshire, boasts the best-preserved of the three surviving Eleanor Crosses in England. *Laxton*, Nottinghamshire, is the only village where the medieval system of open-field farming still operates. The final superlative, not of fact but of opinion, comes from the politician and journalist William Cobbett (1763–1835) who visited many of the villages in this guide during the course of his 'Rural Rides'. On arrival at the village green of *Tilford*, Surrey, he described the oak tree that still stands there as 'by far the finest tree that I ever saw in my life'.

AREA ONE

Cornwall, Devon and Somerset

T he villages mentioned in this section are found in counties as beautiful and yet diverse as any in England. Cornwall, rich in coastal scenery, occupies the extreme SW of England, a region that abounds in ancient crosses, holy wells and Arthurian legend. Inland Cornwall includes Bodmin Moor, a peaty upland where from Brown Willy (1,375ft), the highest hill in the county, there are spectacular views across both Cornwall and Devon. Minerals such as tin, copper and lead are mined, and china clay for pottery is a considerable source of income. Among the coastal villages are *Tintagel*, legendary birthplace of King Arthur; *Boscastle*, with its lovely harbour; *Polperro*, where the smuggler's museum reminds the visitor of the main occupation of former villagers; and *Morwenstow*, with the cliffside hut in which R. S. Hawker composed his poetry.

Devon, like Cornwall, abounds in fine coastal scenery. To the NE of the county is Exmoor, the 'Lorna Doone country' and the home of red deer and a native breed of pony; and to the S is the lofty expanse of Dartmoor, noted for its wildness and crowned by blocks of granite known as tors. Contrasting with these rugged coastal and upland areas, the sheltered parts of Devon give way to pastureland and acres of rich red soil interwoven with a complex pattern of winding high-banked country lanes. This part of Devon specializes in the production of cream and cider. Among the most picturesque of its coastal villages is *Clovelly*;

CORNWALL

Touring Centres

1 St Ives
2 Bodmin
3 Bideford
4 Exeter
5 Minehead
6 Wells

while inland moorland villages such as *Widecombe in the Moor* contrast with more sheltered places like *Broadhembury* and *North Bovey*.

Somerset, washed by the Bristol Channel to the N and with Dunkery Beacon (1,707ft), near *Luccombe*, as its highest point, specializes in dairy-farming and cider-making. In the N are the Mendip Hills with the famous Cheddar Caves; further W are the Quantock Hills and Exmoor where the tiny village of *Oare* has been immortalized in R. D. Blackmore's Lorna Doone. At *Montacute* there is a gracious National Trust house; and at *South Cadbury* memories of King Arthur are rekindled by Camelot Hill.

Stone is the traditional building material of the West Country, ranging from the granites of Cornish villages to the mellow golden stone quarried from Ham Hill and employed in Somerset buildings such as those seen in *Montacute* and *Hinton St George*. Many cottages, particularly in Devon, are built of thick cob walls, thatched and colour washed, like those of *Broadhembury*.

SOMERSET

DEVON

All the tours in this area could be accomplished in a long day's drive, except Tour 2 which takes one and a half to two days. **Tour 1** (120 miles) includes four villages in the toe of Cornwall, taking the motorist on a picturesque route around Land's End. From Bodmin, **Tour 2** explores a variety of Cornish villages in a comprehensive 150-mile trip. Much of the 96 miles of **Tour 3** is on minor roads, covering N Devon and the outstanding cliffside village of *Clovelly*. **Tour 4** (104 miles) covers the edge of wild and desolate Dartmoor before heading E to *Broadhembury*. **Tour 5** runs along the N Somerset coast between Exmoor and the Quantocks in an attractive 97-mile trip. **Tour 6**, in a 110-mile route from Wells through rich Somerset farmland, takes in golden-stone villages and the spectacular *Cheddar* Gorge.

Touring centre

St Ives, Cornwall

Hotels: **Carbis Bay,** Carbis Bay, *Tel.* **(0480) 795311 ❷**
Dunmar, Pednolver Terrace, *Tel.* **(0480) 796117 ❶**

ZENNOR, CORNWALL ★ †

The beauty of this village lies in its remoteness and rugged grandeur, a complete contrast to many of the lusher inland villages of the West Country. The road from St Ives undulates through bare, rock-strewn moorlands, passing a vast cromlech of seven stones capped by a stone 6yds long. This burial chamber, known as the **Zennor Quoit**, lies a mile or so from the road. The village is made up of scattered granite cottages and farmsteads — with the church and inn standing side by side as the focal point.

A famous legend of the village is that of the Mermaid of Zennor. In a side chapel of the **Church of St Senara** stands the Mermaid Chair, on the side of which is the carved figure of a mermaid looking into a mirror while combing her long tresses. The story goes that a beautiful woman used to sit at the back of the church each Sunday evensong, captivated by the voice of Matthew Trewhella, the squire's son. Eventually she enticed him to accompany her to the sea, and the pair set off to Pendour Cove, now known as Mermaid's Cove. They were never seen again, although it is said that on warm summer evenings they can be heard singing a ghostly duet.

On the wall of the church porch is a memorial to John Davey (*died* 1891), claimed to be the last person to have spoken Cornish as his native tongue. There is also a **folk museum** in Zennor with a collection of local implements, working models of tin mines, furniture and archaeological exhibits.

Pub: **Tinners Arms** |Bs|Ra|

MOUSEHOLE, CORNWALL

Memories of the tragedy of December 1981, when the brave lifeboat men of the village gave their lives saving others, are still vivid. But it has to be remembered that along this part of the rugged Cornish coast, deeds of bravery have been commonplace for centuries.

Picturesque granite cottages perch along steep, winding cobbled streets above the tiny artificial harbour, where fishing used to be more prominent than it is today. Many of the older buildings of the village were demolished during a Spanish raid of 1595. Among these was the Elizabethan manor house of Jenkin Keigwin, who was killed by a cannonball, which can now be seen at Newlyn, and whose sword is in Penzance museum.

In the parish **Church of St Paul**, which lies above the village, there is a memorial to Dolly Pentreath (*died* 1777), often claimed to be the last person to have spoken only Cornish, although a tablet outside the church at **Zennor** disputes this (see above).

To the S of Mousehole at **Raginnis** a wild bird hospital, founded in 1928, provides sanctuary for a wide range of both land and sea birds, and can be visited. The South Cornwall Coast Path runs SW from Mousehole, passing **Lamorna Cove**, and then **Logan Rock**, a 65-ton boulder balanced so that it tilts, and on to the **Minack Open Air Theatre**, a beautiful natural amphitheatre on the Atlantic cliffs, where plays are performed during the summer.

A final reminder of the bravery of the people who live in these parts is to record that a Victoria Cross hero, Joseph Trewavas, was born in Mousehole. He won the award during the Crimean War.

Pub: **Lobster Pot** |A|R|Bs| *Tel.* (073 673) 251.

HELFORD, CORNWALL |◆◐|

A pretty though narrow minor road leads from Helston through Gweek, passing wooded glades and occasionally crossing inlets of the River Helford to its estuary on which Helford lies. There is a car park a quarter of a mile above the village, which affords fine views of the river, and in summer cars are not allowed beyond this point. From here there is a short walk down to a ford and a pedestrian bridge, past delightful cottages, some of almost doll's house appearance, before the road loops back to the **Shipwright's Arms**. From here a footpath leads to the Helford boatyard, where there is a coffee and gift shop and where boats can be hired. A pedestrian ferry plies between this point of the river and Helford Passage on the other side.

The Helford River numbers among the most picturesque anchorages in England, and naturally the village boasts a thriving yacht club. Wooded hills crowd down on the river and there are many inlets, among them **Frenchman's Creek**, which provided the background and title of the famous novel by Daphne du Maurier (*born* 1907).

Pub: **Shipwright's Arms** |R|Bs|Ra|

ST JUST IN ROSELAND, CORNWALL |❖|△|†|

If approaching from the W the shortest route to the Roseland peninsula is to take the B3289 and the King Harry ferry across a beautiful wooded stretch of the Fal estuary. There may be delays here in summer and the alternative is the much longer route by the A3078. In any case the area is perhaps best avoided during the high season.

The romantic-sounding name has no connection with roses and probably derives from the old Cornish word *ros*, meaning 'promontory'. However there can be few more romantic places than the lovely sub-tropical gardens of the parish **Church of St Just and St Mawes**. The church lies on the shore of St Just Creek above the broad stretch of water known as Carrick Roads, but it is the garden rather than the church that attracts thousands of visitors every year.

Paths wind through the sloping churchyard through magnificent trees and shrubs, some tropical like the African strawberry tree and the Chilean myrtle that lie among large numbers of hydrangeas, camellias, rhododendrons and polyanthuses. This whole lovely aspect is summed up by H. V. Morton in his book, *In Search of England* (1927):

> *I have blundered into a Garden of Eden, that cannot be described in pen or paint . . . . I would like to know if there is in the whole of England, a churchyard more beautiful than this. There is hardly a level yard to it. You stand at the lych gate and look down into a green cup filled with flowers and arched by green trees. In the dip is the little church, its tower level with you as you stand above. The white grave stones rise up from the ferns and flowers.*

The gardens are perhaps even more beautiful now than when Morton wrote about them, for many of the shrubs were not introduced until 1950.

To the S of St Just in Roseland is the larger village of St Mawes, the tourist centre for the Roseland peninsula. Some rather ugly villas have sprung up in the area, but there are some fine old houses on the waterfront. The well-preserved **St Mawes Castle**, built by Henry VIII in 1542 to guard the harbour, is considered to be among the biggest round castles in England, and is open to the public.

Pub: **Rising Sun Inn** |Bs|Ra|

TOUR TWO
Touring centre
Bodmin, Cornwall

Hotels: **Castle Hill House, Castle Hill,** *Tel.* **(0208) 3009**❷
Westberry, Rhind Street, *Tel.* **(0208) 2772**❷

POLRUAN, CORNWALL |△|†|

There is very little parking space on the quay at the foot of the steep main street, so it is advisable to park at the top and be prepared for a strenuous climb back to the car. From Polruan's quayside there is a regular pedestrian ferry service across the estuary to **Fowey**, and a superb view of the town that was once an important port and now boasts a multitude of crooked cobbled streets. It was described by the sea rat in Kenneth Grahame's *Wind in the Willows* (1908) as the 'little grey sea town that clings along one side of the harbour'. Right on Polruan's quay there is an excellent **guesthouse** close to a pleasant **inn**.

Much of the land around the village is owned by the National Trust. **Pont Pill Creek** is a place of particular beauty. Polruan's parish church, **Llanteglos** (14thC), is 2 miles E of the village in a hollow behind Pencarrow Head, and the well-restored **Churchtown Farm**, beside the church, is also owned by the National Trust.

Pub: Lugger |Bs|Ra|

Guesthouse: **Quayside** |A|R| *Tel.* (072 687) 377.

POLPERRO, CORNWALL |❖|△|★|

This enchanting fishing village lies in a ravine through which the little River Pol flows, bordered by delightful colour-washed cottages. Near the car park above the village (where it is best to leave your car) is an old **water mill**, the site of which is mentioned in the Domesday Book. The heart of the village is a maze of narrow streets, where among the interesting buildings is the **Elizabethan house** of Dr Jonathan Couch, village doctor, naturalist and fossil collector, who practised here for many years in the last century and was the grandfather of Sir Arthur Quiller-Couch. A cellar of one of the other houses has been converted into a **smuggler's museum** — a reminder that in addition to fishing, this part of the Cornish coast was something of a paradise for smugglers right up to a century ago.

Georgian houses stand above the spacious harbour, the entrance to which is so narrow that in rough weather it can be closed by timber booms. In summer months the quayside provides a magnificent setting for the Polperro Fishermen's Choir who perform here. The **Warren**, a mile of cliff above the estuary, has been bequeathed to the National Trust by the novelist Angela Brazil.

Pubs: Crumplehorn Inn |A|R|Bs|Ra| *Tel.* (0503) 72348.

Mermaid Hotel |A|R|Bs| *Tel.* (0503) 72502.

BLISLAND, CORNWALL |❖❖|

Although there has been some modern housing development on the periphery of Blisland — a village on the extreme western edge of Bodmin Moor — its centre remains unspoilt; granite Georgian cottages, shops and an inn surround a village green, which is something of a rarity in Cornwall. Giant sycamore and ash trees once graced the green although recently a number have been felled.

Set in a hollow to the S of the green is the part-Norman **Church of St Protus and St Hyacinth**, celebrated for the painted and gilded rood screen across the chancel and aisles; it is the work of F. C. Eden who was responsible for much restoration in this beautiful church at the end of the 19thC. Another imposing feature of the church is the canopied pulpit, carved with shells and sprays of flowers.

A mile to the N of the village, on **Pendrift Common**, is a natural weather-worn rock of great antiquity that was painted with figures of Britannia to celebrate the jubilee of George III in 1810. A little further to the NE, at **Bradford**, a well-preserved ancient clapper bridge spans the river.

Pub: **Royal Oak** |Bs |Ra|

ALTARNUN, CORNWALL |△|✝|.

Altarnun lies in a valley on the eastern edge of Bodmin Moor. The most picturesque part of the village is by the river, where an old pack-horse bridge links the church on one bank and a group of cottages on the other. The village name derives from the 'altar of St Non', a saint of the 6thC said to be the mother of St David and remembered in Wales through the Holy Well of St Non near St David's Cathedral.

The **Church of St Nonna** as it now stands was built in the 15thC and is known as the 'Cathedral of the Moors'. Among the more notable features are the Norman font and 79 benchends which bear the signature of Robart Daye who carved them between 1510 and 1530. The benchends portray both traditional Christian symbols and various aspects of life in and around the village.

In the churchyard by the gate is a Celtic Cross believed to date from the 6thC. Two of the gravestones were carved by Nevil Burnard (1818–78) who later won fame as a sculptor in London. One of his best-known works is the Lander statue in Truro. Burnard also carved a head of the preacher John Wesley (1703–91) — a regular visitor to the village — over the door of Altarnun's Methodist chapel.

Pub: **Rising Sun** |**A**|**Bs**|**Ra**| *Tel.* (056 686) 636.

A row of fishermen's cottages hugging the hillside in Boscastle. Features which are typical of this part of Cornwall are the thick whitewashed stone walls, slate roofs, distinctive chimneypots, small windows and large porches.

BOSCASTLE, CORNWALL ❖ △ ★ ✝

The village of Boscastle lies in two distinct parts. First there is Boscastle's **harbour** — the only shelter for many miles along this rugged Cornish coastline renowned for its fierce seas. In order to visit the harbour it is necessary to park about a quarter of a mile away. Sir Richard Grenville (1541–91), the Cornishman and hero of the battle against the Spanish in his ship the *Revenge*, built the jetty here in 1584. In rough weather sea spray is thrown across the harbour as the incoming tide surges through a nearby blowhole — a truly spectacular sight. The National Trust-owned **Palace Stables** at the head of the harbour were originally built for the carthorses that worked the capstans used in busier times, and nearby is a **museum of witchcraft**.

In contrast to this rugged scene, the actual village of Boscastle is a placid place. It lies off the main road behind the harbour in the wooded hillside, the steep main street straddled by old houses. A grassy site was once occupied by a castle owned by the Bottreaux family, and it was this castle which gave the village its name. **Forrabury Church**, partly Norman, lies on the cliffs to the W of the harbour and overlooks a common, which, in feudal days, was divided into strips so that agricultural holdings could be shared out fairly.

The poet and novelist Thomas Hardy (1840–1928) wrote of Boscastle as 'Castle Boterel' in his novel *A Pair of Blue Eyes* (1873).

Pubs: **Wellington Hotel** |**A**|**R**|**Bs**| *Tel.* (084 05) 203.

    Napoleon |**Bs**|**Ra**|

TINTAGEL, CORNWALL |❖|△|★|⚬•|

Legendary birthplace of King Arthur, this long, straggling village is of no particular distinction apart from a handful of buildings in the centre. Among them is the **Old Post Office**, which was reopened by the National Trust in 1972 after it had been in disuse for almost 100yrs. This beautiful building was constructed in the 14thC at a time when the Black Prince (1330–76) was the owner of Tintagel Castle. Much later, in Victorian times, the building was used as the village post office and remains furnished as such, with Victorian exhibits.

The English version of the legend of King Arthur owes most to Sir Thomas Malory (*died* 1471), a Warwickshire landowner who wrote *Le Morte d'Arthur* during the final 20yrs of his life, which he spent in Newgate prison after conviction for theft, rape and attempted murder. Malory's literary romance intermingles fact with fiction, and its subject, the story of Tintagel, later became the topic of major works by Tennyson and Swinburne among many others.

In 1933 a **Hall of Chivalry** was built in the centre of the village to contain symbolic objects associated with King Arthur and the Knights of the Round Table. A smaller adjoining hall, known as **King Arthur's Hall**, houses a solid oak Round Table of 13 segments, with the names of the Knights carved upon it in letters of gold. Copies of the banners and shields of the Knights are hung around the hall and on the walls are oil paintings by William Hatherell, which illustrate various events in the lives of Arthur, Queen Guenevere and the Knights.

The ruins of **Tintagel Castle** lie on a peninsula known as 'the Island' to the NW of the village. These are the ruins of a Norman castle, but the castle site is connected with King Arthur and the outline remains of a Celtic monastery (*c.*AD500) can be seen here. Below the castle is a cave known as **Merlin's Cave**, allegedly the actual place of King Arthur's birth. Five miles from Tintagel, near Camelford, is **Slaughter Bridge** where Arthur fought Mordred:

> *Striking the last stroke with Excalibur*
> *Slew him, and, all but slain himself, he fell.*

Pub: **Atlantic View Hotel** |**A**|**R**|**Bs**| *Tel.* (084 04) 221.

PORT ISAAC, CORNWALL |❖|△|

A jumble of fishermen's cottages, many whitewashed with slate roofs, flank the hill that descends sharply to the harbour. Similar cottages, bedecked with window boxes full of flowers, lie in tiers along narrow lanes that diverge from the main street. Some of the cellars where fish used to be stored and salted for export still exist, and a little stream flows down through the village to the sea. The heart of Port Isaac has remained unchanged over the centuries; unspoilt either by modern housing development (except for a certain amount above the village) or by traffic (cars must be left at the top of the hill).

The **harbour**, a narrow inlet between steep cliffs, once boasted a Tudor quay and breakwater, but these have now been replaced by more solid sea walls. A long stone warehouse by the harbour's side is still used by the dwindling number of Port Isaac fishermen.

The National Trust owns part of the coast to the W of the village, including Portquin and Doyden Castle. It seems there is no evidence for the legend that a fishing fleet from Portquin once put out to sea and never returned. Nevertheless today **Portquin** comprises little more than derelict cottages and a few others that have been converted into holiday villas.

Doyden castle, a little octagonal, red-brick folly on the headland above Portquin, commands a magnificent view. It was built in 1820 by a Wadebridge merchant as a summerhouse for entertaining his friends, and today the National Trust lets it out to holidaymakers.

Pubs: **Castle Rock Hotel** |**A**|**R**|**Bs**|**Ra**| *Tel.* **(020 888) 300.**

   Golden Lion |**Bs**|**Ra**|

ST MAWGAN, CORNWALL |△|✝|

Situated a few miles from the W coast of Cornwall, St Mawgan can only be approached by narrow lanes, and the centre of the village takes some finding. However, the effort is well worthwhile. Church, school and inn stand near a ford forming the focal point of this little village of stone cottages; the whole nestling in a green, sheltered valley.

   The **Church of St Mawgan and St Nicholas** was begun in the 13thC but extensively restored in the 19thC. Within the church are monuments to members of the Arundell family, who were responsible over the years for financing many of the rebuilding programmes. Other interesting aspects of the church's interior include the stained glass window with figures of the patron saints and a letter of thanks from King Charles I to the loyal people of Cornwall.

   To the E of the church is a beautiful memorial rose garden where in summer the roses that cling to the E wall form an arbour. A notice in the church and a tablet outside recall how nine men and a boy were found frozen to death in a boat that drifted on to Tregurrian beach in 1846.

   On the cliffs to the NW of the village are the National Trust-owned **Bedruthan Steps** — a dramatic cliff staircase that once had to be closed for reasons of safety but was reopened in 1974.

Pub: **Falcon Inn** |**A**|**Ra**| *Tel.* **(063 74) 225.**

A view of Port Isaac's narrow harbour, with the long stone fish warehouse visible on the right-hand side of the picture.

Touring centre

Bideford, Devon

Hotels: **Royal**, Barnstaple Street, *Tel.* **(023 72) 2005** ❷
Riversford, Limers Lane, *Tel.* **(023 72) 4239** ❶

CLOVELLY, DEVON

❖ △ ❖

This picturesque, world-famous coastal village is best avoided in the height of summer as it tends to be overwhelmed by tourists. At other times, however, a visit to this quaint little fishing village is a delight. Cars must be left on the National Trust land above the village, from where there are fine views across the bay. The walk to the village leads down a steep cobbled street, between whitewashed cottages with window boxes and wooden balconies, many of which were restored at the beginning of the century by Christine Hamlyn and bear her initials. The Hamlyns succeeded the Cary family as lords of the manor when Zachary Hamlyn built Clovelly Court in 1740, and since that time, they have done much to maintain the beauty of the village which is now the property of the National Trust.

Another of the benefactions of the Hamlyn family is the **Hobby Drive**, which was built by Sir James Hamlyn in the 19thC and provides a wooded coastal approach to Clovelly. It is open to motorists from the A39 during the summer (a toll is payable).

Far below the village is the quay where an inn faces the sheltered circular harbour. About half a mile above Clovelly, the part-Norman **Church of All Saints** and **Clovelly Court** lie close together; and on a hilltop a mile or so to the S of the village stands **Clovelly Dykes**, an Iron Age fort.

Charles Kingsley (1819–75), the writer and Anglican divine, spent much of his boyhood in Clovelly while his father was rector here. *Westward Ho!* (1855), his tale of Elizabethan seamen, did much to bring this simple fishing village to public notice, and there is a monument to Kingsley in the church.

Pubs: **New Inn** |A|R|Bs| *Tel.* (023 73) 303.
Red Lion |A|R|Bs| *Tel.* (023 73) 237.

HARTLAND, DEVON

|△|★|†|

A pleasant sleepy little village in the extreme NW of the county, a sparsely populated agricultural area. Among the buildings that surround the small square in the centre of the village are two attractive inns. One and a half miles to the W at **Stoke**, is the **Church of St**

A typical row of cottages with wooden balconies above Clovelly's picturesque harbour.

A Norman font, intricately carved in stone, which can be seen in the Church of St Nectan at Stoke, near Hartland.

Nectan, surmounted by a 128ft pinnacled tower, on the E wall of which is the figure of the Celtic St Nectan. The tower is the highest in Devon and if you climb the spiral staircase, there are magnificent views from the top. An interesting feature of the church is the **Pope's Chamber** where it was customary for the parish priest to sleep and which is now in use as a miniature museum.

A little to the NE of the church, beyond a copse, is a private house, which was built in the mid-18thC; it stands on the site of **Hartland Abbey**, founded in the 12thC and dissolved by Henry VIII.

It is worth taking the tollroad from Stoke to **Hartland Quay** where there is a good hotel and a bar that supplies cider from local farms. The hotel was originally one of the harbour buildings built in Elizabethan days but abandoned at the end of the last century.

From Hartland Quay there are exciting cliff walks towards Bude in the S and Hartland Point to the N, where on occasions it is possible to visit the **lighthouse.** One mile to the E of Hartland Point is an ancient farmhouse, **East Titchberry Farm,** which with 120 acres including 1 mile of cliff, is owned by the National Trust.

Pubs: Anchor |**A**|**R**|**Bs**|**Ra**| *Tel.* (023 74) 414.

Hartland Quay Hotel |**A**|**R**|**Bs**| *Tel.* (023 74) 218.

MORWENSTOW, CORNWALL |△|†|✛|

A remote village consisting of little more than the beautiful **Church of St Morwenna,** the adjacent vicarage, an inn and a few scattered houses. The church occupies a superb position close to the highest cliffs in Cornwall with a churchyard where the bodies of ship-wrecked sailors are buried, victims of the fierce Atlantic gales that rage along this rugged coastline.

Morwenstow will always be linked with the name of the poet Robert Stephen Hawker (1803–75) who was rector here from 1834 until his death and who was responsible for reintroducing the Harvest

Festival, thus reviving a Service that had lapsed since medieval times. Hawker's concern for those at 'peril on the sea' was so great that he habitually preached in oilskins, determined to be among the first of the rescuers. He buried more than 40 ship-wrecked sailors by the upper wall of the churchyard, using the figurehead of the *Caledonia*, wrecked in 1843, as a memorial. The large **vicarage** near the church was built by Hawker. The quaint chimneys depict various church towers within his parish and over the vicarage door the poet priest placed a stone that bears the lines:

> *A house, a glebe, a pound a day,*
> *A pleasant place to watch and pray!*
> *Be true to church, be kind to poor,*
> *O minister for evermore.*

Hawker is best known for his *Cornish Ballads* (1869) and, in particular, his 'Song of the Western Men', an evocation of the proud, independent and defiant Cornishmen who championed their bishop with the words 'And shall Trelawney die?'

Much of his poetry was written in the little **hut** on the cliff edge which can be found by taking a footpath from the church. The hut with a marvellous view of 60 miles of the finest cliff scenery in Cornwall has been preserved by the National Trust. Perhaps it was here that he composed these incomparable lines:

> *What is my wish? Not that an echoing crowd*
> *Publish my praises on some distant strand;*
> *Not that the voices of some men be loud*
> *With whom a strange and nameless man I stand:*
> *'Tis the fond vision that some Western hand*
> *Will turn this page — a native lip proclaim*
> *Him who loved well and long the rocky land,*
> *Hills of old Cornwall! ! in your antique fame,*
> *Oh, that a voice unborn might blend my future name!*

Pub: **Bush Inn** |**R**|**Bs**|**Ra**|

CHITTLEHAMPTON, DEVON |✝|

There is an air of serenity about this isolated village in the midst of farming country, cupped by rolling hills and only approachable by minor roads that are little more than high-hedged lanes. The **church** with its 114ft pinnacled tower, described by the local historian Professor W. G. Hoskins as 'unquestionably the finest church tower in Devon', dominates the little village and faces a spacious square that slopes down towards a number of pretty thatched cottages and the pleasant inn.

The church, which was rebuilt in the 15th–16thC, was originally built over the shrine of the saint to whom it is dedicated, the Celtic St Hieritha (or St Urith). Said to have only been a young girl at the time of her martyrdom, she was set upon by the people of Chittlehampton who killed her with their scythes, allegedly at a place known as St Teara's Well, at the eastern end of the village, where a pump now stands. St Hieritha is also commemorated by a figure on the fine stone pulpit within the church.

First inhabitants of the village were Saxon farmers who moved into the area around the 8thC, and by settling here gave the place its descriptive name 'farm of the dwellers in the hollow'. Chittlehampton remains remote and detached; there may be prettier villages but few of them can rival its tranquility.

Pub: **Bell** |**A**|**Bs**|**Ra**| *Tel.* (076 94) 368.

Exeter, Devon

Hotels: Buckerell Lodge, Topsham Road, *Tel.* (0392) 52451 ❸
Bystock, Bystock Terrace, *Tel.* (0392) 72709 ❷

A view of Widecombe in the Moor, with the pinnacled tower of St Pancras' Church, nicknamed the 'Cathedral of the Moor', soaring above the village and a desolate expanse of Dartmoor.

NORTH BOVEY, DEVON |✝|

In this isolated village, only approachable by twisting narrow country roads, solid whitewashed thatched cottages lie close to a pretty oak-tree green with the **Ring of Bells Inn**, one of the oldest buildings, set back down a narrow lane.

The village cross outside the church has an interesting history; it is one of many ancient granite crosses that were often used on Dartmoor to mark boundaries or define tracks. This one was recovered from the moor in 1829 to replace the former cross that had been demolished in the Civil War. Opposite the cross is a house with a gabled porch, dated 1728, where as recently as 1943 portions of the original village cross were discovered. In the **Church of St John the Baptist**, which dates from the 13thC and 15thC, the waggon roof and rood screen (both of the 15thC) repay close inspection.

North Bovey is typical of many of the smaller and more isolated villages in rural areas and has a declining population. Six hundred people lived here in the middle of the 19thC — now there are probably less than two hundred.

Pub: **Ring of Bells** |**A**|**R**|**Bs**|**Ra**| *Tel.* (064 74) 375.

WIDECOMBE IN THE MOOR, DEVON |★|✝|∞|

The first thoughts of those visiting this delightful village in the heart of the Dartmoor National Park will probably be of Widecombe's famous fair, immortalized by the ballad of Uncle Tom Cobleigh who, with Bill Brewer, Jan Stewer and others, attended the fair from nearby Spreyton. A **monument** depicting the old grey mare and her heavy load commemorates the event and can be seen on the village green. The inn sign, portraying Uncle Tom and his party in bibulous mood, acts as an additional reminder. Widecombe Fair is held annually on the second Tuesday in September and has recently become very commercialized.

St Pancras' Church, with its lofty pinnacled tower, is known as the 'Cathedral of the Moor' and is said to have been built with 'tin money' — recognition that tin miners who once prospered in the area contributed to the cost of building the tower and the general upkeep of the church. On 21 October 1638 lightning struck one of the tower pinnacles killing four people and injuring 62 others, who were all attending an afternoon service. According to local legend the tragedy began when the devil arrived and after tethering his horse to one of the pinnacles entered the church to claim the souls of 'Widecombe Jan' and others who were playing cards in the church.

Among the buildings in the little village square near the lych-gate of the church is the 15thC **Church House**, a granite building formerly used as a school, but now in the care of the National Trust and in use as a village hall and information centre; **Glebe House**, a 16thC building, also granite, and now used as a gift shop; and the 17thC **Old Inn**.

Signs of prehistoric settlements abound on the moors around Widecombe; there is a fine example at **Grimspound**, 3 miles NW of the village, the site of a Bronze Age hutted village surrounded by a 10ft wide protective wall now some 3ft in height.

Pub: **Wooder Manor Hotel** |A|R|Bs|Ra| *Tel.* (036 42) 240.

BUCKLAND IN THE MOOR, DEVON |✝|

High up on Dartmoor, this village has a wooded setting on a tributary of the River Dart mid-way between Buckfast Abbey, built by French Benedictine monks during 1906–32 on the site of a Cistercian monastery, to the south and *Widecombe in the Moor* to the north. Two miles to the southwest of the village is Holne where Charles Kingsley (1819–75), the writer and Anglican divine, was born.

There is a magnificent view across the moors from the church-yard of **St Peter's**, a little medieval church that stands above and on the fringe of the village, with a remarkable clock face on the tower where the letters of MY DEAR MOTHER are used instead of numerals, a memorial placed by a local family.

The tiny village is composed largely of granite thatched cottages, those in the centre forming a picturesque group astride a bubbling stream. The nearby **Buckland Court** was once a distinguished Georgian manor house, but now an overgrown drive leads up to the building which has been allowed to decay.

BROADHEMBURY, DEVON |✝|

Hundreds of years ago this small village was a prosperous wool town. Now it lies far from the beaten track in enviable solitude, a village of thatched cottages — many with picturesque thatched porches, dormer windows and thick cob walls painted in cream and buff. There is a grand approach to the church between huge chestnut trees, culminating at **Church Gate Cottage** believed to be older than the church itself.

St Andrew's Church has an impressive 100ft tower surmounted by gargoyles. The interior of the 14th–15thC church also has much of interest. There is a memorial to the Revd Augustus Toplady, who wrote the famous hymn 'Rock of ages', and was vicar here from 1768 to 1778 (see **Cheddar**). There are memorials to the Drewe family who were connected with the village for centuries, as well as a fine monument in the Sanctuary to Adrian Moore, a relative of the Drewes, who is seen kneeling at a desk. The church is also noted for its fine barrel roof and ancient font.

A mile to the SE of the village on a wooded hillside are earthworks of what was once **Hembury Fort**; this hillside fort was inhabited *c*.200BC and had earlier been a neolithic settlement.

Pub: **Drewe Arms** |**A**|**Bs**|**Ra**| *Tel.* (040 484) 267.

TOUR FIVE
Touring centre
Minehead, Somerset

Hotels: **Benares, Northfield Road**, *Tel.* (0643) 2340❸
Mentone, The Parks, *Tel.* (0643) 5229❶

SELWORTHY, SOMERSET |†|

The village stands beneath **Selworthy Beacon** (1,013ft) which shelters it from the sea to the immediate north. Near to the Beacon is **Bury Castle**, the remains of a large Iron Age hill fort. There is a car park near to the church at the top of the village and from here there is a superb view across Exmoor to Dunkery Beacon (1,705ft).

The stone exterior of the **Church of All Saints** is periodically coated with a mixture of lime and tallow to protect it from the weather, and this white shimmering building can be clearly picked out for miles from the valleys beneath. Interesting characteristics of the church include the S aisle with a 16thC barrel roof and a late Norman font. In the churchyard there is a portion of an early 16thC preaching cross and two yew trees that were planted by Sir Thomas Acland in 1860. The Acland family still own much land in the area, and in fact it was they who presented several local villages to the National Trust in 1944.

The bulk of the village consists of picturesque thatched cottages set amidst sheltered pastures beneath the church. A large 14thC **tithe barn** stands in the grounds of the former rectory. (An information office in the village gives details of places to explore in the locality.)

PORLOCK, SOMERSET |❖|△|★|†|◆◆|

By the alehouse fire of the **Ship Inn** at Porlock, the poet Robert Southey (1724–1843) penned these lines:

Porlock, thy verdant vale so fair to sight,
Thy lofty hills with fern and furze so brown,
The waters that so musical roll down
Thy woody glens, the traveller with delight

Recalls to memory, and the channel grey
Circling it, surges in thy level bay.
Porlock, I also shall forget thee not.

Today Porlock is perhaps better described as a small town than a village. It lies at the foot of Porlock Hill, where the main road is claimed to be the steepest in England. The **Church of St Dubricius** (13thC) in the centre of Porlock is worth visiting, as is the **museum** with its collection of Exmoor birds, reptiles, and documents relating to local history.

Visitors with time to spare should not miss some of the smaller villages nearby, such as West Porlock, Porlock Weir and Culbone. The road to Porlock Weir passes the hamlet of **West Porlock**, where the claustrophobic beehive-shaped prison, once used to incarcerate prisoners of the Monmouth rebellion, has been preserved.

Porlock Weir is an entrancing place. Three delightful terraced cottages washed in pink, yellow and grey stand across a footbridge spanning the channel between the tiny harbour and estuary where colourful boats are moored. Two hotels stand side by side, facing the shore beneath the wooded hills.

A sign behind the **Anchor** in Porlock Weir points to footpaths which lead to **Culbone** 2 miles away, where there is a **pottery** and a **Saxon church** measuring only 35ft by 12ft, the smallest complete parish church in England. It was at a **farmhouse** near Culbone that Samuel Taylor Coleridge (1772–1834) was inspired by a dream to write his well-known poem 'Kubla Kahn'.

Pubs: Ship Inn, Porlock |**A**|**R**|**Bs**|**Ra**| *Tel.* (0643) 862507.

Ship Inn and Anchor Hotel, Porlock Weir |**A**|**R**|**Bs**|**Ra**| *Tel.* (0643) 862753.

OARE, SOMERSET |✝|👓|

Although it comprises little more than a church and a few farmsteads in a lonely part of N Exmoor, this village is mentioned in the Domesday Book, taking its name from Oare Water that cascades through the idyllic setting of a narrow valley wedged between heather-clad hills. Despite its size, it is interesting to note from the church records that Oare supported a chaplain as long ago as 1225, for in that year 'one Robert of Oare killed Walter the chaplain and wounded his son'.

Inside the **Church of St Mary** there is a memorial to R. D. Blackmore (1825–1900), who brought this wild remote area of Exmoor to life with his romance of 17thC moorland life, *Lorna Doone* (1869). In the novel Lorna is brought up from childhood by a family of robbers, the Doones. She falls in love with an honest local farmer, John Ridd, and while the marriage ceremony at Oare church is in progress she is shot and wounded by the jealous Carver Doone. Carver flees to his death and fortuitously Lorna recovers; but Oare church is only one of a variety of local places that form the background to the story.

The road leading W from the church runs in the direction of Badgworthy Water, Doone Valley, and ruins considered to have been the Doone settlements. The road to the E eventually returns to the main road, passing magnificent scenery on the banks of the river and crossing it at **Robber's Bridge**, yet another place where the Doones carried on their trade. Unfortunately both road and bridge are only suitable for very narrow vehicles.

LUCCOMBE, SOMERSET |△|✝|

The most exciting approach to Luccombe is perhaps by way of the A396 from the lovely town of Dunster and the minor road through

Wootton Courtney which descends sharply to this National Trust-owned village in a hollow. The minor road is single track in parts, but there are passing places. The name of the village is said to mean 'enclosed valley' or 'courting valley', both of which are appropriate, since it lies on the NE extremity of Exmoor with the coast to the north and Dunkery Beacon (1,705ft) some 4 miles to the south.

Picturesque thatched cottages with flower-bedecked porches stand near a swiftly flowing stream which is bridged at the foot of the village. The **cottage** facing the lych-gate of the church dates from 1680 and the nearby **post office stores**, another ancient cottage, faces a larger oval shaped thatched building.

The beautiful **Church of St Mary the Virgin** is partly 13thC, and has many interesting features. On entering the door, immediately to the left, on the N wall, is a memorial to a former vicar, Dr H. Byam, a Royalist who escaped with Prince Charles after the arrest of Charles I and who returned to Luccombe when the prince became Charles II.

NETHER STOWEY, SOMERSET |★|∞|

Nether Stowey lies on the slopes of the Quantock Hills, from where a small stream runs merrily past attractive houses, alongside the village's broadest street. Another narrower street leads up to the First and Last Inn, opposite which is a small **cottage** once loaned by Thomas Poole to his friend Samuel Taylor Coleridge (1772–1834). The poet's stay here was only 3yrs, from 1796 to 1799, so it is small wonder that the villagers scarcely feel he was ever one of them. Nevertheless the **parlour** where he wrote his 'Ancient Mariner' is preserved by the National Trust and open to the public on most afternoons. Coleridge is known to have preached in the parish church, and Thomas Poole lies buried in its churchyard.

Originally a beautiful thatched shelter and clock tower graced the centre of the village, but this was pulled down a long time ago and a less elegant clock tower (1897) has taken its place. From here, **Castle Hill** ascends to earthworks where a Norman castle once stood and which affords fine views. There is a footpath leading from Castle Hill through the woods of the Quantocks.

One of the village inns, the **Rose and Crown**, also has literary associations. Preserved inside are some verses by John Taylor, the 'Water Poet', recording the miserable night he spent here in 1649, pestered by fleas and various vermin, before departing as hastily as possible to Dunster. Happily, today the Rose and Crown is a pleasant place at which to call.

Pub: **Rose and Crown Inn** |A|R|Bs|Ra| *Tel.* (0278) 732265.

EAST QUANTOXHEAD, SOMERSET |✝|

The focal point of this small village near the N Somerset coast is the duck pond and thatched cottage that is separated from it by a neat, circular stone wall. A sign at one end of the duck pond points to a footpath to the beach. Also near the pond is a car park, from where another footpath leads to the **Church of St Mary**, which, with the Jacobean Manor house called **Court House**, stands above the village. On the N side of the church's chancel is a monument to Sir Hugh Luttrell (*died* 1522) and his son Sir Andrew, members of the family that has owned land in these parts over many centuries.

In the porch is an interesting example of a coffin squint, a small aperture in the wall enabling the waiting priest to view the arrival of a funeral cortege. The N wall of the church lies only 10yds from the creeper-clad wall of Court House that stands in well-tended gardens.

Touring centre

Wells, Somerset

Hotels: **Swan**, Sadler Street, *Tel.* (0749) 78877❹
White Hart, Sadler Street, *Tel.* (0749) 72056❷

HINTON ST GEORGE, SOMERSET ⊹|✝|

On arrival at this pretty village it is worth strolling down to the end of West Street, a cul de sac, for a marvellous view of the 15thC **Church of St George** across the meadow. In common with the neighbouring village of *Montacute* most of the houses and cottages are constructed of golden stone transported from **Ham Hill**, which lies between the two villages, giving Hinton St George a golden glow when the sun shines. These houses, many thatched, are seen to advantage in West Street, Abbey Street and High Street where there is a 15thC preaching cross with a carving on one side of the figure of St John the Baptist.

In the **Church of St George** there are many monuments to the Poulett family, among them the tomb of Sir Amyas Poulett (*died* 1537) who is reputed to have put in the stocks for drunkenness none other than the young Thomas Wolsey, later the venerable Cardinal! Among the most treasured possessions of the church is the Norman font, remodelled in the 15thC with panels bearing the arms of the Poulett family, many of whom once lived at **Hinton House**, set in a park of some 1,000 acres s of the village.

A peculiar tradition is preserved on the last Thursday of October, Punky night, when the village children parade through the street with candles chanting 'Gie us a candle, gie u.. light, It's Punky night tonight' — thus re-enacting scenes from the Middle Ages when wives searched for their husbands who had failed to return from an all male 'get together' at Chiselborough Fair.

Pub: **Poulett Arms** |Bs|Ra|

MONTACUTE, SOMERSET |❖|△|✝|

As in *Hinton St George* most houses in this village are built from the golden stone brought from nearby Ham Hill. The narrow main street is flanked by these stone houses until it broadens at a small square, **The Borough**, bordered by more picturesque cottages and the **Phelips Arms**. At a corner of the square is the entrance to Montacute House where there is a car park.

In the **church** there are monuments to the Phelips family who were associated with the village from the 15thC until 1930. From the churchyard you can glimpse the outbuildings of **Abbey Farm**, which include a gatehouse of a former Cluniac priory. High above, on the crown of **St Michael's Hill**, is an 18thC folly tower that occupies the position of **Montacute Castle**, which was built during the reign of William the Conqueror, but has long since vanished.

Montacute House (owned by the National Trust) was built in the late 16thC by Edward Phelips. It lies in a landscaped park with formal gardens, and contains a fine display of 17thC and 18thC furniture, as well as Elizabethan and Jacobean portraits in the Long Gallery and adjoining rooms.

Only a mile or so N of the village is another National Trust property, **Tintinhull House**, the pride of which is the garden. A rewarding time to visit is in July when the sweet-scented Regula lilies are in full bloom.

Pubs: **King's Arms Inn** |A|R|Bs|Ra| *Tel.* (0935) 822513.

Phelips Arms |A|R|Bs|Ra| *Tel.* (0935) 822557.

NORTH AND SOUTH CADBURY, SOMERSET |△|✝|

These two villages lie amidst rich farm land, which generations of old Somerset families have farmed for centuries. Although far removed from the village of *Cheddar*, the Cadburys are renowned for the production of Cheddar cheese, often taking the lion's share of the prizes in agricultural shows.

North Cadbury, the larger of the two villages, has expanded recently but most of the modern building has been carried out with taste. Pride of the village is the Elizabethan **Cadbury Court** and the 15thC **Church of St Michael** that stands beside it. Both buildings are approached along a broad avenue of beech trees, but Cadbury Court is privately owned and not open to the public.

The church, built in the perpendicular style from the same grey stone as Cadbury Court, has a wide variety of interesting 16thC bench-ends thought to be the work of Dutch or Italian carvers. The bench-ends are described in detail in the church guide, and their subjects include The Packhorse, Emblems of St Joseph of Arimathea, and The Cat and Mousetrap said to be the only carving of a Tudor cat and trap in existence.

South Cadbury's claim to fame is its location, immediately at the foot of a fort known as **Cadbury Castle**. A sign near the church points to a footpath leading to the summit of the hill, where legend has it that King Arthur once reigned and where excavations are still taking place. Near to the castle is **Arthur's well** and villagers still say that a ghostly Arthur can be seen each Midsummer's Eve riding along the crest of the hills on his way to Glastonbury.

Pub: **Catash Inn, North Cadbury** |Bs|

NUNNEY, SOMERSET |△|✝|

Castles often form an integral part of English country towns, but it is rare to find one in the confines of a small village, Nunney, however, is the possessor of a ruined 14thC **castle** that lies across a small stream from the main village street and is guarded by a moat. It was modelled on the Bastille in France and three of the original corner towers remain. Both Nunney Castle and the adjoining grey-stone manor house are now privately owned.

The castle's demise came about when, as a Royalist stronghold, it was besieged by the Parliamentarians. One of their 30lb cannon-balls is displayed in **All Saints' Church** on the opposite side of the stream from the castle, and approached by an iron footbridge. Inside the church there is a model of the castle as it must once have been. Although a certain amount of modern building has developed above the village, the central part is made up of charming 16th–17thC grey-stone cottages that border the stream. Beside them stands the attractive inn with its sturdy sign (depicting St George slaying the dragon) spanning the road.

Pub: George Inn |A|R|Bs|Ra| *Tel.* (037 384) 458.

CHEDDAR, SOMERSET |❖|△|★|†|⊷|

The famous **Cheddar Gorge**, to the NE of the village, lies in a narrow, mile-long cleft, straddled by almost vertical wooded cliffs which tower some 500ft above it. The National Trust own approximately 300 acres of this area, including cliffs known as the **Lion and Monkey Rocks**, and **Ebbor Gorge**, close to the Wookey Hole and nearer Wells than

Cheddar, which the Trust claims is the loveliest and most unspoilt ravine in the Mendips.

It has to be admitted that the fame of Cheddar Gorge does mean that the area has become over commercialized and is, perhaps, best visited in the low season. Caves known as **Cox's** and **Gough's** (there is a museum near the latter) have yielded the bones of prehistoric men as well as Roman coins. At another nearby gorge, **Burrington Coombe**, the Anglican divine Augustus Toplady (1740–78) wrote the lines of his famous hymn 'Rock of ages cleft for me' while he was sheltering from a storm.

Close to the village is a **motor museum** and the village centre is graced by a fine 15thC market or preaching cross. Not far away is a whitewashed cottage, now used as a Red Cross centre but formerly the home of the philanthropist and writer, Hannah More (1745–1833), who founded Cheddar's first day school and later published her best-known work *Coelebs in Search of a Wife* (1809) . The 14th–15thC **church** has an imposing tower and contains a fine 15thC pulpit carved in stone. The area is famous for the cheese made in local farmhouses since the 12thC, but which is now only a modest cottage industry.

Pubs: **Gordons Hotel** |**A**|**R**|**Bs**|**Ra**| *Tel.* (0934) 742497.

Market Cross Hotel |**A**|**R**|**Bs**|**Ra**| *Tel.* (0934) 742264.

Sheer, heavily wooded cliffs tower above the lakes and lakeside cottages at Cheddar Gorge.

Dorset, Wiltshire, Hampshire and Berkshire

Pleasant holiday resorts overlook Lyme Bay and Weymouth Bay on the coastline of Dorset, a county that is low lying apart from its central chalky heights. Dorset depends on cattle and sheep farming as well as the quarrying of marble and stone used for building. This is Thomas Hardy country, unspoilt and much as it was when the novelist lived in his cottage near *Puddletown* and wrote *Far from the Madding Crowd*. Among the places listed in Dorset are the lovely model village of *Milton Abbas*; Giant's Hill with its 180ft carved figure that dominates *Cerne Abbas*; and *Abbotsbury* where the climate permits the cultivation of sub-tropical plants.

A large part of S Wiltshire is occupied by the huge Salisbury plain, while to the NE are the Malborough Downs and Savernake Forest. The county's chief crop is wheat and there is much pasture land. Avebury and Stonehenge are prehistoric monuments as famous as any found in England. Among the many picturesque villages are the National Trust-owned *Lacock*; and *Castle Combe*, the scene chosen for the filming of *Dr Doolittle*.

The English Channel washes Hampshire's coast and the SW of the county incorporates the New Forest, the royal hunting-ground in Saxon times later enlarged by William the Conqueror. Further N are the Hampshire Downs where sheep are reared and, in the lower parts, cattle are pastured and wheat, hay and fruit are grown.

In the N of Berkshire, which lies S of the River Thames, are the Lambourn Downs, where race horses from the stables nearby are trained. A large area to the E is occupied by Windsor Great Park, a wooded park with magnificent gardens. To the extreme S is Inkpen Beacon, more than 1,000ft in height, in the shadow of which is the little village of *Combe*. Berkshire relies heavily on agriculture, and the area around Faringdon is noted for the rearing of pigs.

Within this widespread area building styles and materials vary enormously. Dorset, in particular, has many cottages built of cob, a mixture of clay, chalk, gravel and straw, coated in lime or plaster to form thick walls such as those seen at *Milton Abbas*. Thatch is in evidence everywhere, and *Wherwell* is one of the villages where thatched black and white timbered cottages predominate. At *Lacock* there is a contrast of styles and periods, stone-built and stone-roofed houses mingling with white-washed half-timbered houses and red-brick cottages.

All the tours in this area can be accomplished in one day if time is short but in most cases an overnight stop would make the trip more enjoyable. **Tour 7** links six typical Dorset villages in a round-trip of 117 miles passing along the coast and through rolling countryside that has changed little since Thomas Hardy's day. Starting at the historic town of Salisbury, **Tour 8** straddles Wiltshire and Hampshire in a 125-mile route much of which passes through the New Forest. **Tour 9** (81 miles) takes the motorist through five recommended Wiltshire villages including the historically important village of *Avebury*; part of the route borders Salisbury Plain. Further E, **Tour 10** is a long day's drive covering 105 miles and comprising seven Hampshire and Berkshire villages known for their picturesque thatched cottages and culminating at *Hambledon*.

Touring centres

35

Touring centre

Dorchester, Dorset

Hotels: **Kings Arms**, High East Street, *Tel.* (0305) 65353❸
Antelope, South Street, *Tel.* (0305) 63001❷

CERNE ABBAS, DORSET |†|

Half a mile to the N of the village is **Giant's Hill** where the figure of a naked man has been cut into the chalky hillside. The **Cerne Giant**, 180ft in height and grasping a club that is more than 100ft long, is a fertility figure believed to date from Roman times, and up until a century ago local women obeyed the superstition that sleeping near the figure would cure infertility. Above the giant is a rectangular earthwork known as the **Trendle**, once the scene of maypole dancing and still the venue for Morris dancing on May Day.

Within the village all that remains of the 10thC Benedictine **Cerne Abbey** is the **Abbot's Porch** with a fine oriel window, once the entry to the Abbot's Hall, a two-storey guesthouse and a barn.

The medieval **church** has an E window made of glass believed to have come from the abbey. In the burial ground where the Abbey church once stood is **St Augustine's Well**, a spring, which according to legend, ·yielded water when the saint prayed for it for baptismal purposes.

In the heart of the village there are a number of timber-fronted Tudor houses and colour-washed thatched cottages. Among the pleasant inns is **New Inn** in Long Street, an early 18thC building.
Pub: New Inn|**A**|**Bs**|**Ra**| *Tel.* (030 03) 274.

WHITCHURCH CANONICORUM, DORSET |†|

This village, sometimes spelt Whitechurch, lies in the Marshwood Vale, renowned for its oak trees and sheltered by hills from Lyme Bay, where, at Charmouth in AD831, hordes of marauding Danish pirates landed, killing hundreds of Christians, among whom may well have been the church's patron saint, St Wite. The **Church of St Candida and Holy Cross** (Candida is the name given to the lady of the West Country formerly known as Wite or Wita) contains one of only two shrines that remain intact in an English church.

The church guide, written by Christine Waters in 1980, gives a wealth of detailed information about Whitchurch in an attempt to solve the mystery of 'Who was St Wite?' It records the discovery in 1900 of a lead casket bearing the inscription 'HIC REQESCT RELIQE

SCE WITE' ('Here rest the relics of St Wite'). Within the casket were the bones of a small woman about 40yrs of age; possibly a Saxon woman martyred on Chardown Hill. The saint may well have lived the life of a hermit, sustained by a well that still exists on the slope of a hill at nearby Morcombelake. After her martyrdom pilgrims flocked to the shrine of St Wite to pray or to be healed by thrusting their injured limbs into the shrine.

The village contains many attractive whitewashed or yellow-stone thatched cottages and at neighbouring **Marshwood**, in the centre of the vale, is the **Shave Cross Inn** where pilgrims on the way to the shrine rested or sought sanctuary. The inn has served Whitchurch as a hostelry since the 14thC, a place visited by countless pilgrims who flocked to the shrine of St Wite, whose mystery is summed up in the lines of Walter de la Mare:

> *But beauty vanishes; beauty passes;*
> *However rare — rare it be;*
> *And when I crumble, who will remember*
> *This lady of the West Country?*

Pub: **Shave Cross Inn, Marshwood** |**Bs**|**Ra**|

ABBOTSBURY, DORSET |△|✝|

This village shelters in a valley about a mile from the coast. At the E end is the 15thC **Church of St Nicholas**, from where there is a good view of the only surviving wall of a 12thC **abbey** outbuilding and the huge tithe barn that was once Abbey property. A sign points to the **swannery**, established by the monks in the late 14thC, where today more than 500 swans, as well as wild geese and duck, can be seen. Crowning the hill above is the little 15thC seamen's Chapel of St Katherine. But perhaps the village's greatest attraction lies to the W, where sheltered frost-free **gardens** are renowned for sub-tropical trees, camellias, magnolias, azaleas and a great variety of wild plants.

The main street of the village itself is straddled by sturdy cottages constructed from local stone. The minor road that leads NE out of the village across Black Down climbs steeply to **Hardy Monument**, preserved by the National Trust. There is a magnificent view from this huge tower, erected in 1846 in memory of Vice Admiral Hardy, Nelson's flag captain at Trafalgar.

Pub: **Ilchester Arms** |**A**|**R**|**Bs**|**Ra**| *Tel.* (030 587) 243.

CORFE CASTLE, DORSET |❖|△|★|✝|

The castle dominates the village from the hill above and a good overall view of it is obtained from the car park. It is best to park here for the streets are narrow with few alternative parking places. Local grey Purbeck stone was used for building both the castle and the shops, inns and cottages that lie below. Strolling down from the car park the first inn to be seen (on the left) is the **Fox Inn**, built in 1568 and claimed to be the earliest of the many old village inns.

In medieval days Corfe Castle was an important centre for the marble carving industry, and each Shrove Tuesday the Ancient Order of Marblers and Stonecutters meet at the town hall and then proceed to the Fox Inn, performing a variety of traditional activities in between. Further down the street from the Fox is another delightful old pub, the **Greyhound** (dating from 1773) which, together with the larger **Banks Arms**, faces the **Church of St Edward**.

The church has a 15thC tower, but most of it was rebuilt in the 19thC. It contains an inscription which reads: 'Edward the Martyr

King of Wessex treachourously stabbed at Corves gate in AD978 by his stepmother Elfrida'. Edward died with a knife in his back; killed either by Elfrida or at her instigation so that her son, Ethelred the Unready, should come to the throne. Edward was only 17, and in AD986 Elfrida attempted to expiate her sin by building a priory at **Wherwell** in Hampshire. A statue to the martyred king stands prominently on the E end of the church roof.

The **castle** was not built until almost 100yrs later and ranks among the most spectacular ruined castles in England. It, too, has a

Strategically perched on a hill, Corfe Castle was an important stronghold from the 11thC to the 17thC. Its history was one of treachery and bloodshed until it was blown up by the Roundheads. Today the brooding ruins are a most impressive sight.

history of bloodshed; it was in the dungeons that King John starved 22 French noblemen to death for supporting his nephew's claim to the throne. The castle remained proudly intact for more than four centuries after John's death, but in 1646 as a Royalist stronghold it was reduced to ruins by the attacking Roundhead troops. A model of it as it was originally can be seen in West Street (near the Fox Inn) and there is a **museum** of local interest in the town hall.

Pubs: Banks Arms |**A**|**R**|**Bs**|**Ra**| *Tel.* (0929) 480206.

     Fox Inn |**Bs**|**Ra**|

MILTON ABBAS, DORSET |△|★|†|

Thatched, well-spaced, whitewashed cottages straddle a broad hillside street where well-tended lawns separate the street from the dwellings. This model village was planned in the 1770s by the Earl of Dorchester to stand a mile from the original market town, which he had ordered to be demolished because it spoiled the view from his recently acquired house. In addition to the cottages the village boasts some older re-erected **almshouses**, the 18thC **Church of St James**, a thatched inn the **Hambro Arms**, and a **museum** of local interest.

On the site of the huge 18thC Gothic **manor**, built by the Earl, a **monastery** had been founded in AD938 by King Athelstan; shortly afterwards it became the original **Milton Abbey**. When the Earl built his mansion much of the abbey was razed to the ground, although part of the house incorporates the 15thC **Abbot's Hall** and the 14th–15thC **church** exists alongside it. The abbey house is now a school that may only be visited during the school holidays but the church is open throughout the year.

Turf steps climb into the woods from the abbey to reach the little Saxon **Chapel of St Katherine**, which was rebuilt by the Normans. The surrounding park, with an artificial lake and woodland backing, was landscaped by Capability Brown (1715–83).

Pub: **Hambro Arms** |A|Bs|Ra| *Tel.* (0258) 880233.

PUDDLETOWN, DORSET |△|†|◆◦|

Puddletown is one of several pretty villages that lie on or near the River Piddle. Other names associated with the river are Piddletrenthide (nearest to the source of the river at Alton Pancras), Piddlehinton, Tolpuddle, Alfpuddle, Briantspuddle and Turnerspuddle. The original name of this village was Piddletown. However, for reasons of propriety, a County Council Debate some 30yrs ago decreed that the name Puddletown should thenceforth be used.

In the village square there are a number of picturesque thatched cottages. The **church**, which is mainly 15thC but has Jacobean furnishings and a late Norman font, incorporates a chapel with interesting monuments to the Martyn family.

Puddletown forms the background for Thomas Hardy's *Far from the Madding Crowd*, and a little out of the village on the Piddlehinton road there is a farmhouse which Hardy used as a model for Everdene's house Weatherby Farm.

The **cottage** where Hardy was born and wrote much of his work is owned by the National Trust and lies near the Dorchester road. This thatched cottage was built by Hardy's grandfather in 1800 and Dorset's best-known writer described it thus:

> *It faces west and round the back and sides*
> *High beeches, bending, hang a veil of boughs,*
> *And sweep against the roof.*

The room where Hardy was born in 1840 and the one in which he wrote *Far from the Madding Crowd* in 1874 can be seen.

In Puddletown Forest is the **Rhododendron Mile**, where the bushes planted either side of the road are best seen in spring. **Tolpuddle** lies 3 miles away, with its National Trust-preserved **Martyr's Memorial** to the farm labourers who were cruelly transported to Australia in 1834 for asking for a living wage. Public outrage saw to it that they were pardoned. The sycamore tree where they first met is preserved to remind us of the event.

Pubs: **Kings Arms** |A|Bs|Ra| *Tel.* (030 584) 335.

Salisbury, Wiltshire

Hotel: Red Lion, Milford Street, *Tel.* (0722) 23334❸
Cathedral, Milford Street, *Tel.* (0722) 20144❷

GREAT WISHFORD, WILTSHIRE ⟨†⟩

The very name of the village has a magical ring about it, and on arrival the visitor will not be disappointed. Great Wishford is a placid place. It is approached by leaving the busy A36 and crossing the River Wyle through broad meadows graced by poplars and willows.

The focal point of the village is the parish **Church of St Giles** on whose wall are inscriptions giving the varied prices of bread from 1800 until recent times. The church stands at the apex of the two main streets, and to the left, as you face the church, are some delightful thatched cottages; to the right, is a row of terraced cottages with tiny dormer windows that were founded as **almshouses** in 1628 by Sir Richard Gorbham for four poor people. Sir Richard is believed to have been the last man to kill a wild boar in nearby **Grovely Wood** and he is depicted on his tomb in the church with his feet resting on a boar's head. Another interesting feature of the church is the fire trailer bought in 1728 by the church wardens for £35.

Next to the almshouses is the **school**, founded in 1722 for the education of 20 poor boys and 20 poor girls. From the school the street continues past an interesting, long wall topped by thatch, beyond which is the creeper-clad **inn**.

Oak Apple Day, which is 29 May, is a special day in the village calendar when the ancient rights of the villagers to collect timber from Grovely Wood is commemorated. After collecting green boughs from the wood there is a procession to Salisbury Cathedral followed by celebrations that include maypole dancing and singing.

Pub: Royal Oak ⟨Bs⟩⟨Ra⟩

STOURTON, WILTSHIRE ⟨❖⟩⟨△⟩⟨★⟩⟨†⟩

The road descends sharply to this tiny village comprising, in the main, the trim, stone-built estate cottages of **Stourhead**, the great house and gardens that most people visiting Stourton have come to see.

As you enter the village, on the left, is the pleasant old **Spread**

Eagle Inn where two huge log fires burn during the winter and prints of famous bare-knuckled pugilists line the walls. The inn forms part of a cluster of buildings that include the Stourton Club, the village war memorial, and an excellent National Trust shop. Nearby is the little **Church of St Peter**, from where there is a good view of **Stourhead Gardens**, perhaps the best-preserved 18thC landscaped garden in Europe; lawns, a huge variety of trees and shrubs, temples, obelisks and grottoes surround an artificial lake formed by damming a section of the River Stour.

Both Stourhead House and Gardens are now the property of the National Trust which has charted an 18thC circuit walk starting at Stourhead House and circumventing the lake by way of fascinating structures that include Watch Cottage, the Pantheon, the Temple of Apollo, Bristol Cross and the Temple of Flora. The Trust has also prepared a pamphlet listing the location of the enormous variety of trees and shrubs, some 400 in all, that are to be seen in the garden.

The house contains paintings and a fine collection of Chippendale furniture, and crowning the surrounding hillside is **Alfred's Tower** where King Alfred rallied his troops before his final battle against the Danes. But it is the Stourhead Gardens that will be remembered long after everything else has been forgotten. The form of the gardens has changed much over the years, but they lie in the unchanged setting that Horace Walpole, author and son of the Prime Minister Robert Walpole, described in 1762 as 'one of the most picturesque scenes in the world'.

Pub: **Spread Eagle** |A|R|Bs|Ra| *Tel.* (0747) 840587.

ROCKBOURNE, HAMPSHIRE |†|

Rockbourne nestles in a hollow in the downs with a stream that meanders alongside the village street. Enchanting houses and cottages, many thatched and dating from the 16th–17thC, are approached from the street by crossing a series of small bridges that straddle the stream. The Elizabethan **manor house** at the N end of the village stands amid medieval farm buildings with a 13thC chapel and a great 14thC barn.

The nearby **Church of St James**, restored in the 19thC, contains some traces of the original Norman structure. The memorials to the Coote family include one to General Sir Eyre Coote (1726–83), the distinguished soldier who took part in Clive's occupation of Calcutta and the battle of Plassey in 1757. The church lies on a hill with good views of both the village and the unspoilt, surrounding countryside.

A little to the SE of Rockbourne are the remains of a **Roman villa**. It was discovered as recently as 1942 and has yielded numerous rooms with geometric mosaic floors as well as ancient coins. To the NW is **Martin**, another charming village of thatched houses, which in 1978 was voted to be Hampshire's best-kept village.

Pub: **Rose and Thistle** |Bs|Ra|

BREAMORE, HAMPSHIRE |△|★|†|

The pride of this village is the red-brick Elizabethan manor house and the Saxon church which stands beside it in a magnificent parkland setting. The manor, **Breamore House**, dates from 1583, and although in 1857 a fire gutted much of the interior, fortunately it did little damage to the exterior. Inside the house there is a fine collection of paintings, furniture and works of art, while outside, in the grounds and stables, a **Countryside and Carriage Museum** demonstrates in particular the development of agricultural machinery. Both house and

The well-preserved Cistercian abbey in Beaulieu, founded by King John in the 13thC.

museum are open to the public on specified occasions during the summer only.

A feature of the peaceful little **church**, one of the few complete Saxon churches in the county and believed to date from around AD1000, is the large Anglo Saxon inscription over one of the arches which translated reads: 'Here is manifested the Covenant to Thee'.

A little to the NW of the village, cut into the turf of Breamore Down, is a maze of about 30yds in diameter. Sometimes known as **Miz-Mazes**, these curious cuttings of intricate pattern are occasionally found near religious institutions and may once have been places where monks paid penance by crawling along them on their hands and knees.

BEAULIEU, HAMPSHIRE

The name tells you that this is a 'beautiful place' and the village undeniably lives up to its name with a woodland setting on the Beaulieu River and one of the few Hampshire lakes on its fringe. A Cistercian abbey was founded here by King John in 1204 and the carefully preserved foundations and ruins include the **refectory**, now in use as a **museum**, where a model of what the abbey once looked like can be seen. In the grounds is the **Montagu Motor Museum**, founded by Lord Montagu in 1952, with a fascinating display of vintage vehicles that include racing cars, trams, a Spitfire, and bicycles used by Edward VII and George V.

Two miles S of the village is **Bucklers Hard**, once an important ship-building centre where New Forest oaks were used for building ships of Nelson's fleet. Red-brick cottages, formerly the homes of the shipwrights, flank the single broad street that leads down to the river and the **House of the Master Builder**, now a hotel with a spectacular view. The **Maritime Museum** includes a model of the 64-gun Agamemnon that was built here and took part in the victorious battle of Trafalgar in 1805.

Pub: **Master Builders House Hotel, Bucklers Hard** |**A**|**R**|**Bs**| *Tel.* (0590) 63253.

Touring centre

Bath, Avon

Hotels: **Pratts, South Parade,** *Tel*. **(0225) 60441 ❸**
Fernley, North Parade, *Tel*. **(0225) 61603 ❸**

CASTLE COMBE, WILTSHIRE |❖|△|†|

The name of this village suggests a castle in a valley. The village does indeed lie in a valley and is approached by a narrow, tree-shaded lane, at the end of which is the car park; cars are strictly prohibited from parking in the village itself. So far as the castle is concerned, it has long since vanished; but there is an effigy in the church dated 1270 to the builder of the original castle, Walter de Dunstaville.

Castle Combe is among England's prettiest villages, and in fact 20yrs ago it was chosen as the winner of the coveted title 'prettiest village in England'. The steep main road leads down by way of picturesque gabled cottages built of Cotswold stone to a sparkling stream and arched stone bridge. In 1966 this stream, the Bybrook, was chosen as the setting for the filming of *Doctor Doolittle* and the village took over the temporary mantle of a bustling seaport.

Castle Combe was once a centre for cloth-making and in front of the church is the 15thC market cross with a hipped roof, where the wool merchants once plied their trade. Another reminder of the wealthy wool merchants is **St Andrew's Church** — for records show that it was they who subscribed to the building of the magnificent perpendicular tower and pinnacle in 1434. The 17thC **manor house** in a splendid setting of well-tended lawns and a river is now a hotel. The **Fosse Way**, the Roman road that ran from Exeter to Lincoln, passes near to the village where there are also relics of a Roman villa and cemetery.

Pubs: Castle Hotel |**A**|**R**|**Bs**|**Ra**| *Tel*. (0249) 782233.

White Hart |**Bs**|**Ra**|

BIDDESTONE, WILTSHIRE |†|

Although close to Chippenham, Biddestone is a remote village, only approachable by minor roads, but certainly worth the trouble. On one side of the village street are a number of imposing Georgian houses, fronted by a green and a war memorial. On the other side is the **White Horse Inn**, part of a handsome row of terraced cottages. Just past the inn, on a green, is a large duckpond, and nearby is an old farmhouse with a Georgian gazebo in the garden; perhaps it was once used for spying on village activity or for watching the arrival of the stage coach at the inn.

44

The **Church of St Nicholas** lies a little beyond the village in peaceful surroundings. It is a Saxon foundation, although the building is basically Norman with a sanctuary built in the 19thC. In Cromwell's days it would seem that the inhabitants of Biddestone were somewhat 'standoffish' for, as the church guide tells, a special gallery with an outside staircase was built in the church to accommodate the parishioners of nearby Slaughterford when their church was wrecked. Meetings between the rival villagers on church territory was not, it appears, the done thing!

Pub: **White Horse Inn** |**Bs**|

Cotswold golden-stone houses line the Bybrook in Castle Combe, the location for the film, Doctor Doolittle.

LACOCK, WILTSHIRE |❖|△|★|†|

The entire village, as well as the abbey around which it grew, is the property of the National Trust. Numbering among England's prettiest villages, Lacock boasts a multitude of building styles and a great variety of buildings, none dating from later than the 18thC. Timbered cottages with gabled roofs intermingle with others of stone and red-brick. The **High Street** is broad, but other narrower streets run off it, each with a jumble of attractive inns, shops and cottages.

The Trust's policy is to ensure that local people with roots in the area continue to live here, and to do this they insist that the beautiful village buildings are not sold or let out as weekend cottages for the invading middle classes. An interesting building in High Street is the two gabled timber-framed **Porch House**. Off High Street, opposite the Red Lion, is a massive 14thC **barn** with eight bays. Another little street is graced by the **Angel Inn**, and the nearby **Carpenters Arms** stands in front of King John's Hunting Lodge where cream teas are served.

The 15thC **Church of St Cyriac** was built on the site of an earlier Norman structure; its patron saint was a child martyr of *c*.AD300. In the church is the tomb of Sir William Sharington who in 1539 bought **Lacock Abbey**, originally founded in 1229. Later the abbey fell, literally if the story of the lover's leap is believed, into the hands of the Talbot family. It is said that the Sharington heiress, locked in the abbey tower by her father who disapproved of her relationship with John Talbot, jumped down from the window into the arms of her lover, and was rewarded by being allowed to marry him.

A descendant, William Henry Fox Talbot (1800–77) was the photographic pioneer who carried out many of his experiments at the abbey, and in particular is credited with the production of the first photographic negative. In a 16thC barn at the abbey gate is a **museum** exhibiting his work and equipment.

Much of the abbey house was altered in the Gothic style in 1753, but there is a great deal to be seen that relates to earlier times, a feature of particular interest being the **Mechlin Pot**, a cooking pot dating back to 1500 which was used by the nuns.

Pubs: **Sign of the Angel** |**A**|**R**|**Bs**| *Tel.* (024 973) 230.

  George Inn |**Bs**|**Ra**|

AVEBURY, WILTSHIRE |△|★|✝|

Historically, Avebury must rank as one of the most important English villages. The bulk of the village lies within the circumference of circles of stones, the outer circle being at one time composed of some 100 stones. The stones date from Neolithic times and encircle an area of 28 acres, some of them weighing more than 30 tons. They look like tall upright figures and may have been intended to represent the male and female body at a place where fertility rites were practised.

Avebury Circle has never had the notoriety of Stonehenge, but the antiquarian John Aubrey (1629–97), the first man to claim Stonehenge as a Druid Temple, thought highly of its importance. He persuaded Charles II to visit Avebury after declaring that it 'exceeded Stonehenge as a Cathedral exceeds a parish church'. A diagram showing the various formations of the stones stands in a field near the small Reformed church.

An old coaching inn, the **Red Lion**, stands at the centre of the village of thatched cottages and farmhouses. There is a legend that at midnight a ghostly coach and four draws up at the inn. It is heard but apparently never seen. The nearby **Church of St James** is partly Anglo Saxon, and through the churchyard is the **Alexander Keiller Museum** where objects are exhibited from Avebury and neighbouring places of antiquity such as **Silbury Hill** and **West Kennet Long Barrow**.

Pub: **Red Lion** |**Bs**|

URCHFONT, WILTSHIRE |✝|

Mentioned in the Domesday Book, the name of Urchfont originates from Funta — a spring which never runs dry. Delightful Georgian houses and thatched cottages surround the green and large duckpond; nearby is a William and Mary **manor house** that was once the home of the statesman and orator William Pitt the Elder (1708–78). It is not open to the public and is now in use as a school.

The large cruciform **church**, mostly 14thC, has a 15thC tower and porch, with much 14thC glass and an interesting 13thC font on pillars. In a nearby field lie the **Plague Graves**. Guarded by a rail and overlooked by massive elm trees, the graves, according to legend, are those of two men who died of the plague and were buried by a third who promptly dug his own grave and died.

Pub: **Lamb Inn** |**Bs**|**Ra**|

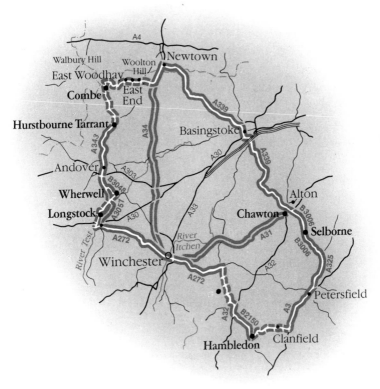

LONGSTOCK, HAMPSHIRE

This village lies astride a quiet minor road where picturesque thatched cottages and a pub are separated from the River Test to the E by lush meadows. Another minor road branches out from the centre of Longstock to cross the river, which is famous for trout fishing, at a point where there is a pretty private house and some nearby ruins of interest. These take the form of a broad channel about 100yds long that runs parallel to the river and is believed to have once been a place where invading Danish long-ships docked.

Pub: Peat Spade | **A** | **Bs** | **Ra** | *Tel*. (026 481) 612.

WHERWELL, HAMPSHIRE |✝|

The location of this charming village, with its many black and white timber-framed thatched cottages, is on a little stream, a tributary of the River Test. In AD986 an **abbey** was established at Wherwell by Queen Elfrida, widow of King Edgar and mother of Ethelred the Unready, as expiation for murdering her stepson King Edward the Martyr (see *Corfe Castle*). The site of the abbey is now occupied by the **Priory**, a 19thC manor house; on a wall near the gate to the house is a notice which recalls how the abbey was destroyed by 'the zeal or avarice of King Henry'.

Only a few ruins of the abbey remain within the grounds of the manor house, next to which is the 19thC village **Church of St Peter**

and Holy Cross. Inside the church are relics of the former building including Saxon sculpture and 14th–15thC monuments; in the churchyard are several strange medieval gargoyles.
Pub: **White Lion** |**A**|**R**|**Bs**|**Ra**| *Tel.* **(026 474) 317.**

Fantastic, distorted heads which can be seen in the graveyard of the Church of St Peter and Holy Cross in Wherwell. Dating from medieval times, they are relics from the original 10thC abbey.

HURSTBOURNE TARRANT, HAMPSHIRE |★|†|✤|

Part of the village lies along the main Newbury–Andover road at the foot of the steep Hurstbourne Hill. However the prettiest part is found along the B3048 to the SE where the school and thatched cottages are fronted by a little stream and faced on the other side of the road by the **Church of St Peter**.

Two remarkable men are associated with the village and in particular with **Rookery Farm**, an old farmhouse that stands on the main road at the southern extremity of the village. Joseph Blount lived here and often entertained his friend William Cobbett (1762–1835), who wrote much of his *Rural Rides* (1830) at the farmhouse.

On the garden wall of Rookery Farm, Cobbett's initials, WC and the date, 1825, are inscribed. This wall is known as the 'Wayfarers' Table' for it was here that the generous Blount would regularly place plates of bread and bacon for the relief of passing agricultural labourers. Perhaps he was influenced by his friend, for Cobbett describes, in *Rural Rides*, how he often gave the price of a meal to wayfarers met on his journeys.

Blount died in 1863, almost 30yrs after Cobbett, and generous to the last if tradition is to be believed, for it is said that he ordered that his tombstone in St Peter's churchyard should be big enough and flat enough for the village children to play marbles on it.

Another notable villager of the past was Anna Lee Merritt, an artist whose painting *Love Locked Out* hangs in the Tate Gallery. A memorial to her on the N wall of the church relates that she was born in Pennsylvania in 1844 and died here in 1930. Her **studio** can still be found in a garden of one of the village houses. Regular painting, craft and sculpture exhibitions are held at the **Bladon Gallery**, which was opened here some 30yrs ago by Augustus John (1878–1961).

Pub: **George and Dragon** |**Bs**|

COMBE, BERKSHIRE |✝|

This is Berkshire's highest village, lying in a remote corner of the county with Hampshire only a mile to the south and Wiltshire a mile to the west. If approached from Inkpen in the north the minor road climbs to a great height, with **Walbury Hill** (974ft) even higher still to the west. Walbury Hill offers one of the most panoramic views in the whole of the south of England and is the location of the largest prehistoric camp, covering some 80 acres, in Berkshire. At this high point on the road, a sign points right to **Combe Gibbet**.

The gibbet stands on the summit of **Combe Hill**, and it was here, overlooking this glorious aspect of the North Downs, that George Broomham of Inkpen and Dorothy Newman of Combe were hanged in 1676 for the murder of two of their children. Few more glorious sites could have been chosen for the man and woman to breathe their last. The gibbet had been specially erected for the occasion and today, it is understood, a local farmer is required to maintain it.

From the gibbet the road drops sharply to the tiny village of Combe which comprises a few farm cottages, a manor and a church. The small 12th–13thC **church** enjoys a tranquil position down a leafy lane close to a hairpin bend in the road. Its main feature is the font: the 14thC base is believed to support a Saxon bowl.

It is said that Charles II and Nell Gwynn used to make visits to Combe, and certainly there can still be few better places to seek peace and solitude after the bustle of town life.

CHAWTON, HAMPSHIRE |△|★|✝|◦•|

The Victorian **Church of St Nicholas** and the 17thC Chawton **manor house** stand in a tree-studded park a little outside the village. Inside the church is a monument with a marble effigy of Sir Richard Knight (*died* 1679). This is of particular interest for two reasons. Firstly, it is one of the few surviving items from the former church that was destroyed by fire. Secondly Sir Richard is the ancestor of Thomas Knight who adopted Jane Austen's brother, Edward, and bequeathed him his estate.

The novelist Jane Austen (1775–1817) was born at Steventon, Hants, and died at Winchester where she is buried in the Cathedral. However she spent almost all the last 8yrs of her life in Chawton, writing her final novels *Mansfield Park* (1814), *Emma* (1816) and *Persuasion* (1818) while in the village. The cottage where she lived and wrote is in the main street, described by Jane in a somewhat uncharacteristic manner in a jingle, declaring 'that when complete, it would all other houses beat'. The cottage is now a museum where the novelist's personal effects can be seen. The donkey cart that she used

'THE WAKES' home of GILBERT WHITE the naturalist 1720-1793

THE OATES MEMORIAL LIBRARY & MUSEUM

THE GILBERT WHITE MUSEUM

for her trips to Alton is on view in the garden. Close to the cottage are some attractive thatched cottages, the inn, and a craft shop.
Pub: Greyfriars |Bs|Ra|

SELBORNE, HAMPSHIRE |❖|△|★|†|❖•|

Selborne's most famous son is the naturalist, Revd Gilbert White (1720–93) who was born here, wrote his *Natural History and Antiquities of Selborne* (1789), and lies buried in the churchyard of the parish church where his memorial window depicts St Francis feeding the birds.

The village clusters around a green, formerly a market place, known as the **Plestor** and described by White:

> *In the centre of the village, and near the church, is a square*
> *piece of ground surrounded by houses, and vulgarly called the*
> *Plestor.... Among the singularities of this place are two rocky*
> *hollow lanes by the traffic of ages and the fretting of water worn*
> *down in many places 16 or 18 feet beneath the level of the*
> *fields....*

Gilbert White's house, **The Wakes**, which lies near the church, is now a museum. Here is his library, together with mementoes of Captain Lawrence Oates (1880–1912), the Antarctic explorer who accompanied Scott to the South Pole, walking to his death in a blizzard — 'a very gallant gentleman'.

A great beech-covered hill (700ft) stands above the village, a favourite retreat of the naturalist and now in the care of the National Trust. A mile to the E of Selborne is **Priory Farm**, the site of an Augustinian priory founded in 1223.
Pub: **Queens Hotel** |A|R|Bs|Ra| *Tel.* (042 050) 272.

HAMBLEDON, HAMPSHIRE |†|

Running through a narrow valley with wooded hills on either side, Hambledon is sometimes credited as being the 'birthplace of village cricket', although there are other villages that dispute this. The ground of the original Hambledon Cricket Club lies some 2 miles away on Broadhalfpenny Down. At a corner of the ground with its thatched pavilion is a monument, engraved with a two stump wicket and a ball between the stumps. E. W. Swanton, the famous writer of cricket, has told how, in the days when the ball passed between the stumps, arguments arose as to whether or not the batsman had been bowled out. Thus a third stump was introduced. Opposite the ground is the 17thC **Bat and Ball Inn**, once the clubhouse of the cricket club, which was formed in 1767 and 10yrs later defeated an All England XI.

The main street of the village is made up largely of Georgian houses and cottages, among them a former coaching inn, the **George Hotel**. Further along the street are vineyards, among the first to produce wine in quantity in England. The short high street leads northwards from the George to the church, flanked by a number of old houses and shops, among them the butchers shop with outward folding shutters which when opened form the counter.

In the churchyard of the flint and rubble **Church of St Peter and St Paul** are the graves of many famous cricketers. This Saxon church was enlarged and restored in Norman times and restored in the 19thC.
Pubs: **Bat and Ball Inn** |Bs|Ra|

The Wakes in Selborne, which was once Gilbert White's house,
and has now been turned into a museum.

Surrey, Sussex and Kent

Parts of the N of Surrey have now been absorbed by the Greater London Council. This commuter county is often described, somewhat scathingly, as the stockbroker belt. Yet despite its proximity to London, Surrey has much delightful wooded countryside in a protected green-belt area. Here picturesque villages, such as *Shere* and *Abinger*, lie in peaceful surroundings, worlds apart from the great city where many of their inhabitants make their daily trip to work.

The south-coast county of Sussex, now divided administratively into East and West, has many popular holiday resorts; among the largest are Worthing, Brighton and Eastbourne. Above these towns are the chalk South Downs that extend eastward past Beachy Head, rising at Ditchling Beacon to 813ft. Sheep are reared on the downs, and further inland there are well-wooded areas and root and cereal crops are grown. Hilaire Belloc (1810–53) spent his boyhood at *Slindon*, writing of the country he loved in prose and verse:

> *If I ever become a rich man,*
> *Or if I ever grow to be old,*
> *I will build a house with deep thatch*
> *To shelter me from the cold,*
> *And there shall the Sussex songs be sung*
> *And the story of Sussex told.*

(From *Complete Verse*)

Among the many beautiful villages are *Alfriston* and *Amberley*, the latter close to the historic Arundel Castle.

Kent in the extreme SE of England embraces the North Downs, S of which is the Weald, a rich area of hop fields, fruit orchards and market gardens that has become known as 'The garden of England'. Along the coast are many holiday resorts, and four of the original Cinque Ports (Dover, Sandwich, New Romney and Hythe). Subterranean passages, cellars and caves are found in the villages of the Romney Marshes, once a haven for smugglers and an area terrorized in the 18thC by the Hawkhurst Gang as well as being the home of Russell Thorndike's fictional Dr Syn.

SURREY
11

WEST
SUSSEX

The older buildings of all three counties are noted for wall-tiling, plain or shaped clay tiles being nailed to wall battens in a variety of patterns. Much white weather boarding can be seen in villages such as *Northiam* and *Smarden*. The row of 16thC and 17thC timber-framed houses of *Chiddingstone* — a National Trust-owned village — remain as unspoilt as any of that period in the country. Kent, in particular, is noted for its many picturesque oast-houses, used for hop drying.

Divided into two circular routes, based on Guildford, **Tour 11** is a two-day tour covering 106 miles and ten villages. Part of the tour follows the high chalk ridge between Guildford and Farnham called the Hog's Back, which affords panoramic views. **Tour 12** (116 miles) is a day trip from the handsome resort of Brighton, taking the motorist to the colourful village of *Amberley* in the heart of the South Downs, and on to *Horsted Keynes*, an ancient village near Ashdown Forest. One long day or a leisurely day and half should be allowed to complete **Tour 13** (77 miles). Starting at Rye, with its delightful cobbled streets, the route explores some of the prettiest villages of the Weald. A 76-mile round-trip, **Tour 14** requires a full day to complete and includes a visit to one of Kent's loveliest villages, *Goudhurst*. A short tour centred on the historic cathedral city of Canterbury, **Tour 15** (53 miles) takes in the picturesque villages of *Chilham* and *Elham*, with their Norman heritage, and the charming riverside village of *Fordwich*, once a bustling medieval port.

Touring centres

11   Guildford
12   Brighton
13   Rye
14   Tunbridge Wells
15   Canterbury

2

53

Hotels: Angel, High Street, *Tel.* (0483) 64555❹
White Horse, Upper High Street, *Tel.* (0483) 64511❸

COMPTON, SURREY |★|†|

The bulk of the village straggles along a lengthy main street close to the Hog's Back. The volume of traffic has increased considerably over recent years, to some extent marring a once peaceful village with a number of picturesque period houses and cottages. However Compton still has two buildings which have to be seen.

Pride of the village is the parish **Church of St Nicholas**, one of Surrey's oldest and loveliest churches. Approaching the church from the main road two immense cedar trees that form its background are visible. They are said to be among the largest cedars in the country. The Saxon tower is of particular beauty and interest; a distinct vertical line can be seen on the tower wall, dividing the work of the original Saxon builders from the later Norman style.

The second building of note is the **Watts Gallery** where some of the works of the painter and sculptor George Frederick Watts (1817–1904) are on display. Perhaps the artist's most famous work as a sculptor is his *Physical Energy*, executed for Rhodes' grave in South Africa with a replica in Kensington Gardens. After Watt's marriage to the actress Ellen Terry had been dissolved he remarried and, with his second wife who was also an artist, is buried in **Watts Chapel** which stands near his gallery.

Pubs: Harrow Inn |**Bs**|**Ra**|
    Withies Inn |**R**|

TILFORD, SURREY |◆◆|

If approached from the Hog's Back, the first sight of Tilford is the large triangular-shaped village green. Dotted around the green are a handful of well-spaced houses and the 17thC inn. The area proved an ideal setting for the filming of that classic village cricket match in A. G. McDonnell's *England their England* when a team of visiting journalists are skittled out by the blacksmith, repairing to the inn for frequent refreshment. Oak trees have been planted at the extremities of the green to commemorate various royal occasions, but these trees are dwarfed by the Tilford Oak, 800yrs old, and considered by William Cobbett (1763–1835) to be 'By far the finest tree I ever saw in my life.'

A number of gracious houses are to be found scattered around the village, among them the 17thC **Tilford House** with a sundial above the front door. It can be found by crossing one of the two medieval bridges that span the River Wey.

Famous people associated with Tilford include the politician, Philip Snowden (1864–1937), who spent the last years of his life here; and Elizabeth Strickland (1794–1875), co-authoress of *Lives of the Queens of England*, who lies buried in the churchyard. The 19thC church is the venue for a Bach Festival held every spring.
Pub: **Barley Mow** |**Bs**|**Ra**|

THURSLEY, SURREY |✝|✦•|

The bulk of this delightful village is found astride a narrow cul-de-sac which winds upwards, petering out at a hillside farmstead. The name Thursley derives from Thunor's Leah, Anglo Saxon for 'a clearing or grove sacred to Thor', so, as the church guide points out, a temple to the old god may well once have existed in a grove of trees somewhere around the village.

The **Church of St Michael and All Angels** lies half-way up the lane, on the right, with a marvellous view from the churchyard across to the Hog's Back. The field next to the church has been preserved by the National Trust in memory of the poet who is buried close to the churchyard wall. The tombstone above this grave is inscribed very simply: 'John Freeman, Poet', commemorating a man who died in 1929; a writer of countryside scenes and events as well as poetry of the Great War that includes these moving lines:

> *There is not anything more wonderful*
> *Than a great people moving towards the deep*
> *Of an unguessed and unfeared future; nor*
> *Is aught so dear of all held dear before*
> *As the new passion stirring in their veins*
> *When the destroying Dragon wakes from sleep.*

Close to the **Poet's Grave** is a well-preserved though somewhat macabre tombstone engraved with the figure of a man pleading mercy from three assailants. Part of the long verse inscription reads:

> *In perfect Health and in the Flower of Age*
> *I fell a Victim to three Ruffians' Rage;*
> *On bended Knees I mercy strove t'obtain;*
> *Their Thirst of Blood made all Entreaties vain.*

The grave, known as the **Sailor's Grave**, is the resting place of an unknown sailor who was battered to death at a nearby beauty spot, the Devil's Punchbowl.

The murder took place in 1786 and was sensational enough for Charles Dickens to refer to it through the lips of Nicholas Nickleby when he and Smike are on their way to Portsmouth:

> *They walked upon the rim of the Devil's Punchbowl and Smike*
> *listened with greedy interest as Nicholas read the inscription*
> *upon the stone which, reared upon this wild spot, tells of a*
> *murder committed there by night. The grass upon which they*
> *stood had once been dyed by gore; and the blood of the*
> *murdered man had run drop by drop, into the hollow which*
> *gives the place its name. 'The Devil's Bowl', thought Nicholas*
> *as he looked into the void, never held fitter liquor than that.*

The murderers were hanged in chains on Gibbet Hill, a lofty point above the Punchbowl.
Pub: **Three Horseshoes Inn** |**R**|**Bs**|

CHIDDINGFOLD, SURREY †

The central point of this large village is the green, surrounded by some splendid houses as well as the church, inn and village store. Outside the store an ancient thorn tree believed to be 500yrs old has been preserved. The village has the distinction of having been the principal glass-making centre in England up to the 16thC, and there are records to show that as long ago as 1227 Lawrence, the first glass-blower, was granted 20 acres of land here.

Strangely the **Church of St Mary** contains only one window made of Chiddingfold glass, the lancet window in the W wall. The churchyard is entered by an interesting lych-gate, beneath which is one of the few coffin rests of its type to be seen in this area. Close to the lych-gate is the barely decipherable gravestone of an 18thC village blacksmith with the strange epitaph:

> *My fire is out, my forge decayed,*
> *And in the dust my vice is laid,*
> *My coal is spent, my iron gone,*
> *My nail is drove, my work is done.*

The name of the author of these moving lines is not known. But the epitaph is not unique to Chiddingfold as a number of others are to be found around the country, among them one at Meavy in Devon.

The **Crown Inn**, opposite the church, was built in 1285, and is among the oldest inns in the country and possibly the oldest in Surrey. It is a large building and was first used as a rest home for Cistercian monks before being established as an inn in 1383, when it was rented for four shillings a year. King Edward VI is believed to have stayed here in 1552, while his men camped on the adjoining green.

Pubs: **Crown Inn** |A|R|Bs|Ra| *Tel.* **(042 879) 2255.**

HASCOMBE, SURREY |△|†|

The beauty of this village is its position for, as the name implies, it lies in a combe or valley. Picturesque old cottages nestle beneath wooded hills, the highest of which is **Hascombe Hill** (644ft). A ridge known as **Telegraph Hill** was the site of a signalling station in Napoleon's time.

The little village **church** is Victorian, although the painted screen and font, relics of an older building, have been retained.

Just beyond the village on the Godalming road is **Winkworth Arboretum**, a 100-acre area of National Trust land where colourful trees and shrubs adorn a hillside, beneath which there are two lakes. In spring the area is carpeted with bluebells and daffodils, amid trees, such as cherries, oaks and magnolias, and a variety of tropical plants.

The charming inn sign of the **White Horse** was painted in 1946 by Gertrude Jekyll, the much respected local artist.

Pub: **White Horse Inn** |R|Bs|

SHERE, SURREY |✝|✦•|

Many people consider Shere to be Surrey's prettiest village. A little willow-clad stream, the Tillingbourne, passes through the centre of the village and many of the timbered houses and cottages were constructed from ship's timbers brought in barges from Deptford to Guildford. Lines of elm trees separate the Tillingbourne from Shere's lovely **church** with its Norman tower and octagonal shingled spire.

Among the many old houses of the village is the **Oak Cottage**, built in 1500 and now a restaurant. Another very old building is the **White Horse Inn**, built originally as a farmhouse in 1475 but later converted into an ale house when the resident farmer started to grow hops. A cut in the ceiling of the bar marks the spot where access to the first floor was once by a barn ladder. Logs burn in two fine fireplaces, one with the original wattle and daub above it; the other with an Elizabethan carved chalk-stone mantle.

Among the famous artists and writers who stayed at the White Horse are Samuel Pepys (1633–1703), J. M. Barrie (1860–1937), Augustus John (1878–1961) and Sir Max Pemberton (1863–1950) who recorded that 'there were sheep stealers, smugglers and brigands at the White Horse, for Shere was formerly one of the wildest parts of Surrey'.

Pub: **White Horse Inn** |Bs|

Attractive period buildings grouped around Chiddingfold's large triangular green and duckpond.

ABINGER, SURREY †|••|

There are two parts to the village of Abinger: on the slopes of wooded Leith Hill is Abinger Common, and 2 miles away in the valley beneath lies Abinger Hammer. At **Abinger Common**, the church and inn face each other, the church fronted by a green with the village stocks and a tiny pond where ducks appear to thrive in abundant numbers.

The figure of a blacksmith strikes a bell with his hammer to mark the hours on this unusual clock in Abinger Hammer.

In 1944 a flying bomb exploded near the church, destroying all but the 13thC chapel which survived almost intact. The church was restored, but in 1964 a further disaster occurred when the tower was damaged during a thunderstorm; this was also restored and today the **church**, which has a lofty setting and fine views from the churchyard, is well worth visiting.

Abinger lays claim to being the 'oldest village in England'. In a meadow a few hundred yards from the church a **Mesolithic pit dwelling**, dating from 5000–4000BC, was unearthed, and excavated in 1950 by Dr L. S. B. Leakey and Sir Edward Beddington-Behrens who believe the settlement to be the oldest man-made and preserved dwelling in Britain.

Abinger has many literary associations. John Evelyn (1620–1706), the diarist, built the **manor house** here. Sir Max Beerbohm (1872–1956) once lived at **Manor Cottage**. E. M. Forster (1879–1970) wrote a collection of essays under the title *Abinger Harvest* (1936). Even the village **stocks** have a literary connection for it is said that Riccabocca, heroine of the Bulwer Lytton novel of the same name, was put in them.

Abinger Hammer is a less placid place for it lies astride the busy Dorking–Guildford road, and has a huge green. Its name derives from the iron-forging hammer in use when the iron industry flourished here in the 16thC. Above some tea rooms (once the site of a forge) and overlooking the main street, a quaint **clock** projects, the figure of a smith striking the hours with his hammer, a reminder of a vanished industry. The clock was erected in 1909.

Pub: **Abinger Hatch, Abinger Common** |R|Bs|Ra|

FRIDAY STREET, SURREY |◆•|

Friday Street is approached through a glorious woodland setting in the heart of Surrey's green belt. The car park lies above the hamlet and after a short descent on foot Friday Street comes into view — first the lake, then a handful of cottages, finally the inn where the metalled road ends and a little footpath leads through the woods. Friday Street, taking its name like the day of the week from Frigga, goddess of Earth and Love, is a remote, enchanting place that was busier in the past. It is believed that the lake was originally one of a number of hammer ponds in the area, providing power for a local iron works.

Many of the cottages are still owned by the lords of the manor, the Evelyn family from nearby Wootton, and are occupied by those who work on the estate. The family are descendants of the diarist and author, John Evelyn (1620–1706), a Royalist and a friend of Samuel Pepys. John Evelyn would have welcomed the preservation orders ensuring the area's tranquillity for, in his days, trees were being felled at an alarming rate to provide timber for fuel, causing him to protest: 't'were better to purchase all our iron from America than thus to exhaust our woods at home'.

The **inn**, which is modern but on the site of an old building, takes its name from Stephan Langton, the Archbishop of Canterbury who defied King John and forced him to sign the Magna Carta. Although it is generally understood that Langton was born in Lincolnshire, local legend disputes this and claims that he was born in Friday Street in about 1150 (he died in 1228). Two interesting pamphlets are available from the inn, *The Story of Friday Street* and *The Story of Stephen [not Stephan] Langton and the Silent Pool*; the latter relates much of the folklore that surrounds one of England's greatest archbishops.

Pub: **Stephan Langton Inn** |R|Bs|

BLETCHINGLEY, SURREY |✝|

The village high street forms part of a busy main road. Heavy traffic hurtles along it but, fortunately, the street is spacious and the houses well set back, so the hurly-burly of traffic does not detract too much from the charm of the place. Among the oldest buildings is the **Whyte Hart Inn**, which dates back to 1388. In a little lane, sheltered from the main road, are a number of picturesque period cottages, among them **Nicholas Wolmer's Cottage**, built in 1552.

The **church** also lies apart from the high street, and in the S chancel chapel a huge monument to a Lord Mayor of London can be seen. Sir Robert Clayton and his wife Dame Martha are dressed in the robes of their office, surrounded by cherubs, urns and painted shields and guarded by a massive iron railing. Sir Robert, the son of a carpenter, built up a huge fortune as a London money-lender and before his death in 1707 had become the owner of the 'rotten borough' of Bletchingley. This rags-to-riches success prompted the Lord Mayor to make many charitable donations. His generosity did not, however, protect him from the satirical Dryden who described him as being: 'As good a Saint as userer ever made'.

Not far from the Clayton tomb is a humble hermit's cell believed to have been occupied in the 13thC by Roger of Bletchingley. An edict declared that according to the King's pleasure a quarter of corn was to be given to the hermit every 8 weeks for sustenance.

Pub: **Whyte Hart Inn** |**A**|**R**|**Bs** *Tel.* (0883) 843231.

GREAT BOOKHAM, SURREY |△|✝|••|

Although in the middle of London's commuter belt, Great Bookham, unlike many neighbouring villages, has retained its village atmosphere. The heart of the village is the narrow main street, a place where villagers shop and gossip just as if London was 100 miles away. In the old oak-beamed inn, the **Royal Oak**, there are records that tell of Bookham's famous cricketing victory when their unfortunate opponents failed to score a run, their final total of one being attributed to a leg bye.

At the foot of the high street is the **Church of St Nicholas**, surmounted by an ancient timber tower, and with a strange memorial near the church door to a man who was killed in Africa by a buffalo. Inside the church there are memorials to the Howard family, a reminder that Lord Howard of Effingham (1536–1624), who commanded the fleet which defeated the Spanish Armada, once lived at nearby **Effingham Court Place**, the relics of which are now contained in a farmhouse.

There are many literary associations with the village. Fanny Burney (1752–1840) wrote her novel *Camilla* (1796) while staying at a house now called **The Hermitage**. Jane Austen (1775–1817) stayed here when visiting her godfather, and is believed to have based the Hartfield of her novel *Emma* (1816) on the village.

Two miles away, preserved by the National Trust, is **Polesden Lacey**, a Regency house built on the site of the country home of the playwright Richard Sheridan (1751–1816). King Edward VII was a frequent guest at Polesden Lacey and King George VI and his bride spent their honeymoon there. Both the house, with its collection of tapestries, furniture, china and paintings, and the extensive grounds, with their open-air theatre, lawns, terraces and lovely rose gardens, are open to the public. Apart from its ownership of Polesden Lacey the National Trust also preserves many acres of land around Bookham.

Pub: **Royal Oak Inn** |**Bs**|

Brighton, East Sussex
Hotels: **Old Ship, Kings Road,** *Tel.* **(0273) 20091❹**
Royal Promenade, Marine Parade, *Tel.* **(0273) 697376❸**

SLINDON, WEST SUSSEX ⛺✝️👓

> *The great hills of the South Country*
> *They stand along the sea;*
> *And it's there walking in the high woods*
> *That I would wish to be,*
> *And the men that were boys when I was a boy*
> *Walking along with me.*

(Hilaire Belloc, *Complete Verse*)

One of the charms of this village on the southern slopes of the South Downs is that there is no focal point. Little streets with cottages of flint or brick roughly form the shape of a square, along which are dotted around a church, a manor house, an inn, a duck pond, a thatched post office and a tree of idleness that lies in a miniature square of its own.

The village was once a retreat for the Archbishops of Canterbury, and the site of the palace where Stephan Langton died in 1228 is now occupied by Slindon House (a private school, which is not open to the public). The flint-built **church** dates from the 11thC and contains a tablet recording that Archbishop Langton was the 'upholder of English liberties in Magna Carta' (see *Friday Street*). Perhaps the church's most notable possession is the effigy carved in oak of Anthony St Leger (*died* 1539) in the armour of the late Wars of the Roses, the only example of a wooden effigy to be found in Sussex.

Slindon stands on the edge of a glorious park of beech woods, part of the National Trust-owned **Slindon Estate** of 3,500 acres. From the duck pond, footpaths lead to the woods which the poet Hilaire Belloc (1870–1953), who spent his boyhood here, loved and wrote about.

Pub: **Newburgh Arms** | **Bs** |

AMBERLEY, WEST SUSSEX |†|

Amberley lies on a hill in the heart of the South Downs, overlooking the River Arun and the flat marshy land that spreads out from the river and is known as the Amberley Wildbrooks. There can be few more colourful villages in England: little streets twist and turn past a variety of cottages; thatched and timbered buildings mingle with others built of flint, brick or stone that peer out behind creeper-clad walls overhung by shrubs and hedges.

On the very edge of this hilltop village are the lovely Norman **church**; the ruins of **Amberley Castle**, a former retreat of the Bishops of Chichester; and the **manor house**, which, standing amid the castle ruins, is privately owned and not open to the public.

At another corner of the village is the **Black Horse Inn** with its spacious restaurant, which over the centuries has fulfilled various functions, among them serving as a barn, a court room and a doss-house for Irish labourers when they were building the railway beneath the village. The largest of the two bars, appropriately named the **Village Bar**, could almost be described as a miniature museum. Some monstrous fish, caught locally, and collections of sheep bells and shepherds' crooks are on display. On one wall there is a letter of appreciation to the landlord from Lord Selwyn Lloyd, one-time Cabinet Minister, written during the course of his walk along the South Downs Way.

Pub: **Black Horse Inn** |R|Bs|

LINDFIELD, WEST SUSSEX |❖|†|

Few villages can boast a finer high street than Lindfield. It slopes gradually downwards from the church at the top to the duckpond and huge green at the bottom; a broad gracious street flanked by lime trees and a blend of Tudor and Georgian houses. Among the most splendid of the older buildings is an **Elizabethan house** behind the church. This was once the home of the Chaloners, a family who flourished here in the 16thC and 17thC, and now forms part of the adjoining mansion, **Old Place**.

The **Church of All Saints**, mainly 14thC with a prominent broach spire 116ft in height, stands squarely at the head of the high street. An old building next to the church carries an inn sign displaying the fact that this was once the **Tiger Inn**; its role as an inn ceased in 1916 when it was purchased to serve as a church house.

At the foot of the high street, near the pond and common, are a number of 19thC houses and villas, among them several one-storey buildings which form **Pelham Place**. These are part of the original dormitory buildings of an industrial school for distressed workers founded in 1825 by William Allen, the great Quaker chemist who was associated with Wilberforce in the movement to abolish slavery.

The common provides ample space for both cricket and football. Cricket has been played here for centuries attested by records such as that of a schoolmaster in 1759: 'left off school at 2 o'clock, having heard the spellers and readers a piece, to attend a cricket match of the gamesters of Mayfield against those of Lindfield and Chailey'. A little later, in 1788, another diarist attending a match at Lindfield Common 'soposed that there were upwards of 2,000 people present'.

Pub: **Bent Arms Hotel** |A|R|Bs| *Tel.* (044 47) 3146.

HORSTED KEYNES, WEST SUSSEX |★|†|

Horstede, mentioned in the Domesday Book, was land given to a

Norman, William de Cahagnes, which accounts for the village name. The village in Normandy from which the knight came, Cahagnes, is now 'twinned' with Horsted Keynes and exchange visits take place.

Set in a clearing of dense woodland near to Ashdown Forest, Horsted Keynes lies in two parts. Around the green are two pleasant inns and some Tudor houses, and a colourful sign on the green itself combines the name of the village with a pictorial representation of the former Norman lord of the manor. Set apart from the green is the Norman **church**, enclosed by earthworks of Saxon origin, and a handful of buildings, among them two medieval cottages. From here a bridle path and a footpath lead off, enticingly, into the woods.

An interesting feature of the church is the miniature 13thC **effigy** of a crusading knight, set in a niche on the left of the altar. It is believed to commemorate a de Cahagnes, possibly being a heart shrine; the heart of the warrior used to be buried in an English church and his body in the foreign land where he fell.

A mile away is Horsted Keynes **station**, the northern terminus of the Bluebell Railway, from where steam trains ply their way nostalgically through a 5-mile stretch of lovely countryside to Sheffield Park. An interesting collection of old coaches can be seen at Horsted Keynes station. At **Sheffield Park** there is a small railway museum, some famous National Trust gardens, and the Wings Haven Bird Sanctuary and Hospital.

Pubs: Green Man|**Bs**|**Ra**|

　　 Crown Inn|**Bs**|

ALFRISTON, EAST SUSSEX　　　　　　|❖|△|✝|

The narrow high street is flanked by many old buildings, some timber-framed with overhanging storeys and strange carved emblems. Among several ancient inns is the **Market Cross Inn**, close to the medieval village cross and once the haunt of the Alfriston smugglers; the 15thC **Star Inn**, adorned with numerous quaint carvings including a figurehead of a ship in the shape of a lion; and the timbered **George Inn**, also built in the 15thC. In addition to the inns are a number of tea and curio shops, making Alfriston a popular tourist centre, best avoided at weekends.

A footpath, signed from the High Street, leads to the **South Downs Way**, a long-distance walk that follows an ancient ridgeway to the W of the village. At the end of the high street is the spacious village green, one corner displaying a mine washed up in the River Cuckmere in 1943. Dominating the green is the 14thC **St Andrew's Church**, a building of such size that it has become known as the 'Cathedral of the South Downs'. The church is built in the form of a Greek cross from local flints, which were carefully selected and fitted to yield one of the finest examples of church flintwork to be found in the country.

Alongside the church and close to the river is the thatched, oak-framed **Clergy House**. Designed for a small community of parish priests, it was built in about 1350 with separate apartments and a large communal dining and recreation hall. In 1896 it was bought by the National Trust for £10 and restored; it is one of the few clergy houses to have survived.

A footpath from Alfriston church leads to **Lullington church**, a pleasant 15-minute walk to one of the smallest churches in England that lies almost hidden in a clump of trees.

Pubs: Star Inn|**A**|**R**|**Bs**| *Tel.* (0323) 870248.

　　 George Inn|**Bs**|

　　 Market Cross Inn|**Bs**|

WINCHELSEA, EAST SUSSEX |★|✝|

Together with its neighbour, Rye, this village was once one of the
Cinque Ports and stood at the sea's edge. Throughout the 13thC
storms battered Winchelsea, and in 1288 the greatest storm of them
all virtually demolished what had once been an important coastal
stronghold. Fortunately the disaster had been anticipated. The new
Winchelsea was already taking shape, this time built on a secure hill-
top in the pattern of a French defensive town of the period, the streets
laid out on a grid plan and the whole protected by walls and tower
gates.

Only three of these gates remain — **Strand Gate, Pipewell** and
New Gate. It was by way of the New Gate that the French penetrated
during one of the many raids that they made during the 14thC and
15thC. In another raid they destroyed the greater part of **St Thomas's
Church** that stands in the heart of the village.

Near the church is **Wesley's Tree** where John Wesley preached in
1790, recognizing that this once important town was by now little
more than a wayside village with his words 'that poor skeleton of
Ancient Winchelsea'. Despite the description of a 'poor skeleton',
Winchelsea is a pleasant place in which to linger. Rye is a town of
much old world charm and bustle, while Winchelsea retains much of
the charm without the bustle.

The 14thC chancel of St Thomas's Church as well as some fine
tombs have to be seen. The 14thC **Court House** is now a museum,
numbering among the exhibits a model of Winchelsea as it was in
more prosperous times, and the ruin of a 14thC **Franciscan church** lies
in a garden not far away.

Pub: **New Inn** |**A**|**R**|**Bs**| *Tel.* (079 76) 252.

SEDLESCOMBE, EAST SUSSEX |△|

A long village that straggles along the Hawkhurst–Hastings road. The **church**, which is mainly Victorian but with a 15thC tower, and a group of houses lie to the north. The prettiest part of the village, however, is known as **Sedlescombe Street**, where the sloping village green and broad high street are flanked by 16thC and 17thC shops and houses, some thatched alongside others of brick and tile. Prominent on the green is the covered village **water pump**, installed in 1900.

At the extreme S end of the village is the **Pestalozzi Children's Village** (visited only by appointment). Named after the Swiss educationalist, Johann Heinrich Pestalozzi (1746–1827), the village was founded in 1958 for children from the Third World with the intention that their education here would enable them eventually to play a helpful part in their countries of origin. Children from a variety of nations are housed in separate dormitories that are dispersed within the gardens of a 19thC country house.

Pub: **Brickwall Hotel** |**A**|**R**| *Tel.* **(042 487) 253.**

NORTHIAM, EAST SUSSEX |△|★|†|

A number of massive oak trees grace the series of greens that lie between Northiam's main street and church. **Queen Elizabeth's Oak**, the largest, is said to have sheltered Elizabeth I when she paused here on her way to Rye in 1573, removing her green high-heeled shoes and presenting them to the villagers as souvenirs. Not far from the oak is a pump presented to the village in 1907.

A complex of modern building has sprung up to the N of the village, but the centre remains unspoilt and comprises a number of white weatherboarded houses and cottages.

The oldest part of the **church** is the lower section of the tower, built of iron sandstone in Norman times, beneath a stone spire rebuilt and raised in 1860. Among interesting features of the churchyard are the ancient yew tree, reckoned to be 600yrs old, and two scratch dials, primitive sundials in use up to the 16thC.

On the outskirts of Northiam, to the NW, is a fine timber-framed 15thC manor house, **Great Dixter**, which was converted and enlarged by Sir Edwin Lutyens in 1911. It stands in lovely gardens and is open to the public.

Three miles to the W of Northiam is an even more impressive building, the National Trust-owned **Bodiam Castle**, described by Lord Curzon when presenting it to the Trust as 'the most fairy of English Castles'. Built in 1385, it stands above a lake-moat, which is carpeted by water lilies in summer. Both the castle and nearby **museum** are open to the public.

Pub: **Hayes Hotel** |**A**|**R**| *Tel.* **(079 74) 3142.**

SMALLHYTHE, KENT |★|†|

It is hard to believe that the few scattered buildings in this flat marshy area were, in medieval days, within the embrace of an important port that served Tenterden to the N of the village. Before the recession of the sea, the River Rother flowed wide and deep, permitting the passage of ships of reasonable size to carry cargo to and from the Continent.

In this village there is a lovely half-timbered house with an overhanging storey named **Smallhythe Place**. Built in the late 15thC, it was a port house and shipyard; in the garden, traces of the original repair dock can still be seen. Later, after the channel had silted up, the house became the property of yeomen farmers until, in 1899, it was bought by the famous actress, Dame Ellen Terry (1842–1928), who lived there until her death.

Now owned by the National Trust and open to the public, Smallhythe Place has been preserved as a museum in memory of Dame Ellen. The actress's bedroom, much as it was when she lived there, can be seen, and other rooms of the house contain theatrical relics associated with Dame Ellen and other players such as Siddons, Bernhardt and Henry Irving.

Close to Smallhythe Place is the little 16thC **Church of St John** where the actress worshipped, presenting the ancient millstone in which the 15thC font is set. Standing beside the church is another old timbered building of approximately the same period, the **Priest's House**.

SISSINGHURST, KENT

The village and castle lie 2 miles apart, and it is **Sissinghurst Castle**, approached by a narrow minor road to the N of the village, that most visitors to the area have come to see.

In 1930 Sissinghurst Castle was acquired by the historian and biographer, Sir Harold Nicolson (1886–1965) and his wife Vita Sackville-West, the novelist. At that time the Castle was only a 'shell' of the former great, moated, Elizabethan manor house, a house of such importance that the Queen visited it in 1573. Later the fortunes of the owners declined. In 1750 it was used as a prison for captured French troops during the Seven Years War; later still it fulfilled the function of a workhouse.

By the time the Nicolsons bought the property it had fallen into decay, the greater part of the existing buildings and gardens owing their beauty to the creative imagination of their new owners. Among the original buildings is the tower, climbed by a spiral staircase, to give a marvellous view of the woods, lakes and oast houses that surround the estate as well as the six-acre garden beneath it.

The garden, described by Harold Nicolson as combining 'the element of expectation with the element of surprise', consists of several separate gardens, the most admired of which, the **White Garden**, is made up entirely of white flowering plants. Within the gardens are the **Priest's House**, built in 1560, and another of the remaining earlier buildings, home of the novelist Richard Church until his death in 1972. The gardens and parts of the castle, now owned by the National Trust, are open to the public.

Sissinghurst village contains a number of weatherboarded houses, some dating from the 16thC. **Sissinghurst Place** and **Sissinghurst Court**, to the S of the village, have gardens that are occasionally open to the public.

Pub: **Bull Inn** |**Bs**|

BIDDENDEN, KENT

At one end of the main street the small triangular green is dominated by the village sign depicting two young women in blue gowns, evidently Siamese twins for they are joined at hip and shoulder. The twins, always known as the Biddenden Maids, were born here in 1135 and named Elizabeth and Mary Chulkhurst. They lived to the age of 35, bequeathing land in the village, the proceeds from which were required to provide bread and cheese for the poor of the parish.

From the green the road curves towards the **church**, flanked on one side by a line of bow-shaped half-timbered houses and on the other by inns, shops and cottages of red brick. The timbered houses were formerly the homes of cloth-makers, and Biddenden was once an important cloth-making centre, the cloth being assembled at Old Cloth Hall, a seven-gabled half-timbered house that lies N of the main street. The timbered houses display some quaint carvings, in particular the head of a man framed above a doorway known as the **Tate Door**. Another house of interest is **Ye Mayde's Restaurant**, where

The Biddenden Maids are so well-known in this village that they even appear on the village sign. Elizabeth and Mary Chulkhurst were 12thC Siamese twins who survived here for 35yrs.

the Biddenden twins are again commemorated, this time in a stained-glass window.

The **church**, at the end of the street, stands in a beautiful garden setting of trees and lawns through which public footpaths lead towards fields that touch the edge of the village. The most frequent question asked by visitors to the church is 'where are the Biddenden Maids buried?' The church guide informs you that the answer is uncertain, although it is believed that they were taken to Battle Abbey for burial.

Pubs: **Three Chimneys Inn** |**R**|**Bs**|**Ra**|

    Chequers Inn|**Bs**|**Ra**|

SMARDEN, KENT |✝|

A narrow, pavementless street winds through the heart of Smarden, making the pedestrian's journey from one end of the village to the other a somewhat hazardous adventure. It is well worth the trouble, however, for this old wool village and Elizabethan market place is full of half-timbered and weatherboarded buildings of interest. Among these are the 16thC **Cloth Hall**; 17thC **Hartnup House**, named after Mathew Hartnup whose name is carved on the beams; the **Dragon House**, decorated with a frieze of dragons; and the **Pent House** beneath the upper storey of which the path to the church leads.

The **Church of St Michael**, among the largest of Kent's parish churches, has a timber roof both 36ft in height and span, above a wide 15thC nave, and is known affectionately as the 'Barn of Kent'. On the S wall is a copy of the charter of 1576 whereby Queen Elizabeth allowed the holding of a weekly market and annual fair.

Pubs: **Bell Inn** |**A**|**Bs**|**Ra**| *Tel.* (023 377) 283.

    Chequers Inn |**A**|**Bs**|**Ra**| *Tel.* (023 377) 217.

APPLEDORE, KENT |△|✝|

Before the recession of the sea, which is now several miles away, Appledore was an important ship-building centre. Today it is a village which lies on the edge of Romney Marsh; its wide main street is flanked by a number of charming houses of various periods, among them the **Swan Hotel** which is faced by the timbered **Swan House**. Next door is the **Village Blacksmith**, where a wrought-iron craftsman proudly displays his work in front of the shop.

Near the church and the ivy-clad **Red Lion Hotel** the road broadens still further, forming a small square where markets were once held. At this point a notice has been erected, giving a 'potted history' of Appledore and Appledore men.

Over the centuries the village suffered pillage from the Danes and later the French who burned down the 13thC church. In 1381 the villagers took part in the Wat Tyler revolt, attacking a medieval farmhouse, **Horne's Place**, that still stands to the N of Appledore. Almost a century later the villagers marched again, this time taking part in the Kentish rebellion under Jack Cade.

In 1805 the **Royal Military Canal** was constructed as a means of defence during the Napoleonic Wars, an operation supervised by the Prime Minister, William Pitt, at a cost of £200,000 and taking only a year to complete. The canal was never put to military use, and today a $3\frac{1}{2}$-mile stretch of it, between Appledore and Warehorne, is preserved by the National Trust. This part of the canal is a place of great natural beauty, a signpost from the main street points to the bridle path which leads to the canal banks.

Pub: **Red Lion Hotel** |**A**|**R**|**Bs**|**Ra**| *Tel.* (023 383) 206.

Touring centre
Tunbridge Wells, Kent

Hotels: **Spa, Mount Ephraim,** *Tel.* **(0892) 20331 ❸**
Wellington, Mount Ephraim, *Tel.* **(0892) 42911 ❷**

GROOMBRIDGE, KENT AND EAST SUSSEX |△|✝|

This village combines the old and the new. Kent Water, a tributary of the Medway, bisects the village and defines the county boundary, the old part of Groombridge lying in Kent, the new part in East Sussex. In the older part the triangular village green is overlooked by picturesque rows of tile-hung and weatherboarded 17thC and 18thC cottages and the charming 16thC **Crown Inn**.

Across the road is **Groombridge Place**, a moat-surrounded Jacobean mansion rebuilt on the site of a former Norman castle. This H-shaped building of mellow red brick stands among terraced gardens, the park of the estate sweeping down to the main road where the **church**, built in 1625 as a chapel to the estate, stands above a lake.

Inside the church are monuments to the Packer family. Above the door a Latin inscription reads 'Because of the happy return of Charles our Prince from Spain', written by the new owner of Groombridge Place, John Packer, in gratitude for the safe return of the Prince of Wales, later Charles I. Packer, as Clerk to the Privy Seal, had accompanied the prince to Spain at the time of his unsuccessful attempt to woo the infanta.

Pub: **Crown Inn** |**A**|**R**|**Bs**| *Tel.* (089 276) 361.

PENSHURST, KENT |△|✝|⬥⬤|

Beneath wooded hills near the junction of the Medway and Eden rivers, Penshurst is a compact group of shops and cottages clustering around the church and the fringe of the lovely park that surrounds Penshurst Place.

Entry to the **church** is through a square of little timbered cottages, a cottage at the end constructed on stilts forming a natural archway into the churchyard. Inside the church is the **Sidney Chapel** with many monuments to that famous family, among them the soldier and poet Sir Philip Sidney (1554–86). They were the ancestral owners of Penshurst Place after Edward VI awarded it to them in 1552.

The main feature of **Penshurst Place** is the **great hall**. Built in 1340 by Sir John de Pulteney, it is 60ft long and 40ft wide beneath a beamed roof of chestnut. On display at one end of the hall is the helmet worn by Sir Philip Sidney in battle and carried at his funeral. Parts of Penshurst Place, including the hall, state rooms and picture gallery, as well as the grounds with a formal Italian garden and lake, are open to the public during the summer.

Pub: **Leicester Arms Hotel** |**A**|**R**|**Bs**| *Tel.* **(089 284) 870551.**

CHIDDINGSTONE, KENT |△|†|

The single street of this village, the property of the National Trust, is made up of 16thC and 17thC houses that face the parish church. The houses, brick and half-timbered, have picturesque gables; a striking example is a 16thC house with three overhanging gables, the middle one forming the porch. **St Mary's Church**, largely rebuilt in sandstone after a fire in the 17thC, stands in a churchyard dotted with yew trees and contains a fine decorated font.

A 14thC manor house with an Elizabethan façade, Penshurst Place stands in beautiful grounds, and was the Sidneys' ancestral home.

The 19thC **Chiddingstone Castle** has been reconstructed in mock-Gothic style on the site of an earlier 17thC building. In the castle grounds is a large sandstone rock, the 'chiding stone', from which the village is said to take its name. Various legends surround the origin of the chiding stone. One account suggests that it may once have been a Druidic judgement stone; another belief is that it was here that offending wives were brought to be chided for their misdeeds.

Two miles to the W is **Hever Castle**, a restored fortified manor house which Henry VIII once visited, falling in love with Mary Bullen (better known as Boleyn) and taking her away to Court. It was of course her younger sister, the fated Anne Boleyn, whom Henry eventually married. Hever Castle is set in magnificent gardens that include a 35-acre lake, a maze formed by yew trees, and an Italian garden with various Roman statues and busts.

Pub: **Castle Inn** |**Bs**|

BRENCHLEY, KENT |†|

A hill-top village where the focal point is the small green and oak tree. Scattered around the green and the roads that converge on it are a number of Tudor cottages, some of which are conversions of larger houses to make shops or modest dwellings. Among the most impressive buildings is the **Old Palace**, sometimes called the **Gatehouse**, a half-timbered line of separate dwellings, which was once the home of the lords of the manor, the Roberts family, and was restored in 1964.

The path to the sandstone **church** is lined on either side by yew trees, shaped like sentinels and believed to be 400yrs old. Near the lych-gate is a white, weatherboarded cottage, the 14thC **Old Vicarage**. The poet and First World War hero, Siegfried Sassoon (1886–1967) spent his boyhood years in a rambling house that still stands to the NW of the village. Brenchley is the Butley of his semi-autobiographical novel, *Memoirs of a Fox Hunting Man* (1928), with his vivid description of hunting and playing cricket on the local village greens. In his diary (22 March 1921) he wrote: 'Brenchley bells, across the meadows, will always be music, whereas Big Ben's booming is an automatic episode in the calendar.'

Perhaps, however, Sassoon is best remembered for his *War Poems* (1919), in which he expressed the disgust of his generation of fighting soldiers for war and the ambitious politicians, aided by the 'yellow' press and armchair patriots, who glorified in it:

> *The House is crammed: tier beyond tier they grin*
> *And cackle at the Show, while prancing ranks*
> *Of harlots shrill the chorus, drunk with din;*
> *'We're sure the Kaiser loves our dear old Tanks.'*
>
> *I'd like to see a Tank come down the stalls,*
> *Lurching to ragtime tunes, or 'Home, sweet Home',*
> *And there'd be no more jokes in Music-halls*
> *To mock the riddled corpses round Bapaume.*
>
> ('Blighters', 4 February 1917)

Pubs: **Bull Inn** |R|Bs|Ra|
  Rose and Crown Inn |R|Bs|Ra|

HORSMONDEN, KENT |△|†|

At one time the local population was spread widely throughout the 5-mile length of the parish, and so today the church and a handful of buildings are separated from the existing village by almost 2 miles.

Horsmonden's most famous 'son' was John Browne, the gunsmith who cast guns for Charles I, and who later, according to the church guide, was equally happy to work for the Commonwealth. Accordingly the village grew around Browne's **Furnace Pond**, a 'hammer' pond that provided power for the gunsmith's thriving industry.

The village surrounds a handsome square green, with the **Gun Inn** recalling past glories. SW of Horsmonden is the National Trust-owned **Sprivers**, an 18thC mansion set in 108 acres of glorious parkland, orchards and woods.

The **Church of St Margaret** contains no monument to John Browne, although his wife is buried beneath the chancel arches. On the S wall is a memorial to another native of the village, whose trade though not romantic was certainly practical. This is the sculptured head of John Read, described as a 'very ingenious mann', the inventor of the stomach pump which he demonstrated to the Royal Society in 1823.

There is a fine view across undulating countryside from the churchyard — a view which reminds you that this lonely spot lies in the very heart of 'The Garden of England'.

Pub: Gun Inn |Bs|

GOUDHURST, KENT |△|†|

In every sense a lovely village. The narrow main street climbs sharply up from the large duck pond, passing tiled, weatherboarded and half-timbered houses until it broadens at the top to reach the square towered **Church of St Mary**. Next to the church are two adjoining inns, the **Star and Eagle** and the **Eight Bells**. They stand above the street, approached by a flight of steps; it is believed that at one time the timbered Star and Eagle was connected to the church by a secret underground passage, a hideaway for the Hawkhurst Gang of smugglers who terrorized the county in the 18thC.

In his novel, **The Smuggler**, G. P. R. James wrote that: 'Of all counties the most favoured by nature and art for the very pleasant sport of smuggling is the County of Kent.' The gang who came from nearby Hawkhurst were certainly the most notorious of the smuggling fraternity, on occasions virtually taking over local towns and villages.

In 1747 the gang invaded Goudhurst, waging a pitched battle with the militia in the churchyard while the villagers hid inside the church. The gang were defeated but accounts of the fate of their leader, Richard Kingsmill, vary. Some say he was shot during the course of the battle, others that he was hanged at Tyburn, while yet another account tells that his execution took place at *Horsmonden*.

Much of **St Mary's Church** dates from the 13thC. There are many monuments to the Bedgebury and Colepeper families, the most important being the painted wooden effigies of Sir Alexander Colepeper and his wife.

Pubs: Star and Eagle |A|R|Bs| *Tel.* (0580) 211512.

    Eight Bells Inn |Bs|

    Vine Inn |Bs|

BURWASH, EAST SUSSEX |△|†|••|

The long high street is lined with brick and timber-framed shops and cottages. The village stands on a ridge between the Rivers Rother and Dudwell, the village sign emphasizing that Burwash was once a centre for iron-making.

Inside the **Church of St Bartholomew** there is a 14thC iron tomb-slab, one of the oldest of its kind in the country. Near the door is a plaque commemorating John Kipling, son of Rudyard, who was killed in the Great War. Rudyard Kipling (1865–1936) bought a 17thC house named **Bateman's** in 1902, living there until his death 34yrs later. Bateman's and the beautiful gardens in which it lies is now the property of the National Trust, and is open to the public. Here can be seen the study where Kipling described the local countryside in *Puck of Pook's Hill*, a room furnished as it was when the writer worked there.

Kipling's assessment of Bateman's when he first visited it is worth recording: 'At first sight the Committee of Ways and Means [Mr and Mrs Kipling] said: 'That's her! The Only She! Make an honest woman of her — quick!' We entered and felt her Spirit — her Feng Shui — to be good.'

Pubs: Admiral Vernon Inn |A|R|Bs| *Tel.* (0435) 882230.

    Bear Inn |A|R|Bs| *Tel.* (0435) 882540.

    Bell Inn |A|R|Bs| *Tel.* (0435) 882304.

MAYFIELD, EAST SUSSEX |†|

The main street of the village lies along a high ridge; from the car park there is a marvellous view of the surrounding Sussex countryside. Among the most prominent buildings are **Walnut Tree House** and the fine Tudor inn, **Middle House Hotel**. Across the road from the inn is the 15thC **gatehouse** to a convent school, the site of a former palace of the Archbishops of Canterbury until 1545, Cranmer's time. The original palace was built of wood in the 10thC by the Saxon Archbishop, St Dunstan, as was the **church**, which was then rebuilt in the 13thC and again in the 15thC.

The village sign depicts a maid among children at play, possibly accounting for the village name, 'Maid's Field' (old English, Maghfeld). The sign also portrays a famous piece of folklore, St Dunstan's encounter with the devil, when he is supposed to have gripped the devil's nose with the red hot tongs he was using for his forging; the devil reputedly leaping into a nearby lake to cool down.

Pub: **Middle House Hotel** |**A**|**R**|**Bs**| *Tel.* (043 55) 872146.

TOUR FIFTEEN
Touring centre
Canterbury, Kent

Hotels: **Chaucer, Ivy Lane,** *Tel.* (0227) 64427❹
Falstaff, St Dunstans Street, *Tel.* (0227) 62138❷

CHILHAM, KENT |❖|△|★|†|

Considered by many to be Kent's prettiest village, Chilham stands perched on a hill — a medieval oasis aloof from the traffic that thunders along the two main roads which lie beneath and on either side of the hill. The focal point of the village is the compact little square around which crowd delightful half-timbered Tudor and Jacobean shops and houses as well as a picturesque inn.

Facing each other across the square are the gates of **Chilham Castle** and **St Mary's Church** with a tall flint-built 15thC perpendicular tower. Narrow lanes lead down from the extremity of the square past other attractive period cottages.

All that remains of the original Norman castle is the keep that stands near the existing Jacobean house built by Sir Dudley Digges in 1616. Sir Dudley, it seems, was a popular and generous squire, for his will of 1638 decreed that a race was to be held annually on 19th May (his birthday) — 'the race to be run by young maidens and bachelors of good conversation, the fastest maid and the fastest man to receive £10 apiece'.

The castle grounds, laid out by Capability Brown with terraced lawns and rose gardens, are occasionally open to the public, and activities here include displays of jousting and falconry. The castle is also the home of the **Kent Battle of Britain Museum**.

Pubs: **White Horse Inn** |**Bs**|**Ra**|
    Alma Inn |**Ra**|

ELHAM, KENT †

This charming village in the Nailbourne Valley has two distinct areas of interest. Firstly, set back from the main street, there is a quiet little square, around which are the flint-built Norman **church** with its battlemented tower and some red-brick as well as timbered houses, among them the **Kings Arms Inn**. The square was once the scene of a market; the charter to hold one here having been granted by Prince Edward before he became Edward I.

Elham's high street also contains notable buildings, in particular the **Abbot's Fireside Hotel** and the **Rose and Crown Inn**, which face each other. The Abbot's Fireside, once known as the Smithies Inn, was built in the 15thC. This timbered building, its upper storey supported by brackets carved to resemble strange human figures, was used by the Duke of Wellington as his headquarters during the Napoleonic Wars. The **Rose and Crown**, another timbered building that once served as a coaching inn, incorporates the former court room.

Pubs: Rose and Crown |**A**|**R**|**Bs**| *Tel.* (030 384) 226.
    Kings Arms |**Bs**|**Ra**|

FORDWICH, KENT

It seems hard to believe that this charming little riverside village was once a bustling port. In medieval days ships from the Continent anchored here, offloading food, wine and building materials for Canterbury Cathedral a few miles to the west.

A cluster of buildings huddles above the banks of a lovely section of the River Stour; among these buildings are the Fordwich Arms, the town hall, the church and the village shop. The 16thC **town hall**, said to be the smallest in England, has an overhanging upper storey filled with herringbone brick that once served as a court room, above a solid brick base where the cells were. Today the town hall houses a small **museum**, where the exhibits include the ducking stool, which used to be lowered by crane into the river for the immersion of recalcitrant wives. Outside the town hall are the village stocks.

The **Church of St Mary the Virgin** has an angled 'broach' style spire, covered with wooden shingles. Two objects of particular interest stand side by side against the N wall. One of these is known as the **Fordwich Stone**, a block of carved Norman stone which according to popular superstition was once the tomb of St Augustine. Next to the Fordwich Stone is a rough-hewn wooden seat with a high back, made from wood of great antiquity — an object far older than the adjacent stone. The origin of the seat is uncertain. It is known as the 'Penitent's Chair' because, according to folklore, people who erred in the Middle Ages were required to be seated there in its uncomfortable embrace.

Pubs: **George and Dragon Hotel** |**A**|**R**|**Bs**| *Tel.* (0227) 710661.
    Fordwich Arms |**Bs**|

Cambridgeshire, Essex, Suffolk and Norfolk

Historically East Anglia was taken to mean the former Saxon kingdom that corresponded, roughly, to Norfolk and Suffolk. Nowadays, however, although the total area of East Anglia is not precisely defined, it is generally assumed to embrace the additional counties of Essex and Cambridgeshire. East Anglia is among the less populated and less well-known areas of England, primarily a rural as opposed to an industrial locality.

The low-lying fen county of Cambridgeshire is a grain-producing district where, also, fruit is grown, dairy foods are produced and sheep are reared. Cambridge University is one of the oldest European universities, believed to date from the 12thC, although the earliest of the existing colleges, Peterhouse, was not founded until 1284.

Much of the countryside on the borders of Suffolk and Essex is known as 'Constable Country', scenery made famous by the landscape painter who was born at East Bergholt and who depicted the area in many famous works that include *Flatford Mill*, *Dedham Vale* and *The Hay Wain*. Essex, bounded in the S by the Thames estuary and the E by the North Sea, is predominantly low-lying with rich soil that produces heavy crops of vegetables and sugarbeet. The villages described include the much photographed *Finchingfield* and *Great Bardfield*, a place of great architectural interest.

Much of Suffolk's low, undulating surface is under the plough, producing wheat, barley and sugarbeet. Race horse breeding and training take place in the many stables that surround Newmarket. Suffolk's coastline is flat; the two coastal villages described are *Walberswick*, much favoured by artists, and the remote and ghostly village of *Dunwich*. Further S is Aldeburgh, renowned for its music festival and close to the Minsmere bird sanctuary.

Norfolk, the largest of the eastern counties, covers some 2,000sq. miles. The coastline is mainly flat and inland the reed-bordered lakes, known as the Broads, are famous for their wild-life and the sailing and motor-cruising which take place there. The chief crops include oats, wheat and barley; and turkeys are reared for the London markets. The beaches of *Blakeney* form a natural bird sanctuary and impressive medieval ruins can be seen at *Castle Acre, Castle Rising* and *Castle Hedingham*.

 Material used for many buildings in East Anglia is flint, either to form brick-and-flint walls, or knapped flint used in conjunction with plaster, a method known as flushwork, seen on a grand scale at Eye (close to Tour 18). Suffolk and Essex also preserve much timber-framing, such as that seen at *Lavenham*. Many of these 16thC and 17thC timber-framed buildings are embellished with pargeting, a method of modelling ornamental patterns with plaster while it was still wet; a fine example of this craft can be seen on the Fox Inn at *Finchingfield*.

At least one day should be allowed for each of the tours in this area. **Tour 16** (113 miles) covers the low-lying area around Cambridge. Constable Country is explored in **Tour 17**, a 107-mile round-trip. **Tour 18** (98 miles) and **Tour 19** (82 miles) both include picturesque coastal and inland villages.

Cambridge, Cambridgeshire

Hotels: **University Arms, Regent Street**, *Tel.* (0223) 63421 ❹
Arundel House, Chesterton Road, *Tel.* (0223) 67701 ❷

Delightful timbered houses built right on the bank of the River Ouse at Hemingford Grey.

GRANTCHESTER, CAMBRIDGESHIRE ✝ ◆■

And is there honey, still, for tea?

Rupert Brooke (1887–1915) immortalized Grantchester with his famous poem, 'The Old Vicarage, Grantchester'. Born at Rugby, he won a fellowship to Kings College, Cambridge and settled at the **Old Vicarage** here before becoming involved in the First World War, during which he died as a result of blood poisoning on the Greek isle of Scyros.

The **Church of St Andrew and St Mary** is noted for its magnificent decorated chancel, the design of which has been compared to the one at Ely. As the village name implies (chester means camp) there must have been a Roman settlement here and fragments of the ruins of a Roman villa lie near the school. Cambridge lies just 2 miles away. There is a lovely walk there along the bank of the river that glides as sweetly as in the days when Brooke saw it. But unhappily the mill that the poet gazed upon some 70yrs ago was burned down in 1928:

> *And laughs the immortal river still*
> *Under the mill, under the mill.*
>
> ('The Old Vicarage, Grantchester')

Pub: **Blue Ball Inn** │**Bs**│**Ra**│

HEMINGFORD GREY, CAMBRIDGESHIRE ✝

Some modern building has sprung up nearby, but this does not impair the enchantment of this riverside village. Brick and timber-framed thatched cottages reach down towards a lovely point of the reed-fringed River Ouse. Here houseboats and motor cruisers are moored; the river curving gracefully and flowing within a few feet of the 12thC **Church of St James** that stands beneath its perpendicular tower and curious truncated spire. Willows droop over the river bank and across the water from the village cows graze in lush meadows.

There are marvellous towpath walks, and to the W of the village is a 12thC manor house, perhaps the oldest English home to have remained under permanent occupation. A beautiful garden stretches to the river's edge and a moat surrounds the other three sides of this sturdy stone building, a house of two storeys which, at one time, was entered by a staircase that led to a first-floor door, the ground floor merely acting as the storeroom.

Another building of interest is the red-brick **Hemingford Grey House** (built in 1697), noted for containing in the garden one of England's biggest plane trees (planted in 1702).

Pub: **Cock Inn** |**Bs**|

DALHAM, SUFFOLK |†|

Attractive thatched cottages line the banks of the River Kennet in a secluded valley; little arched footbridges span the river to give added delight to the scene. The street then ascends sharply by way of a cul-de-sac, winding its way through a copse up to Dalham's most impressive buildings, the church and the hall.

The 14thC **Church of St Mary** stands on the site of a Saxon church mentioned in the Domesday Book: 'One church with 40 acres of land, and half a plough team, value five shillings'. The 40 acres (the church ley) remain the property of the church and can be seen by looking across the valley from the church door. The church guide observes that although five shillings seems a small amount, it is necessary to remember that in 1087 the whole manor of Dalham had an annual value of only 60 shillings.

The church has a gracious pinnacled tower and it is believed that the spire fell during the gale which caused havoc in England on the night that Oliver Cromwell died in 1658. It is noted for its fine monuments to previous lords of the manor, the Stutevilles, the Afflecks and the Rhodes.

Dalham Hall stands next to the church; it is a superb Queen Anne mansion in grounds of 3,000 acres, which, after the death of Cecil Rhodes of Africa (1835–1902) who purchased the Dalham estates in 1900, became the property of his brother, Colonel Francis Rhodes. In memory of his famous brother, Francis Rhodes restored the church's 15thC roof, but only outlived him by 3yrs. Francis Rhodes' body was brought back from Capetown in 1905 and is buried here with this proud epitaph:

> *Long travel in this churchyard ends*
> *A gentleman who knew not fear,*
> *A soldier, sportsman, prince of friends,*
> *A man men could but love, lies here.*

Pub: **Affleck Arms** |**Bs**|

CASTLE HEDINGHAM, ESSEX |△|★|†|

The **castle** after which the village is named was built in the mid-12thC as a residence and stronghold of the De Vere family, Earls of Oxford. This massive building dominated the valley of the River Colne, and although much of it was demolished in the 16thC, the mighty keep, 100ft in height and reached by a bridge across the moat, remains to give some idea of the castle's former strategic importance. It is open to the public on specific occasions.

The **Church of St Nicholas**, in the centre of the village, was begun shortly after the castle was built and underwent much restoration in Tudor times. Among several impressive monuments is one in black marble to the 15th Earl of Oxford and his wife; the figures of their eight children surround the tomb.

The village is composed of a jumble of narrow streets and alleys, many with medieval houses and cottages. A focal point, near the church gate, is **Falcon Square** with a large, picturesque half-timbered house that once served as an inn on one side.

A mile or so out of Castle Hedingham, on the A604 road to Great Yeldham, is the **Colne Valley Railway**, an interesting reconstruction of a typical railway station of the Victorian era. It has a small museum, where you can see old steam and diesel engines, as well as carriages, among them the renowned 'Brighton Belle'. Meals and refreshments are served, appropriately, in an old and well-appointed buffet car.

Pubs: **Bell Inn** |**Bs**|**Ra**|
     Vine Inn |**Bs**|

FINCHINGFIELD, ESSEX

This much photographed village, among the most attractive in Essex, tends to become crowded with sightseers at weekends. Its focal points are the lovely white-railed pond and the nearby split village greens. Around the greens and along the streets that converge on them, houses and cottages, many colour-washed and gabled, cluster in an unplanned fashion and yet each one of them appears to fit perfectly into the scene.

Georgian houses, together with a line of older cottages, face the gabled **Finchingfield House**. Close to the pond is an old coaching inn, the **Fox**. The hill-top **Church of St John** with its Norman tower dominates the village, and inside there is an inscription relating to William Kemp, an early owner of the Elizabethan red-brick manor house, **Spains Hall**, which lies a mile to the W of the village. After unjustly accusing his wife of adultery Kemp was struck with remorse, vowing to keep silent for 7yrs and to dig a pond in the grounds of Spains Hall for each of the years of his penance. The present lake is a composite result of his efforts.

In the 17thC Spains Hall passed to the Ruggles-Brise family and a plaque in the church to Sir Evelyn Ruggles-Brise reads: 'We shall remember him as one who had faith in his fellow men' — a reminder that Sir Evelyn was the prison reformer who devised the borstal system for the training of young offenders.

Pub: **Red Lion** |**Bs**|**Ra**|

GREAT BARDFIELD, ESSEX

Great Bardfield is a place in which to linger for there is much to see both in the village and the immediate surrounding countryside. In 1982 Norman Clift, the Rector, and Stanley Hyland, Chairman of the Great Bardfield Historical Society, produced a booklet *Great Bardfield and its Church*. This is available in the village bookshop and is well worth obtaining for it tells far more about the locality than a few lines in this guide can hope to do.

The name most associated with Great Bardfield is that of William Bendlowes, Sergeant at Law and Member of Parliament among a variety of offices, who was born here and died in 1584 after

Just E of Great Bardfield, the tower windmill, Gibraltar Mill, was built in 1661, enlarged in the 18thC, and is now a private house.

founding a local charity which is still used to help the poor and needy. The timber-framed **Place House** in the Dunmow Road was the lawyer's home. It bears his initials and the date 1564. A tiny thatched cottage, inhabited until 1958 when it became unfit for human habitation, was taken over by the Bendlowes Charity and converted into a cottage **museum**.

Other buildings of interest include the 19thC **town hall**; the 15thC timbered **Gobions** and adjacent **Town House**; the **White Hart Inn**, also 15thC and now a private house; and the **Friends' Meeting House** on the old village green in the middle of the High Street.

The 14thC **Church of St Mary the Virgin** possesses a beautiful stone screen, one of only three in the world. The brass to William Bendlowes is missing, but the one to his wife, Alienor, remains. The manor house, **Bardfield Hall**, stands on the hill by the church with an ancient barn nearby. It is now used as a farmhouse and specializes in the growing of orchids.

There is much to see in the outskirts of the village, notably a windmill known as **Gibraltar Mill**, now part of a private house that lies along the road leading to a group of farms and cottages that form the hamlet of **Waltham Cross**.

Pubs: Bell Inn |**Bs**|
     Vine Inn |**Bs**|

THAXTED, ESSEX |△|★|✝|

In medieval days this large village was one of England's foremost centres for cutlery. Thus the two most impressive buildings, the church and the guildhall, owe much to the patronage of wealthy tradesmen.

The **Church of St John the Baptist** is numbered among the finest of Essex churches and is also dedicated to Our Lady, and St

Lawrence, the patron saint of cutlers. This hill-top church with an imposing spire, some 180ft in height, dominates the village and a feature of historic interest is the chapel dedicated to John Ball, leader of the Peasants' Revolt, who was executed in 1381 after delivering his famous lines: 'When Adam delved and Eve span, Who was then the gentleman?' Near the church a path leads between a picturesque double row of almshouses to a little windmill which contains, on the lower floor, a rural **museum** of local interest.

The central point of the village is the timbered 14thC **guildhall**, a three-storeyed building, first used by the cutlers as a market place, and subsequently housing the grammar school and council chambers. A narrow alley close to the guildhall is lined with a variety of ancient houses, among them **Dick Turpin's Cottage** where the highwayman, born at nearby Hempstead in 1706 and executed at York in 1739, is said to have lived at one time. The 16thC **Recorder's House** is now in use as a restaurant and next door is a house where the composer Gustav Holst (1874–1934), famed for his orchestral suite **The Planets**, lived between 1917 and 1925.

Pub: Star Inn |Bs|Ra|

TOUR SEVENTEEN
Touring centre
Hadleigh, Suffolk
Hotel: Edgehill, High Street, *Tel.* (0473) 822458 ❶

KERSEY, SUFFOLK |✝|❖▪|

Henceforth my wooing mind shall be expressed
In russet yeas, and honest Kersey noes.
(speech by Biron, Love's Labour Lost, Act V, scene 2)

The famous Kersey cloth woven in this lovely village is mentioned at least twice in the plays of Shakespeare, who, in this quotation, pays the village a deserved compliment.

The main street sweeps down past timbered cottages which once contained the looms used to weave the cloth. At the head of the street is the ancient village water pump and buildings of note include the **Bell Inn**, a variety of gabled weavers' cottages and the 'horse doctor's house' with a horse's tail on the gable end.

At the foot of the street a ford crosses a tributary of the River Brett where the 15thC River House stands. The street then ascends sharply past more medieval houses before arriving at the **Church of St Mary**, where, from the churchyard, the best overall view of the village is obtained. Outstanding features of the church which was greatly restored in the 19thC include the screen in the N aisle, the S porch roof, and the lectern with a carved eagle, all of which are more than 500yrs old.

Just outside the S porch a memorial stone in the graveyard is inscribed:

Reader pass on nor waste thy time
On bad biography or bitter rhyme
For what I am this humble dust enclose,
And what I was is no affair of yours.

Pubs: **Bell Inn** |**Bs**|
     White Horse |**Bs**|

LAVENHAM, SUFFOLK |△|★|†|⬥●|

The woollen industry was already well established in East Anglia by the time Edward III was encouraging Flemish weavers to settle here. In those days Lavenham was a prosperous wool town; today, while Lavenham retains many picturesque medieval buildings, it is more accurate to classify it as a village — a large compact village full of historic associations.

The **guildhall** in Market Place is preserved by the National Trust. This timber-framed building, among the finest to be found in England, was built in the 1520s by the Guild of Corpus Christi, one of the four social and religious guilds in Lavenham at a time when the wool trade was flourishing. Later it served various uses, among them as a prison, a workhouse and a wool store. It was restored in 1887 and now houses a **museum** with exhibits of local history and industry, including the medieval wool trade.

Market Place is also graced by a preaching cross, dating back to 1501, and the **Angel Hotel** which belongs to the same period. Little streets with many of the original weavers' cottages lead off Market Place — among them Shilling Street, named after a Flemish weaver, Schylling, who came to Lavenham to instruct in cloth-making. Through an upper oriel window of a house that still stands in Shilling Street the stars were watched by Jane Taylor, prompting her to compose her famous jingle, 'Twinkle, twinkle, little star'. The old **Wool Hall** now forms part of the Swan Hotel and many other notable Tudor buildings are to be found in a network of streets such as Water Street, Church Street and Lady Street that are near Market Place.

The lovely **Church of St Peter and St Paul** stands on the site of the original building, retaining its chancel. The 140ft tower serves as a landmark for miles around, yet surprisingly only a glimpse of the church can be seen from Market Place by taking up a position near the preaching cross. The church contains many memorials to the De Vere family, Earls of Oxford, and is well worth visiting if only for the marvellous view obtained by climbing the tower.

Pub: **Angel Hotel** |**A**|**R**|**Bs**| *Tel.* (0787) 247388.

LONG MELFORD, SUFFOLK |△|†|

The high street extends for 3 straight miles along a Roman highway. The original ford, now replaced by a bridge, gives the village its name, 'the ford by the mill'. Attractive old buildings straddle the high street, among them the **Bull Inn**, which contains ancient carved beams and has served as an inn for more than 400yrs. The real beauty of the village, however, begins where the road enters the area of a huge triangular green with Melford Hall on one side and Suffolk's loveliest church, the Church of Holy Trinity on the other.

Melford Hall, a gracious turreted Tudor mansion, has changed little since Elizabeth I visited it in 1578. It is owned by the National Trust and a number of rooms, including the original panelled banqueting hall, a Regency library and a Victorian bedroom, are open

Arguably the most beautiful church in Suffolk, Holy Trinity, Long Melford was reconstructed in the 15thC by the Cloptons. A large building gracing one side of the green, it has almost 100 windows.

to the public. Exhibits include period furniture, paintings and Chinese porcelain, and the walled garden contains a charming, octagonal Tudor pavilion.

On the other side of the green, a lane passes between a line of terraced cottages and the restored Elizabethan Trinity Hospital, culminating at the church, which is a magnificent spectacle. The **Church of Holy Trinity** was almost entirely rebuilt in the late 15thC by the Clopton family. Apart from the tower, which was rebuilt in 1903, little of the structure of this huge building, which is 260ft in length and boasts almost 100 windows, has changed. The church's most precious window, the **Lily Crucifix**, can be seen in the Clopton Chapel and shows the cross in the form of a lily. The Lady Chapel dates from 1496 and the many memorials to Long Melford families include those to the Cordells, the Cloptons and the Martyns.

It was Sir William Cordell, lawyer and Speaker of Parliament, who entertained Elizabeth I at Melford Hall. The Clopton family were the owners of **Kentwell Hall**, to the N of the village and occasionally open to the public. **Melford Hall**, at the other end of Long Melford, was the home of the Martyns.

Pubs: Crown Inn |**A**|**R**|**Bs**|**Ra**| *Tel.* (0787) 77666.

Bull Inn |**A**|**R**|**Bs**| *Tel.* (0787) 78494.

NAYLAND, SUFFOLK |✝|

Once an important centre for the wool trade, this village is today a colourful place with a feast of houses and cottages washed in pinks, browns, whites and yellows. The River Stour, separating Suffolk from Essex, flows peacefully past the edge of Nayland, beneath a bridge first designed in wood by a wealthy clothier, William Abell, who was also responsible for notable additions to the **Church of St James** in the early 16thC.

The most interesting feature of the church is undoubtedly the Constable painting of *Christ Blessing Bread and Wine.* John Constable (1776–1837) was born at nearby *East Bergholt*, and this was among his earlier works, being commissioned as a gift for the church and remaining there since it was painted in 1809.

In the High Street, next to one of several of Nayland's ancient inns, is the **Old Guildhall**, built in 1470, and on the other side of the street is a quaint obelisk milestone which informs you that London lies 55 miles away.

In Church Street is **Alton Court**, which was begun in the 15thC, and has fine carved timbering and various additions, including a huge 18thC cowled doorway and mullioned windows.

Pub: Queens Head |**Bs**|

STOKE-BY-NAYLAND, SUFFOLK |△|✝|

The glory of the village is the **Church of St Mary the Virgin**, one of Suffolk's largest churches and subject of several of the paintings of John Constable (1776–1837) who was born at nearby *East Bergholt*. Set amidst trees this hill-top church is graced by an immense pinnacled tower, 120ft in height and a landmark for miles around as well as being the focal point of Constable's famous *Rainbow* picture.

Inside the church, there are numerous memorials in stone and brass to former inhabitants of the village. Among them, in the S chapel, is the fine sculptured figure of Lady Ann Windsor, robed in a fur-lined cloak with her little son at her feet and her two daughters at her head.

Near the church is the timber-framed **guildhall** with an

overhanging storey that dates from Tudor times. Another building of this period is the **Maltings**, once a hall but now converted into four residences. Two fine old inns, the **Crown** and the **Black Horse**, are in the middle of the village, and 2 miles away, on the road to *Dedham*, is **Thorington Hall**, an oak-framed, gabled house that dates from 1600. It belongs to the National Trust and is now in use as a guest house.

Pubs: Angel |**Bs**|**Ra**|

    Black Horse Inn |**Bs**|

    Crown |**Bs**|

DEDHAM, ESSEX |△|★|†|

The village first grew up along the main road between Ipswich and Colchester, later known as the 'King's Highway'. It has been immortalized by the paintings of John Constable (1776–1837), who was born at nearby *East Bergholt* in Suffolk but was educated at Dedham's grammar school. The Vale of Dedham is known as 'Constable Country' and he wrote of it: 'I love every stile and stump and lane . . . these scenes made me a painter and I am grateful.'

The house where the artist was born no longer stands. But **Flatford Mill** beside the River Stour with its wooden bridge and **Willy Lott's Cottage**, one of Constable's favourite subjects, remain as they were in the days of his boyhood. Dedham Mill, like Flatford Mill, was once owned by Constable's father, and is the last working mill on the Stour, but it is the third on the site since Constable's day and bears little resemblance to his paintings.

The **Church of St Mary the Virgin** (1492) with its gracious pinnacled tower appears in many Constable paintings and dominates the main street of the village. Another famous artist, Sir Alfred Munnings (1878–1959), lived at **Castle House** where a gallery of his work is displayed and can be seen by the public during specified summer afternoons.

Among many Essex and Suffolk families that emigrated to America in 1630 were three Sherman cousins from whom important figures in public life were descended; among them General William Tecumseh Sherman (1820–91), Commander of the Federal Army, whose famous march through the Southern States brought the Civil War to a close. **Sherman Hall**, home of the General's ancestors is opposite the church, and a little further along the same street is the timber-framed **Marlborough Head Inn** (built *c*. 1500), once the home of a wealthy clothier.

Among other old buildings that should be seen are the **Sun Inn**; the timber-framed **Southfields** with its imposing gateway; and the Georgian **grammar school**.

Pubs: Marlborough Head |**A**|**R**|**Bs**| *Tel.* (0206) 323124.

    Anchor |**Bs**|**Ra**|

    Sun |**Bs**|

ORFORD, SUFFOLK |△|†|

At one time an important seaport, Orford today, is little more than a charming backwater — a place in which to linger and admire the immense castle keep; the market square and picturesque brick and timber buildings that encompass it; and the quayside that now caters for small craft which ply their way down the River Ore. Opposite the quay is the **Jolly Sailor Inn**, one of the finest waterside pubs, where legends of former smuggling days abound and secret cupboards can be seen to add weight to the legends.

The best overall view of the village and many miles of

surrounding sea and landscape is obtained by climbing the spiral stair-case of the polygonal **castle keep**, which is 90ft high with walls more than 10ft thick and was built in 1165 by Henry II as one of East Anglia's foremost strongholds.

Even the castle has its legend, for it is said that in the dungeons a merman was once incarcerated. This wild hairy creature, half man half fish, was trapped in the nets of local fishermen, but after interrogation by the governor of the castle, he managed to escape and return once more to the sea. A portrait of the merman hangs on a sign over a shop in Market Square, where, incidentally, markets no longer take place.

Orford **church**, which is mainly 14thC, but with imposing Norman arches at the E end of the aisle, was the venue of some of Benjamin Britten's first compositions, among them *Noyes Fludde* (1958) and *Curlew River* (1964).

The village is famed for its smoked fish, in particular 'Orford Butleys' a variety of smoked herring.

Pubs: Kings Head |**A**|**R**|**Bs**|**Ra**| *Tel.* (039 45) 271.

Jolly Sailor Inn |**Bs**|**Ra**|

TOUR EIGHTEEN
Touring centre
Norwich, Norfolk
Hotels: **Lansdowne, Thorpe Road,** *Tel.* **(0603) 20302❹**
Oaklands, Yarmouth Road, *Tel.* **(0603) 34471❷**

OLD BUCKENHAM, NORFOLK |✝|

In contrast to compact New Buckenham, the village spreads out in a haphazard fashion; inns and cottages with strange names straggle around a vast green. The oldest feature is the mound and a few frag-mentary ruins of a **castle** built in the 12thC by William de Albini and later handed over by him for use in the building of an Augustinian priory. These few traces of the castle and priory can be seen near Abbey Farm.

Turf from Australia was brought to Old Buckenham Hall, producing a pitch which a leading English cricketer, Sir Jack Hobbs (1882–1963), declared to be among the finest on which he had ever played on.

Tucked away down a cul-de-sac at the edge of the green is the delightful **Church of All Saints**, lying in a churchyard of roses with a roof of thatch. The church is also distinguished by its polygonal tower.

Pub: **Kings Head** |**Bs**|**Ra**|

NEW BUCKENHAM, NORFOLK |✝|

The focal point of this village is the large, tree-clad village green with the prominent whitewashed Market House, from which extends a handsome line of cottages. The upper floor of the **Market House** is supported by wooden pillars, the central pillar once acting as a whipping post for dealing with village delinquents. At one time it was planned to make use of this building as a museum but the scheme appears to have fallen through.

A number of Georgian houses stand around the green of the old market place and the remainder of New Buckenham is made up of streets laid out in a symmetrical grid-iron design. The streets have conventional names such as King Street and Queen Street, but in contrast there is a strangely named Boosey Walk with a picturesque thatched cottage dated 1731.

The pinnacled tower of **St Martin's Church** overlooks the village, and the church interior has roof timbers supported by effigies in stone of the twelve apostles.

Pub: **Kings Head** |**Bs**|**Ra**|

LAXFIELD, SUFFOLK |✝|

Probably no one man has had a greater influence on the state of the stained glass and internal treasures of Suffolk's churches than William ('Smasher') Dowsing, born here with a tablet to his memory on his wife's tombstone in the church. This fanatical Puritan, carrying out the orders of Parliament for the destruction of superstitious objects in churches, went far beyond his brief and Arthur Mee relates how 'in 50 days he smashed his way through 150 old churches in Suffolk'.

At Stradbroke, 5 miles from his native village, Dowsing took pleasure in recording '8 angels off the Roof and Cherubims in wood to be taken down; and 4 crosses on the steeple; and 17 pictures in the upper window; and organs which I break'. Many of the village churches mentioned in this guide suffered at his hands, among them those at *Walberswick* and *Coddenham*, though in the latter case the alabaster Crucifix escaped his attentions by being buried underground before his arrival.

Apart from the shadow of William Dowsing, Laxfield is a charming, compact village where the church, the timbered guildhall and the inn lie close together. The **church**, mainly 15thC and screened by arched lime trees, stands beneath a graceful pinnacled tower. There is much fine wood carving; some pews are labelled 'For Men Only' and 'For Women Only'; and the basin of the 15thC font is carved with figures illustrating the Seven Sacraments.

Pub: **Kings Head** |**Bs**|**Ra**|

WESTLETON, SUFFOLK |△|✝|

To the E of the village, barely a mile away, is **Dunwich Heath** where the National Trust have preserved the gorse-covered hills and a mile of beautiful Suffolk coastline. The prevention of the erosion of these cliffs by sea and weather is just one of the varied tasks of the Trust.

In contrast to the austere hills that lie above it, Westleton nestles amid green fields, a charming village with a wide main street, a church with a rustic thatched roof, a pleasant inn, the **Crown**, near a large duck pond, a triangular green, a gabled Elizabethan house and thatched cottages.

The chancel of the **church** is graced by a soaring 14thC arch and other features of interest are the angels attended by lions that guard the 15thC font. The church holds an annual flower festival, using only wild flowers, and every summer a fair is held on the village green.

Pub: **Crown Inn** |**A**|**R**|**Bs**| *Tel.* **(072 873) 273.**

DUNWICH, SUFFOLK |△|★|✝|

It is hard to believe that this remote little hamlet on the edge of a shingle beach was once a large and important centre of Christianity. At the time of the Norman Conquest Dunwich had already become a sizeable town and by the 13thC boasted nine churches; many of them serving seafaring men. The decline soon began. A great storm in 1326 washed away numerous buildings, among them three churches. Successive centuries saw continued erosion until, today, Dunwich consists of little more than an inn, a handful of cottages, the ruins of the priory on farmland above the village, and the Victorian **Church of St James**. Much of the history of the village which now lies under the invading sea is contained in the small **museum** near the inn.

Fishing continues to a limited degree; in one of the fishermen's huts on the beach there are plans that demonstrate the amount of erosion over the past century. The fascination of Dunwich is the contemplation of a great town that lies close at hand buried in the deep — contemplation enhanced by tales of fishermen said to have heard the ghostly peal of church bells from beneath.

To the S of Dunwich, 214 acres of cliff, heathland and beach, together with a row of coastguard cottages, have been preserved by the National Trust. Along this section of the coast there is also **Minsmere**, a bird sanctuary of the Royal Society for the Protection of Birds.

Pub: **Ship Inn** |**A**|**Bs**|**Ra**| *Tel.* **(072 873) 219.**

WALBERSWICK, SUFFOLK

One of the most picturesque Suffolk coastal villages, Walberswick nestles on the southern shore of the estuary of the River Blythe. A passenger ferry plies its way across the river to Southwold, a larger resort to the N of the village. Walberswick was at one time a place of some importance, but today cattle graze near the derelict quays at the mouth of the river from where ships and fishing vessels once sailed.

The 15thC **Church of St Andrew**, formerly a great and noble building, has now been reduced to an ivy-clad ruin with only the tower, the S aisle and porch remaining. Although the village's importance as a trading centre has vanished, it has today assumed the role of a select, unspoilt seaside resort. There is a small sandy beach and pleasant coastal walks. Gracious old houses from various periods cluster around village greens, making Walberswick a favourite subject for artists.

Pub: **Anchor Hotel** |**A**|**R**|**Bs**| *Tel.* **(0502) 722112.**

Touring centre

King's Lynn, Norfolk

Hotels: **Dukes Head, Tuesday Market Place,** *Tel.* **(0553) 4996❹**
Stuart House, Goodwins Road, *Tel.* **(0553) 2169❷**

CASTLE RISING, NORFOLK |△|✝|

Rising was a seaport town
When Lynn was but a marsh.
Now Lynn it is a seaport town
And Rising fares the worse.

This old rhyme tells how Castle Rising was once an important port on the River Babingley until larger ships were unable to navigate the river, when King's Lynn took over the trade.

The **castle** is one of several built by William de Albini in the 12thC and is believed to stand on a Roman site. The huge keep remains and it was here that Edward III imprisoned his mother, the 'She-Wolf of France', after her complicity with the murderers of her husband. In the 16thC the castle passed to the Howard family.

The mellow red-brick, single-storey **almshouses** opposite the church were established by Henry Howard, Earl of Northampton, under the terms that they were to be occupied by a governess and 11 inmates who should be 'of honest life and conversation, religious, grave and discreet, able to read if such a one may be had, single, 56 at least, no common beggar, harlot, scold, drunkard, haunter of taverns, inns or alehouses'. Today the rooms, furnished in Jacobean style, continue to be occupied and on special occasions the occupants comply with tradition by attending church dressed in red cloaks adorned with the Howard badge and wearing cone-shaped hats.

The **Church of St Lawrence**, set in the midst of trees, is noted for its Norman W front and doorway. On the nearby village green is a large 15thC cross.

BLAKENEY, NORFOLK |△|✝|

The high street of this enchanting village on the N Norfolk coast leads past flint cottages to the broad quayside. In medieval days Blakeney was a busy seaport; but the estuary has long since silted up and today the harbour caters only for small boats, yachts and motor launches, making a colourful scene in the heart of the village.

Evidence of Blakeney's former importance can be seen in High Street where the former **guildhall**, which is now a hotel, has a 14thC vaulted undercroft. Near the quay is a superb Georgian mansion. The hill-top **Church of St Nicholas** has in addition to its 15thC W tower, a lofty, slender turret which contains a beacon light; it once served as a landmark and guide to approaching ships.

The sand dunes, mud flats and creeks that surround Blakeney make it an area much loved by bird-watchers and naturalists. **Blakeney Point** was acquired by the National Trust in 1912 and can either be approached on foot from Cley (2 miles to the E of Blakeney) or by boat from Blakeney Quay when the tide is high.

A long shingle beach to the seaward side of the point protects it from incoming tides, leaving a sheltered area that forms a natural bird sanctuary where 256 different species have been sighted. Among scarcer varieties of bird life seen here annually are the long-tailed duck, wryneck, bluethroat and Lapland buntings. The area is also a haven for botanists; 190 species of flowering plants have been recorded, including a kind of sea lavender that normally only flourishes in the Mediterranean climate. Seals are not unknown off this part of the coast. An old life-boat house in the dunes is now used to accommodate visiting students.

Pub: **Blakeney Hotel** |A|R|Bs| *Tel.* **(0263)** 740797.

LITTLE WALSINGHAM, NORFOLK |△|†|

A colourful village where houses of red-brick blend pleasantly with timber-framed whitewashed cottages. A square called **Common Place** is graced by a 16thC brick-built **pumphouse**, octagonal in shape. At the foot of the high street is another square, known as **Friday Market**, where there is a splendid red-brick Georgian house. The nearby **Church of St Mary** has two fonts, one of which is considered to be among the finest in Norfolk, showing the seven sacraments and the Crucifixion on the bowl. In the N chapel is a famous sculpture by Sir Jacob Epstein (1880–1959), *The Risen Christ*.

Little Walsingham has been a place of pilgrimage since the 11thC. According to legend, Lady Richeld saw a vision in 1061 commanding her to build a replica of the House of Nazareth where Gabriel appeared to the Virgin Mary. Pilgrims flocked to the resultant shrine of 'Our Lady of Walsingham'. In the 12thC the Augustinians built a **priory** here and a century later the Franciscans followed with a **friary**.

At the time of the Reformation the shrine, the priory and the friary were all destroyed, lamented by a pilgrim in words which are preserved in the Bodleian Library, Oxford:

Bitter, bitter, oh to behoalde
The grass to growe
Where the walles of Walsingham
So stately did showe.

Remains of the priory and the friary can still be seen here, however, and in the 20thC pilgrimages recommenced to the new shrine where a replica of the original statue is contained.

CASTLE ACRE, NORFOLK |△|★|†|

William de Warenne, son-in-law of William the Conqueror, was responsible for founding the two structures that make this lovely fortress village a place to which admirers of ancient ruins are drawn. Most of the compact hillside village was once contained in the outer bailey of the **castle** after which it is named; an impressive entrance runs beneath the arched Bailey Gate, the narrow street ascending to join the wide main street and green. The castle was dismantled in the 14thC, providing material for the building of surrounding houses. Only the N gateway and fragments of the keep remain, but they stand in extensive earthworks that give an idea of the size and scope of the original building.

Much the most impressive of Castle Acre's ruins, however, are those of its **Cluniac priory**, set amidst lawns at the edge of the village. The dominating feature of these well-preserved remains is the lofty W front of the **priory church**, presenting a wealth of finely carved Norman ornamentation. The most complete building on the site is the gable-roofed **prior's lodging**, a handsome Tudor structure which now houses a **museum** of relics from the priory.

Pub: Ostrich |**A**|**R**|**Bs**|**Ra**| *Tel.* (076 05) 398.

The W front of the Cluniac priory church, embellished with detailed Norman carving. In an attractive setting away from the village centre, it is the most outstanding of Castle Acre's ruins.

AREA FIVE

Buckinghamshire, Hertfordshire, Bedfordshire and Northamptonshire

NORTHAMPTON SHIRE

BEDFORD SHIRE

BUCKINGHAM SHIRE

HERTFORD SHIRE

Touring centres
20 Aylesbury
21 Bedford
22 Oundle

The villages in this area lie within four counties in an area called the Chilterns and Mid-Anglia — a loosely defined and somewhat arbitrary title. The range of chalk hills known as the Chilterns extend from a point N of Reading, stretching east-ward in a curve of some 60 miles as far as Hitchin in Hertford-shire. Thus the bulk of the Chilterns form a loop through South Buckinghamshire and Hertfordshire, their highest points being Ivinghoe Beacon and Coombe Hill at Wendover (850ft).

Buckinghamshire, an agricultural county, incorporates the

fertile Vale of Aylesbury and is noted for its beech trees in the extreme south. The poet, William Cowper, lived and wrote much of his poetry at *Weston Underwood*; and *Penn* is associated with the Quaker of that name, founder of Pennsylvania. Another of Buckinghamshire's famous 'sons' is the statesman, John Hampden, who was born at Great Hampden. His refusal to pay Ship Money in 1636 led to the Civil Wars and his ultimate death from wounds inflicted at Chalgrove Field.

The Chilterns run through Hertfordshire from SW to NE; sheep are grazed on the chalky uplands while elsewhere fruit and specialized products such as flowers, early vegetables and water-cress are grown. Ashridge Park with its famous golf course and acres of lovely wooded countryside overlooks the delightful village of *Aldbury*. There is also much woodland surrounding the village of *Sarratt*.

Bedfordshire, another agricultural county, lies mainly in the lowlands of the Ouse basin. The county town is associated with John Bunyan, the religious writer, who drafted much of his *Pilgrim's Progress* while confined in Bedford gaol, and who was born at nearby *Elstow*.

Cattle-raising and crop-growing are among the chief occupations of Northamptonshire. The county town is the centre of the boot and shoe industry. Among the villages described is *Geddington*, at the heart of which is the best-preserved of the three remaining Eleanor Crosses; the others being at Northampton and Waltham Cross.

Variations of building materials are considerable. Northamptonshire depends much on stone, many village buildings comprising pale grey limestone with slate or thatch roofs. Typical examples of these thatched stone cottages are seen at *Wadenhoe*, where unusual buildings are the polygonal tollhouse and the circular dovecot with 500 nesting boxes. The other three counties rely more on brick and half-timber. At *Aldbury*, Hertfordshire, there are timber-framed, brick-and-tile cottages. *Hambleden*, Buckinghamshire, is remarkable for the uniformity of its brick-and-flint buildings. *Elstow*, Buckinghamshire, has a picturesque row of black and white cottages. This village is also noted for its Moot Hall, former market place and now a Bunyan Museum, a brick and timber building with an overhanging storey; and the Swan Inn, built of timber and herringbone brick.

Tour 20, centred on Aylesbury, is approximately 110 miles; a couple of days and an overnight stop are needed to complete the tour comfortably. The route takes you first to *Quainton*, with its attractive timber-framed cottages, then down to the picturesque Hambleden valley. Allow one and a half days to complete **Tour 21**, which ranges across three counties, covering 178 miles and seven villages. **Tour 22**, a day trip from the delightful town, Oundle, is just 37 miles and leads through the ancient Rockingham Forest to six recommended villages.

Touring centre
Aylesbury, Buckinghamshire
Hotels: **Bell, Market Street,** *Tel*. **(0296) 89835❹**
Kings Head, Market Street, *Tel*. **(0296) 5158❸**

QUAINTON, BUCKINGHAMSHIRE
⎮★⎮†⎮

Quainton is graced by a large triangular green, around which are
dotted attractive 17thC and 18thC timber-framed cottages. The green
slopes up to the pedestal and mutilated shaft of the 15thC market
cross, believed to have been erected by the Knights Hospitallers, who,
before the Reformation, had a hospice close by. Beyond the cross is an
18thC farmhouse and the tower of a windmill built in 1870, which has
been restored by the local Windmill Society.

A lane from the green leads to the **Church of St Mary and Holy
Cross** with its sturdy 15thC battlemented tower. Here is the tomb of
Sir Richard Winwood (*died* 1689), a bewigged figure in the armour of
a knight with his wife by his side, who provided the Winwood almshouses 2yrs before his death. The **almshouses**, red-brick and gabled,
with fine chimneys and porches surmounted by heraldic shields, stand
at the gates of the churchyard.

Among the other interesting tombs is that of James Lipscomb,
18thC sailor and surgeon, father of George Lipscomb, the Buckinghamshire historian, who lived at a cottage called Magpie on the green
but who, despite a varied and successful career, died penniless in a
London garret.

The Quainton Railway Society have taken over the disused
railway station outside the village where a **collection** of steam loco-
motives and rolling stock is on view.

BRILL, BUCKINGHAMSHIRE |△|✝|

A remote, windswept, hilltop village where red-brick houses cluster around a variety of spacious greens. Brill stands more than 600ft above sea level and one of the steep roads that descends from it, Tram Hill, was once the start of a tramway, which connected the village with the main railway line from *Quainton* to London.

There are three 17thC inns and on a grassy knoll near one of them, the **Pheasant Inn**, there is a 17thC red-brick windmill that has been restored by the National Trust. Flanking the central village green is the 12thC parish **church**, largely restored in the 19thC, and the **Red Lion Inn**. Nearby is the red-brick, gabled Elizabethan **manor house** with handsome gate posts.

Set behind glass in a wall of the main street is a barometer in memory of Sir Edmund Verney, a Crimean war veteran, inscribed: 'in grateful recognition of Sir Edmund Verney's devotion to the welfare of the people of Brill'.

Two miles to the W of Brill, through a wooded valley, is the National Trust-preserved **Boarstall Tower**. This is the stone gatehouse of a 14thC fortified house, now demolished. To the NE of the village is **Wotton House**, built in 1704 to a plan similar to that used for Buckingham Palace, in grounds landscaped by Capability Brown.

Pubs: Pheasant |**Bs**|
    Red Lion |**Bs**|
    Sun |**Bs**|

LONG CRENDON, BUCKINGHAMSHIRE |△|✝|

On one side of the square of this former lace-making centre is the 15thC gabled **Long Crendon Manor**. It can be seen through an imposing stone gatehouse that leads into the courtyard. On the other side of the square is the long main street that runs from the Churchill Arms, by way of delightful thatched houses and cottages of the 16thC and 17thC, culminating at the court house and church.

Among the many fine buildings passed on the way are the 17thC **Manor House** (not to be confused with Long Crendon Manor) and **Madges** with its 18thC facade of chequered brickwork. The street lies along the spur of a hill, permitting occasional glimpses between the houses of the rolling countryside beneath.

Undoubtedly Long Crendon's most impressive building is the early 15thC **court house** near the church. It was bought by the National Trust in 1900 and was one of its first acquisitions. Initially built as a wool-store, the building came into use as a court house during the reign of Henry V (1413–22) and fulfilled that function over several centuries. It has a long overhanging upper storey with five bays, four of which form one huge room.

The walls of the medieval **Church of St Mary** contain Norman masonry and the 15thC tower is adorned with many strange gargoyles. The finest monument inside the church is the tomb of Sir John Dormer (*died* 1622), an armoured figure by the side of his wife with her head resting on a cushion.

Pubs: Chandos Arms |**Bs**|**Ra**|
    Churchill Arms |**Bs**|**Ra**|

TURVILLE, BUCKINGHAMSHIRE |✝|

This village lies at the head of the Hambleden valley in the heart of some of the finest Chiltern scenery, overlooked from the immediate ridge above by a black-capped windmill. Timbered and dormered cottages stand near the little circular village green; nearby is the black and white **Bull and Butcher Inn** and the flint-built **Church of St Mary the Virgin**.

The church, which is 14thC with much subsequent restoration, has a small stained glass window designed by John Piper (*born* 1903) and its finest monument is the altar tomb of William Perry, builder of **Turville Park**, whose arms, a muzzled bear and porcupine, occupy a window.

A mile away from Turville is another pretty village, **Fingest**, noted for its **church** with a tall sturdy Norman tower, topped by a rare double saddleback roof that was added in the 18thC. The flint-and-brick-built **Chequers Inn** is believed to have served as a hostelry for over 500yrs.

Pubs: Bull and Butcher, Turville |Bs|Ra|

Chequers Inn, Fingest |Bs|Ra

HAMBLEDEN, BUCKINGHAMSHIRE |△|✝|

The name describes this as a 'village in a valley'; a glorious valley sheltered by a backdrop of beech-clad hills that run from Fingest to the Thames a mile to the south. A narrow stream glides past houses of brick and flint. Some of these date from the 17thC while others are estate buildings, put up by W. H. Smith (1825–91), politician and co-founder with his father of Britain's greatest chain of bookshops. Smith bought the Hambleden estate in 1871 and lived in a large Victorian house near the Thames, now a staff college.

At the heart of the village is the church and little green where the water-pump, in use as a main supply until recently, is sheltered by a giant chestnut tree. The **Church of St Mary the Virgin** contains a magnificent 17thC alabaster monument to the D'Oyley family, at one time lords of the manor. The kneeling figures of Sir Cope D'Oyley (*died* 1633) and his wife (*died* 1618) are surrounded by their ten children, some with skulls in their hands that indicate they died before their parents. The oak chest near this monument belonged to the Seventh Earl of Cardigan who was born here and who led the Charge of the Light Brigade (1854).

To the E of the church is the **manor house**, built in 1604. At Mill End, a mile from the village, the huge white weatherboarded **Hambleden Mill** stands near the weir. A mill is said to have stood here before the Domesday Book was written in 1086, when the owner paid a yearly rent of £1. The weir was constructed during the reign of Henry V (1413–22).

Pub: **Stag and Huntsman** |A|Bs|Ra| *Tel*. (049 166) 227.

PENN, BUCKINGHAMSHIRE |✝|

This long village straggles along a high ridge of the Chilterns. At one end is the large green with a duckpond surrounded by 17thC cottages. At the other end of the ridge, half a mile away, is the 14thC creeper-clad **Crown Inn**, from whose garden there is a superb, panoramic view. A view of equal beauty can be had from the 14thC tower of the **Church of the Holy Trinity** opposite the inn.

There are many monuments in the church to the family who share their name with the village, ancestors of that great Englishman, William Penn (1644–1718), founder of Pennsylvania. Son of Admiral Sir William Penn (1621–70), he joined the Quaker movement in 1667 and on being granted land in America in settlement of a debt owed by Charles I to his father, he emigrated there in 1681. A year later he founded the 'city of brotherly love', Philadelphia, intending to foster a State governed by Quaker principles.

Large, white and weatherboarded, Hambleden Mill dominates the weir at Mill End.

His spiritual values gained acceptance but his plans were not realized in practical terms and 4yrs later, disillusioned, he returned to England. On his death, many years later, William Penn was laid to rest in the Quaker burial ground at Jordans. However several of his decendants, as well as his ancestors, lie here at Penn.

Pub: **Crown Inn** |**R**|**Bs**|**Ra**|

SARRATT, HERTFORDSHIRE |**✝**|

Set amid wooded countryside, Sarratt has a long village green that runs by a variety of houses and cottages for some quarter of a mile, with a 17thC farmhouse in the background, the **Boot Inn** central to the green, and at the extreme end the **Cricketers' Inn** near a pretty duck pond. At this point there is still no sign of the church. It lies tucked away amidst another group of buildings, among them the Baldwin almshouses, founded in the 16thC, and the little **Cock Inn**.

The **Church of the Holy Cross** is distinguished by its gabled saddleback roof, the only one of its kind in Hertfordshire.

Pub: **Cock Inn, Sarratt** |**Bs**|**Ra**|

IVINGHOE, BUCKINGHAMSHIRE |**✝**|**◆●**|

The National Trust own much land in these parts, in particular **Ivinghoe Beacon** that towers over the village some 800ft above sea level, and the old **windmill** in a nearby field. The **Kings Head**, a restored 15thC creeper-clad inn with original oak beams and fireplaces stands by the village green. Here, also, is a handsome Georgian house used as a youth hostel.

The **Church of St Mary the Virgin** is 13thC, although it was altered extensively over the following two centuries, and lies in a huge churchyard. It is noted for its spectacular roof, from which carved figures of angels with outspread wings look down. Another feature of the church is the intricate, richly panelled Jacobean pulpit.

Ivinghoe is said to have given Sir Walter Scott the name for his novel *Ivanhoe* (1819), perhaps inspired by local rhyme when he visited the village:

> *Tring, Wing, and Ivanhoe*
> *Hampden of Hampden did forgo*
> *For striking of ye Prince a blow*
> *And glad he might escapen so.*

Pub: **Kings Head** |**R**|**Bs**|**Ra**|

ALDBURY, HERTFORDSHIRE |**✝**|**◆●**|

This village nestles at the foot of **Ashridge Park** where, at the summit of these beech-clad hills is the massive 200ft high column in memory of the Duke of Bridgewater (1736–1803), father of British inland navigation. At the core of the village is the green. The stocks that stand prominently here are restored versions of those in use more than 100yrs ago. A new oak replaces the old elm that stood on the green for centuries until disease accounted for it in 1976; the lime that stands nearby was planted in Victoria Jubilee Year, 1897.

The green fringes a fine duck pond from where Stocks Road leads northward, straddled by picturesque houses and cottages. Alongside the pond is one of Aldbury's oldest buildings, the timbered **manor house** with lattice windows, which today provides two dwellings. Built in the early 16thC the manor house was the home of a succession of yeomen farmers, the initials BW on one of the chimneys being those of Benedict Winch whose family lived here for about 100yrs. Next to the manor house is the creeper-clad **Greyhound Inn**; a little further along the street are three black-beamed terraced almshouses.

The **church**, set back a little from the green, dates mainly from the 14thC with a square tower of the 15thC. In the Pendley chapel is the tomb and sculptured figure of Sir Robert Whittingham, builder of nearby **Pendley Manor**. Sir Robert, a Lancastrian killed at the battle of Tewksbury, lies by his wife with the family shields carved on the tomb. Another person of distinction to be buried here is the novelist and social reformer Mary Augusta Ward (1851–1920), known as Mrs Humphry Ward. Her best known novel, *Robert Elsmere*, was published in 1888, and in another novel, *Bessie Costrell*, there is a vivid description of Aldbury. The entrance to her former home, **Stocks House**, can be seen on the left of the road that leads from the village to *Ivinghoe*.

Pubs: **Valiant Trooper** | **Bs** | **Ra** |
      Greyhound | **Bs** |

TOUR TWENTY-ONE
Touring centre
Bedford, Bedfordshire
Hotels: **Bedford Swan, Embankment,** *Tel.* **(0234) 46565 ❸**
     De Parys, De Parys Avenue, *Tel.* **(0234) 52121 ❷**

WESTON UNDERWOOD, BUCKINGHAMSHIRE |△|✝|❖•|

A stone archway marks the entrance to the village. Little else remains of the manor house owned over the centuries by the Throckmorton family, who befriended the poet William Cowper (1731–1800) when he lived and wrote here. Much of Cowper's creative life was spent at nearby **Olney** in a house now preserved as a **museum** with many of his relics.

Many of Cowper's middle years had been plagued with bouts of insanity, but the final and happiest years of his life were spent at Weston Underwood, in the two-storey house with seven prominent dormer windows that can be seen in the single main street. Nearby is the inn, the **Cowper Oak** named after him. Close to the inn a path leads across the fields to a sheltered alcove with an inscription from one of his poems: 'The summit gained, behold the proud alcove that crowned it'. **Cowper's Alcove** commands glorious views across the rolling countryside and from it he gathered inspiration for much of his later work.

Another view much loved by the poet was that from the church-yard. Inside the **church**, noted for its magnificent chancel window, there are many monuments to the Throckmorton family who had succoured and encouraged the poet throughout his time in the village.

Pub: **Cowper Oak** |**Bs**|

STOKE BRUERNE, NORTHAMPTONSHIRE |△|★|†|

The main street descends past some delightful thatched cottages before reaching the bridge across the Grand Union Canal. Here, from the towpath, colourful craft can be seen as they pass through the canal locks. On one bank is the **Boat Inn**, constructed from a number of ter-raced houses to form bars and a restaurant; on the other bank is the fascinating **British Waterways Museum**, a conversion of an old grain warehouse.

To the S of the village are **Stoke Park Pavilions**; two pavilions in a great park that originally flanked an Inigo Jones house designed in 1630 in the Italian style but which burnt down in 1886. The pavilions are open to the public on specified occasions during the summer months.

In the churchyard of the Norman **Church of St Mary** that stands on the hill above the village is a tribute to the daughter of a former coachman at Stoke Park, Sister Elsie Bull. Her name is inscribed proudly on the war memorial, a marble obelisk, in memory of her death in 1918 from a plague of typhus in Serbia. She had nursed victims of the First World War with selfless devotion.

Pub: **Boat Inn** |**Bs**|

ELSTOW, BEDFORDSHIRE |★|†|◦•|

The heart of the village, famous as the birthplace of the religious writer John Bunyan (1628–88), is the huge green where Bunyan played as a child and where he heard the voice that changed the course of his life: 'Will thy leave thy sins and go to heaven, or have thy sins and go to hell?'

At present a busy main road means that traffic thunders through the village, but a by-pass is under construction and shortly Elstow hopes to regain the peace found there in Bunyan's day. The cottage where the writer was born no longer exists; a stone in a field near the road to Harrowden, hard to find, marks the site. Another cottage where he spent his youth has also disappeared but a notice opposite the school on the road to Bedford indicates where it once stood.

On the edge of the green is the timbered **Swan Inn** of herring-

A familiar sight in the village of Stoke Bruerne, a long boat passing through a lock on the Grand Union Canal. The buildings on the left of the picture include the recommended Boat Inn.

bone frontal design and the **Moot Hall**, a timbered medieval market hall. This two-storeyed building now houses a **Bunyan museum** with interesting manuscripts and relics that relate both to the writer and the period in which he lived. Among the relics are the doors of Bunyan's cell in Bedford gaol where he began his *Pilgrim's Progress* in 1678.

Across the green from the Moot Hall is the fine **Church of St Mary and St Helen** with the separate 15thC bell-tower where Bunyan once rang the bells. Inside the church is the font where the author was baptised and stained glass windows illustrate both his *Pilgrim's Progress* and his later *Holy War* (1682).

Pubs: Red Lion |**Bs**|**Ra**|

     Swan Inn |**Bs**|

OLD WARDEN, BEDFORDSHIRE |★|†|

Before 1500 Old Warden was known simply as Warden (watch-hill). At that time there stood here the earliest house of the Cistercian order in Bedfordshire, the **Abbey of St Mary de Sartis**, founded in 1135. The monks were famous for the cultivation of pears which they made into Warden pies, causing the clown in Shakespeare's *Winters Tale* to exclaim 'I must have saffron, to colour the warden pies'. The site of the abbey, pulled down in the reign of Henry VIII, is now occupied by a Tudor house with mullioned windows that lies just outside the village.

The prize possession of the parish **Church of St Leonard** perched on the hill above Old Warden is the stained glass in the N wall of the nave that came from the abbey. The church is also noted for rich wood carving, in particular a number of panels from the private chapel in Bruges of Anne of Cleves, fourth wife of Henry VIII, identifiable by the initials AC beneath the royal crown.

Across the valley from the brown cobbled church is **Old Warden Hall**, a huge Victorian building of yellow brick with a large clock tower, built for Joseph Shuttleworth. The hall, set in a magnificent park, is used today as a College of Agriculture and Forestry. In the grounds is a small **aerodrome**, owned by the Shuttleworth Trust, with a display of vintage aircraft.

The village lane meanders past a variety of quaint little

buildings of no particular shape or design. Honey-coloured thatched cottages mingle with those of red brick. In the garden of one of the cottages, the well is surmounted by mock gallows.

ASHWELL, HERTFORDSHIRE ★ †

This large village lies above the River Rhee; its name deriving from the springs that form the source of the Rhee, a tributary of the River Cam. There are a host of period properties here, many of which have been restored and boast fascinating names. The oldest houses are **Bear House**, once an inn at the corner of Bear Lane, and **Ducklake Farmhouse** near the springs. The **Chantry House** at the W end of Ashwell is said to have been occupied since 1400. The **Guildhouse** in High Street, a long timbered and whitewashed building with an overhanging storey, was established as the Guildhall of St John the Baptist in 1476. Other 15thC buildings in the high street include **Kirby Manor**, the **Foresters' Cottages** and the **Rose and Crown Inn**, which is timbered with overhanging gables.

The former manor house, **Ashwell Bury**, dates from Victorian times and was redesigned by Sir Edward Lutyens during the 20thC. It is now used for offices. The **Old Mill**, at the end of Mill Street, has been much altered and the huge mill wheel renovated. The timbered 15thC **Town House**, used for a great variety of purposes over the centuries, was scheduled for demolition in the 1920s. Resourceful villagers came to the rescue, however, and formed a Museum Committee to purchase the building. Thus by 1930 it had been bought and restored, and today it houses a **museum**, managed by local people, illustrating life in Ashwell from prehistoric times to the end of the 19thC.

Dominating the village is the glorious 176ft tower of the 14thC church; the tower is topped with an octagonal lantern and a tall slender spire. The **church** is believed to be unique for the amount of graffiti on its pillars and walls. On these, over the centuries, men and

---

A vast mansion in a lovely parkland setting, Old Warden Hall boasts a beautiful interior of dark carved oak and a fascinating collection of rare aircraft in its grounds.

women have given vent to their frustrations by scratching feelings of all kinds, ranging from those of the medieval architect who wrote: 'The corners are not pointed correctly, I spit at them' to the young man who described his one-time lover as a barbarian.

Pubs: **Three Tuns Hotel** |**A**|**R**|**Bs**| *Tel.* (046 274) 2387.

Rose and Crown |**Bs**|

WESTMILL, HERTFORDSHIRE †|◆•|

A minor road leads away from the busy Ware–Royston road (A10), dropping sharply to a secluded valley and crossing a stream before entering this enchanting village. On the left is a large farm building and a line of colour-washed tree-fronted cottages that face the church and inn.

The **church** with traces of its Saxon origins has seen much recent restoration. The inn, the **Sword in Hand**, next to the church, has an entrance protected by two huge trees and beyond it is the triangular village green surrounded by picturesque cottages and enclosing a water-pump, which is sheltered by a beehive-shaped pavilion with an inscription that reads: 'Traverse the Desert and then you can tell What Treasure exists in this cold deep Well'.

A notice on the green of this much photographed village records that it won the award for being the best-kept village in Hertfordshire in 1975, 1977, 1979 and 1981. A mile from Westmill, at **Cherry's Green**, is a thatched cottage, once the property of the essayist and critic Charles Lamb (1775–1834). The cottage is preserved by the Royal Society for the Arts, although ironically Lamb never lived there despite recording his visit to his only landed property thus:

> *When I journeyed down to take possession, and planted foot on my own ground, the stately habits of the donor descended upon me, and I strode (shall I confess the vanity?) with larger paces over my allotment of three quarters of an acre with its commodious mansion in the midst, with the feeling of an English freeholder that all betwixt sky and centre was my own.*

Pub: **Sword in Hand** |**Bs**|**Ra**|

MUCH HADHAM, HERTFORDSHIRE |◆•|

The greater part of the village lies along either side of a long main street, timbered medieval cottages with overhanging storeys harmonizing with old inns, Regency houses and Victorian almshouses to make Much Hadham one of Hertfordshire's most gracious villages. Among many handsome buildings are **Much Hadham Hall**, a seven bay, brick house built in 1735 with a central Venetian window, and, at the extreme end of the village, The Lordship, also 18thC, a long, two-storey house with stables, which was once the home of the poet and social reformer William Morris (1834–96).

The **Red Lion Inn** recently ceased to be a hostelry having been turned into a number of dwellings. At one time it is said that a secret passage from behind the panelling of the inn led to the Bishop's Palace. The palace, country home of the Bishops of London for more than 800yrs, is near the church by the River Ash, a little to the E of the main street. It was here that Henry V's widow gave birth to Edmund Tudor whose son was to become Henry VII, founder of the Tudor dynasty. This long low building once served as a farmhouse. It underwent extensive restoration in the 16thC and was enlarged in the 18thC.

Pub: **Bull Inn** |**Bs**|**Ra**|

Touring centre
Oundle, Northamptonshire
Hotel: **Talbot, New Street,** *Tel*. **(0832) 3621 ❹**

ROCKINGHAM, NORTHAMPTONSHIRE |✝|◆●|

This charming village was once the hub of the vast **Rockingham Forest**, a hunting centre as well as a defensive stronghold used by kings and princes from Norman to Tudor times. Old thatched cottages mingle with newer buildings of flint-stone in the wide main street where the market cross is believed to mark the central point of the ancient forest.

On the summit of the tree-clad hill above the village is **Rockingham Castle**, which was started by William the Conqueror as a hunting lodge, and although the present building is largely Elizabethan some traces of the original Norman work remain. In 1530 the castle was granted by Henry VIII to the Watson family. By this time it was falling into decay; but successive generations of the family restored it over the centuries, loyal to the intention of Sir Edward Watson, who in 1579 had cut on the beams of the renovated great hall: 'The house shal be preserved and never will decaye/Where the Almightie God is honored and served daye by daye.' The Watson family still live at the castle, the oldest house in Northamptonshire to have been occupied continuously. The novelist Charles. Dickens stayed at the castle as a guest, writing much of his *Bleak House* (1853) here and dedicating David Copperfield to Mr and Mrs Watson.

The 13thC **Church of St Leonard** near the castle was largely rebuilt in the 19thC. There is a fine Jacobean pulpit and many memorials to the Watsons.

GEDDINGTON, NORTHAMPTONSHIRE |△|✝|

The stone and thatched cottages of the village lie on either side of the Rive Ise, joined by a narrow, four-arched, medieval bridge. The centre of Geddington is graced by a 40ft high Eleanor Cross. Eleanor of

Castile, daughter of Ferdinand III of Castile, and wife of Edward I of England, died at Harby in Notts in 1290. The king ordered that crosses were to be erected at the 13 stopping places of his Queen's funeral cortege to Westminster Abbey. Only three remain, those at Northampton, Waltham Cross and Geddington, and of these Geddington's Eleanor Cross is the best preserved.

Mounted on seven steps and pinnacled, the cross incorporates three statues of Queen Eleanor in niches. A modern imitation of the Eleanor Crosses can be seen outside Charing Cross station in London. Overlooking the scene is the **Church of St Mary Magdalene**, entered through a 13thC doorway, but mainly dating from the 15thC. The imposing tower is crowned by an octagonal spire.

A mile or so to the SE is **Boughton House**, which is often open to the public in the summer.

TITCHMARSH, NORTHAMPTONSHIRE |✝|∞|

In common with so many remote English villages, Titchmarsh has suffered a steady decline of its population. In 1841 registers show that 905 people lived here; today that figure has dwindled to a little over 400. The pride of the village is the **church tower**, said to be the finest village tower outside Somerset. Ninety-nine feet in height and built in four stages, it soars majestically above the sleepy scene, a noble landmark above which the 'Tychemersle Beacon' was erected in the reign of Elizabeth I when the invasion of the Spanish Armada was feared.

The early lords of the manor were the Lovel family, and a grassy mound visible from the high street marks the site of Lovels Castel (*c.*1300). In 1553 the manor of Titchmarsh was bought by Gilbert Pickering whose descendant, Sir Gilbert Pickering, became Lord Chamberlain to Oliver Cromwell. When the family became extinct in 1778 the manor house was pulled down; but the group of **almshouses** near the church, thatched with dormer windows, remain as a memorial to the Pickering family who donated them.

The poet John Dryden (1631–1700), poet laureate for 20yrs, was born at nearby *Aldwincle* but spent much of his boyhood here. Dryden was related to the Pickerings through his mother and it is believed that his parents, Erasmus and Mary Dryden, lived at Brookside farmhouse near the village.

Pub: **Dog and Partridge** |Bs|Ra|

ALDWINCLE, NORTHAMPTONSHIRE |✝|∞|

Attractive stone cottages line the street that curves through this remote village. A sign whose centrepiece has been removed suggests that the building behind it was once the inn.

Aldwincle is mentioned in the Domesday Book as Eldwincle. It is said that over the ages there have been at least 17 variations of the village name. Aldwincle is commonly used, and in the chancel of All Saints' Church is a brass to William Aldewyncle. 'Wincle' is believed to derive from 'wincel', a bend or corner; the River Nene having a great double bend nearby.

Before 1879 Aldwincle comprised two manorial villages which accounts for the presence of two churches, St Peter's and All Saints'. **St Peter's** is the church used today; it is graced by a magnificent tower and a broach spire considered to be the finest in the county.

At the extremity of the village is **All Saints' Church**, no longer in use but preserved with many interesting features. Here the poet John Dryden (1631–1700) was christened; he was born at the rectory which was originally opposite the church and later spent his boyhood at nearby *Titchmarsh*.

Another famous literary son of Aldwincle is Thomas Fuller (1608–61), author of *A Church History of Britain*. The house where he was born is no longer standing, but his name is commemorated in the tower window of the Church of St Peter with the words: 'A scribe instructed into the Kingdom of Heaven'.

WADENHOE, NORTHAMPTONSHIRE |★|†|❖|

Picturesque stone cottages, many of them thatched, cluster around this charming agricultural village that lies above the banks of the River Nene. A cul-de-sac leads down to the **Kings Head Inn** which has a lovely garden bordering the willow-lined river. A footpath (sign-posted to *Aldwincle*) rises sharply across the fields from the inn, arriving at the hill-top **Church of St Michael and All Angels** with its rare saddleback Norman tower. From this lonely little church the spires of the churches at Aldwincle can be seen, as well as the lovely stretch of river that flows by the old water mill below.

The stained glass window in the N aisle of the church is a memorial to the Rt Hon. George Ward-Hunt, Chancellor of the Exchequer in Disraeli's government, who once lived at the gabled **Wadenhoe House** in the village and who is said to have installed the first rural telegraph office here to enable him to keep in touch with Whitehall.

Interesting structures include a house with a polygonal end, once the **tollhouse**; and a fine round **dovecot** in a farmyard at the centre of the village. To the W of Wadenhoe are earthworks called **Castle Close** (its origin is unknown) and 2 miles to the E of the village is **Lilford Hall** where the outbuildings have been turned into a craft museum and an antiques centre.
Pub: **Kings Head** |Bs||Ra|

BARNWELL, NORTHAMPTONSHIRE |†|

This village lies in two parts, divided by a tree-lined brook where, at the foot of the street, a little arched stone bridge connects the village store with the **Montagu Arms**. There were once two villages here, each with its own medieval church. Today only the **Church of St Andrew** remains complete; the main village street climbs gradually past pretty stone cottages before reaching the church and the **Latham alms-houses**. 'Cast thy bread upon the waters' is the inscription on the gateway to the almshouses, rebuilt in the 19thC but founded in 1601 by Nicholas Latham who was parson at St Andrew's for 51yrs. There is a bust to him in the church which has a handsome 13thC tower from which rises a lovely spire.

Further along the stream, standing forlornly on the bank at the edge of the village, is all that remains of **All Saints' Church**, which is the 13thC chancel with many memorials of the Montagu family, original occupants of Barnwell Castle. Among the most moving of these memorials is that to a little boy of three who was drowned in 1625; the inscription reads: 'A witty and hopeful child, tender and dear in the sight of his parents and much lamented by his friends.'

Standing in the grounds of the big Elizabethan **manor house**, formerly the home of the Montagus, but now the property of the Duke of Gloucester, are the ruins of the original **Barnwell Castle**, built by Berengar le Moine in the mid-13thC. The grounds are normally open to the public once a year in April.
Pub: **Montagu Arms** |Bs|

Warwickshire and Leicestershire

Touring centres

23 Banbury
24 Stratford-upon-Avon
25 Uppingham
26 Melton Mowbray

LEICESTERSHIRE

WARWICKSHIRE

Among the villages grouped in this area are two, *Lyddington* and *Edith Weston*, which originally lay within the borders of Rutland, England's smallest county until it disappeared in the boundary changes that occurred in 1974, and these villages are now part of the county of Leicestershire.

Within the boundaries of Warwickshire coal and iron are found, as well as much rich agricultural land. Indeed there can be few counties where the old and the new blend in such close proximity. Near to the industrial towns of Birmingham and Coventry with its fine modern cathedral is Stratford-upon-Avon, birthplace of William Shakespeare. Close at hand are old towns of great historic interest, Warwick and Kenilworth, and the spa town of Leamington. Associations with England's greatest poet are found at *Aston Cantlow*, where Shakespeare's parents are believed to have married, and at Wilmcote where Mary Arden, the poet's mother lived as a child. Above *Radway* is Edge Hill, scene of the first major battle of the Civil War. Near *Long Compton*, astride the county boundary with Oxfordshire, are the Rollright Stones, smaller than those at Stonehenge but believed to date from earlier times.

Leicestershire, mainly a low-lying county, has much loamy soil affording rich pastureland. Here cattle graze in fields dotted with clumps of woodland and divided by broad thorn hedges — an area that provides some of the best fox-hunting in England with world-famous packs such as the Quorn and Belvoir. The Vale of Belvoir is dominated by Belvoir Castle near *Bottesford*, where the lovely church with its tall spire is known as the 'Lady of the Vale'. Other notable landmarks of Leicestershire are the huge reservoir of Rutland Water that fringes *Edith Weston*, and the parish church of *Breedon on the Hill* which overlooks the surrounding countryside from the heights of the huge limestone bluff above the village.

Picturesque thatched timbered buildings can be seen in many Warwickshire villages, among them *Welford-on-Avon* and *Aston Cantlow*. Elsewhere building materials range from the rich honey-coloured Hornton stone seen at *Warmington* to the golden iron-stone used in the construction of the model village of *Horninghold*. Iron-stone, quarried locally, forms the substance for the cottages of *Edith Weston*. *Ilmington* is close to the Cotswolds and can be compared, naturally, with a typical Cotswold stone village.

With Banbury as its touring centre, **Tour 23** (covering 76 miles and six villages) takes you from Oxfordshire into Warwickshire and one of this county's most attractive villages, *Warmington*. The 46 miles and four villages of **Tour 24** can be covered in a leisurely day's drive. Beginning at Stratford, the route leads through countryside rich in Shakespearean associations. A short day trip from Uppingham, **Tour 25** covers 36 miles and four villages, from *Hallaton*, with its pretty thatched cottages, up to *Edith Weston* and views of Rutland Water. **Tour 26** (89 miles) can also be accomplished comfortably in one day. The route from Melton Mowbray includes the villages of *Gaddesby*, *Breedon* and *Bottesford*.

Touring centre
Banbury, Oxfordshire
Hotels: **Whateley Hall, Horse Fair,** *Tel.* (0295) 3451❹
Banbury Moat House, Oxford Road, *Tel.* (0295) 59361❹

WHICHFORD, WARWICKSHIRE |✝|

This village lies in a valley beneath rolling hills close to the boundary with Oxfordshire. Around the spacious green are stone houses, some thatched with mullioned windows, the old Victorian school house and the **Norman Knight Inn**, a name which gives the clue to Whichford's long history. From the green the road rises to the **church**, which like the long vanished castle was built by a Norman knight, De Mohun. In the chapel, built by a mother in memory of her soldier son, is the coffin lid of the last of the male line of this family, Sir John Mohun of Dunster, who was killed at the Battle of Boroughbridge in 1322.

The treasures of the church are the tombs of two men, both of them 16thC rectors to the Earl of Derby. One is that of John Merton (*died* 1537), the alabaster effigy dressed in rich garments; the other is the richly carved tomb of Nicholas Asheton (*died* 1582), engraved with his portrait in brass. The pulpit is unusual in that it is approached by steps from the chapel.

Whichford House, close to the church and once the rectory, dates from the early 17thC and stands in a pleasant garden.
Pub: **Norman Knight** |**Bs**|

LONG COMPTON, WARWICKSHIRE |△|★|✝|

The name gives weight to the fact that the village straggles for a considerable distance along the main street which inevitably has led to recent development. Fortunately many old grey-stone cottages remain to enhance the scene; and the entrance to the church is of particular interest. Here the lych-gate takes the form of a small, two-storey building, the arch leading to the churchyard is surmounted by an upper room with quaint windows and a thatched roof. This tiny cottage is thought originally to have been a priest's house and is known to have been occupied more recently by the village cobbler. Today it houses the **museum**.

The **Church of St Peter and St Paul** dates from the 13thC.

Approached by a regimented line of clipped yew trees, you can see that the battlements of the church contain loopholes through which muskets were fired during the Civil War. Within the porch is the ancient stone effigy of a lady, a sad and lonely figure if only because it is anonymous.

Many visitors to Long Compton have come to see the **Rollright Stones**, to be found on the windswept heights that lie just across the borders of Oxfordshire. Older than Stonehenge (they are believed to predate 1500BC), the origin of the stones is a mystery. Highest placed of the Rollright Stones are a circular group known as the **King's Men**. A quarter of a mile from these is a further group of five stones called the **Whispering Knights**. A solitary stone, almost 9ft in height and enclosed by railings, is dubbed the **King's Stone**. This last stone lies just within the border of Warwickshire.

RADWAY, WARWICKSHIRE |△|✝|❖•|

Clusters of stone cottages, some thatched, nestle around the village green and pond; the whole overshadowed by the wooded Edgehill, scene of the first and indecisive battle of the Civil War (see *Warmington*).

Near the church is **Radway Grange**, a gabled manor house built in Tudor times and converted with Gothic features by the architect Sanderson Miller in the 18thC. After the conversion the grange became a place renowned for its social gatherings. Among Miller's guests at this time was the novelist Henry Fielding, whose masterpiece, *Tom Jones* (1730), was written here, and Lord Chatham, a friend of Fielding's since Eton days, who is known to have planted a number of trees in the park. Subsequently Radway Grange became the home of Field Marshall Earl Haig (1861–1928), whose name is recorded on the lych-gate of the church along with others from the village who served in the First World War.

A reminder of much earlier conflicts can be seen inside **St Peter's Church**, rebuilt in 1866 on the site of an earlier church. There is the mutilated effigy of a soldier who fell during battle in 1642 on the hill above, Captain Henry Kingsmill.

Another of Sanderson Miller's creations is the lofty tower on **Edgehill**, sited on the spot where Charles I raised his standard before the battle. This is now the **Castle Inn**, which affords fine views.

Two miles to the S of Radway is the National Trust property, **Upton House**, built of rich yellow Warwickshire stone and remodelled in 1927 while retaining the style of the original 17thC building. The house, set in terraced gardens, is noted for its Flemish, Italian and English paintings, as well as collections of 18thC porcelain and furniture.

Pub: **Castle Inn** |**Bs**|

WARMINGTON, WARWICKSHIRE |✝|

Set in a hollow, the church towering above it, Warmington numbers among Warwickshire's most attractive villages. At the top of the spacious, sloping green is the small duckpond, tucked away and barely visible from the road, overlooked by the 17thC manor house. All around the green are delightful cottages built of Hornton stone; the road then narrows as it climbs towards the 17thC **Plough Inn** from where it climbs still further towards the church, which is approached by a flight of steps from the main road.

The **Church of St Michael**, built like the village houses of Hornton stone, stands at the threshold of Edgehill, scene of the first

Built of russet stone similar to that used in the village, the 17thC mansion, Farnborough Hall, stands in a magnificent landscaped garden, and is now owned by the National Trust.

and indecisive battle of the Civil War. It was here on 23 October 1642 that the foot soldiers of Lord Essex almost broke the line of infantry which formed the centre of the Royalist forces; King Charles only escaped capture with the arrival of his cavalry under the command of his nephew, Prince Rupert. Most of the victims of this bloody encounter will have been buried in unknown graves around the battlefield; but the name of at least one of those buried in the churchyard here is known. Recorded on a stone is the name of a Scots 'captaine', Alexander Gourden.

Pub: **Plough Inn** |**Bs**|**Ra**|

FARNBOROUGH, WARWICKSHIRE |△|✝|

Some modern building has developed at the eastern extremity of the village, but the core of Farnborough is still a pleasant composition of russet stone cottages, and among many attractive buildings are the 17thC inn, the **Butchers Arms**, the **school** and the **village store**. Across the road from the store a lane leads up to the church, set on a plateau above the village.

The **Church of St Botolph**, with its Gilbert Scott spire, has memorials to the Holbech family of Farnborough Hall, now a National Trust property open to the public. From the war memorial at the edge of the churchyard there is a fine view across the park of **Farnborough Hall**, a landscaped garden with a lake, temples, an

obelisk and a long terraced walk. The hall, built in the 17thC of russet stone, contains Italian paintings and sculpture.
Pub: **Butchers Arms** |**Bs**|**Ra**|

NAPTON ON THE HILL, WARWICKSHIRE |†|

Known as Neptone in the Domesday Book, the name Napton derives from cnaepp (hilltop) and tun (homestead). The hill, on which the village stands, rises to 450ft and is crowned by the **Church of St Lawrence**. Around the village green and streets that cling to the lower slopes of the hill are picturesque thatched cottages and Georgian as well as Victorian houses. Intermingled with these older buildings are some modern villas, sited to take advantage of the view, but not unfortunately to enhance the general scene.

Local folklore tells how the lofty church was planned originally to stand where the village green now is. But each night, so the story goes, the stones on the site disappeared to be found at the hill's summit, perhaps moved there by the spirits. The obvious conclusion was to build the church in its present dominant position, and there it stands, so high above the surrounding flat countryside that it is possible to stand in the churchyard and gaze across six counties. The church dates from Norman times with subsequent restoration that includes the tower, added in the 18thC.

Across the ridge is the Napton **windmill**, an ancient landmark, the predecessors of which can be traced back to 1543. The Oxford Canal curves round the foot of the hill, and to the N the Napton reservoir was built at the junction of the Oxford and Grand Union canals to maintain water levels.
Pub: **Napton Bridge** |**Bs**|**Ra**|

Touring centre

Stratford-upon-Avon, Warwickshire

Hotels: Falcon, Chapel Street, *Tel.* (0789) 5777❹
Haytor, Avenue Road, *Tel.* (0789) 297799❸

HONINGTON, WARWICKSHIRE |✝|

There is a delightful entry to this parkland village. Standing aloof by
the side of the main road is the little Tollgate Cottage, from where the
approach road to Honington passes between the stone pillars of a
former gateway, topped by pineapples. The road then crosses the
River Stour by way of a little bridge, adorned by 24 stone balls, before
reaching the focal point of the village, the gates to the grounds of
Honington Hall. Here the road divides. To the right it leads past
houses of brick and stone, fronted by lawns, before arriving at a small
green and a sign to indicate that Honington was Warwickshire's best
kept village.

To the left the road winds to the **church** with a Norman tower
but otherwise dating from the late 17thC when it was restored by Sir
Henry Parker, builder of the adjacent hall. At the W end of the church
is the marble monument to Sir Henry and his son, Hugh, the two men
bewigged with flowing cloaks. There are other monuments to the
Townsend family, later occupants of **Honington Hall**. The hall, not
open to the public, has a remarkable red-brick facade with six oval
recesses containing the busts of Roman Emperors. Near the house is
an octagonal dovecot with a sundial.

The village boasts neither a shop nor an inn.

ILMINGTON, WARWICKSHIRE |△|✝|

As befits an area that lies only a little to the E of the Cotswolds, this is a village with many Cotswold-style stone houses and cottages — a place of some importance a century ago when it was fashionable to 'take the waters' and the spring here was said to contain properties 'not often used by parishioners but frequently by visitors'. Ilmington can only really be seen to advantage on foot. The village streets, in any case, are usually blocked by bollards so that the church, the two greens and the groups of houses spread over a wide area are joined by a series of footpaths. One of these footpaths leads from the green by the inn, the **Howard Arms**, and the village shop to the church, passing on the way the chapel that was once the school-house as well as a spacious meadow and duckpond.

The **Church of St Mary**, mainly Norman and 13thC with later additions, has woodwork carved by the 'Mouseman of Kilburn' (see *Kilburn*). Two miles to the SW is the National Trust-owned **Hidcote Manor**, a 17thC house in a delightful 11-acre garden where rare trees, shrubs and plants thrive in an area sheltered from cold winds.

Pub: Howard Arms |**Bs**|

WELFORD-ON-AVON, WARWICKSHIRE |✝|

The River Avon is constantly at hand, forming a loop around the village and embracing it on three sides. There are three inns and from one of these, the **Bell**, the road leads to the river by way of the church, a picturesque cluster of timbered and thatched houses standing in Church Road and Boat Lane. The **church**, built in Norman times on a Saxon site, has a lych-gate much loved by artists. It was built in the 14thC and stood here for almost 600yrs until old age finally caught up with it in 1966 when it was dismantled. It was rebuilt in 1969, a careful replica of the original in seasoned wood and exact in design and measurement.

The village green, off the long main street, has a grassy mound topped by a tall maypole, surmounted by a ball and weathervane. Behind the green is the **Shakespeare Inn**; but an inn with an even more delightful setting lies just outside the village, by the river bridge on the road to Stratford. This is the **Four Alls Inn**, where a visit to the public bar gives a clue to the strange name. There is a stained-glass window depicting four figures:

The king who rules over All
The parson who prays for All
The soldier who fights for All
And the farmer who pays for All.

Pubs: Bell Inn |**Bs**|
    Four Alls Inn |**Bs**|
    Shakespeare Inn |**Bs**|

ASTON CANTLOW, WARWICKSHIRE |✝|

Facing each other across the long main street is the 17thC **Kings Head Inn** and the black and white timbered guild house with an overhanging storey. The **guild house**, once the scene of a thriving market, has a modern extension to the rear and is now in use as the village hall.

On the River Alne there was once a castle, built by the Norman family of de Cantelupe from which the village gets its name. No trace of the castle today remains; but the family are remembered by a depiction in the E window of the **Church of St Thomas de Cantelupe**,

The house at Wilmcote near Aston Cantlow, where Mary Arden once lived, is a fine example of a timber-framed building, with leaded windows, a tiled roof and walls that have bowed visibly with age.

a former Chancellor of England and Bishop of Hereford, who died in 1282.

The **Church of St John the Baptist** is believed to be the place where the marriage took place of John Shakespeare of Snitterfield and Mary Arden of Wilmcote, parents of England's greatest poet. At

Wilmcote, 2 miles to the SE, is the lovely timbered farmhouse where Mary Arden, mother of William Shakespeare, lived as a child. The house and charming garden in which it lies is maintained by the Shakespeare Birthplace Trust and is open on occasions to the public.
Pub: **Kings Head** |**Bs**|

Uppingham, Leicestershire

Hotels: **Falcon, High Street,** *Tel.* (057 282) 3535❸
Central, High Street, *Tel.* (057 282) 2352❷

HALLATON, LEICESTERSHIRE |★|†|

The white-railed duck pond and the **Fox Inn** stand at the top of this charming hillside village. Nearby is the 18thC grey-stone **Hallaton Hall**, not open to the public and now occupied by the Torch Trust for the Blind. The main street descends past picturesque thatched cottages to the village green with the war memorial and cone-shaped market cross.

By the green is a pretty little walled garden with a plaque which tells of 'the ancient custom of Hallaton Bottle Kicking'. The plaque gives details of the rough and ready rules of an extraordinary Easter Monday contest between Hallaton and neighbouring Medbourne, involving a hare pie distributed by the rector. After disposal of the pie and much 'toing and froing' on the outskirts of the village with beer bottles, the victors and vanquished of this strange contest retire to the local inns for celebration.

The **Church of St Michael and All Angels**, set among chestnut trees and cypresses, is graced by a 13thC spire and has a clock which plays a melody every third hour. A number of enchanting narrow lanes diverge from the main street, and in one of them, Hog Lane, is a small **museum** of local interest.

Hallaton Castle, half a mile away on the Goadby road, is a well-preserved grass earthwork where pottery from Roman times has been discovered.

Pubs: **Bewicke Arms** |**A**|**R**|**Bs**|**Ra**| *Tel.* (085 889) 217.
    Fox Inn |**Bs**|
    Royal Oak |**Bs**|

HORNINGHOLD, LEICESTERSHIRE |†|

Landlord-planned villages in England are far from uncommon. Within the pages of this guide a few that spring to mind are

Blanchland in Northumberland, *Milton Abbas* in Dorset and *Sudbury* in Derbyshire. Horninghold is another, smaller than those mentioned but singular in that it must be one of the last of these villages to be built.

The houses here, built from local golden iron-stone, are the creation of a wealthy local farmer, Thomas Hardcastle, and were newly built or reconverted at the beginning of the 20thC. They lie in a secluded valley among sycamores, chestnuts and a variety of trees and ornamental shrubs; the focal point of the village being the small triangular green.

From the green there is a pleasant approach to the church, passing a restored, lawn-fronted **Tudor cottage** that once served as the rectory. Far and away the oldest building is the **Church of St Peter**, 700yrs old, but with considerable restoration in Victorian days. Figures engraved on the Norman doorway include demons and animals, among them a lamb, a lion and a dove. One of the older relics within the church is the 13thC font, and in 1951 the limestone coffin lid of a cross bearer to the Knights Templar was discovered, dated 1260.

There is no inn today in Horninghold; the original inn having been converted into cottages.

LYDDINGTON, LEICESTERSHIRE |△|†|

Charming iron-stone cottages line the long main street of Lyddington, a village once part of Rutland, England's smallest county.

The building of greatest interest in the village is **Bede House**, part of the manorial retreat used by the Bishops of Lincoln, established in 1200 and rebuilt by Bishop Russell in the late 15thC. This long two-storey building by the churchyard is classified as an ancient monument and is open to the public in the summer.

In the days when Bede House served as an episcopal residence, the upper floor contained the banqueting hall and living quarters, and the ground floor was used for storage. In 1547 the manor was surrendered to Henry VIII, and subsequently his daughter, Queen Elizabeth I, granted it to Lord Burleigh, whose son, the Earl of Exeter, converted the building into almshouses. The ground floor was partitioned into a number of small rooms to accommodate a warden, 12 men and two women. A stone-roofed verandah was added to run the full length of the building and overlook the lawns to the north. The look-out tower, built above the village street at the corner of the garden, has a public path running through it and is known as the 'Bishop's Eye'.

An unusual feature of the **Church of St Andrew**, which is mainly 15thC, is the position of the altar, at some distance from the E wall and completely surrounded by rails. The position arose as a result of ecclesiastical dispute and it is believed that no other church in England has such an arrangement.

Pubs: **Marquess of Exeter** |**A**|**Bs**|**Ra**| *Tel.* (057 282) 2477.

White Hart |**Bs**|**Ra**|

EDITH WESTON, LEICESTERSHIRE |†|

This village of stone cottages, some thatched and others slate-roofed, was formerly incorporated in England's smallest county, Rutland, and stands above Rutland Water. The focal point is **Well Cross**, around which, grouped in a U-shape, is a cluster of cottages. Well Cross is so called because the little green contains an ancient well, now covered and acting as the support for the stem of the ancient village cross which originally stood on the other side of the road.

From Well Cross the road narrows past stone-built terraced cottages, a farmhouse and a barn until it reaches the church. This road, named King Edward's Way, acts as a reminder of the origin of the village name; Edith was the wife of Edward the Confessor, who gave her much of the western part of Rutland.

The edge of the churchyard allows a good view of Rutland Water, a reservoir with a 24-mile perimeter, where fishing and sailing take place. The **Church of St Mary the Virgin**, built of limestone, has traces of work begun in 1170 and a battlemented tower with grotesque gargoyles at each corner. Among charities administered by the church, one is of particular interest, that of William Louth. Although only a humble labourer who died in 1850 at Uppingham workhouse, Louth gave £100 during his lifetime for distribution to the poor of the parish.
Pub: **Wheatsheaf Inn** |Bs|

The Church of St Matthew at Normanton, half a mile from Edith Weston, stands on a spit of land jutting out into Rutland Water. It was designed by a London architect, Thomas Cundy, in the 19thC.

Touring centre

Melton Mowbray, Leicestershire

Hotels: **George, High Street**, *Tel*. (0664) 62112❸
Kings Head, Nottingham Street, *Tel*. (0664) 62110❷

GADDESBY, LEICESTERSHIRE |✝|

The creeper-clad **Cheney Arms**, once a guesthouse of the nearby manor, is the focal point of this remote village. A narrow lane behind the inn winds past some picturesque cottages and the entrance to Gaddesby Hall. From here a footpath leads past a meadow to the lovely **Church of St Luke**, with an impressive 13thC spire that soars above it. The footpath allows a glimpse across the hedge to **Gaddesby Hall**, built originally in the 18thC and once the home of the Cheney family after whom the inn is named.

An interesting monument in the church is the equestrian statue in marble of Colonel Edward Cheney of the Royal Scots Greys who fought at the Battle of Waterloo in 1815. Brought from the hall and placed here, the statue portrays Colonel Cheney astride his fallen horse with his sword upraised. A panel beneath depicts him warding off a French officer who is attempting to recapture one of Napoleon's standards, the eagle. A more ancient monument is the altar tomb of a 15thC knight in armour, his feet resting on a lion.

In farmland near the church a racehorse is buried. Bendigo, first winner of the Eclipse Stakes in 1886, is much revered in the village, where he was trained.

Pub: Cheney Arms |**A**|**R**|**Bs**|**Ra**| *Tel*. (066 472) 228.

BREEDON ON THE HILL, LEICESTERSHIRE †

The name is misleading for much of the village lies along the main road at the foot of the hill, where there are a number of old houses and two of the three village inns. At a point near the **Horseshoes Inn** the road narrows alarmingly and opposite the inn is the forbidding conical-roofed village 'lock-up' — impossible to see out of if incarcerated there so, when in use, it was termed the 'blind-house'. From here a footpath is signposted to the church which stands in glorious isolation on a 180ft limestone bluff above the village.

There is, fortunately, a motorable road to the church which begins the ascent at the war memorial and passes some of the more attractive village cottages, among them the ancient **Hollybush Inn**. Much of the hill of magnesium limestone on which the church stands and dominates the landscape has been quarried away. In the quarries, which produce stone for building and lime for agricultural purposes a stone axe head was discovered, pointing to very early habitation. The church stands on a site where an iron age fort, a Saxon monastery and a Norman priory had stood in turn.

Behind the altar and continued in the S aisle of the **church** are more than 70ft of intricately carved friezes, presumed to have originated from the Saxon monastery, depicting foliage, birds, animals and human figures. The most interesting Saxon sculpture of all, however, is not contained in this group but is in the tower ringing chamber. It is the figure of an Angel giving Byzantine blessing and can only be seen by arrangement.

Pubs: **Horseshoes Inn** |**Bs**|
      Lime Kiln Inn |**Bs**|

BOTTESFORD, LEICESTERSHIRE △†

'Please drive slowly, Ducks cross here' is the quaint road sign displayed at the bridge across the river by the church gates, a place often subject to flooding. The **Church of St Mary the Virgin** is set back from the main road, and around it a number of lanes are worth exploring for a view of the attractive, red-brick 17thC houses that lie dotted around them. The church, sometimes called 'The Lady of the Vale', is one of the largest village churches in England, providing ample space for the tombs of the Lords of Belvoir. Among these monuments is the Witch-craft Tomb, the only tomb in the country to bear an inscription which unashamedly attributes death to be the result of 'wicked Practice and Sorcerye'. The tomb is that of the male heirs of the Sixth Earl of Rutland, two sons who died in their infancy and for whom scapegoats were needed.

After the death of the boys in 1617 six women were arrested and accused of witchcraft, among them Joan Flower and two of her daughters. During her examination Joan Flower called for bread and butter, wishing to prove her innocence by declaring that 'it would never go through her if she were guilty'. After eating the bread Joan died immediately, confirming her as a witch as well as her unfortunate daughters who were hanged a year later at Lincoln Gaol.

Belvoir Castle, still the house of the Dukes of Rutland, lies some 2 miles to the S of the village on an isolated spur where the battle-mented walls and towers dominate the valley. Parts of the castle and the gardens that surround it are open to the public on specified occasions. During the summer months there are a variety of displays that include falconry and jousting.

Pubs: **Red Lion**|**Bs**|**Ra**|
      Bull |**Bs**|

Avon, Gloucestershire and Oxfordshire

The Cotswold hills start near Bristol, Avon, and extend for some 50 miles north-eastwards as far as Chipping Campden, Gloucestershire. The average height of the range is 500ft, although it rises to more than 1,000ft at Cleeve Hill near Cheltenham. Cotswold villages are, of course, renowned for the uniformity of their golden-stone buildings. The limestone of the Cotswolds, the fabric of the older houses and cottages, is a calcareous rock formed from small grains of carbonate of lime, resembling the hard roe of a fish and consequently known as oolite (egg-stone). Various layers of this rock are used for the building of both walls and roofs; the material for the latter, although often described as Cotswold slate, is in fact composed of thin layers of sandy limestone. The shortage and expense of this material means that it has not been used much in recent building. But strict planning regulations ensure that the material used for walls and roofs resembles the original, thus safeguarding the appearance of some of England's most beautiful villages.

This section contains descriptions of villages in three counties. The new county of Avon is an area that previously lay within the boundaries of Gloucestershire and Somerset, and has two listed villages: *Marshfield* and the ducal village of *Great Badminton*.

Although Gloucestershire is associated in particular with its picturesque Cotswold villages, the county also embraces within its SW boundary the former royal Forest of Dean. The forest occupies some 20,000 acres in a triangular shaped area, bounded by Ross, Chepstow and Gloucester, where hundreds of footpaths make it an ideal centre for rambling. The most central point of the forest is marked by a stone opposite the Speech House Hotel, built on the site of the headquarters of the Court of Verderers, who once administered the forest laws, and some of whose customs are maintained. *St Briavels*, where the remains of a medieval castle stand above the River Wye, lies in the heart of the Forest of Dean.

Oxfordshire, mostly in the Thames basin, is the home of the oldest of the British universities, University College dating from 1249. At *Kelmscot*, one of the villages listed, lived William Morris who did much to popularize the Cotswolds in the 19thC, as well as helping to preserve them by founding the Society for the Protection of Ancient Buildings. Despite the industrialization of the fringe of the city of Oxford, the county retains much of the charming rural scenery depicted by Matthew Arnold more than 100yrs ago:

> *Screen'd is this nook o'er the high, half-reaped field,*
> *And here till sun-down, Shepherd, will I be.*
> *Through the thick corn the scarlet poppies peep,*
> *And round green roots and yellowing stalks I see*
> *Pale blue convolvulus in tendrils creep;*
> *And air-swept lindens yield*
> *Their scent, and rustle down their perfum'd showers*
> *Of bloom on the bent grass where I am laid,*
> *And bower me from the August sun with shade;*
> *And the eye travels down to Oxford's towers . . . .*

('The Scholar Gipsy')

Touring centres
27 Bath
28 Cirencester
29 Gloucester
30 Cheltenham
31 Oxford
32 Witney
33 Chipping Norton

Tour 27 (40 miles), requiring half a day, starts from Georgian Bath, dips into the Cotswolds, and brings the motorist back via Chippenham. **Tour 28**, from Cirencester and through many typical Cotswold villages, is a 42-mile day trip, much of it on minor roads. **Tour 29** from Gloucester is a short day's drive (69 miles) going W, through the Forest of Dean, across the River Severn and through the remote village of *Bisley*. Leading through the heart of the Cotswolds, **Tour 30** covers 50 miles and five villages, and will take a full day. a 73-mile day trip, **Tour 31** traces a route to the S of Oxford. **Tour 32** (28 miles) could be completed in half a day, however, *Burford*, *Kelmscot* and *Minster Lovell* deserve more than a brief stop. Taking one day, **Tour 33**, a 41-mile route along many minor roads, encompasses more delightful golden-stone villages.

TOUR TWENTY-SEVEN

Touring centre

Bath, Avon

Hotels: **Pratts, South Parade,** *Tel.* **(0225) 60441**❸
Fernley, North Parade, *Tel.* **(0225) 61603**❸

The traditional procession, performed by the Marshfield Mummers every year on Boxing Day. Ringing his bell, the town crier leads the Mummers through the village. They are dressed in colourful costumes and masks made from shredded paper. A vital part of Marshfield's history, the Mummers even have a bar named after them in the Crown Inn.

MARSHFIELD, AVON ✝

Marshfield lies some 600ft above sea level at the southern extremity of the Cotswolds, a large village yet a peaceful one where the lack of bustle conveys a feeling of yesteryear. Conspicuous buildings on entry to the village are the **Nicholas Crisp almshouses**, built for eight old people in 1625. The almshouses peer out from behind a stone wall, the coat of arms over the porch and the whole surmounted by a clock-tower and spire with a weathervane. From here the long straight high street leads past houses of grey stone to give ever increasing delight.

Towards the end of the street are three ancient inns, the **Catherine Wheel** on the right, the **Crown** on the left and the **Lord Nelson** at the extreme end. All three inns entice but the Crown is of particular interest; a 17thC coaching inn, it once serviced the Bristol–Chippenham–London stage. It has a Mummers' Bar, so called because every Boxing Day the Marshfield Mummers perform a traditional English folkdance. The dancers, led by the town crier ringing his bell, are dressed in costumes made from newsprint and coloured paper. The cellar under the Mummers' Bar was once the gaol and the restaurant was the village shop. A plaque on a house near the Crown tells that it lies 103 miles from Hyde Park.

Detached from the High Street is the small Market Square, flanked by Marshfield House and smaller picturesque houses and cottages the names of which convey their former functions: the Old Inn, Bakehouse Cottage and Saddler's Cottage among them. Near Market Square is the **church**, its tall pinnacled tower and golden weather vane dominating the full length of the high street.

An interesting feature of the high street has been **Bodman's General Store**, founded in 1840 and owned, until his death in 1983, by Mr Christopher Bodman, grandson of the shop's founder. Run more as a museum than a shop, Bodman's was fitted with Edwardian and Victorian relics which the local council intend to preserve. The shop has now been put up for auction and at present its future is uncertain.

Pubs: Crown Inn |**R**|**Bs**|
    Catherine Wheel |**Bs**|
    Lord Nelson |**Bs**|

GREAT BADMINTON, AVON |△|†|

Badminton House, home of the Beaufort family, stands in parkland of some 15,000 acres (a perimeter of nearly 10 miles). There are many associations attached to the name. It was here that the game with shuttlecocks, introduced from India, was first played in 1860; the rules being drawn up in 1876 and the Badminton Association forming in 1895. Badminton is also, of course, internationally famous for the three day horse trials which take place here; and the kennels of the hounds of the Beaufort Hunt can be visited at specified times throughout the year.

Badminton House was originally built for the First Duke of Beaufort in 1682. The house, remodelled by the Third Duke in about 1740, is approached by a 3-mile avenue of beech trees. It is open on various occasions during the summer for the public to view valuable paintings and furniture as well as elaborate wood carving by Grinling Gibbons.

The park is renowned both for the trees that grace it, planted by stages over generations, and the variety of follies that are scattered around it. A rose arbour leads to the 18thC **church** where there are monuments to the Beaufort family and some impressive Italian paintings.

In the village the large green is well supplied with playing fields. The main street of 17thC buildings leads to the gates of Badminton House where one of the houses is the home of the village club. Two miles away is **Little Badminton** with a tiny Norman church roofed with Cotswold tiles. In the nearby field is an ancient turreted pigeon house.

SAPPERTON, GLOUCESTERSHIRE |✝|

Sapperton lies on a hillside at the head of what is sometimes called the 'Golden Valley', a wooded valley where the superb autumnal tints are best seen from the churchyard which overlooks them. Many of the more modern houses in Sapperton were built by architects and craftsmen of the William Morris 'school', Ernest Gimson and Ernest and Sidney Barnsley, who were men of international reputation. Across the Golden Valley from the village is Daneway House (part 14thC) where Gimson had his workshop and showrooms. All three men are buried in the churchyard and their graves can be seen by the yew trees near the top of the churchpath.

An earlier tombstone of interest is that of Rebekah Mason who died in 1759. She was the wife of the astronomer, Charles Mason, the co-originator, with Jeremiah Dixon, of what came to be known as the Mason-Dixon Line, separating the northern from the southern States of America before the Civil War. Within the church a slab under the altar marks the burial place of Henry Wentworth, Major General to Charles I.

The 18thC **Daneway Inn** lies near one end of the Sapperton tunnel, a tunnel no longer in use but originally built beneath the hill to accommodate a 2-mile stretch of canal.

Pub: **Daneway Inn**|**Bs**|

WITHINGTON, GLOUCESTERSHIRE |△|✝|∞|

The focal point of this quiet village of the Coln Valley is the lovely **St Michael's Church**, crowned by its magnificent tower with corner pinnacles, battlements and projecting gargoyles. The church certainly seems large for a small village which does not even have a shop. It was described by William Cobbett when he visited it in 1826 during one of his 'Rural Rides' as being: 'A Church like a small Cathedral . . . which is as sound as it was 700 or 800 years ago'. Although much restored the church retains many Norman features, in particular the N and S doorways, the latter rich in ornamentation. The most

131

imposing of the internal monuments is that to Sir John Howe (*died* 1642) and his wife Bridget, their eight children kneeling at a desk below.

Although Cobbett had much praise for the church he was more critical of the village, complaining that 'Withington is very prettily situated; it was, and not very long ago, a gay and happy place; but it now presents a picture of delapidation and shabbiness scarcely to be equalled.' At least Cobbett praised Withington for its pretty situation; and certainly few inns can rival the picturesque site of the **Mill Inn**. The inn, with lawns running down to the stream, faces the old Mill House where more than a century ago corn was ground. The inn is split into a variety of small rooms where log fires burn as hospitably as they did in 1682 when Thomas Baskerville wrote:

> *a man told us we might find a good Inn to lodge at, so blundering in the dark as well as we could to our great comfort at last thither we came, where we found excellent ale, of which we drank freely, a good dish of steaks, or fried beef, a dish of birds we had killed, well roasted, strong water, and for breakfast bread and cheese and cold meats, tongues well boiled, hay and each horse his peck of oats, and all this for 17 shillings.*

Pub: **Mill Inn** | **A** | **R** | **Bs** | *Tel.* (024 289) 204.

BIBURY, GLOUCESTERSHIRE |△|★|†|

Bibury has been described by the poet William Morris (1834–96) as 'the most beautiful village in England'. The River Coln runs parallel to the main road, crossed at one end by a bridge that dates from 1770. On one side of the bridge is the creeper-covered **Swan Hotel**, a former coaching inn. On the other is **Arlington Mill**, a 17thC cloth and corn mill, now a **museum** with collections of furniture among the many items displayed. Near to the mill is a large trout farm.

In addition to the road bridge several small stone foot bridges span the river, giving access to the water meadows on the other side. Across one of these bridges is **Arlington Row**, an enchanting row of early 17thC cottages built for weavers from a much older wool store. A National Trust property not open to the public, Arlington Row stands by a 4-acre field known as Rack Isle, which is bounded by water on three sides and so called because it was here that wool was hung on racks to dry.

At the northern end of Bibury, set apart from the main road, is the Saxon **Church of St Mary** overlooking a square of stone-built houses and set in a churchyard of outstanding beauty. At a corner of the churchyard is the Jacobean **Bibury Court**, a wing of which is said to have been designed by Inigo Jones (1573–1652), the celebrated architect, whose masterpiece was the Banqueting House in Whitehall.

Pubs: **Bibury Court Hotel** | **A** | **R** | **Bs** | *Tel.* (028 574) 337.
    Swan Hotel | **A** | **R** | **Bs** | *Tel.* (028 574) 204.

BARNSLEY, GLOUCESTERSHIRE |△|†|

Farmhouses and cottages with dormer windows and fronted by neat walled gardens overlook the narrow main street. At one end of the village is **Barnsley House**, the former rectory, which was built in the late 17thC and where the gardens with a Gothic summerhouse and Adam temple are occasionally open to the public.

In the centre of Barnsley is **The Village Pub**, appropriately named for it is the only inn and also appears to be the sole commercial enterprise in an unspoilt village that does not even boast a shop.

Facing the inn is the **church**, much restored in the 19thC, approached through an arch of yews and surmounted by an Elizabethan tower.

Barnsley Park, a 17thC house in wooded grounds, once contained in its library some 900 volumes from the collection of Sir Isaac Newton (1642–1727); these now are in the keeping of the Royal Society.

Pub: **The Village Pub** |**Bs**|

Tour Twenty-nine
Touring centre
Gloucester, Gloucestershire

Hotels: Tara, Upton Hill, *Tel.* (0452) 67412❹
New Wellington, Bruton Way, *Tel.* (0452) 20022❸

ST BRIAVELS, GLOUCESTERSHIRE |△|✝|

This village is high above the wooded valley of the River Wye in the heart of the Forest of Dean, a great primeval forest of more than 20 million trees. Here are the remains of a 13thC castle, built as a fortified stronghold to resist marauders from Wales and at one time used by King John as a hunting lodge. Principle surviving relic of the original castle is the gatehouse with its two rounded towers.

The **Church of St Mary**, Norman with 13thC additions and much restored, is noted for its E window where the figures of the Madonna, John the Baptist and St John are resplendent above smaller pictures of the wise men and shepherds visiting Bethlehem.

The surrounding areas of forest are much favoured by ramblers. There are numerous woodland paths and wildlife and flowers abound. The people who live in and around the Forest of Dean are known as Foresters, preserving many of their traditional customs.

Pub: **George Hotel** |**A**|**R**|**Bs**|**Ra**| *Tel.* (0594) 530228.

FRAMPTON-ON-SEVERN, GLOUCESTERSHIRE |✝|

At one end of the huge village green, more than 20 acres in

dimension, is the **Bell Inn**. From here the road runs from end to end, bisecting the green until it reaches the bulk of the smaller houses in the village. The green is fringed by a number of Georgian houses, among them **Frampton Court**, built by Richard Clutterbuck who in about 1740 had reclaimed the land around the green which until then had been little more than marsh. Next to Frampton Court is a strange white, Gothic-style building. However the oldest house stands behind the pond on the other side of the green: **Manor Farm**, a 15thC black and white building with a stone roof, tall chimneys and gables was the seat of the early lords of the manor, the Cliffords. Frampton is said to have been the birthplace of 'Fair Rosamund', mistress of Henry II, and so it might be assumed that Jane Clifford was brought up in the house that preceded this old manor.

At the end of the green the road narrows, flanked by cottages on either side. Here, from the lych-gate a path leads across the water meadows to the church which stands at the canal's edge. Within the **church** is an effigy of William Clifford in knight's armour, his hand on his sword and a dog at his feet. His wife lies by his side. Outside, overlooking the churchyard, is a Judas tree.

Pubs: **Old Vicarage Country Hotel** |**A**|**R**| *Tel.* (0452) 740562.

  Bell Inn |**Bs**|

BISLEY, GLOUCESTERSHIRE |✝|

Grey-stone houses cling in tiers along the edge of this remote hillside village. High in the village is the **Bear Inn**, originally the court house with an upper storey supported by pillars. Next to the inn is the old village 'lock-up'. Nearby is the church, the school, and **Over Court**, a fine stone house granted to Elizabeth I as part of her estate before she became queen.

The **Church of All Saints** has many features of interest. It is an ancient church with a 13thC chancel and 14thC tower; but large parts of it were restored by the Revd Thomas Keble who was vicar here from 1827–73, and was the younger brother of the more famous John Keble (1792–1866), Anglican divine and religious poet. It was Thomas Keble who in 1863 instituted the ceremony of dressing the wells on Ascension Day, a picturesque occasion more generally associated with villages in Derbyshire.

Near the S porch is the 13thC **well head** which contained the 'poor souls' light', used to hold candles when Masses were said for the souls of those in purgatory. It is believed that the well was built over after a priest had fallen into it and drowned on a dark night when visiting a parishioner.

The Revd Thomas Keble was succeeded by his son, also Thomas, who was vicar here for 30yrs from 1873–1903. It was this Thomas Keble who created the legend of the 'Bisley Boy' and Queen Elizabeth. Elizabeth I is reputed to have stayed at the adjoining Over Court as a young child. Centuries later, workmen excavating a nearby site came upon a medieval coffin containing the bones of a girl. From this sprang the fable that these were the bones of Elizabeth who had died during her visit. The villagers, fearful of Henry VIII's wrath, needed a substitute to send back to Court, and eventually substituted a boy, who was the only child with a likeness to Elizabeth. Thus the 'Bisley Boy' reigned as Queen of England, never marrying for obvious reasons.

Near to the village is **Lypiatt Park**, the house where the conspirators of the Gunpowder Plot once hid. A letter, still in existence, is addressed to Robert Catesby at Lypiatt and refers to the plot.

Pub: **Bear Inn** |**A**|**R**|**Bs** *Tel.* (045 277) 265.

Touring centre

Cheltenham, Gloucestershire

Hotels: Carlton, Parabola Road, *Tel.* (0242) 514453❹
Royal Ascot, Western Road, *Tel.* (0242) 513640❷

BOURTON-ON-THE-WATER, GLOUCESTERSHIRE　❖★✝

The clear waters of the River Windrush flow through the heart of this village. Willows droop over the sparkling stream which is spanned by graceful little stone footbridges, connecting the lawns and houses of Cotswold stone that lie on either side. The fact that Bourton is often styled 'the Venice of the Cotswolds' seems something of an absurdity, conjuring up in the mind of the expectant visitor a vision of gondolas, until, on arrival, he or she sees that the river here is the shallowest of streams.

⸱ Once the allusion to Venice is forgotten, however, Bourton is a charming place in which to wander during off-season periods. The **Model Village**, located in the gardens of the Old New Inn, is of particular interest. There is a replica of Bourton here; an accurate reproduction of the village in stone on a scale of one ninth. On the other side of the river is **Birdland**, a collection of foreign birds ranging from penguins to exotic and colourful parrots and flamingos.

The **Church of St Lawrence** was modernized in 1890. The chancel, however, dates from 1328 and the 18thC tower has an unusual diamond-shaped clock. Apart from Bourton's more obvious attractions, it is of interest that one of the few Saxon dwellings to have survived in England was discovered here. Among the relics unearthed were the primitive knives, cups and cooking implements used by the Saxons.

Pubs: Old New Inn |A|R|Bs|Ra| *Tel.* (0451) 20467.
　　　Brookside Hotel |A|R|Bs| *Tel.* (0451) 20371.

THE SLAUGHTERS, GLOUCESTERSHIRE　△✝
LOWER SLAUGHTER

The River Eye links the twin villages of Lower and Upper Slaughter. In Lower Slaughter the stream flows through the centre of the village, straddled by little footbridges of ancient weathered stone; it is a place to which artists are drawn to recreate a lovely scene which, unlike Bourton, has not been commercialized.

135

The **manor house**, now a hotel, was in the possession of the Whitmore family from the beginning of the 17thC until they sold it in 1964. The **Church of St Mary** was rebuilt completely in 1866 after it had become so unsafe for occupation that services had to take place at the manor. The finest features of the new church are its tower and beautiful spire which rises gracefully above the tree-clad village.

At one end of the village street is a large brick-built 19thC corn-mill and water-wheel, in use until quite recently. Along the river bank, old houses and cottages blend pleasingly with others built more

Lower Slaughter's picturesque river and large brick early-19thC corn-mill and water-wheel, which only ceased to operate in the 1960s.

recently. Among the older buildings is **Washbourne's Place**, situated near the main bridge and acquiring its name from its 15thC owner. Nearby is the **village hall**, modern in contrast for it dates from 1865.

In Malthouse Lane there are a number of picturesque cottages, and the little village square has a water pump in the shape of a lion.

UPPER SLAUGHTER

Upper Slaughter lies a mile away from its 'twin', a cluster of typical Cotswold stone houses, the last of them built as long ago as 1904. Upper Slaughter stands on a hill above the stream, a place of great antiquity for it encompasses the site of a Bronze Age burial ground. To the E of the church is the **castle mound** where the Norman castle, a wooden building with stone walls, once dominated the village. Outside the village is the beautiful Tudor **manor house**, open on specified occasions to the public.

In the village itself the **Lords of the Manor Hotel** is so called because in 1854 the rector became lord of the manor and from that time the parsonage became known as 'the manor'. The church, much restored in the 19thC, retains its original 15thC chancel.

Pubs: **Lord of the Manor Hotel, Upper Slaughter** |**A**|**R**|**Bs**| *Tel.* (0451) 20243.

Manor Hotel, Lower Slaughter |**A**|**R**|**Bs**| *Tel.* (0451) 20456.

GUITING POWER, GLOUCESTERSHIRE |✝|

The tall war memorial cross stands on the sloping green in the heart of the village. Here, also, there is a tribute to Mrs Cochrane who 'gave much to Guiting Power'. In the 1970s the Cochrane family, the local landowners, set up a trust in order to stabilize the rents of many of the village houses, thus ensuring the continued occupancy by local people.

Houses and cottages of Cotswold-stone, many with gables, mullioned windows and trim gardens cluster around the green and the little streets that lead from it. **St Michael's Church**, Norman but much restored, lies in a peaceful setting at the edge of the village, distinguished by its castellated tower and Norman doorways. In Well Lane is the **Old Bakery**, built in 1603 but now a private house. In 1970 the Rare Breed Survival Centre of the Cotswold Farm Park was started. It lies about 2 miles to the N of Guiting Power and here among a variety of breeds of farm animals can be seen the Cotswold Lions, which are heavily fleeced sheep.

Pub: **Farmers Arms** |**A**|**Bs**|**Ra**| *Tel.* (045 15) 358.

STANWAY AND STANTON, GLOUCESTERSHIRE |★|✝|
STANWAY

At the crossroads at the edge of the village is the huge war memorial, a bronze figure of St George slaying the dragon. The engravings are by the celebrated sculptor, Eric Gill (1882–1940). From here, round a curve in the minor road, is a magnificent **gatehouse** of golden-stone, surmounted by a coat of arms and intricate carvings of scallop shells. This is the entry to **Stanway House**, property of the Earl of Wemys.

Set among the lawns and trees of Stanway House, a honey-coloured Jacobean mansion, is a medieval **tithe barn** with massive buttresses and timbers believed to date from 1400. The barn is best seen from the N wall of the churchyard over which it lies. In the churchyard is the grave of Thomas Dover (*died* 1742), the physician who discovered the use of quicksilver for medical purposes. Dover, incidentally, was among those who took part in the rescue of the marooned Scottish sailor, Alexander Selkirk, who gave Defoe the idea for Robinson Crusoe.

Across the road from Stanway House is the cricket ground. Here the thatched pavilion, raised on stilts, was presented by the playwright, Sir James Barrie (1866–1937), at a time when country house cricket was often played.

STANTON

Stanton lies some 2 miles to the N of Stanway. The main street climbs sharply past gabled houses of Cotswold stone, mostly of the 16thC and 17thC, until at the top it reaches the **Mount Inn**. Prominent in the street is the ancient village cross, the medieval base surmounted by an 18thC shaft. **Stanton House**, a Jacobean manor house where the gardens are occasionally open to the public, is the former home of Sir Philip Stott, the architect responsible during his time here for ensuring that this lovely village remained unblemished.

A feature of the **church**, which catches the eye on entry is the fact that it has two pulpits. They stand side by side. The one in use is of 17thC panelled oak and from here John Wesley (1703–91) once preached. Standing humbly by its side and retired from duty is the second pulpit. It dates from the 14thC, and is one of the few wooden pulpits of this great age to have survived in England. Some pews at the back of the church are also of interest. The distinctive grooves in the woodwork are said to have been made by the leashes of sheepdogs, secured there impatiently while their masters attended service.

Two miles to the E is **Snowshill Manor** (owned by the National Trust), which houses a museum with a wide collection of antique items ranging from musical instruments to hobby horses and bicycles. Pub: **Mount Inn, Stanton** |Bs|Ra|

Marking the entrance to Stanway Hall is an outstanding honey-coloured stone Jacobean gatehouse. The gables and pediment are decorated with carvings of scallop shells, and the windows are leaded.

Touring centre

Oxford, Oxfordshire

Hotels: Randolph, Beaumont Street, *Tel.* (0865) 47481 ❺
Eastgate, Merton Street, *Tel.* (0865) 48244 ❸

STANTON HARCOURT, OXFORDSHIRE |✝|◆•|

The first distant view of this village is of two tall towers that appear to protrude from the church. Once in the village, however, it becomes clear that one of these towers is not part of the church, but lies inside the walls of the manor house gardens that surround the churchyard. The **manor** was the home of the Harcourt family from the 12thC to the 18thC. The three-storey tower in its grounds is known as Pope's tower, for it was here, between 1715 and 1718, that the poet and satirist Alexander Pope (1688–1744) stayed as a guest, translating Homer's *Iliad* and leaving a record of the fact on a pane of glass. Another outstanding manor building is the **great kitchen**. This curious medieval kitchen, among the most complete to be found in England, has an octagonal pyramidal roof that is crowned by a weathercock in the form of a griffin.

    St Michael's Church, cruciform in shape with a square Norman tower, stands beside the manor. The Harcourt Chapel, completed in about 1470, blends well with the earlier building and is filled with monuments to the family. Among the many interesting tombs is that of Sir Robert Harcourt KB, standard bearer to Henry VII at the Battle of Bosworth Field in 1485; the tattered standard that he bore that day hanging above the tomb. It is of interest that the close neighbours of the Harcourts, the Lovells from *Minster Lovell*, fought on the side of Richard III in that fateful battle, an *allegiance* which is recorded in the famous jingle:

> *The Cat, the Rat, and Lovell the Dog*
> *Ruleth all England under the Hog [Crest of Richard III]*

Harcourt Manor, St Michael's Church and Parsonage House form a close knit group, the outstanding buildings in a trim little village with a pleasant inn, the **Harcourt Arms**, and a number of thatched cottages.

Pub: Harcourt Arms |**Bs**|**Ra**|

UFFINGTON, OXFORDSHIRE |△|✝|◆•|

Uffington lies in the Vale of the White Horse, an area which has been immortalized by Thomas Hughes (1822–96), author of **Tom Brown's School Days**, the story of Rugby under Thomas Arnold. Hughes was born here and is buried in the churchyard of the lovely **Church of St Mary** with its 13thC octagonal tower.

Describing the area in his novel Hughes wrote: 'I pity people who weren't born in a Vale. I don't mean a flat country bounded by hills. The having your hill always in view if you choose to turn towards him, that's the essence of a Vale.' The writer, perhaps, sensed that the real romance of Uffington lay not in the village itself but the hills that surround it.

White Horse Hill (856ft) is so called because of the great white horse carved in the chalky hillside, a galloping figure that dominates the scene and according to legend was cut out of the turf by King Alfred. **Uffington Castle**, a prehistoric fort, crowns the hill and a rounded hill nearby, **Dragon Hill**, is traditionally the place where St George slew the dragon. A mile to the SW of the village is a megalithic barrow, named **Wayland's Smithy** after a mythological figure who shod the horses of travellers when they rested here overnight, but who was never seen.

Pub: White Horse Inn |**Bs**|**Ra**|

SUTTON COURTENAY, OXFORDSHIRE |✝|◆•|

A number of important buildings flank the green and the main road that passes through this Thames-side village. At one end of the road a row of period cottages backs on to a lovely stretch of the river, a good view of which can be obtained from the footpath and bridge behind the cottages. It was in a house on this stretch of river that the Earl of Oxford and Asquith, Prime Minister from 1908 to 1916, spent the years of his retirement.

Central to the green, facing the church, is **Norman Hall**, or **Court House**, a 12thC stone building with Norman doors and lancet windows. Beyond the southern edge of the green, partially hidden by trees, is the larger gabled **manor house**. At the southern extremity of the green a driveway gate marks the entrance to the **abbey**, which is not in fact an abbey, but a 14thC building with a great hall, built originally as a retreat for monks. None of these buildings are open to the public.

The **Church of All Saints** has a Norman tower and 13thC chancel. In the churchyard is the tomb of Lord Asquith (*died* 1928). Set amidst an avenue of small yews is a simple headstone marking the resting place of E. W. Blair, better known as George Orwell, the writer of works such as *Down and Out in London and Paris* (1933), *Homage to Catalonia* (1938), *Animal Farm* (1945) and *Nineteen Eighty-four* (1949). He died in 1950.

Pub: George and Dragon |**Bs**|

CLIFTON HAMPDEN, OXFORDSHIRE |✝|◆•|

The little **Church of St Michael and All Saints**, approached by a flight of stone steps, stands on a knoll at one end of the village, commanding a fine view of the Thames and the bridge which crosses the river into Berkshire. The church was much restored in 1844 by the architect Sir George Gilbert Scott (1811–78). The entire village, apart from the inn on the other side of the river, lies in Oxfordshire.

Standing above the water meadows, there are a number of picturesque timber-framed Elizabethan cottages, and across the bridge, reconstructed by G. G. Scott some years after he designed the church, is the **Barley Mow Inn**. Built in 1350 as a farmhouse, this thatched building with its half-timbered walls of cruck construction began its life as an inn in about 1400. A serious fire in 1975 did much damage to the upper parts of the building; but it was restored, faithfully, and reopened 2yrs later. Jerome K. Jerome (1859–1927) chose the Barley Mow as a setting for the most famous of his novels, *Three Men in a Boat* (1889), in which his description of the inn is as accurate now as it was then:

> *It is, without exception, the quaintest, most old-world inn up the river. Its low-pitched gables and thatched roof and latticed windows give it quite a story-book appearance, while inside it is even still more once-upon-a-timeyfied. It would not be a good place for the heroine of a modern novel to stay at. The heroine of a modern novel is always 'divinely' tall, and she is ever 'drawing herself up to her full height'. At the Barley Mow she would bump her head against the ceiling each time she did this.*

The Barley Mow remains as quaint as it was then and the ceilings do not appear to have been heightened an inch.

Pub: **Barley Mow** |**A**|**R**|**Bs**|**Ra**| *Tel.* **(086 730) 7847.**

EWELME, OXFORDSHIRE |✝|♠|

Houses of brick and flint are built in tiers on the gentle slope of the hillside where Ewelme lies. The three buildings of outstanding interest are the church, the almshouse and the school, grouped on terraces with the church at the top overlooking the almshouse and school beneath.

The **Church of St Mary** is associated with the Chaucer family. It was built in 1430 on the site of an older church and contains the altar tomb of Thomas and Matilda Chaucer. Thomas was the son of the poet Geoffrey Chaucer (1340–1400). The daughter of Thomas and Matilda, Alice, was married here to William de la Pole, first Duke of Suffolk, at about the time the church was due to be rebuilt. She died in 1475 and her fine tomb with her alabaster effigy, hands folded together in an attitude of prayer, stands under a canopy of panelled stone with intricate carving.

The **almshouse** was built by the Duke of Suffolk and his wife, the statutes providing for a 'Corporation of two chaplains and thirteen poor men'. The 13 dwellings, grouped round a square courtyard, date from 1437, the only brick buildings of such an early date known in this part of England.

Ewelme Foundation School, founded at about the same time as the almshouse, claims to be the oldest of our church schools now incorporated in the state system, and using its original building. The provision in the statutes was that a Grammar Master should be appointed to teach the children of Ewelme 'freely without exaccion of any Schole hire'. The school, now in use as a Church of England primary school, has been modernized without changing its external appearance.

Witney, Oxfordshire

Hotels: **Fleece Hotel, Church Grove,** *Tel.* **(0993) 2263 ❷**
Red Lion, Corn Street, *Tel.* **(0993) 3149 ❶**

MINSTER LOVELL, OXFORDSHIRE |△|✝|

At one end of this attractive village on the River Windrush are the
church and the ruins of Minster Lovell Hall. From here the road
descends gradually past stone-built thatched and tiled cottages to the
Old Swan Hotel, the Mill Conference Centre, and the ancient bridge
across which is the solitary thatched Bridge Cottage, for centuries the
property of Eton College.

It is at **Minster Lovell Hall**, open to the public and in the care of
the Ministry of the Environment, that most visitors feel inclined to
linger. The ruins are dispersed among grassy banks above the willow-
lined river, the ghostly remains of the manor house built in the first
half of the 15thC by William, Seventh Baron Lovell of Tichmarsh.
The principal remains are the great hall with its entrance porch and
the SW tower beside the river.

In 1485, Francis Viscount Lovell, loyal to the king, shared in
Richard III's defeat at Bosworth Field and fled to France. Two years
later he rallied to the cause of the Pretender, Lambert Simnel, and
after a further defeat fled to Minster Lovell Hall. Here, it is said, he
was befriended by a solitary servant who hid him in a concealed and
locked room. More than 200yrs later, during repairs, a room was
opened revealing a skeleton seated at a table with the skeleton of a dog
at his feet. Some theories suggest that the skeleton may have been that
of Francis Lovell, left to die of starvation by the death or desertion of
his servant.

Among the surviving buildings of the manorial farm to the NE
of the hall is an interesting **dovecote**, a small circular building with a
conical roof. The **church** beside the manor was also built by William
Lovell and inside there is the effigy of a knight in plate armour,
believed to represent either William or his son John.

Across the river from the older buildings are some more modern
houses, but they are not without significance. It was here that Feargus
O'Connor (1794–1855), an influential member of the Chartist move-

ment, founded a bungalow settlement, **Charterville**, for the re-habilitation of impoverished townsmen.

Pub: Old Swan Hotel |**A**|**R**|**Bs**|**Ra**| *Tel.* (099 387) 614.

BURFORD, OXFORDSHIRE |❖|★|✝|

During the Middle Ages Burford was a prosperous wool town and as early as 1100 was administered by a Guild of Merchants. At the Tolsey, now a museum, the merchants met and received payments which they exacted for the holding of markets and fairs.

Burford is known as the Gateway to the Cotswolds, a composition of golden Cotswold stone houses in a compact setting with an atmosphere that is, perhaps, more village than town and justified its inclusion in this guide.

At the foot of the long, broad high street is the River Windrush, spanned by a narrow three-arched bridge. Almost every building in High Street is of interest. There is, for example, the **Tolsey**, where the **museum** has many notable collections, among them a doll's house with 18thC rooms and costumes; the **Bull Hotel**, the only brick-faced building due to a recent fire; the archway of the former **George Hotel** where Charles II stayed with Nell Gwynne; and **Falkland Hall**, built for a clothier in 1558. Many other houses in High Street, too numerous to mention in detail, date from before the 16thC.

Other interesting buildings grace the streets that adjoin High Street, in particular Sheep Street, Priory Lane and Lawrence Lane. In Sheep Street the 15thC **Lamb Inn** is believed to be the oldest inn in Burford, although some say the cellars of the Bull are older still. Next to the Lamb is the **Bay Tree Hotel**, birthplace of Sir Lawrence Tanfield (1554–1625) who bought the lordship of the manor, and by doing so put an end to the monopoly that the Guild of Merchants had held until then. In Priory Lane is the **priory**, which is a medieval offshoot of Keynsham Abbey, and was rebuilt in the 16thC as a dwelling house.

At the foot of High Street is **St John the Baptist Church**, among the largest churches in Oxfordshire, and the **grammar school** founded in 1571 by Simon Wysdom, a prosperous mercer, who was also responsible for the original building of the weavers' cottages near the river.

There is an interesting account of the visit to the church by William Morris (see *Kelmscot*) in 1876, while the church was being restored. A protest by Morris to the vicar that the restoration was in poor taste drew the response: 'This Church, Sir, is mine and, if I choose to, I shall stand on my head in it.' As a result of the interview, Morris founded the Society for the Protection of Ancient Buildings.

Pubs: Lamb Inn |**A**|**R**|**Bs**|**Ra**| *Tel.* (099 382) 3155.

Bay Tree Hotel |**A**|**R**|**Bs**| *Tel.* (099 382) 3137.

Bull Hotel |**A**|**R**|**Bs**| *Tel.* (099 382) 2220.

KELMSCOT, OXFORDSHIRE |✝|❖•|

Stone cottages and farmhouses straggle across a wide area in this flat, rural countryside close to the upper reaches of the Thames. Yet Kelmscot is only a tiny village — too small to warrant a shop. In the middle of the village is the old **Plough Inn**, and from here a road leads to **Kelmscot Manor**, the former home of William Morris (1834–96), the poet, craftsman and founder of the Socialist League.

The **manor house**, largely hidden by a high garden wall, is gabled with mullioned windows and contains furniture and textiles designed by Morris. It is occasionally open to the public. Between the manor and the inn are two cottages, on the front of which is a relief of

Morris, a reclining figure with his hat at his feet, designed from a drawing by his architect friend Philip Webb (1831–1915).

The little **church**, unfortunately normally locked, lies in an isolated position at the opposite end of the village to the manor. In a corner of the churchyard an unpretentious tombstome marks the spot where William Morris lies buried.

Pub: **Plough Inn** |**Bs**|**Ra**|

A grey-stone Elizabethan house, Kelmscot Manor was the home of William Morris for 25yrs; his work is now exhibited here.

Touring centre
Chipping Norton, Oxfordshire
Hotels: **White Hart, High Street,** *Tel.* **(0608) 2572❹**
Crown and Cushion, High Street, *Tel.* **(0608) 2533❷**

CORNWELL, OXFORDSHIRE

Both the village and the manor house were planned by the architect Sir Clough Williams-Ellis (1883–1978), famous for the construction of the colourful Italianate village of Portmeirion in North Wales, as well as being responsible for Llangoed and Bolesworth Castles, and contributing to Stowe School. Brown stone-built cottages hang in tiers above a little stream, the village road forming a loop from the main road and crossing the stream at a ford by the **village hall**. This building, once the school, is conical at one end with a domed roof and tall slender windows; the whole surmounted by a quaint chimney stack.

The building next to the hall was once the village shop, now alas closed like so many such establishments in the remoter parts of England. The village green is enclosed by walls and serves as the childrens's playground. The **manor house** (not open to the public) overlooks formal gardens and an artificial pool, all landscaped by Williams-Ellis. There is no church or inn, simply a charming huddle of cottages in a remote and peaceful setting.

ADLESTROP, GLOUCESTERSHIRE |△|✝|◆◆|

> *Yes, I remember Adlestrop —*
> *The name — because one afternoon*
> *Of heat the express train drew up there*
> *Unwontedly. It was late June.*
> *The steam hiss'd. Someone clear'd his throat.*
> *No one left and no one came*
> *On the bare platform. What I saw*
> *Was Adlestrop — only the name.*

These words, engraved on the seat on the bus shelter, are those of Philip Edward Thomas (1878–1917), the poet killed in the Great War at Arras. Today there is no railway station at Adlestrop, but the nameplate seen by Thomas stares prominently from the shelter above the words with which he immortalized the village.

Picturesque cottages of golden-stone form the nucleus of Adlestrop. The Georgian manor house, **Adlestrop Park**, lies in land-scaped gardens that are not open to the public for the house is now a school. Nearby is the **Church of St Mary Magdalene** with monuments to the Leigh family, lords of the manor since the 16thC. A member of this family was Thomas Leigh who, when Rector here, entertained his grandaughter Jane Austen (1775–1817), the novelist.

DEDDINGTON, OXFORDSHIRE |✝|

Deddington Castle is shown prominently on many maps, which is somewhat misleading as the Norman castle was in ruins by the 15thC and today the castle mound is barely visible. It lies beyond playing fields across the road from the church. It was in the castle that Piers Gaveston, favourite of Edward II, is said to have been held between his capture at Scarborough and his ultimate execution by the king's enemies at Kenilworth.

The village was once a flourishing medieval market place. Among the older buildings of Market Square is the 17thC **Kings Arms** and some of the finest houses are in New Street; for example, the **Crown and Tuns Inn** and **Grove Farm House**, as well as a number of other 17thC buildings.

Much of the **Church of St Peter and St Paul** dates from the 13thC. Its eight-pinnacled tower replaced the earlier tower which collapsed during a storm in 1653, the collapse bringing down the massive church bells which were sold to Charles II who needed the metal for munitions.

Pubs: **Crown and Tuns** |**A**|**Bs**|**Ra**| *Tel.* (0869) 38343.

   Holcombe Hotel |**A**|**R**|**Bs**| *Tel.* (0869) 38274.

   Hotel Russell |**A**|**R**|**Bs**| *Tel.* (0869) 38339.

GREAT TEW, OXFORDSHIRE |✝|

Many of the buildings in this remote village lie derelict. Great Tew has now, however, been designated as an Outstanding Conservation Area and improvements to existing houses and cottages appear to be under way. The village has been described as being one where 'thatched cottages engulfed in gardens lie in a valley enriched by trees'. On the tree-shaded village green are the somewhat delapidated old village stocks. Facing the green is the 18thC **Falkland Arms** and a row of thatched cottages.

The **Church of St Michael** stands on a wooded hill above the village, and entry to the churchyard is beneath an 18thC stone archway; from here a tree-lined path stretches for some 300yds to the church itself. It is believed that an earlier village green was sited to the right of this path, while to the left of it are the walls of the **manor house gardens**.

A tablet in the church to the memory of Lucius Carey, second Viscount Falkland, tells how it was at the manor that he 'entertained his learned friends' during the reign of Charles I. There is also a brass to one of the early lords of the manor, Sir John Wilcotes, and his wife Alice. Later owners were the Boulton family, a monument of particular interest being one by Sir Francis Chantrey (1781–1841), famed for his *Sleeping Children* in Lichfield Cathedral. This work shows Mary Anne Boulton, a book open on her lap with the words 'Thy Will be Done'.

Pub: **Falkland Arms**|**Bs**|**Ra**|

Derbyshire, Staffordshire and Nottinghamshire

NOTTINGHAM SHIRE

DERBY SHIRE

STAFFORDSHIRE

35

34

36

Touring centres
34 Ashbourne
35 Bakewell
36 Newark-on-Trent

Few areas of England can compare with the natural, unspoilt beauty found in the Peak District National Park. Nor can there be many finer views than that from Mam Tor, across the green valley that shelters the little village of *Edale* from the heights of rugged moorland that tower above and beyond it. Edale, the northern-most of the villages in this area, marks the start of the Pennine Way, a walk only taken by the fittest of ramblers for it stretches for 250 miles as far as the borders with Scotland. Near to Edale is *Castleton*, crowned by Peveril Castle in an area of caverns, and *Hathersage*, the reputed burial place of Robin Hood's lieutenant, Little John. It seems hard to believe that the lovely remote scenery that embraces these Derbyshire villages has, close at hand, the huge industrial conurbations of Manchester to the West and Sheffield to the East.

Further S these tracts of sandstone country give way to lower and flatter land where sheep graze and dairy farming is also important. The Dove, one of England's loveliest rivers, divides Derbyshire from Staffordshire, winding its way through narrow gorges past the matchless scenery of Dovedale, Beresford Dale and Wolfscote Dale. These dales, inaccessible from the road, can be appreciated from the footpath that is signposted from *Hartington*. Other Derbyshire villages of interest include *Tissington*, famous for its well dressing ceremony, *Edensor*, the estate village of Chatsworth House, and *Ashford-in-the-Water* where the River Wye is spanned by the graceful 17thC Sheepwash Bridge.

Staffordshire, despite its association with the Black Country and the pottery towns, has much unspoilt and peaceful countryside. Among many of its picturesque villages is *Ilam*, near the entrance to Dovedale, which boasts connections with literary figures, including William Congreve, Samuel Johnson, who was born at Lichfield, and Charles Cotton who fished the local streams with Izaak Walton and wrote of them:

> *Oh my beloved nymph, fair Dove,*
> *Princess of rivers, how I love*
> *Upon thy flower banks to lie.*

Although coal-mining and various other industries take place in Nottinghamshire, first thoughts of that county are of Sherwood Forest, known the world over as the home of Robin Hood and his Merry Men. In Robin's day Sherwood Forest was a vast tract of dense woodland that covered a fifth of the county. Today the remnants are mostly parkland in an area known as the Dukeries, comprising the estates of Welbeck, Clumber and Thoresby. At the edge of the Dukeries is Edwinstowe, close to *Wellow*, where tradition has it that Robin married Maid Marian.

The range of materials used in the construction of the villages in this widespread area is considerable. Derbyshire villages tend to depend on local stone. The cottages of *Edale*, for example, comprise gritstone while those at *Hartington*, like many nearby villages, are of limestone quarried from the surrounding hills. Further to the SE, buildings in the Nottinghamshire villages rely much on red brick, some with pantile roofs, such as those seen at *Wellow* and *Blyth*. Few half-timbered black and white houses are in evidence, exceptions being the fine timbered buildings in *Abbots Bromley* and a handful of cottages in *Repton*.

Tour 34 (94 miles) is a two-day tour, neatly divided into two circular routes based on Ashbourne, and taking the motorist to eight villages. **Tour 35**, a 47-mile trip to six villages, covers the Low Peak region, and takes one day. **Tour 36** from Newark is a 114-mile drive through attractive country including Sherwood Forest and the Vale of Belvoir; an overnight stop would make this journey leisurely and enjoyable.

Touring centre

Ashbourne, Derbyshire

Hotels: **Green Man, St John Street,** *Tel.* **(0335) 43861 ❸**
Brookfields, Station Road, *Tel.* **(0335) 43330 ❷**

SUDBURY, DERBYSHIRE

|△|★|†|

Red-brick cottages, mainly of the 17thC straddle the curved village street. The gabled **Vernons Arms**, built of stone and brick with an arch through which stage coaches once passed, dates from 1671. The inn, named after the lord of the manor, was one of the many village buildings moved here to replace their counterparts which had previously stood directly in front of Sudbury Hall to the west.

Sudbury Hall, now the property of the National Trust, had been owned by the Vernon family since 1513, but it was not until 1659 when George Vernon inherited the estate that the hall as it is seen today was begun. For the next 35yrs, during which time the village buildings were removed to their present site, George Vernon was at work on the existing building, transforming what had previously been little more than a small manor house.

The Hall, with its red-brick diamond-patterned facade, faces N towards the main road. The terraces to the S of the hall overlook a lake and the valley of the River Dove, across which are the former hunting grounds of kings, **Needwood Forest**.

The Hall is built to an E plan and incorporates a **long gallery** (138ft). Craftsmen who worked here between 1659 and 1694 include Grinling Gibbons whose carving in the drawing-room was executed in 1678 at a cost of £40; and Edward Pearce whose masterpiece, among other work, is the gorgeous staircase. In 1691, during George Vernon's old age, Louis Laguerre was called in to contribute many mural designs.

Sudbury Hall is open to the public on specific occasions in the summer. A wing of the hall, added in the 19thC, now serves as a **Museum of Childhood** and is administered by the National Trust jointly with the County Council.

Hidden from the hall in a grove of yew trees is **All Saints' Church**, where the oldest memorials are to the Montgomery family, lords of the manor from the Conquest until the marriage of Ellen Montgomery to Sir John Vernon in 1513.

Pub: **Vernon Arms** |**A**|**R**|**Bs**|**Ra**| *Tel.* **(028 378) 329.**

REPTON, DERBYSHIRE |★|†|

Scattered around this ancient village are the buildings, old and new, of one of England's oldest public schools, founded in 1556 by Sir John Port. A monastery was established here in AD633. It was sacked by the Danes, but in AD975 the existing church was built and much enlarged over the coming centuries.

In a niche above the porch door of the **church** is St Wystan, its patron saint, and soaring upwards to a height of 212ft are the tower and slender spire. The feature of greatest interest inside the church is the Saxon crypt, desecrated during the Dissolution, and only discovered at the end of the 18thC when a man fell into it while digging a grave. The crypt, 17ft square with a vaulted roof resting on four central pillars, is approached from a steep, narrow stairway and has been described as the most perfect specimen of Saxon architecture on a small scale to be seen.

Alongside the Church of St Wystan a priory was founded in 1172. After the Dissolution the priory fell into ruin but the original gateway remains leading into two of the school's most interesting buildings. Viewed from the gateway, the larger building, on the right, is **Pears' School**, named after Dr S. A. Pears, headmaster from 1854–74, and known as the school's 'second founder'. Pears School was built in 1886 on the site of the nave of the priory church. The old stone building, on the left, is approached by a 16thC cobbled causeway. This building also incorporates part of the priory and today houses the **Repton School Museum** which can be seen by appointment.

From the church and school the broad main street leads by way of Georgian brick and timbered houses to the market cross, mounted on steps and topped by a stone sphere.

Pub: **Shakespeare Inn** |**Bs**|**Ra**|

ABBOTS BROMLEY, STAFFORDSHIRE |†|

This village, with its charming old brick as well as black and white timbered houses, was once a thriving market place; the butter cross on the village green acting as a reminder of the fact. Abbots Bromley once lay in the heart of the huge **Needwood Forest**, the hunting ground of jealous kings, and the Horn Dance for which the village is famous may originate from the need of its inhabitants to stress their rights to certain privileges in the surrounding forests.

The **Horn Dance** is performed annually on a Monday early in September. Those that take part are Robin Hood, who rides a hobbyhorse, Maid Marian, a jester, a boy with a bow and arrow, and six men wearing ancient reindeer horns. The troupe of dancers parade around the local farms; when they have finished, they return their gear to the church where the horns are hung on the wall and there they remain until the next year's festival.

The **Church of St Nicholas** was restored in Victorian times, but retains its 14thC arcades and 17thC balustraded tower. The **Bagot Almshouses** (built in 1705) and the **Bagot Arms** are named after the family who, at the time of the Norman Conquest, settled at the manor house at Bagots Bromley a mile away. Here they lived until

1811, entertaining visiting kings who came to the forest to hunt, before they moved to Blithfield. A stone in Monument Field marks the site of the former manor house.

Pubs: Bagot Arms |**A**|**Bs**|**Ra**| *Tel.* (0283) 840371.

Coach and Horses |**Bs**|**Ra**|

Royal Oak |**Bs**|**Ra**|

ILAM, STAFFORDSHIRE |△|✝|↔•|

This model village, built during the 19thC, by Jesse Watts-Russell, stands near the junction of the Rivers Dove and Manifold. While Watts-Russell was rebuilding the village he was also at work on the

The Abbots Bromley Horn Dance, said to originate in medieval times when villagers established their rights in the surrounding Needwood Forest, bears some resemblance to a beating the bounds ceremony; participants enact the characters of Robin Hood and Maid Marian.

Tudor-Gothic **Ilam Hall**, a building surmounted by towers, turrets and lofty, crooked chimneys. The hall, now a youth hostel, stands in a lovely wooded park in a loop of the Manifold; it is owned by the National Trust and is always open to the public. At the heart of the village, near the river bridge, is the 30ft high Eleanor-style cross which Watts-Russell erected in memory of his wife.

Everywhere in Ilam there are literary associations. It was in the grounds of Ilam Hall that the dramatist William Congreve made his name with the first of his comedies, *Old Bachelor* (1693). Here, too, came Doctor Samuel Johnson, finding the inspiration for his philosophical romance *Rasselas* (1759). 18yrs later Johnson returned to Ilam with his biographer, James Boswell, refusing to believe that the underground stream which emerges in the park was the Manifold until, in Boswell's words, they 'had the attestation of the gardener, who said he had put in corks where the Manifold sinks into the ground, and had caught them in a net placed before one of the openings where the water burst out'.

Two more literary figures were attracted to Ilam before the days of Congreve and Johnson. They were Izaak Walton and his friend Charles Cotton, who both loved to fish in the local rivers (see *Hartington)* and who were friends of Robert Port. Port is buried in the chancel of Ilam's church with lines by Cotton which end:

> *Beloved he lived, and died o'ercharged with years,*
> *Fuller of honours than of silver hairs;*
> *And to sum up his virtues, this was he,*
> *Who was what all we would but cannot be.*

Among many monuments in the church, which was restored by Sir Gilbert Scott in 1884, the most impressive is that to David Pike Watts by Sir Francis Chantry. This magnificent white monument of 1826 depicts a death-bed scene, the dying man bidding farewell to his daughter and her three small children.

Pub: **Izaak Walton Hotel** |**A**|**R**|**Bs**| *Tel.* (033 529) 261.

HARTINGTON, DERBYSHIRE |✝|

No parking problems exist in this spacious village where, at the centre, a number of roads converge on the two greens and the duckpond. On one of the greens, a water pump with a lion's head commemorates the Coronation of King Edward VII in 1902. Well spaced around the green, once the site of the market place, are limestone houses and cottages, as well as the two inns, the **Charles Cotton Hotel** and the **Devonshire Arms**.

The Charles Cotton Hotel acquired its name from the poet and translator, Charles Cotton (1630–87), a friend of Izaak Walton (1593–1683), famous for his *Compleat Angler*. The two men used to fish in the nearby waters of **Dovedale** and **Beresford Dale**, among the most beautiful of the Derbyshire dales, which can be reached by a footpath, which is signposted across the road from the hotel.

Crowning a knoll above the village is the **Church of St Giles**, built in red sandstone and surmounted by a sturdy battlemented tower. An unusual memorial, behind the main door on the W wall, is one to Thomas Mellor, 'who lived a remarkably sober, steady life with the enjoyment of his mental faculties to the day of his death, the 6th of December 1822, aged 103'.

The **cheese factory** in the village is noted for its Stilton and visitors are welcome by prior arrangement.

Pubs: **Charles Cotton Hotel** |**A**|**R**|**Bs**| *Tel.* (029 884) 229.
Devonshire Arms |**Bs**|

PARWICH, DERBYSHIRE |✝|

This remote village of limestone cottages stands amidst hilly country-side at an intersection of several minor roads, overlooked by the Georgian **Parwich Hall** where the gardens are occasionally open to the public. At the heart of the village are two greens, one in use as a children's playground, and the **Church of St Peter**, rebuilt in Victorian times but with Norman relics. Among these are the W door, over which are intricate Norman carvings that include two serpents intertwined, a boar, a stag, and a wolf.

Pub: **Sycamore Inn** |**Bs**|

BRADBOURNE, DERBYSHIRE |✝|

Perched on a windswept hill above the valley that divides the village from grassy Haven Hill are a charming group of buildings, the Old Parsonage, the church and the hall. Standing prominently in front of this group is a stone plinth surmounted by a wrought-iron lantern, presented by the village in memory of the 60yr reign of Queen Victoria. From here a lane leads past the timbered **Old Parsonage**, on the right, to the church gates; just inside the gates by the church path is Bradbourne's oldest possession, the remains of an 8thC Saxon cross, about 3ft in height, the carving of foliage and figures still discernible.

Across the churchyard wall is **Bradbourne Hall**, a gabled, stone-built Elizabethan manor house in an old-world garden. This was once the home of the Bradbourne family, later passing to the Buckstons who have memorials in the **Church of All Saints**. Among these memorials is one to Thomas Buckston, who fought at Culloden in 1746, and when he died in 1811 at the age of 87, is described as one of the oldest officers in the army.

TISSINGTON, DERBYSHIRE |✝|

Mellow stone houses surround the green in Tissington which lies in delightful seclusion in the southern fringe of the Peak District National Park. **Tissington Hall**, home of the Fitzherbert family for more than 300yrs, is not open to the public, but this broad-fronted Jacobean mansion beneath a massive array of chimney stacks can be seen from the road.

St Mary's Church, raised above the road amidst an array of sycamore and yew trees, contains fine memorials to the Fitzherberts. This Norman church was much restored in the 19thC, and among its notable possessions is the two-tier, canopied pulpit.

The village's chief claim to fame, however, is not its hall or its church but the fact that Tissington is the first of the Derbyshire villages to institute the annual floral festival of well-dressing (see *Ashford*). A notice outside a shop in the village gives a diagrammatic description of the position of the five wells which are dressed with flowers on Ascension Day, a custom possibly originating from pagan times and said to have subsequently relieved the village from the Black Death, as well as a severe drought in the 17thC.

The wells can be seen during the course of a short circular walk around the village by way of **Hands Well**, named after some former villagers, **Coffin Well**, so-called because of the shape of its trough, **Town Well**, **Yew Tree Well**, and finally **Hall Well**, opposite Tissington Hall. Close to Yew Tree Well and the duck pond is a building bearing the initials FF and the Fitzherbert coat of arms. This was originally the school-house built by Frances Fitzherbert, but since the school's closure, it acts as a tea room during the summer season.

Touring centre

Bakewell, Derbyshire

Hotels: **Rutland Arms, The Square,** *Tel.* **(062 981) 2812❹**
Milford House, Mill Street, *Tel.* **(062 981) 2130❷**

EDENSOR, DERBYSHIRE |△|†|

This estate village stands at the threshold of **Chatsworth Park,**
ancestral home of the Cavendish family, the Dukes of Devonshire.
Prior to 1839 Edensor lay in full view of Chatsworth House. But in that
year the sixth Duke of Devonshire decided that the village should be
demolished and rebuilt a mile away in its present position. This work
was assigned to Sir Joseph Paxton, the duke's gardener and great
friend, who was already at work landscaping the gardens of Chatsworth House and who, many years later, in 1851, designed Crystal
Palace. Evidently Paxton was allowed full rein to experiment.

Grouped at random along the lower slopes of the hill, a jumble
of houses of every shape and style emerged; Swiss chalet type buildings mingle with others in the Italian style amidst a complex pattern
of irregular roofs and chimneys, turrets and battlements. In the centre
of this conglomeration is **St Peter's Church**, built in 1867 and
designed by Sir Gilbert Scott on the site of a Norman church, a photo-
graph of which can be seen in the present church.

On the S side of the chancel is the great Cavendish monument,
erected in 1625 to the memory of the two sons of Bess of Hardwick,
builder of the original Chatsworth House. On the N side of the altar is
the memorial to John Beton, Comptroller to Mary, Queen of Scots,
who had helped her to escape, before he was captured and imprisoned
with her at Chatsworth where he died. At the top end of the sloping
churchyard, among monuments to the Cavendish family, a stone
commemorates the visit of the President of the United States, John
Kennedy, to his sister's grave.

It is worth climbing to the top of Edensor for the view of the
deer park in which Chatsworth House lies. The present house is the
second to be built on the site. The first was designed by Sir William
Cavendish and his wife, Bess of Hardwick. It was completed in 1555,
but all that remains to be seen today is the **Hunting Tower** and **Queen
Mary's Bower**. The present building, standing on a rising slope above
the River Derwent, was built in the Palladian style. Begun in 1687 for

the first Duke of Devonshire, the work developed over the next two centuries until the completion of the N wing in 1820.

BASLOW, DERBYSHIRE |†|

The village lies in two distinct parts, each in its own way equally picturesque. The smaller part, known as **Goose Green**, comprises a neat, tree-shaded, triangular green across from the village stores and the stone-built **Devonshire Arms**. Behind the inn a lane leads to a cluster of delightful thatched and tiled cottages that huddle around the bridge across the stream. A footpath bordering the stream is signposted to **Chatsworth House** (see *Edensor*).

From Goose Green the main road rises, passing the **Cavendish Hotel** before dropping down to the larger part of Baslow half a mile away. Here two bridges cross the River Derwent. The newer of these bridges carries the main road traffic, diverting it from the village street which runs parallel to the river towards the older packhorse bridge. At the end of this graceful three-arched bridge is a tiny quaint stone structure, once a shelter for the toll collector but now rebuilt and only capable of containing the smallest of pygmies.

St Anne's Church occupies a lovely position on the riverside between the two bridges. The oldest parts of the church, which was restored in 1853, are the tower, built in the 13thC, and the N aisle, originally the nave of the church. The porch contains stones found during the rebuilding of the church, which is believed to have once formed part of an earlier Saxon church. By the main door in a glass case is a leather dog whip and a pitch-pipe. The former was once used by the churchwardens to keep dogs at bay; the latter was an instrument used for tuning the organ. Another interesting feature is the church clock; the E dial reads VICTORIA 1897 in place of the usual numbers.

Pubs: Cavendish Hotel |**A**|**R**|**Bs**| *Tel.* (024 688) 2311.

Devonshire Arms |**Bs**|

HATHERSAGE, DERBYSHIRE |†|✧•|

Situated on high ground above the Derwent valley, Hathersage existed before the Domesday Book, the name possibly deriving from 'heather's edge'.

The **Church of St Michael**, built in the 14thC but extensively restored in Victorian times, occupies a commanding position above the village. There are many memorials in the church to the Eyre family, the first dated 1459, supporters of James II until the king's retreat to France when they were also forced to flee their homes. During the 16thC the Eyres built many houses in the surrounding moors; among those that survive is **North Lees Hall**, a house mentioned in Charlotte Bronte's novel, *Jane Eyre* (1847). Charlotte Bronte used to stay at the vicarage here and took the name of Hathersage's oldest family for that of her heroine, describing Hathersage in her novel under the name of Morton.

Near the porch of the church is a grave 14ft long, reputedly that of Robin Hood's henchman, Little John. The grave lies beneath yew trees and is maintained by the Ancient Order of Foresters. In his youth, Little John is said to have been brought up in Hathersage, serving his apprenticeship as a nail-maker before joining the rebels under Simon de Montfort in 1265. After many years as an outlaw, it is said, he returned to his native village, brokenhearted after laying Robin Hood to rest at Kirklees.

No proof exists that the grave is that of Little John; but centuries after the time he would have died, the grave was opened, revealing a thigh bone more than 30 inches long which could only have been that of a gigantic man.

Pub: Hathersage Inn |**A**|**R**|**Bs**| *Tel.* (0433) 50259.

CASTLETON, DERBYSHIRE |❖|△|✝|∞|

Towering above this peakland village of the Hope Valley are the ruins of **Peveril Castle**, sometimes known as the Castle of the Peak, built by William Peveril at the time of the Conquest and immortalized by Sir Walter Scott in his *Peveril of the Peak* (1825). The castle walls, the gateway and the immense roofless keep (built 100yrs later) still stand; the village houses lying snugly beneath these dramatic ruins.

Derbyshire is famous for its caverns, four of them being located in or around Castleton. Among the most impressive of these is **Peak Cavern**, its massive entrance penetrating the face of the cliff beneath the castle. Guided tours of Peak Cavern take some 40 minutes, through passages which lead for 1 mile beneath the hill, by way of a variety of chambers with intriguing names such as Roger's Rain House, Devil's Cavern, Bell House and the Orchestral Chamber. At

The miniature stone-built tollhouse at the end of the old packhorse bridge in Baslow, allegedly the smallest of its kind in England.

157

one time the cavern was entered by lying prone in a punt, an adventure which the poet Lord Byron described thus:

> *I had to cross in a boat a stream which flows under a rock so close upon the water as to admit the boat only to be pushed on by the ferryman, a sort of Charon, who wades at the stern, stooping all the time. The Companion of my transit was M. A. C. [Mary Chaworth], with whom I had long been in love and never told it, though she had discovered it without. I recollect my sensations but cannot describe them, and it is as well.*

Other caves to be seen near Castleton are **Speedwell Cavern**, **Treak Cliff Caverns** and the **Blue John Caverns**, containing the unique blue john stone which is made into ornaments and jewellery and can be purchased in the village shops.

The Norman **Church of St Edmund** was much restored in 1837. Its library includes a Breeches Bible of 1611, so named because in Genesis the word breeches is used instead of aprons, which is found in the Authorised Version.

Pubs: Castle Hotel |**A**|**R**|**Bs**| *Tel.* (0433) 20578.
     Ye Old Nags Head |**A**|**R**|**Bs**| *Tel.* (0433) 20248.

EDALE, DERBYSHIRE |△|

Glorious scenery encompasses Edale, tucked snugly in the valley of the River Noe and overshadowed by the rugged heights of the Peak District. Mam Tor, to the S, separates the dale from that of *Castleton*, and from here there is a magnificent view of the village and the hills beyond.

Mam Tor, known as the 'Shivering Mountain' because of the layers of grit and shale that occasionally give way to landslides, is one of many National Trust hills in the area. Even higher than Mam Tor is **Kinder Scout** (2,088ft) to the NW of the village.

One of Derbyshire's splendid walks starts at Edale, crossing the Kinder Scout range along a track known as Jacob's Ladder to Hayfield, passing on the way a medieval boundary stone called **Edale Cross**. The village is also the starting point for a much longer walk, the Pennine Way, a trek of some 250 miles northwards as far as the village of **Kirk Yetholm** across the border of Scotland.

To the immediate SW of Edale is **Lord's Seat** (owned by the National Trust), a 7ft barrow which is the burial place of a tribal chieftan; to the NE are the Howden Moors and three huge reservoirs, an area sometimes called the 'Lake District of Derbyshire'. The gritstone houses and pretty gardens of Edale make a sharp contrast with the rugged scenery that encircles the village. The inn, the **Rambler**, is more than 300yrs old.

Pub: Rambler |**A**|**R**|**Bs**|**Ra**| *Tel.* (0433) 70268.

ASHFORD-IN-THE-WATER, DERBYSHIRE |†|

The River Wye meanders past Ashford, crossed by three bridges that connect the village with the main road. One of these bridges was built in 1664, but the other two are older still, dating from medieval times. The narrow **Sheepwash Bridge** is named appropriately, for the stone pen, where sheep were herded before being dipped in the clear waters of the river, can be seen here.

Near to the bridge is the **well** where the old Derbyshire custom of well-dressing takes place on Trinity Sunday (see *Tissington*). It is not known when the ceremony first took place in Ashford; but having fallen into disuse for some 40yrs, the custom was revived in 1954.

Close to the village of narrow streets and limestone cottages are the quarries that were once the source of Ashford's principal industry, marble. The marble works were established in 1748 and continued to operate until the beginning of the 20thC. The industry was founded by Henry Watson, a memorial to whom, in Ashford marble, can be seen in the church near the main door; its inscription tells how he 'Was the first Who formed into ornaments The FLUORS and other FOSSILS Of this County'.

The **Church of the Holy Trinity**, much restored in the 19thC, stands on the site of a Norman church.

Pubs: Devonshire Arms Hotel |**A**|**Bs**| *Tel.* **(062 981) 2725.**

Bulls Head |**Bs**|**Ra**|

Tour Thirty-six
Touring centre
Newark-on-Trent, Nottinghamshire
Hotels: **Robin Hood, Lombard Street,** *Tel.* **(0636) 703858❹**
Midland, Muskham Road, *Tel.* **(0636) 73788❷**

Colston Bassett, Nottinghamshire |✝|

A little stone bridge marks the entry to the village, spanning the River Smite before the road arrives at the inn, the **Martins Arms**, and the village cross, its 15ft high stem rising gracefully from a flight of steps and medieval base. From here the road passes between the 90 acre park of the hall and the church.

From the churchyard there is a good view of Colston Manor and the park. In the church a winged figure, sculptured in marble, commemorates Alice Knowles. A memorial tablet, removed from St Mary's Church, is to the Martin family, earlier lords of the manor after whom the inn is named.

Pub: **Martins Arms** |**Bs**|**Ra**|

WELLOW, NOTTINGHAMSHIRE |△|✝|

The village green is set back from the main road, and is overlooked by two inns and red-brick, pantile-roofed cottages of the 17thC and 18thC. Other buildings to note are the small **Methodist chapel**, dated 1847, and the white **Rock House** at the corner of the green with its overhanging storey. The green is dominated by a tall red and white maypole, more than 60ft in height, and erected in 1966 in place of the earlier one, which had been blown down in a gale. The maypole, surmounted by a weathervane and surrounded by a seat, is one of few permanent structures to be found in England.

The much restored **church** with its sturdy 14thC pinnacled tower can be approached by a footpath from the green. One of its most ancient treasures is the Norman font bowl, no longer in use as a font. The stone pulpit has a figure of St Swithin to whom the church is dedicated. The clock face on the tower was constructed locally to commemorate the coronation of Queen Elizabeth II in 1953.

On the main road at the extremity of the village a sign directs you to **Jordan's Castle Farm**, the site of the former 13thC moated manor house. A mile to the SW of Wellow is **Rufford**, once a Cistercian abbey, the park of which is open to the public and contains an exhibition demonstrating the changing scene of the locality over the centuries. A little to the NW of the village is **Edwinstowe**, once in the heart of the old Sherwood Forest where, according to tradition, Robin Hood took Maid Marian as his bride.

Pubs: **Durham Ox** |**Bs**|
    Red Lion |**Bs**|

BLYTH, NOTTINGHAMSHIRE |✝|

There are no less than four inns in the village, testimony to the fact that Blyth was once a bustling coaching stop on the Great North Road. Now, however, it is bypassed by the A1 and can be viewed in peace.

There are two village greens, the largest of which is oval in shape, long and sloping, with, at its head, the former Hospital of St John the Evangelist, built initially in the 12thC as a leper hospital. Later it fulfilled a variety of functions, acting as a resting place for weary travellers as well as a school, until in 1964, by then a derelict building, it was rebuilt to form two dwellings and acts as a memorial.

Along the main street there are modern bungalows, but facing them beside the slip road on the other side of the green there is a row of attractive houses that includes the White Swan Inn as well as houses of red brick and pantiles, one with a carriage entrance.

The smaller green, triangular in shape, is bisected by a broad path that leads to the church, and is surrounded by gracious houses that include the former rectory and three inns. The oldest of these, the **Angel Hotel** dates back to 1274 and must be one of the most ancient surviving coaching inns in the county; while among other buildings in the same row there is one appropriately named **Ye Olde House**.

The **Church of St Mary and St Martin** is all that remains of the priory, built in 1088 as a Cell of the Abbey of St Catherine at Rouen in France. During the Reformation, the monastic part of the priory and the living quarters were destroyed, the western parts of the priory church surviving to form a nucleus of the present church.

Pubs: Angel Hotel |A|Bs|Ra| *Tel.* (090 976) 213.

Fourways Hotel |A|R|Bs| *Tel.* (090 976) 235.

GRINGLEY ON THE HILL, NOTTINGHAMSHIRE |†|

The busy main road from Sheffield to Gainsborough passes beneath Gringley. From this road there is a sharp climb to the little village past charming houses of red brick, the bulk of Gringley lying, as the name indicates, along the ridge of a hill and sited to give magnificent views. At one end of the narrow main street is the village cross; the church and neighbouring buildings positioned high above one side of the street overlooking the inn and the adjacent cottages on the other.

The Early English **Church of St Peter and St Paul** has been restored during the 20thC. The old **Blue Bell Inn** has recently come under new ownership and has been modernized internally. A green mound at the extremity of the main street stands some 50ft above the ridge, offering panoramic views across Yorkshire to the N as well as the gleaming towers of Lincoln Cathedral some 20 miles away to the south-east. Here, on **Beacon Hill** as it is known, Prince Rupert camped in 1644 before riding to the relief of Newark.

Pub: Blue Bell Inn |Bs|Ra|

LAXTON, NOTTINGHAMSHIRE |△|†|

The first impression on entry to Laxton is the wealth of farmhouses, farmyards and barns within such a small village. This is not so surprising when you learn that Laxton is unique among English villages in that the open-field system of farming has survived here, unchanged in its essentials, since Saxon times. Throughout all those centuries open-field farming has been practised on a co-operative basis in large hedgeless fields; and today it is estimated that some 483 acres continue to be farmed on this basis, a system of rotation whereby wheat and spring corn are grown on two huge fields while the third lies fallow.

The Laxton Trail, a pamphlet issued by the Newark District Council, gives suggestions for a 1½hr walk around the village, visiting 17 places of particular interest. The walk begins at **High Street Farm**, one of the typical farm buildings in the village, and ends at St Michael's Church in the heart of Laxton. Among places visited along the way are the **Motte and Bailey Castle** (approached by a footpath to the N of the church); **West Field**, one of the three fields that still form part of the open-field system (the others are Mill Field and South Field); and the **Pinfold**, a walled enclosure in which an official known as the Pinder once held stray cattle, the owner of the cattle being fined for his negligence by the Court Leet. Even today a court is appointed, acting for the lord of the manor, now the Minister of Agriculture, to administer a system which has survived to function very much as it did in medieval times.

St Michael's Church was built at the same time as Lincoln Cathedral, and is believed to have numbered among the finest of medieval churches until it was largely rebuilt in 1861. A stone terrier set in the N wall of the tower gives details of the land which formed part of the parson's benefice in the 18thC.

Pub: Dovecote Inn |Bs|

AREA NINE

Hereford and Worcester and Shropshire

40

SHROPSHIRE

Touring centres

37 Ross-on-Wye
38 Worcester
39 Leominster
40 Shrewsbury

39

HEREFORD and WORCESTER

38

37

I n medieval days the boundary areas of England and Wales saw scenes of pillage, raids and counter raids, cross-border activity not dissimilar to that which took place along the frontiers of Scotland and England. These troubled regions were held by feudal families, known as the Earls of March, families such as the Mortimers and Bohuns who, as Sir Winston Churchill remarked, 'exploited their military privileges against the interests alike of the Welsh and English people'. The Norman marcher barons, though conquering much of South Wales, met strong resistance in the north from Llewelyn I (1194–1240) and Llewelyn II (1246–82); and it was not until the latter's death that Wales first came under English rule after its total defeat by Edward I.

The villages described in this section lie in these border areas of Hereford and Worcester, and Shropshire, territory which, for historical reasons, is known as the Welsh Marches and to the W of which are the foothills of the Welsh mountains, that chain of defence which delayed the advance of the English.

Herefordshire, now joined administratively with Worcestershire, is watered by the picturesque River Wye and its tributaries. The county embraces the beautiful Malvern Hills as well as much flat pastureland where the famous Hereford cattle are reared. The chief river of Worcestershire is the Severn, which, with its tributaries, forms the vales of Teme and Evesham, an area of market gardens and fruit orchards of which John Drinkwater (1882–1937) wrote:

> *Who travels Worcester county*
> *Takes any road that comes*
> *When April tosses bounty*
> *To the cherries and the plums.*

The countryside of Shropshire is relatively flat, contrasting with that to the S of the county, where the Shropshire Hills rise to almost 1,800ft at Brown Clee Hill. In the county, which was described by A. E. Housman in his well-known poem, 'A Shropshire Lad', cattle and sheep are reared and cheese is produced. There can be few more enthralling towns than Ludlow (close to Tour 39) with its Norman castle and fine market square about which Housman wrote:

> *Oh, come you home on Sunday when Ludlow's streets are still*
> *And Ludlow's bells are calling to farm and lane and mill.*
> *Or come you home on Monday when Ludlow market hums*
> *And Ludlow chimes are playing The Conquering Hero Comes.*

('A Shropshire Lad')

The villages of the Welsh Marches are renowned, in particular, for the beauty of the timbered black and white buildings that abound there. Among villages outstanding in this respect are *Weobley*, known as the capital of black and white, *Pembridge* and *Elmley Castle*. One of Worcestershire's most remote villages, *Abbots Morton*, is distinguished both for its picturesque timbered cottages and the quaintness of their design. Here every imaginable shape of building is to be seen, and even the post office, as if intent on sharing the originality of the scene, is fronted by a thatched post-box.

Only half a day is needed for **Tour 37** (54 miles), apart of which takes the motorist along the beautiful Wye valley. Based on Worcester, **Tour 38** (70 miles) can be accomplished in one day, leaving plenty of time to stop in the quiet and pretty villages listed. It is also possible to complete **Tour 39** (92 miles) in one day, although visits to the celebrated black and white villages merit a more leisurely pace. **Tour 40** is a day trip of 138 miles through the attractive country by the Welsh border.

Ross-on-Wye, Hereford and Worcester

Hotels: Chase, Gloucester Road, *Tel.* (0989) 3161❹
Chasedale, Walford Road, *Tel.* (0989) 2423❷

GOODRICH, HEREFORD AND WORCESTER |△|◆●|

Overlooking the village, on a ridge above the River Wye, are the ruins of **Goodrich Castle**, once Godric's Castle with a history of siege and counter siege that dates back at least as far as the 12thC. The castle's fate was sealed finally when it fell to the Parliamentarians during the Civil War. Cannonballs that did the damage can be seen in the castle grounds; while the cannon that fired them, the oddly named 'Roaring Meg', is preserved in Hereford.

The village, named after the castle, comprises grey-stone houses, the **Church of St Giles** with a 14thC tower, and an inn, **Ye Old Hostelrie**, pinnacled with Gothic windows. The castle had a strange fascination for William Wordsworth who, while wandering through the ruins in 1793, met the little girl who features in his poem 'We are Seven':

> *I met a little cottage Girl;*
> *She was eight years old, she said;*
> *Her hair was thick with many a curl*
> *That clustered round her head.*

In a preface to the poem, written in 1798, Wordsworth wrote:

> *I revisited Goodrich Castle, not having seen that part of the Wye since I met the little girl there in 1793. It would have given me greater pleasure to have found in the neighbouring hamlet traces of one who had interested me so much; but that was impossible as unfortunately I did not even know her name. The ruin, from its position and features, is a most impressive object. I could not but deeply regret that its solemnity was impaired by a fantastic new Castle set up on a projection of the same ridge.*

Wordsworth was referring to a folly, Goodrich Court. This was later shipped brick by brick to America, leaving the old ruins in their present peaceful surroundings.

Pub: **Ye Old Hostelrie** |**Bs**|

FOWNHOPE, HEREFORD AND WORCESTER †

A wide variety of buildings make up this village in the Wye valley. Black and white timbered houses mingle with others of plain stone and red brick. The church, which is large for a village of this size and consequently known as the 'Little Cathedral', has a Norman tower carrying an attractive 14thC broach spire roofed with wooden tiles. Near the churchyard the old village stocks and whipping post have been retained.

Among several old inns is the 15thC black and white **Green Man**, formerly known as the Naked Boy. In the 18thC, the Petty Sessional Courts were held in this building, and it is still possible to see the prisoner's cell and the iron bar to which he was chained, as well as the judge's bedroom with its four-poster bed. In the bar there is a picture of Tom Spring, the champion bare-knuckle fighter who was born at Fownhope in 1851.

At the entrance to the yard of this old coaching inn an amusing jingle runs: 'You travel far, you travel near, its here you find the best of beer. You pass the East, You pass the West, if you pass this you pass the Best.' Every June, villagers of the Heart of Oak Club parade through the village with flowered sticks before arriving at the Green Man.

Pubs: **Green Man** |**A**|**R**|**Bs**| *Tel.* (043 277) 243.

    Forge and Ferry |**Bs**|**Ra**|

Dominating the River Wye, the impressive red sandstone ruins of Goodrich Castle, built in the 12thC and destroyed by Cromwell's men.

EASTNOR, HEREFORD AND WORCESTER

Eastnor has associations with two castles; one old and one new. The former, **Bronsil Castle**, was built in the 15thC by Richard Beauchamp and all that now remains is the moat and two-gate houses a mile to the E of the village. **Eastnor Castle**, in the heart of the village, is a 19thC mansion built in Norman style with turrets and towers, overlooking a lake and extensive parkland with many rare trees. It is open on specified occasions so that the public can view the state rooms, paintings, tapestries and armour, as well as the arboretum.

On the edge of the castle estate there are only a handful of houses, among them the picturesque black and white thatched post office. The small triangular village green has a drinking fountain beneath a pyramid roof presented by the temperance campaigner Lady Henry Somerset with the inscription: 'If any man thirst let him come unto me and drink.' A worthy inscription but, regrettably, the fountain does not appear to operate in the 1980s, and as the village has never boasted a pub Eastnor can be something of a 'dry' place.

The **church**, apart from the 14thC tower, was almost entirely rebuilt by Sir Gilbert Scott in 1853. An important Iron Age **fort** that has yielded pottery during recent excavations stands on nearby Midsummer Hill.

TOUR THIRTY-EIGHT
Touring centre
Worcester, Hereford and Worcester

Hotels: Star, Foregate Street, *Tel.* (0905) 24308 ❸
Park House, Droitwich Road, *Tel.* (0905) 21816 ❶

OMBERSLEY, HEREFORD AND WORCESTER |✝|

A quiet village now that the main Kidderminster–Worcester road by-passes it. The most picturesque part of the village is the street in which the two inns stand. The **Kings Arms**, mainly 15thC, is a timbered black and white building with an overhanging storey. Next to it is the white-fronted **Crown and Sandys**, across the street from which a lane leads into the churchyard of the 19thC church. The path to the church runs by the remains of an older church, now used as a mausoleum for the Sandys family.

The **Church of St Andrews**, built in 1829 for Lord Sandys in the grounds of the older **Ombersley Court**, retains some fine original box pews. One of particular interest is the private family pew, complete with fireplace for the occupants. The centre of the village is also graced with fine buildings, two of these being black and white cruck houses.

At the central crossroads, on a little green, is a large rectangular trough of solid stone known as the **Plague Stone**. Formerly it stood at the edge of Ombersley, and in the 14thC, at a time when the Black Death swept the area, the Plague Stone acted as a place of exchange. Traders reluctant to enter the village for fear of disease would deposit their wares in the stone after collecting coins placed there by the villagers.

Pub: Kings Arms |**Bs**|**Ra**|

ABBOTS MORTON, HEREFORD AND WORCESTER |✝|

This village is hard to find for it is tucked away on a loop road off the narrowest of lanes. The effort is well worthwhile, however, for Abbots Morton has an almost 'fairy tale' appearance; the single road through it is straddled at generous intervals with a variety of quaint black and white houses and cottages of every imaginable shape and design. At one end of the village, near the church, the black and white **Corner Thatch Cottage** has a small, unique pillar box roofed with thatch attached to it.

Abbots Morton is small, boasting neither a pub nor a shop, yet it is considered to be among the oldest of English villages. A Saxon church stood here before the Norman Conquest. The existing church, on the same site, stands aloof and above the village, with a N wall that is a relic of another, later 12thC church.

In a field to the NE of the churchyard cattle now graze, as oblivious as most humans to the fact that in AD700 this was the site of the rest house of the Abbot of Evesham. Here is the mound where the Abbots moated house once stood. The pool, nearby, was then known as the Fish Pond, stocked with fish for the monks.

ELMLEY CASTLE, HEREFORD AND WORCESTER |✝|

Reckoned to number among England's prettiest villages, the broad main street contains a host of picture-book black and white cottages and is bordered by a tree-lined stream. Only a fragment or two survives from the castle to which the village owes its name.

Elmley Castle was built in the 11thC by Robert le Despenser, but by the 16thC was already a ruin. Some idea of what the castle once looked like is given by a matchstick model in the church, which has been based on old drawings found there.

The colourful inn sign outside the **Elizabeth I** has a portrait of the monarch on one side, while on the other she is seen visiting the village on 20 August 1575. Two other pleasant inns grace this snug little village beneath the slopes of Bredon Hill.

The **church**, mainly 15thC, contains a monument in alabaster to the Savage family who owned the manor here for more than 300yrs. Amidst the tombstones in the churchyard are two 17thC sundials.

Pubs: Old Mill Inn |**Bs**|**Ra**|
  Queen Elizabeth I |**Bs**|**Ra**|
  Plough Inn |**Bs**|

Leominster, Hereford and Worcester

WEOBLEY, HEREFORD AND WORCESTER ❖†

Weobley, pronounced Webley, is sometimes known as the 'capital of the black and white', for almost the entire village is made up of picturesque half-timbered inns, shops, houses and cottages, many dating from the 14thC and 15thC. A fire in the 20thC gutted some of the central buildings, and thus the main street, appropriately named Broad Street, allowed enough space for the introduction of a sunken rose garden and bus shelter. Nearby is the attractive **Unicorn Inn**, behind which is a private house, **The Throne**, once an inn where King Charles I rested in 1645 after the Battle of Naseby. Other notable buildings include the **Red Lion Inn**, one of many 14thC buildings, and the Jacobean **grammar school**.

The **Church of St Peter and St Paul** stands somewhat aloofly in fields on the very edge of Weobley. It is of Norman origin with much early stained glass, but perhaps is most notable for its magnificent 14thC tower and spire that dominates the village. In the sanctuary is a marble statue of Colonel John Birch (*died* 1691) the Parliamentary Commander who settled in the neighbourhood after the Civil War. The churchyard contains a medieval preaching cross which according to legend has associations with conjuring up the devil.

Pubs: Red Lion Hotel |**A**|**R**|**Bs**|**Ra**| *Tel.* (054 45) 220.

Unicorn Inn |**A**|**R**|**Bs**| *Tel.* (054 45) 230.

EARDISLEY, HEREFORD AND WORCESTER †

This village comprises primarily one long main street lined with pretty half-timbered black and white cottages. At one end of the street is the church and school; at the other are the two village inns. The **Church of St Mary Magdalene** (begun in the early 12thC) has a famous Norman font in perfect condition with deeply carved figures that include warriors in combat, a saint, a lion, and a figure which has been interpreted as Christ snatching Adam from the devil.

At the other end of the village is the old **Tram Inn**, so-called because a century ago ponies hauled coal-trucks along rails from Brecon to Eardisley. The little black and white cottages behind the inn are conversions of the former stables.

At one time Eardisley lay in a clearing of a vast forest and a remnant, known as the Great Oak, 30ft in circumference, is to be found about half a mile along the minor road behind the Tram Inn near to a building that was once the school-house.

Pubs: **Mountie** |**Bs**|

      Tram Inn |**Bs**|

PEMBRIDGE, HEREFORD AND WORCESTER |†|

In common with nearby *Weobley* this village is made up almost entirely of half-timbered black and white houses. Pembridge, however, is larger than Weobley, less compact, and perhaps rather less sophisticated — giving the impression that the village today appears very much as it must have done centuries ago. The focal point is the 16thC **Market House** with an open grooved floor and tiled roof supported by eight pillars.

From the Market House steps lead up to the **Church of St Mary**, where, in the pretty churchyard there is a huge detached bell-house of pyramidal design, similar in appearance to buildings found in Scandinavia. Apertures in the walls of this structure suggest that it may once have been used as a stronghold by archers repelling Welsh raids.

Alongside the Market House is the black and white **New Inn Hotel**, built in 1311 as a coaching inn, and at one time bearing the odd title 'The Inn without a Name'. One of the hotel bedrooms was once a court room, and the beer cellars were formerly a prison. Pembridge lies within 6 miles of Mortimer's Cross, scene of the final battle of the Wars of the Roses in 1461, and it is believed that the treaty confirming the Yorkist victory was signed in the court room of the New Inn.

A feature of many of Pembridge's black and white houses is the overhanging first floor. Notable buildings include the 16thC **Greyhound Inn**, the **Trafford Almshouses** (1686) and the **Duppa Almshouses** (1661), both of which have been modernized internally, and the **Old Steppes**, now a village store but once the rectory with wood carvings on the gable depicting fruit, flowers and dragons.

Pubs: **New Inn Hotel** |**A**|**R**|**Bs**| *Tel.* (054 47) 427.

      Greyhound Inn |**Bs**|

EARDISLAND, HEREFORD AND WORCESTER |△|

The most picturesque view of this delightful village is undoubtedly found on the bridge across the River Arrow. Here, on either side of the river, Georgian red-brick and white-painted houses, fronted by lawns and a variety of shrubs, face each other across the stream. Also overlooked from the bridge is the purpose-built school-house of 1652, which ceased its educational function in 1825 and is now a private residence. The whipping post can be seen here, which, according to the villagers, was surprisingly only used in chastising women.

Nearby is the 16thC court house, across the road from which and adding grace to the scene is a tall, four-gabled, brick **dovecote**. The oldest building in the village, at its northern extremity, is **Staick House** (part 14thC), a large, rambling, timber-framed mansion, built partly in the 14thC and believed to have been a 'mote' house.

Pubs: **Cross Inn** |**A**|**R**|**Bs**| *Tel.* (054 47) 249.

      White Swan |**Bs**|

CLUN, SHROPSHIRE △ ★ † ☙

A large border village that has witnessed tumultuous scenes over centuries. Part of the village nestles beneath the 11thC ruined castle keep on one side of the river. On the other side, across a narrow medieval bridge, are dwellings and the church.

The village name derives from the Celtic 'llan' (a settlement or meeting place), a settlement so old that it would be impossible to define the precise point at which it began. Within the hipped roofed Georgian **town hall**, formerly the court house, is the **Clun Trust Museum** where relics from the Bronze Age, as well as flint and stone tools, give witness to the village's antiquity. Perhaps in those very early days, as in more recent times, the words of the poet A. E. Housman ring true:

Clunton and Clunbury,
Clungunford and Clun
Are the quietest places
Under the sun. ('A Shropshire Lad')

In between times, however, Clun has witnessed battles between British and Romans, English and Normans, and English and Welsh who frequently attacked the castle and burned the village.

A path from the edge of the village is signposted to the **castle** and here, perched on a tree-covered slope are the spectacular riverside ruins, consisting primarily of the Norman keep, the 13thC semi-circular tower and the earthworks. This provides a romantic setting for the game of bowls which the villagers play regularly on the flat grass plateau beneath the ruin.

A number of inns are scattered around the village, and at one of them, the **Buffalo**, the novelist Sir Walter Scott (1771–1832) is reputed to have stayed, possibly featuring the castle in his novel *The Betrothed*.

St George's Church is believed to occupy the site of a Druidic Seminary. It stands beneath a massive Norman tower, and suffered considerable damage during the Civil War, seeing much subsequent restoration. Among other old buildings in Clun are the stone-built **rectory** (1700) and the **Hospital of the Holy and Undivided Trinity**, completed in 1614 as almshouses for twelve poor men and to be staffed by 'a Warden, a sub Warden, a nurse and a barber'.

Pubs: **Sun Inn** |**A**|**R**|**Bs**|**Ra**| *Tel.* (058 84) 277.

      White Horse Inn |**Bs**|**Ra**|

YARPOLE, HEREFORD AND WORCESTER |△|†|

This very old village is mentioned in the Domesday Book. The bulk of the village runs along a little stream where black and white houses mingle with others washed in a variety of colour schemes. An interesting structure that stands right on the stream is a small, square medieval building with archways known as the **Old Bakehouse**. In fact, over the centuries, this building has fulfilled other functions than that of once housing the bakery, for it has also served as a gatehouse to the original manor, the village gaol and an illicit Quaker meeting house.

    St Leonard's Church, which is 14thC with 19thC extensions, stands on the site of an even earlier church and shares with Pembridge the distinction of having a detached belltower in the churchyard. This tower, possibly 13thC, in common with the Pembridge tower, bears a similarity to Scandinavian church buildings, and today houses three bells dated 1450, 1605 and 1652.

    Three of Yarpole's attractive timber-framed 17thC houses can be seen from the churchyard — **Church House**, **Vicarage Farm** and **Tudor House**.

Situated in beautiful rolling countryside, just 9 miles from the Welsh border, Clun is a quiet and peaceful place today, but the ruins of its 11thC castle serve as a reminder of a more violent past.

Touring centre

Shrewsbury, Shropshire

Hotels: **Prince Rupert, Butcher Row,** *Tel.* **(0743) 52461 ❹**
Beauchamp, The Mount, *Tel.* **(0743) 3230 ❸**

LLANYBLODWEL, SHROPSHIRE |✝|

This tiny village, perhaps hamlet is a better description, lies down a
leafy lane off the A495 in a setting so beautiful that the diversion
ought not to be missed. The Welsh sounding name (derived from
'village of flowers') indicates that Llanyblodwel lies within a mile of
the border with Wales.

The first building to be seen along the lane, on the left, is one
surmounted by extraordinary turrets and gables, a **house** that might
have stepped right out of the pages of a Hans Andersen fairy tale. It is
a private house now but was once the school-house, a building both
designed and paid for by the benevolent Revd John Parker, who spent
much of his income on endowments to the village and church.

A little further along the lane a medieval bridge, on the left, spans
the river to arrive at an enchanting scene: on the banks of the river, is
the delightful black and white 16thC **Horseshoe Inn**, joined to a
timbered barn and faced by picturesque black and white, slate-roofed
cottages. Wooden tables and benches stand outside the inn along the
river; it is a place of refreshment hard to equal for its charm and
tranquility.

From the bridge there is a good view of the church and strange
tower and spire, the shape of which is due to the Revd John Parker,
incumbent here from 1845–1860. It was John Parker who designed the
104ft tower and spire, personally footing a large part of the bill and
assisting in the construction until the spire's completion on 14 August
1856, when he recorded:

On this day we removed all the scaffolding from the
tower.... The appearance of my spire, when disencumbered
from the scaffolding was exactly what I wished and
expected.... The convex outline of the spire has, I think, a
certain degree of scientific and geometrical grandeur; and it also

appears to me far more beautiful than the ordinary form.

Further evidence of Parker's bizarre talents are found within the church where colourful texts appear to adorn every available space on the walls. Near to the church is the 18thC **Blodwel Hall** and the whole colourful scene is overlooked by steep, wooded hills.

Pub: **Horseshoe Inn** |**Bs**|

ACTON BURNELL, SHROPSHIRE |△|✝|

Black and white cottages and some large Georgian houses range themselves along the four prongs of this pretty village. The most interesting buildings are found at the extremity of the village, along the eastern prong. Here is **Acton Burnell Hall**, set in a park, built in Georgian style on the site of an earlier building that burnt down in 1914. It now houses a college.

Near to the entrance to Acton Burnell Park are the ruins of **Acton Burnell Castle** and the church. Although styled as a castle, the well-preserved ruins are really those of a fortified manor house, a red sandstone building, built by Bishop Burnell during the reign of Edward I, cornered by four 40ft towers over one of which the branches of a massive cedar spread. Nearby across the lawn are the remains of a huge **barn**, which predates the castle and is believed to have been the venue for a meeting of Parliament when King Edward visited the bishop in 1283.

The **Church of St Mary**, which is mainly 13thC, contains the tomb of one of Bishop Burnell's descendants, Sir Nicholas Burnell (*died* 1382). In a recess are the full length figures of Sir Richard Lee and his wife (*died* 1591), ancestors of the American statesman Richard Henry Lee, a signatory of the Declaration of Independence of 1776; and of General Robert E. Lee (1807–70), recognized as one of the world's greatest military strategists who commanded the Southern forces in the American Civil War.

CLAVERLEY, SHROPSHIRE

Claverley lies on wooded slopes a mere 5 miles to the W of Wolverhampton, and is only approachable by minor roads. The central part of the village is made up of picturesque black and white cottages, as well as those of Georgian red brick. The two delightful inns, the **Plough** and the **Kings Arms**, are close to each other, and opposite the Plough, is a beautiful **sunken garden**.

The large black and white 15thC building near the church lychgate, which is also black and white, was once the vicarage. The most remarkable feature of the **Church of All Saints** is the equestrian frieze, dating from *c*.1200, on the N side of the nave. The painting is in the style of the Bayeux Tapestry with 15 armed equestrian knights, ten of them engaged in active combat. After the discovery of the painting, it was first believed that it represented the Battle of Hastings. Subsequently, however, it has been concluded that the battle between the knights was based on an allegorical poem that told of the conflict between the seven Christian virtues and the seven pagan vices.

In the chapel there is a magnificent monument to Sir Robert Broke who lies with his two wives above the figures of their 16 children and daughter-in-law. In the churchyard a cross dated 1349 serves as a memorial to victims of the Black Death.

Pubs: **Crown Inn** |**Bs**|**Ra**|
     Kings Arms |**Bs**|**Ra**|
     Plough Inn |**Bs**|**Ra**|

Cheshire, Lancashire and Cumbria

Cheshire, with suburban Manchester towns to the NE and the borders with Wales to the W, has as its principal rivers the Mersey, Dee and Weaver. The county is renowned, of course, for its cheese as well as for the Cheshire Cat, the literary creation of the Revd Charles Dodgson, whose pen-name was Lewis Carroll, and who was born at Daresbury.

Lancashire, with Greater Manchester and Merseyside to the S, contains a number of industrial conurbations, yet also has some delightful rural areas such as the Forest of Bowland to the north-west. Throughout the county there are huge expanses of open moorland within close proximity of the urban areas. Along the miles of coastline are many popular holiday resorts.

Cumbria, fringed by the Solway Firth and the borders with Scotland to the N and the Irish Sea to the SW, embraces the Cumbrian Mountains that tower above the glorious lakeland scenery. The fact that the Lake District became a National Park in 1915 owes much to the conservationists of the 19thC. Foremost of these was William Wordsworth, who as early as 1846 was bombarding the national press with protest in both verse and prose, asking: 'Is there no nook of England ground secure from rash assault?'

Wordsworth, born at Cockermouth, educated at *Hawkshead*, and spending much of his later life at *Grasmere* and Rydal, summed up his feelings with the clarion call:

> *be joined by persons of pure taste throughout the whole island who, by their visits (often repeated) to the Lakes of the North of England, testify that they deem the district a sort of national property, in which every man has a right and interest who has an eye to perceive and a heart to enjoy.*

Sixty years after Wordsworth's death, Lakeland became a national property and the poet's dream had become a reality.

Throughout the NW building materials vary. Red sandstone, millstone grit and limestone are much used; and grey-blue Cumbrian slates are the fabric of many attractive roofs. Despite the predominance of stone buildings, Cheshire villages such as *Malpas* and *Great Budworth* are graced by a number of timbered cottages. Buildings of interest to be found in Cumbria are the pele towers, constructed as protection against the Scots.

Tour 41 recommends four outstanding villages within a 97-mile route through the countryside E of Chester; one day should be allowed.
Tour 42 is a long day's drive covering 103 miles, much of it on minor roads leading across the moors to the E of Lancaster. The 123-mile route linking seven recommended villages in **Tour 43** provides a comprehensive tour of the Lake District and an overnight stop is advisable in order to appreciate the spectacular scenery to the full. **Tour 44** (72 miles) incorporates three villages and takes the motorist through the northern part of the Lake District National Park, on to Carlisle and back; this route can easily be completed in one day.

44

CUMBRIA

43

42

LANCASHIRE

41

CHESHIRE

Touring centres

41 Chester
42 Lancaster
43 Kendal
44 Keswick

175

Chester, Cheshire

MALPAS, CHESHIRE ︱✝︱

A large hillside village, the oldest part of which is to be found around
the church, where there are a number of black and white overhanging
timbered houses and cottages as well as some 16thC almshouses.
Among several old inns is one that contains an oak chair on which it is
said James I once rested.

A mound to the N of the church was the site of the Norman
Malpas Castle, a reminder that the villagers once lived in constant fear
from Welsh raiders; a fear which they expressed in *c.*AD1300 when
asking that Services should be conducted at the nearby Cholmondeley
Chapel on the grounds that: 'No Englishman dared to come to the
said parish church [St Oswalds] on Easter Sunday to receive the Body
of Christ for fear of the Welsh.'

Today, undoubtedly, **St Oswald's Church** is the pride of Malpas.
It was built in the second half of the 14thC on the site of an earlier
church and is approached through superb wrought-iron lych-gates. At
first sight of the church, the eye is drawn to an astonishing array of
gargoyles; monkeys hand in hand, grotesque grinning twins, a man
with his tongue out, and a musical angel are but a few of this strange
gathering. There is also a muzzled bear, alms of the original owners of
Malpas. The muzzle on the bear has an interesting origin. History
relates that a member of the Brereton family 'was guilty of an excess of
ardour while fighting in France and pushed an advantage too far. The
King who witnessed this brave fault and thought it called for a mild
rebuke, exclaimed ''I shall put a muzzle on that bear'' and directed it
to be notified to the Herald's College'.

Items of interest within the church abound. They include a 13thC iron-bound chest, two 16thC Flemish windows and a window commemorating Bishop Heber (1783–1826), writer of that famous hymn 'From Greenland's Icy Mountains', who was born in the village. The Cholmondeley and Brereton Chapels contain magnificent monuments to these families.

LOWER PEOVER, CHESHIRE ⟨△⟩✝⟨◆•⟩

This village lies in two parts. Near the green stand a handful of thatched timbered cottages with a village sign to identify them, and half a mile away, down a cobbled lane, are the church, school and inn.

The **Church of St Oswald**, a timbered church with oak beams that date back to the late 13thC, has an early 16thC square stone tower. Memorials within the church include those to the Cholmondeley, Shakerley and de Tabley families; a member of this last family, John Byrne Leicester Warren, Lord de Tabley (1835–95), gained a reputation as a poet late in life. His tombstone in the churchyard bears these lovely lines, proving that his reputation was justified:

> *Peace, there is nothing more for men to speak;*
> *A larger wisdom than our lips' decrees.*
> *Of that dumb mouth no longer reason seek;*
> *No censure reaches that eternal peace*
> *And that immortal ease.*

The tiny chapel of the church contains two objects of particular interest. One of these, a hand nailed to the wall, is thought to have been hung outside the church in medieval times to signal that buying and selling was permitted when fairs were held. There is also a massive oak chest, the lid of which, legend relates, had to be lifted by prospective farmers' wives to prove that they were strong enough for their role. Outside the church is the inn, once known as the Warren de Tabley Arms Hotel but now known more simply as **Bells of Peover** after a former landlord.

Lower Peover is also known as Peover Inferior to distinguish it from Over Peover (or Peover Superior), 2 miles to the SE. Over Peover is graced by **Peover Hall**, an Elizabethan mansion surrounded by a moat and set in lovely gardens and woods.

Pub: Bells of Peover ⟨**Bs**⟩⟨**Ra**⟩

ROSTHERNE, CHESHIRE ⟨△⟩★⟨✝⟩

There is a glorious view of Cheshire's largest lake, the 100 acre Rostherne Mere, from the churchyard of **St Mary's Church**. The lake, now a bird sanctuary, is more than 100ft deep and was used during the last war for training parachutists to descend on water.

The main entrance to the churchyard is by way of an unusual gate, dated 1640, that pivots on a central beam. In the churchyard there is a massive monument to Joseph Simpson, and inside the church there are memorials to the Egertons of Tatton among others. The road to the church is lined with neat brown-brick cottages, all named after shrubs and trees; Willow, Rose, Lilac and Virginia are just some of them.

At the end of the village is a square of some 12 houses built for estate workers by Lady Margaret Egerton in 1909; the Egerton crest adorns the buildings. The famous National Trust property, **Tatton Park**, lies just 2 miles to the S of Rostherne. There is much to see here. Inside the house are displays of furniture, silver, ceramics and paintings, and there is a **museum** of veteran cars. The huge gardens include a Japanese water garden, a terraced Italian garden and an orangery among many others.

GREAT BUDWORTH, CHESHIRE |△|✝|

The village was once the largest parish in Cheshire, hence the prefix. In fact Great Budworth is only a small village, but it stands proudly on a hilltop with meadows and lakes, among them Budworth Mere, beneath. It is something of a fairy-tale place; a piece of Tudor England with a network of thatched black and white cottages, as well as others of red or brownish brick with twisted chimneys set at strange angles.

At the head of the main street is the church, near to which is an old Shakespearean **school-house**, built by John Deane, and the 19thC **George and Dragon Inn** with an impressive wrought-iron sign. Between the church and inn is a **fence** where peculiar mottoes are carved, such as, 'Rest all ye nigh aleyard and Kirkyard' and 'Beware ye Beelzebub'.

The **Church of St Mary and All Saints** was built in the 14thC–15thC. In the N chapel Sir Peter Leycester, one of Cheshire's foremost historians, is buried. In the Warburton Chapel is the armoured figure of Sir John Warburton (*died* 1575), although the effigy has been badly mutilated.

One mile to the SW of the village is a fine park that once surrounded **Marbury Hall**, and a little further to the SW are the splendid gardens of **Arley Hall** which are open to the public.

The 14th–15thC Church of St Mary stands at the top of Church Street, Great Budworth's main street.

Lancaster, Lancashire

Hotels: **Royal Kings Arms, Market Street,** *Tel.* **(0524) 2451 ❸**
Ye Old Registry, Cable Street, *Tel.* **(0524) 34455 ❸**

INGLEWHITE, LANCASHIRE |△|

It seems hard to believe that this isolated village on the SW edge of the Forest of Bowland was once a flourishing trading centre. Today it is a 'sleepy' little place where stone-built houses and cottages are tucked away, hidden down twisting lanes. One of these lanes, Button Row, is a reminder that in the 18thC buttons were made here; while silk was woven at a mill close by. Naturally, in those times, accommodation for local workers as well as casual traders demanded a number of inns and hostelries. These are now private houses and only the **Green Man Inn** near one of the two village greens remains. On this green, once a busy market place, all that remains is a solitary market cross surmounted by the carved figure of a green man. The origins of the figure are uncertain; perhaps he represents some mythical pagan being conjured up from the forests.

Approximately 4 miles to the S of the village is **Chingle Hall,** full of priest holes and considered to number among England's most haunted houses. The severed head of a Franciscan monk beheaded in 1679 is said to be hidden here, the place of his birth.
Pub: **Green Man Inn** |**Bs**|

CHIPPING, LANCASHIRE |✝|

Neat stone cottages, many with mullioned windows and fronted by cobbled pavements, form the framework of this delightful village.

Chipping is set in magnificent country on the southern edge of the Forest of Bowland with Lancashire's industrial belt only a few miles to the south.

The name Chipping indicates that it began as a market place. Later the village became an important wool centre, and the 17thC heralded the arrival of a variety of cottage industries. Among the most important of these was chair-making, and today Chipping boasts a thriving century-old chair factory, located by one of the bridges across the stream. The wheel once used to provide water power for this factory can still be seen.

Chipping's most famous 'son' is John Brabin who, on his death in 1683, bequeathed the old **grammar school**, which was followed a year later by a row of terraced **almshouses** with the inscription: 'Let him that loveth God, love his brotherhood'. The school and almshouses are in Windy Street, at the end of which, at the junction with Talbot Street, is the **Sun Inn**, raised high above the street and approached by steep stone steps.

The **post office**, in Talbot Street, was once John Brabin's home and further down the street, by the bridge, a former mill has been tastefully converted into a modern restaurant. The **Church of St Bartholomew**, which is mainly 16thC but was restored in the 19thC, lies at the heart of the village with chancel screens made by local craftsmen.

A little to the NW of Chipping, at **Bleasdale**, a circular area marked by submerged wooden posts was discovered indicating prehistoric habitation. For reasons of preservation the posts are now housed in the Preston Museum, and their former positions are marked with concrete posts.

Pubs: Sun Inn |**Bs**|**Ra**|

Talbot Inn |**Bs**|**Ra**|

RIBCHESTER, LANCASHIRE |❖|★|†|

It is written on a stone in Rome
That Ribchester is as rich as any town in Christendom.

The antiquarian William Camden (1551–1623) in his *Britannia* (1586) recorded this traditional village quotation when he visited Ribchester. Roman history and tradition is everywhere in this village. The most quoted story is of the schoolboy truant who accidentally kicked up a Roman helmet and visor in 1795, which is now in the British Museum.

The whole village is built over the site of a massive Roman fort, established c. AD70, and the **Ribchester Museum**, near the church, is the place that reveals the facts. The uncovered part of the fort has exposed a section of two large granaries — sufficient to support the garrison with grain for a year. Handfuls of charred barley, recognizable as such, are one of the museum's most interesting exhibits.

There are two inns the **White Bull** and the **Black Bull**. The porch of the early 18thC White Bull is supported by pillars said to have once been part of a Roman building; and the inn was built over existing Roman cellars. Around this inn the village is spread out, but from here a warren of narrow streets diverge, flanked by small stone cottages and several craft shops.

The **Church of St Wilfrid** has a fine position above the fast-flowing River Ribble. It dates from the 13th–14thC, and it is believed that stones from the Roman ruins were used in the building, among them the pillars that support the organ loft.

Pubs: Black Bull |**R**|**Bs**|**Ra**|

White Bull |**R**|**Bs**|**Ra**|

DOWNHAM, LANCASHIRE ✝

This village is divided into two parts on the slopes of a gentle hill, with the lofty Pendle Hill (18,27ft) to the S and the Forest of Bowland to the N. In the upper part of the village are the church, hall, inn and green. A field within the parish, called Kirkacre, suggests that a church may well have stood on the site of the existing church in pre-Conquest times. The **Church of St Leonard** is known, in any case, to have stood here for at least 800yrs, and it includes many memorials to the Assheton family, who have been benefactors to the village over centuries. Their benefactions include the free school, bequeathed by Ralph Assheton in 1705, and the present school, built by his descendant William Assheton in 1839.

The Asshetons, now titled Clitheroe, occupy **Downham Hall**, and quite naturally the nearby inn is named after them. Near to the **Assheton Arms** is a tiny green with village stocks, fringed by some pretty, stone-built terraced cottages, bow-shaped above the green.

The White Bull Inn in Ribchester, which dates from 1707, and has a remarkable Roman portico. Roman cellars have also been discovered beneath the inn.

The road then descends past a cottage, reminiscent of a dolls house, and a grey pillar box, painted unconventionally to harmonize with the village buildings, before reaching the lower part of Downham, where there is another green, a further cluster of grey-stone cottages, a large Tudor house with mullioned windows and a stone bridge that straddles the stream. A Roman road that runs N of the village links the forts at York and *Ribchester*.

Pub: **Assheton Arms** |Bs|

BOLTON-BY-BOWLAND, CUMBRIA

This village lies on the eastern fringe of the Forest of Bowland. The focal point is the **Church of St Peter and St Paul** with a green on either side of it. The lower green, edged by a brook and the war memorial, embraces both the base of the old market cross and the village stocks. The **Coach and Horses Inn**, some pretty whitewashed cottages and a larger house, dated 1835, are nearby. The upper green is well protected by trees and flanked by the **Old Courthouse**, once used to proclaim on forest law. Almost directly opposite, an avenue of trees leads to the point where **Bolton Hall**, seat of the lords of the manor from the 14thC to the 18thC, once stood.

There are many memorials to the lords of the manor, the Pudsays, in the church; in particular, one to Sir Ralph Pudsay (*died* 1468) and his three wives and 25 children. Another feature of interest is the oak door, made in 1705, which the church guide declares has 560 studs that, if observed from the inside, are seen to be square pegs in round holes!

The oak cover to the font was carved by Robert Thompson, the 'mouseman of Kilburn', carrying his 'mouse' trademark, which is found on furniture in so many northern churches. At **Sawley**, 2 miles to the S of this village, are the ruins of a **Cistercian abbey** sometimes known as Salley, as opposed to Sawley, Abbey. Sawley is spread out along a bank of the River Ribble.

Pubs: **Copy Nook** |Bs|Ra|
   Coach and Horses |Bs|

SLAIDBURN, LANCASHIRE |t|

In a hollow in the heart of the Forest of Bowland, Slaidburn is something of a sanctuary after crossing the moors that lie on every side of it. An elegant bridge straddles the River Hodder where the lush green meadow on the edge of the village strikes a vivid contrast with the stone houses, mainly grey, that form the nucleus of the village above the river. One of these buildings, in a central position, is the long, low, oddly named **Hark to Bounty Inn**. It appears that the local vicar, who was also the squire, a frequent visitor to the inn, once owned a dog named Bounty which he would leave tied up outside. Whenever it barked he would turn to his drinking companions with the words 'Hark to Bounty'.

Slaidburn has another connection with dogs, for displayed in the **church** are dog whips once wielded to keep the farm dogs in order when their masters attended the serivce. Next to the church is a handsome two-storey building that dates from 1712. Formerly the **grammar school** it is now the primary school, and displays a carved plaque above the door, with the information that it was 'erected and endowed by John Brennand, late of Panehill in this Parish, Gentleman, who died on the 15th day of May in the year of Our LORD 1717'.

Pub: **Hark to Bounty** |A|R|Bs|Ra| *Tel.* (020 06) 246.

Kendal, Cumbria

Hotels: **County, Station Road,** *Tel.* **(0539) 22461 ❹**
Kendal, Highgate, *Tel.* **(0539) 24103 ❸**

TROUTBECK, CUMBRIA |△|✝|

A small hillside village where the houses, farms and cottages, many 17thC, straggle along a mile of narrow minor road that loops off the busy main road and runs parallel to it. At one end of the village is the inn. At the other is Townend, a National Trust property that is well worth visiting.

The interest of **Townend** is its difference from the 'run of the mill' stately homes, which are normally associated with the older aristocracy. This house was built in 1623 by yeomen farmers, and the same family, the Brownes, lived here for almost three centuries until the last of the male line died in 1914. The whole house with its furniture, pictures, library and domestic utensils provides a record of the habits and good taste of a typical, literate yeoman family.

At the other end of the village, near a further group of farms and cottages, is the **Mortal Man** with its quaint inn-sign depicting a fat, jolly, hard-drinking man defending himself:

> *O mortal man that lives by bread,*
> *What is it makes thy nose so red?*
> *Thou silly fool, that looks't so pale,*
> *'Tis drinking Sally Birkett's ale.*

The parish **church** is isolated from the village, lying on the main road beneath. An interesting feature is the E window of 1873, the joint work of Edward Burne-Jones, William Morris and Ford Madox Brown.
Pub: **Mortal Man Inn** |**A**|**R**|**Bs**|**Ra**| *Tel.* **(096 63) 3193.**

183

GRASMERE, CUMBRIA |❖|△|★|†|☞|

Associations with the poet of the Romantic school, William Wordsworth (1770♣1850), are everywhere. Wordsworth spent 14yrs of his life
in the village (1799–1813), living in three houses here, although the
greater part of the period was spent at **Dove Cottage**, where he was
married and where three of his children were born. Although he later
moved to Rydal he was buried at St Oswald's Church, together with
his wife, his sister, and three of his children.

Much of the beauty of the village is its setting in a lakeland
valley overlooked by Helm Crag, Nab Scar and more distant peaks
and crags. Among the inns, shops, and houses, tile-roofed and built
of local grey and green stone, is the whitewashed **Swan Hotel**, a 17thC
coaching inn where the novelist Sir Walter Scott (1771–1832) once
stayed, and about which Wordsworth wrote in his long poem 'The
Waggoner'. In the same poem Wordsworth refers to his own home,
for Dove Cottage had earlier been an inn known as the Dove and
Olive Bough:

> *For at the bottom of the brow,*
> *Where once the Dove and Olive Bough*
> *Offered a greeting of good ale*
> *To all who entered Grasmere Vale;*
> *And called on him who must depart*
> *To leave it with a jovial heart.*

The Dove Cottage Trust have preserved Dove Cottage much as it was
when the poet lived there. It is open to the public as is the nearby
Wordsworth Museum, which houses many important manuscripts.
After Wordsworth left Dove Cottage, he leased it to his friend Thomas
De Quincey (1785–1859), famed for his *Confessions of an English
Opium Eater* (1821).

St Oswald's Church has a memorial to Sir John Richardson (*died*
1865) the Arctic explorer. The church is the scene of an annual rush-
bearing ceremony held each August.

Pubs: **Red Lion Hotel** |A|R|Bs|Ra| *Tel.* (096 65) 456.

    Travellers Rest |A|Bs|Ra| *Tel.* (096 65) 378.

HAWKSHEAD, CUMBRIA |❖|△|★|†|☞|

The central part of Hawkshead is a honeycomb of squares and court-
yards interconnected by narrow cobbled alleyways, making it one of
Lakeland's most picturesque villages. Immediately to the S is
Esthwaite Water with Lake Windermere farther away to the east.
Among many interesting old buildings is the **grammar school**, built in
1585, with mullioned windows and a big sundial over the door. The
poet William Wordsworth (1770–1850) was schooled here from the
age of 8, lodging in the village with the Tyson family at **Green End
Cottage** after the death of his mother. The school is now a **museum**
where, among other exhibits, is the desk where the poet once carved
his name.

The 15thC National Trust owned **court house**, where manorial
courts were once held consists mainly of a single long chamber above a
small archway. It lies half a mile to the N of the village and houses a
Lakeland Museum. St Michael's Church, which dates back to the
15thC, is no longer whitewashed and so does not agree with Wordsworth's vision of it in 1788 as 'snow white — like a throned lady'.

At **Near Sawrey**, 2 miles to the S of the village, is **Hill Top Farm**,
once the home of the imaginative authoress Beatrix Potter
(1866–1943), which, together with much of the surrounding wood-

land, she bequeathed to the National Trust. Part of the farm contains a **museum** open to the public. The Trust also own the small pub, **Tower Banks Arms**, next door to the farm.

Pubs: **Red Lion** |**A**|**R**|**Bs**|**Ra**| *Tel.* (096 66) 213.

      Tower Banks Arms, Sawrey |**A**|**R**|**Bs**|**Ra**| *Tel.* (096 66) 334.

CONISTON, CUMBRIA |★|†|✥|

The name derives from the Anglo Saxon 'king's village'. Although the identity of the king who once took occupation is open to surmise there can be no doubt that the surroundings are worthy of a king. Coniston is the centre for climbers wishing to make the ascent of the massive 'Old Man of Coniston' (2,635ft) to the west.

Whitewashed cottages, together with those of more sombre grey local stone, form the bulk of the village, where, in the churchyard, a cross with one side depicting an artist at work marks the grave of John Ruskin (1819–1900), the writer, critic, artist and social reformer. It is perhaps fitting that Ruskin should lie in the heart of the lake district, for it was he, together with Wordsworth, who helped to prevent the spread of industrialization to the area and who pioneered the idea of a Lakeland national park. His life and work are illustrated in the **Ruskin Museum** in Yewdale road.

To the E of the village is the tree-lined $5\frac{1}{2}$-mile long **Coniston Water** where Donald Campbell died in 1967 during his attempt to break the water speed record. Marvellous views of Coniston Water are obtained from the minor road that runs above its E bank, where **Brantwood**, Ruskin's home during his latter years, stands. It is open to the public and some 250 of Ruskin's paintings can be seen.

The National Trust own much of the land in the area, including **Tarn Hows** to the NE of the lake, where, from the high ground above, there are further splendid views of the lake and the lofty features that surround it.

Pub: **Crown Hotel** |**A**|**R**|**Bs**|**Ra**| *Tel.* (096 64) 243.

BROUGHTON IN FURNESS, CUMBRIA |†|

Broughton in Furness could be described either as a small town or a large village, although there is so much of the sleepy atmosphere characteristic of a village about Broughton that it deserves to fall into the latter category.

The village lies 1 mile to the E of the River Duddon where it broadens into the Duddon Sands estuary, a place of some strategic importance throughout centuries of seaborn invasion. The name, Broughton, derives from an old English word meaning stronghold, and its importance, strategically, was because of the need to repel Scottish raiders, as well as those from overseas. As in other villages in the border counties it became necessary to build a pele tower here to resist frequent forays by the Scots. Therefore, in 1322, **Broughton Tower** was built and although a ruin today, it still dominates the village.

Neat houses and cottages of grey stone cluster around the spacious square and lofty obelisk that mark the central point of Broughton. Each August the historic Elizabethan charter permitting a market to be held here is proclaimed. **The Church of St Mary** lies outside the village, to the south. Although largely rebuilt in 1873 the 12thC S porch remains, and within the church ancient relics include an Elizabethan bible and a bell that once peeled triumphantly at the defeat of the Spanish Armada.

The village lies to the extreme S of a beautiful and much

neglected part of Cumbria, the Duddon valley. A minor road follows the course of the Duddon; a river about which Wordsworth wrote a series of sonnets in 1820. In a preface to the sonnets he declared: 'I have many affecting remembrances of this stream', and in his 'Afterthought' to the sonnets he wrote:

> *For, backward, Duddon, as I cast my eyes,*
> *I see what was, and is, and will abide:*
> *Still glides the stream, and shall for ever glide:*
> *The form remains, the function never dies.*

Pub: **Old Kings Head** |**A**|**R**|**Bs**|**Ra**| *Tel.* (065 76) 293.

BEETHAM, CUMBRIA |△|✝|

If you approach Beetham by the A6 from the south, before reaching the village, the first object of interest (seen to the left) is a **fortified farmhouse**, home of Sir Thomas Beetham more than 500yrs ago. Parts of the protective wall remain, as do the adjoining great hall and pele tower.

When the compact little village of Beetham was last visited, the sign to it had been removed; perhaps the inhabitants of this tranquil place were anxious that it should not be disturbed by the traffic that thunders along the main road. The central point of the village is the **Wheatsheaf Hotel**, faced by an ample car park with neat cottages of grey stone both along the main street and the street which leads to the church.

In the chancel of **St Michael's Church** is the tomb of Sir Thomas Beetham and his wife; the effigies are badly defaced as a result of Cromwellian visits. During reconstruction work in the 19thC a hoard of about 100 old Norman coins were discovered in the church.

Of more recent interest is the creche made by German prisoners of war when they were held at nearby Bela Camp during the Second World War. They presented the creche to the church in memory of the good relations that existed during their stay here.

Outside the village, on a stretch of the River Bela, is a working mill alongside the **Heron Mill**, which was restored by a charitable trust to function as it had done in the 18thC. The water wheel, 14ft in diameter, drove millstones that ground corn up until 1930. The mill is open to the public daily.

Pub: **Wheatsheaf Hotel** |**A**|**Bs**| *Tel.* (044 82) 2123.

DENT, CUMBRIA |✝|

This must rank as one of Cumbria's remotest yet most picturesque villages. It lies to the extreme west of the Yorkshire Dales National Park, in a cleft of the Dee valley beneath the towering Pennines which include Whernside (2,419ft) to the immediate southeast.

The main street through the village is part of a minor road that could be used as a short cut between Sedbergh and Ingleton. This street is cobbled, pavementless and so narrow that it only permits single-line traffic. The occupants of the stone cottages that flank it are probably grateful that through traffic is light. The grey stone cottages, surmounted by sturdy roofs of local gritstone, blend nicely with a handful of others, whitewashed with colourful doors and window frames.

The street broadens slightly at the village centre where the church gate lies opposite the **George and Dragon Inn**. At this point stands a huge slab of Shap granite, a drinking fountain commemorating Adam Sedgwick (1785–1873), who was a native of Dent and later became a renowned pioneer of geology.

There are several monuments to the Sedgwick family in the **Church of St Andrew** (*c.*1100) and their descendants still live in the village. Marble extracted from neighbouring quarries was used for paving the floor of the church's sanctuary and has provided the material for construction in numerous other churches.

Pubs: **George and Dragon** |**A**|**R**|**Bs**| *Tel.* (058 75) 256.

    Sun Inn |**A**|**Bs**|**Ra**| *Tel.* (058 75) 208.

TOUR FORTY-FOUR
Touring centre

Keswick, Cumbria

Hotels: **Royal Oak, Station Road,** *Tel.* **(0596) 72965 ❹**
Walpole, Station Street, *Tel.* **(0596) 72072 ❷**

MUNGRISDALE, CUMBRIA

Only a couple of inns, a few scattered farmhouses, and a small church make up this remote hamlet. It lies amid fells, across which John Peel and his fellow huntsmen once rode, repairing for refreshment to the 16thC **Mill Inn** on the banks of the River Glendermacklin with a fine view of the Skiddaw range of fells to the west. This is an area of Cumbria that is little known, a favourite place for ramblers who like the kind of solitude that made one local man declare proudly, 'even on Bank holidays the place seems deserted'. The tiny **church**, white-washed with box pews, lies along the narrow road to the north.

Pubs: **Mill** |**A**|**R**| *Tel.* (059 683) 659.

    Mill Inn |**A**|**Bs**| *Tel.* (059 683) 632.

CALDBECK, CUMBRIA |✝|♠•|

Caldbeck lies at the northern edge of the Lake District National Park, its name indicating that this is the place of the 'cold brook'. At one time these waters were harnessed to drive a great variety of mills, used both for weaving and grinding corn. The stream is an integral part of this pretty village and there is a handsome 15thC packhorse bridge that leads to a group of 18thC stone cottages.

Caldbeck is much associated with the local huntsman John Peel, whose grave, surmounted by a tombstone carved with a hunting horn, can be seen to the left of the church path. The words of the famous song 'D'ye ken John Peel' were written by his friend John Woodcock Graves, who worked in the mills that once turned out articles such as the 'coat so grey' to which the song refers. There is a memorial shelter to both men near the church.

Another 'personality' buried in the churchyard is Mary Robinson, the 'Beauty of Buttermere', who married her first husband in 1802 only to see him hanged for forgery soon afterwards.

Among many interesting buildings in the village is the old brewery that once supplied no less than 16 inns in the village. At present you have to rely on the 15thC black and white **John Peel** that occupies a central location.

Pub: **John Peel** |**Bs**|

WETHERAL, CUMBRIA |△|✝|

The focal point of this spacious village is the large triangular green, graced by a stone cross at one end and surrounded by 18thC stone houses and a 19thC *Château*-style mansion. At one corner of the green a 17thC purpose-built barn, later the blacksmith's shop, has now been tastefully converted into an excellent restaurant.

The **Church of the Holy Trinity** is dedicated to St Constantine, and three caves, or cells, said to have been used as a hermitage by Constantine are to be found in a redstone gorge above the River Eden. Six and a half acres of woods along this part of the river are preserved by the National Trust. The church occupies a commanding position above the river, faced on the other side by **Corby Castle**, seat of a branch of the Howard family.

Within the Howard memorial chapel of the church is one of the most important sculptures of Joseph Nollekens (1737–1823). The work was carried out for £1,500, a huge sum in those days, to commemorate the death of Lady Maria Howard and her baby in 1789. The monument comprises a figure, Faith, pointing upwards with one hand while supporting with the other the head of the dying mother, her baby cradled in her lap. Wordsworth was moved enough to write a sonnet beginning:

> *Stretched on the dying Mother's lap, lies dead*
> *Her new-born babe; dire ending of bright hope!*

The poet had in fact seen Nollekens at work on the monument in his studio, describing the visit in a preface to his sonnet:

> *Before the monument was put up in the Church at Wetheral, I saw it in the sculptor's studio. Nollekens, who, by the by, was a strange and grotesque figure that interfered much with one's admiration of his works, showed me at the same time the various models in clay which he had made, one after another, of the Mother and her Infant; the improvement on each was surprising; and how so much grace, beauty, and tenderness had come out of such a head I was sadly puzzled to conceive.*

A quarter of a mile down the river from the church is **Wetheral Priory**. All that remains of the Benedictine priory are the 15thC gateway and porter's lodge.

Pub: **Crown Inn** |**A**|**Bs**|**Ra**| *Tel.* (0228) 61888.

The sparkling stream that gave Caldbeck its name. Typical Cumbrian stone cottages line its bank.

Lincolnshire, Yorkshire and Humberside

T he 25 villages in this section lie
within the boundaries of three
counties, and range over a
considerable area. The flat
fenland county of Lincolnshire
stretches from N to S along more
than 100 miles of coastline; some of
the best scenery lying in the wolds to
the NE of the county.

Prior to the Local Government
Act of 1972, Yorkshire, England's largest
county, was split administratively into three
Ridings — North, West and East. After the
Act, however, parts of these areas were hived
off into the new counties of Humberside and
Cleveland, and into Lancashire and Cumbria.

Geographically Yorkshire remains much
as it was. In the E is the upland heather-clad
surface of the Yorkshire Moors. The centre is
dominated by the great Plain of York; while throughout the
Pennine range in the W are the Yorkshire Dales, valleys of great
beauty, such as Wensleydale, Swaledale, Midderdale and
Wharfedale.

The Yorkshire villages described in this section lie scattered
throughout these three basic areas of moors, plain and dales.
Goathland, for example, lies in the heart of the moors which
stretch eastward to the coast and the historic fishing villages of
Staithes and *Robin Hood's Bay*. Among the villages of the
central plain are *Aldborough* and *Kilburn*. The wolds village of
Sledmere, once in East Riding, is now part of Humberside.

Building materials are varied in both Lincolnshire and
Yorkshire. Many buildings in Lincolnshire are of stone, but
others are red brick as at Doddington (near Tour 45). In Yorkshire
materials range from the grey limestone seen in the dales villages
to the golden sandstone of villages further E such as *Hovingham*.
At *Thornton Dale*, considered by many to be Yorkshire's
prettiest village, there is a rare example of a cruck-built thatched
cottage. Cruck-building, a constructional method common in
the Middle Ages, depends on the use of pairs of curving timbers,
clamped low on the walls and joined to support the roof ridge.

WEST
YORKSHIRE

48

47

Tour 45 from Lincoln (143 miles) is a day's drive, linking four pretty villages in typical Lincolnshire fenland. Starting from historic York, **Tour 46** is a long day trip (125 miles) through six remote Yorkshire villages. Only a short day is needed for **Tour 47**, a route of 75 miles through the varied countryside of the southern Yorkshire Dales; drystone walls, gentle valleys and bare fell are among the features of the journey. **Tour 48**, a short day's drive of 75 miles, complements its predecessor by covering the northern Yorkshire Dales, particularly Wensleydale. More than one day should be allowed for **Tour 49** from Whitby, as it links seven villages in a 129-mile round-trip taking in the wide open moorland of the North York Moors and some stunning cliff scenery.

49

NORTH
YORKSHIRE

46

HUMBERSIDE

SOUTH
YORKSHIRE

LINCOLNSHIRE

45

Touring centres
45   Lincoln
46   York
47   Skipton
48   Richmond
49   Whitby

191

Lincoln, Lincolnshire

Hotels: **White Hart, Bailgate,** *Tel.* **(0522) 26222❹**
Grand, St Mary's Street, *Tel.* **(0522) 24211❸**

FULBECK, LINCOLNSHIRE |†|

Picturesque old cottages nestle along the narrow lanes that lie tucked away from the main road in this pretty hillside village. Splendid wrought-iron gates and an avenue of lime trees lead to the gracious stone-built **Hall**, built as the home of the Fane family after their move from another manor house in 1733. (It is not open to the public.)

Near to the Hall is the **church** with an impressive 15thC tower topped by eight leafy pinnacles and containing many memorials to the Fanes. Among these is a tribute from Sir Francis Fane, an early and celebrated member of the Royal Society, to his faithful servant Thomas Ball who died in 1673 after travelling with his master

> *into Holland, Denmark, Germany, Lorraine, Switzerland, Italy, Naples, France, and Flanders, where he considered ye Courts and camps of most of ye European princes, their splendour and mutabilitie, concluding, with ye preachers there was nothing new under ye sun and yet all was vanity, and only one thing necessary, to fear God and keep his Commandments. Soe doth F.F. who fixed this stone.*

Pub: **Hare and Hounds** |Bs|Ra|

FOLKINGHAM, LINCOLNSHIRE |△|†|

A spacious village headed by a market square from which leads the broad main street lined with gracious stone-built houses and inns. Folkingham was at one time an important coach staging centre and undoubtedly its most impressive building is the **Greyhound Inn** that stands in a commanding position, dominating both the market square and main street. This Queen Anne coaching inn was transformed in 1789 with a Georgian facade of mellow red-brick.

At the same time a magnificent assembly room was adapted from what once served as a Quarter Sessions and Magistrate's Court. Today the room caters for public gatherings, but the brass studs marking the position of the dock, witness box and justice's bench can still be seen. The original prisoner's hall is now the bar, over which can be seen the ostler's bell that once summoned travellers to their departing coaches.

Several other village buildings also once served as coaching inns, among them the **Five Bells** that stands at the head of the main street and is now a restaurant. Nearby is the **Old Correction House** which, from 1609–1808, was the place where delinquents were held, together with the able-bodied poor who, if found travelling without a 'pass', were put to work by the constable.

Folkingham would appear to have been something of an unruly place in bygone days — for as soon as the Old Correction House fell into disuse a larger house of correction was built in 1809. It stood on the site of Folkingham Castle and its austere grey-stone gateway still stands on a mound above the Billborough road.

The **Church of St Andrew** with its noble 15thC tower crowned with 16 pinnacles, four gilded weathervanes and a flagstaff also provides testimony that justice was swift and summary in those days. From 1600 it was a requirement of the churchwardens to provide the stocks and whipping post that are still preserved in the church. It seems unlikely that they were put to much use from the mid-19thC onwards; for historical records of this later period listing petty crimes make no mention of them, confining typical entries such as the following: 'Fine for calling the constable a liar 2/- paid on the spot to the constable.'

Pub: **Greyhound Inn** |**A**|**R**|**Bs**| *Tel.* (052 97) 301.

Old Bolingbroke, Lincolnshire |△|†|

It is hard to believe that this tiny village in the foothills of the wolds, which is approached along leafy lanes, was once a place of pomp and grandeur. John of Gaunt lived here; time-honoured Duke of Lancaster and father of Henry IV (1367–1413), whose boyhood days were spent at **Bolingbroke Castle**. Today sheep graze among the rugged castle walls and mounds which are under a gradual process of excavation and lie in a field close to the **Black Horse Inn**.

The centre of the village is graced by a bed of Lancastrian roses, presented by the town of Provins in France, where Henry's coat of arms is displayed. The **Church of St Peter and St Paul**, with a 14thC aisle and, much recent restoration, was perhaps begun by John of Gaunt. Interesting features are the two heads by the doorway, believed to represent John of Gaunt's parents, Edward III and Queen Philippa.

Pub: **Black Horse Inn** |**Bs**|

Somersby, Lincolnshire |†|♠|

The seven elms, the poplars four,
That stand beside my father's door. ('Ode to Memory')

Set in a wooded hollow in the heart of the wolds the most prominent buildings are the church; a square, red-brick, **battlemented house**, which faces the church and was built in 1722 by Sir John Vanbrugh

(1664–1726), architect of Blenheim Palace; and the former **rectory** where Alfred Tennyson, later to become Poet Laureate, was born in 1809. Even before the onset of Dutch elm disease, the trees to which Tennyson referred in his 'Ode to Memory' had vanished. But the long rambling yellow building, almost opposite the church, which was the poet's home for the first 26yrs of his life still stands, but is not open to the public.

The **Church of St Margaret**, dating from the 15thC and constructed from local green stone is graced by the original 15thC churchyard cross that stands near the porch. A sundial above the door dated 1751 carries the reminder 'Time Passeth'. The church contains a replica bust of the Poet Laureate placed there in 1911 by the Tennyson Centenary Committee. Near the SW corner of the short squat tower is the grave of the Revd George Clayton Tennyson, the poet's father.

From Somersby a lane leads westward to Salmonby, crossing 'The Brook' of Tennyson's poem on the way. When the family finally left this enchanting place in 1837 their sorrow is related by Tennyson in his 'In Memoriam':

We leave the well-beloved place
Where first we gazed upon the sky;
The roofs, that heard our earliest cry,
Will shelter one of stranger race . . . .

I turn to go; my feet are set
To leave the pleasant fields and farms;
They mix in one another's arms
To one pure image of regret.

The old market cross and the stocks in Ripley's attractive main cobbled square.

RIPLEY, NORTH YORKSHIRE |△|✝|

Ripley Castle and **All Saints' Church** face each other across a cobbled, tree-shaded square. Ripley, home of the Ingilby family for more than 700yrs, was remodelled in 1827 by Sir William Ingilby in the style of an Alsatian village. The older thatched cottages were replaced by those of sturdy stone, built in Gothic style, and Sir William decreed that henceforth the village hall would be known as the Hôtel de Ville.

Yet despite these strange innovations older features, such as the market cross and village stocks, were retained and can still be seen. Earlier members of the Ingilby family entertained both James I and Oliver Cromwell at Ripley Castle, although the latter, it is said, was watched over all night by the staunch Royalist, Lady Ingilby, with pistols at the ready.

Monuments to the family in the church include the tombs of Sir Thomas Ingilby (*died* 1369) and Sir William Ingilby (*died* 1617) with a tablet of verse that includes the lines:

Readers desolve in tears els blame thine eyes,
Worthe honour virtue here entombed lies:
The Bee which honie from each flower brought
Lives now eternallie on what he wrought.

When Oliver Cromwell visited the tomb he was unimpressed, carving in capitals words which stand out more clearly than the original inscription:

NO POMPE NOR PRIDE
LET GOD BE HONOURED.

In the churchyard is the base of an ancient weeping cross, surrounded by a number of recesses where penitents knelt in some discomfort to beg forgiveness.

Ripley Castle, built in the 16thC with an earlier gatehouse, contains rooms that are finely furnished and decorated, and boasts a secret hiding place. It is set in grounds landscaped by Capability Brown, has an orangery and lake, and is open to the public on specific occasions.

ALDBOROUGH, NORTH YORKSHIRE |★|✝|

The focal point of Aldborough is the large village green with a tall maypole where traditional maypole dances take place annually in May. At one end of the green is a raised platform — all that remains of the **Old Court House**. An inscription recalls that 150yrs ago Aldborough was an Ancient Borough and that it was from this spot that the elections of Members of Parliament were announced. Beneath the relics of the Old Court House are what appear to be very well-preserved village stocks, although in fact they are replicas of the originals.

Handsome red-brick cottages are grouped around the green and nearby is a small museum, a reminder that this quiet, unassuming village stands on the foundations of what was once a thriving Roman city of vital strategic importance. The **museum** is crammed with excavated remains from this ancient city, and close at hand there are traces of the original walls and pavements.

The **Church of St Andrew** was built in 1330 on the site of the Norman church destroyed by the Scots in 1318. It also has a Roman connection, for it is believed to stand on the site of a former Temple of Mercury. A statue of Mercury, found near the church, has been installed near the sturdy 15thC battlemented tower, built with stones from the Roman walls.

In the churchyard beneath the tower is the tomb of one of the village's greatest benefactors, Mark Smithson. In 1783 Smithson presented the church with the tower clock, and in his will he decreed that 30 freshly baked loaves were to be left in the church every Sunday for poor parishioners. The shelves where these loaves were deposited can be seen in the church.

Among the oldest buildings of Aldborough is the **Ship Inn**. This house of low ceilings and oak beams lies across the road from the church and was once the churchwarden's house.

Pub: **Ship Inn** |**Bs**|**Ra**|

KILBURN, NORTH YORKSHIRE |✝|

Neat stone houses flank the little brook that flows through Kilburn. The central area of the village contains the **church**, the inn, the **Foresters Arms**, and the **woodcraft workshops** and display room which have made the village famous.

Robert Thompson, the 'Mouseman of Kilburn', was born here in 1876. While helping his father at simple joinery he spent his leisure time in carving from oak timber, an ancient and dying craft. After some initial work for Ampleforth School, orders for carvings in churchs, schools and country houses grew until Thompson was able to set up a factory in the village.

When Robert Thompson died in 1955 his work could be seen in 700 churches throughout the country, among them Westminster Abbey and York Minster. All his later work can be identified by the inclusion of his trademark, a carved mouse, an idea which came to him and about which he once said:

I was carving a beam on a church roof when another carver, Charlie Barker, murmured something about us being as poor as church mice, and on the spur of the moment I carved one. Afterwards I decided to adopt the mouse as a trademark, because I thought how a mouse manages to scrape and chew away the hardest wood with its chisel-like teeth, and it works quietly; nobody takes much notice. I thought that was maybe like this workshop hidden away in the Hambleton Hills. It is what you might call industry in quiet places, so I put the mouse on all my work.

Robert Thompson's work continues in Kilburn today under the guidance of two of his grandsons. His Elizabethan timber-framed **cottage**, once described as a 'dream in oak', must be seen, as does the memorial to him in the parish church.

High above the village on **Hambleton Hill** and visible for miles is a **White Horse**, 314ft long and 228ft high, carved by the village schoolmaster and his pupils in 1857.

Pub: **Foresters Arms** |**Bs**|

COXWOLD, NORTH YORKSHIRE |△|★|✝|✵|

The main street is steep, broad, tree-lined and straddled by stone houses and honey-coloured cottages, which are fronted by greens and cobbled verges. Two famous names are associated with the village. Oliver Cromwell's daughter, Mary, married Thomas, Earl of Fauconberg, after whom the pleasant 17thC **inn** bearing the family crest, is named. On the N side of the street is a long line of almshouses, single-storied with mullioned windows, endowed in 1662 by Lady Fauconberg. Cromwell's body is believed to have been buried, secretly, by his daughter at **Newburgh Priory** after the restoration of Charles II.

The writer Laurence Sterne (1713–68) is the other notable name connected with Coxwold for he was vicar here for the final 8yrs of his life. **St Michael's Church**, in which he preached, stands at the top end of the village, and is distinguished by its tower, which is octagonal from its base upwards. Sterne's novels, humerous and bawdy, include the classic *Life and Opinions of Tristram Shandy* (1760), and the house that the writer bought at the extreme N of Coxwold was named **Shandy Hall** by him after his novel. Today it is administered by the Sterne Trust and is open to the public as a **museum** displaying rooms where his novels were written between 1760 and 1768, and still furnished in the period of Sterne's lifetime.

Pub: **Fauconberg Arms** |**A**|**Bs**|**Ra**| *Tel.* (034 76) 214.

HOVINGHAM, NORTH YORKSHIRE ✝

Hovingham Hall occupies a central position in this village of sturdy stone cottages with flower gardens, which are a pleasure to behold. The Hall, built and designed around 1760 by Thomas Worsley, a friend of George III, is not open to the public, and at present is the home of Sir Marcus Worsley, brother of the Duchess of Kent. Within the Hall boundaries, however, is a cricket ground used by the village cricket team, and concerts take place in a riding school which forms part of the main entrance to the Hall. Important Roman remains including a bath-house have been excavated near the Hall's grounds.

Much of **All Saints' Church** was rebuilt in 1860, but the W tower is Anglo Saxon and contains an Anglo Saxon slab, once possibly an altar, carved with eight figures.

Pub: **Worsley Arms Hotel** |**A**|**R**|**Bs**|**Ra**| *Tel.* (065 382) 234.

SLEDMERE, HUMBERSIDE ✝

This village is in the heart of the wolds, 400ft above sea level, amid splendid agricultural land. The richness of this land is to the credit of the Sykes family of Sledmere House, in particular Sir Christopher Sykes who in the late 18thC transformed the surrounding open fields by planting trees and hedges, building roads and growing grain. A Classical temple near the gates of Sledmere House pays tribute to his work of cultivation in 'a bleak and barren tract of country'.

Sledmere House, first built in 1751 but rebuilt in Georgian style after a fire in 1911, stands in a fine park landscaped by Capability Brown. The house and park are open to the public on occasions. The parish church within the park has an old tower, but the bulk of it was rebuilt in 1898.

For such a small village there is no shortage of monuments. At one end of Sledmere is the 60ft Eleanor-style cross, built by Sir Tatton Sykes in 1900, which later came into use as the Great War memorial. Nearby is a fascinating construction designed by Sir Mark Sykes who had raised a company of 1,200 men of the wolds for service in the First World War. The **Waggoner's Monument**, as it is called, is packed with engraved figures that give a pictorial history of events — showing farmers, for example, exchanging their domestic tools for weapons of war before engaging the enemy.

Yet another monument stands on **Garton Hill**, a memorial to the first Sir Tatton Sykes, a famous sporting 'all-rounder' who is pictured on horseback. From this site on Garton Hill there is a marvellous view of the surrounding wolds.

The village inn, the **Triton**, once an 18thC coaching inn, boasts a sign indicating that the landlord is 'licensed to let post horses'.

Pub: **Triton Inn** |**A**|**Bs**|**Ra**| *Tel.* (0377) 86644.

Touring centre
Skipton, North Yorkshire
Hotels: **Midland**, Broughton Road, *Tel*. (0756) 2781❷
Highfield, Keighley Road, *Tel*. (0756) 3182❷

MALHAM, NORTH YORKSHIRE |△|★|❖|

Solid stone cottages and farmhouses cluster round the little hump-backed bridge across the River Aire. Among them are two inns, ideally situated to refresh the footweary who have come to this oasis from across the surrounding moors and fells.

There is a National Park Information Centre in the village and nearby are three features of particular topographical interest: Malham Cove and Malham Tarn to the N, Gordale Scar to the northeast. Perhaps the most unique of all three is **Malham Cove**, a curving cliff of solid limestone almost 300ft in height which inspired Wordsworth to write:

> *Was the aim frustrated by force or guile,*
> *When giants scooped from out the rocky ground,*
> *Tier under tier, this semicirque profound?*

> ('Malham Cove')

Gordale Scar, a precipitous rocky cleft down which water tumbles for some 300ft is the subject of an early 19thC painting by James Ward hung in the Tate Gallery. **Malham Tarn**, to the N, covers 150 acres and at 1,200ft is one of England's biggest mountain lakes.

At the head of the tarn is the 19thC house where Charles Kingsley once stayed. It is now leased by the National Trust as a field studies centre. While staying here Kingsley was asked to suggest the reason for the black streaks on the white face of Malham Cove. His imaginative reply that a chimney sweep must have fallen over the edge gave him the idea for his *Water Babies* (1862), much of which is set in the locality (see *Arncliffe*).

Pub: Buck Inn |**A**|**R**|**Bs**| *Tel*. (072 93) 317.

ARNCLIFFE, NORTH YORKSHIRE |✝|❖|

The mountain road from the SW descends sharply into Littondale, offering a superb view of the valley of the River Skirfare on the banks of which, evenly spaced, are Halton Gill, Litton, Hawkswick, and the principal village of this lovely dale, Arncliffe. Here there is a large, 'rough and ready' green, not close cropped and all the more beautiful for its lack of formality in this peaceful and remote setting. White-washed and grey-stone cottages line one side of the green, among

St Oswald's Church by Cowside Beck at Arncliffe, the main village in lovely Littondale.

them the **Falcon Inn**, which at one time featured in the well-known television series *Emmerdale Farm*.

Below the village the stream cascades beneath a picturesque bow bridge, providing a charming background to the little church on its banks. It is believed that there has been a church on this lovely point above the stream since Saxon times. The present church, **St Oswald's**, is mainly 19thC with a number of interesting earlier relics, as well as inscriptions, informing you that 'nine Arncliffe bow and billmen' attended the Battle of Flodden in 1513, as well as one with 'able horse and harness'.

Charles Kingsley wrote part of his *Water Babies* (1862) while staying in the village and his hero, Tom, fell into the waters of the Skirfare before becoming a water baby.

Pubs: **Amerdale House Hotel** |**A**|**R**| *Tel.* (076 677) 250.

    Falcon Inn |**Bs**|

200

GRASSINGTON, NORTH YORKSHIRE. |❖|△|★|✝|

This large hillside village, once an important lead-mining centre, today depends largely on tourists who find it an ideal centre from which to explore the dales. Narrow lanes of grey limestone buildings converge on the cobbled market square; a friendly, intimate little square, yet busy in the high season as befits a village that has been dubbed the 'capital of Upper Wharfedale'. The square is surrounded by shops, guesthouses, hotels, as well as a building that houses a **folk museum**. Nearby are two cottages, where in 1807 the actor, Edmund Kean, made his stage debut, 7yrs before his sensational appearance as Shylock on the London stage that made his name.

Other buildings of historic interest are a 16thC **barn**, where it is said that John Wesley (1703–91), the founder of Methodism, once preached; and, on a macabre note, a shop, which was once a forge — the place of work of the notorious 18thC murderer, Tom Lee, the blacksmith who was hanged for the brutal murder of the village chemist.

A pleasant stone bridge built in 1603 crosses the River Wharfe below the village, where, at **Linton** the lovely 14thC riverside church, shared by both villages, is found. During the rainy season the **Linton Waterfalls**, just above the village, cascade merrily.

North of Grassington are the ramparts of a **Celtic encampment**, and some 5 miles to the E of the village, beyond Hebden, are **Stump Cross Caverns**, where there is an extensive network of underground caves, open to the public for guided tours; they have intriguing names such as the Cathedral, Jewel Box, Butcher's Shop and Chamber of Pillars.

Pub: Black Horse Hotel |**A**|**R**|**Bs**|**Ra**| *Tel.* (0756) 752770.

RAMSGILL, NORTH YORKSHIRE |△|❖•|

A visit to Ramsgill is worthwhile if only because it means taking the lovely little road northward from Pately Bridge through the heart of Nidderdale. The first point of interest is at **Warth** where sycamores, oaks and firs cluster and where, at the nearby mill, a gigantic water wheel is to be seen. From Warth the road continues northwards along the western shore of the beautiful **Gouthwaite Reservoir**, a bird sanctuary famous for Canadian geese. A footpath hugs the eastern fringe of the reservoir for a more intimate view of the wildlife that thrives there.

Ramsgill stands at the head of the reservoir. A handful of old cottages, a church, built in 1842, a small green and the ivy-clad **Yorke Arms Hotel**, where peacocks strut, are all that make up this tiny village. It seems hard to believe that this peaceful place became the centre of one of England's most sensational murder trials in 1745. Eugene Aram was born here in humble circumstances in 1704, soon became the 'local boy made good' as a successful schoolmaster and later achieved distinction as a philologist. His trial in 1745 for the murder of the local shoemaker shook the village.

Aram was acquitted but subsequently a skull was discovered in a cave at Knaresborough, evidence that led to his retrial, conviction and execution. Lord Edward Lytton (1803–73) made the affair the subject of his book *Eugene Aram* (1832) and the poet Thomas Hood (1799–1845) also wrote lyrics that gave Aram an everlasting place in literature. The house where the murderer was born no longer exists; but a carved head on the old school-house is alleged to represent him.

Pub: **York Arms Hotel** |**A**|**R**|**Bs**| *Tel.* (0423) 75243.

Touring centre

Richmond, North Yorkshire

Hotels: Frenchgate, Frenchgate, *Tel.* (0748) 2087 ❸
Kings Head, Market Place, *Tel.* (0748) 2311 ❷

REETH, NORTH YORKSHIRE ⭐

The largest and most sophisticated of the Swaledale villages where black and white houses, among them hotels and inns, congregate around the spacious village green. Along the western edge of the green is **High Row**, lined with a number of shops, houses and inns of the 18thC. Local pottery is sold here and there is a **folk museum**, housed in the former Sunday School. Of particular interest in the museum is a genealogical tree of a Swaledale family, and a record of the life of the local doctor, illustrating the dedication needed by a GP in treating patients spread out in this remote and rugged area.

Reeth was once a centre for lead, mined in the nearby hills, and has always been a market place where an annual show is held in September. It is a hillside village, standing at a point where Swaledale and Arkengarthdale meet. Consequently it makes a popular centre for tourists wishing to explore Swaledale, either along the narrow valley to Birkdale Common in the W or by a road of outstanding beauty to Richmond in the east. The road to the NW runs through Arkengarthdale where the inn, **Tan Hill**, is reputed to be the highest in England.

Pubs: Black Bull Hotel |A|R|Bs|Ra| *Tel.* (0748) 84213.

Tan Hill Inn |A|R|Bs|Ra| *Tel.* (0833) 28246.

C. B. Hotel, Arkengarthdale |A|R| *Tel.* (0748) 84265.

MUKER, NORTH YORKSHIRE

Swaledale is the most rugged and remote of the Yorkshire Dales, hemmed in on either side by wooded hills. The road from the S reaches Muker by way of the Buttertubs Pass, so called because of weird geological features, some 50ft deep, shaped like butter tubs.

The River Swale rises to the W of the village, running almost due E to Richmond past some enchanting villages of which Muker is only one. Houses perch on the hillside in tiers, linked by narrow alleys and steps with a fine view of the valley beneath.

The **Chapel of Ease** above Muker dates from 1580, but was restored in 1890. A plaque on the side of the school-room records that

Richard and Cherry Kearton were educated here. Cherry Kearton (1871–1940) became well known for his films and photographs of wildlife in Africa and Australia.

At one time the only consecrated ground in Swaledale was at **Grinton** to the east. Consequently bodies for burial from Muker and other villages had to be transported manually to Grinton churchyard, giving this eastward road the somewhat macabre name, Corpse Way.

HUBBERHOLME, NORTH YORKSHIRE |✝|

Hubberholme Church in beautiful Wharfedale,
Wharfedale so sweet and fair
Nothing in England can with
Thee compare.

The little **church**, originally built as a chapel of ease to the Church of St Oswald at *Arncliffe*, stands near the river bank in a setting that justifies the proud boast of the quoted verse which can be seen inside the church.

Hubberholme lies in a wooded cleft of Wharfedale. Giant fells tower above the village on either side, among them **Buckden Pike** (2,302ft). Much of the church has stood for 700yrs, despite periodic flooding, which on one occasion was so deep that fish swam in the nave. The pride of the church is its ancient rood loft, dated 1558 and one of few that remain in England. There is also some modern wood-carving by Robert Thompson, the 'Mouseman of Kilburn' (see *Kilburn*).

Across the humpback bridge is the **George Inn**, until recently church property, where on New Year's Eve the village 'parliament' meets and according to custom the vicar auctions off the tenancy of a field; the proceeds go to charity.
Pub: George Inn |**A**|**Bs**|**Ra**| *Tel.* (075 676) 223.

MIDDLEHAM, NORTH YORKSHIRE |△|✝|

Once the capital of Wensleydale and an important market town, Middleham today is best styled as a village, a quiet compact place with houses of local stone, best known for the castle that dominates it and the racehorses that train on the surrounding moors. The Norman **castle** was eventually acquired by Richard III in 1471, and was subsequently the scene of Richard's son's birth and later his death. The gatehouse, massive keep and lofty walls give some idea of the immensity of the castle before its destruction during the Civil War.

There are two cobbled squares in the village, each with a monument, the market cross on the upper square bearing a carving of an animal, possibly the white boar that was Richard's emblem. The **church**, mainly 14thC is dedicated to St Akelda, a Saxon princess martyred by the Danes. According to legend the **Well of St Akelda**, near the church, was once a place where eye ailments were cured.

The clearly defined though scanty ruins of **Jervaulx Abbey**, a Cistercian abbey and monastery, lie a few miles to the SE in a beautiful setting near the River Ure. The abbey was founded in 1098 and dissolved in the 16thC when the last abbot was hanged at Tyburn for complicity in the Pilgrimage of Grace. This abbot, Adam Sedbar, was lodged in the Tower of London in a room where his name and date are inscribed on a wall. The monks were well known as horse breeders, and interestingly this tradition persists. Middleham became a centre for the training of racehorses long before Newmarket.
Pub: **Millers House** |**A**|**R**| *Tel.* (0969) 22630.

Touring centre
Whitby, North Yorkshire

Hotels: Saxonville, Ladysmith Avenue, *Tel*. (0947) 602631 ❸
Marvic, Whitepoint Road, *Tel*. (0947) 602400 ❷

STAITHES, NORTH YORKSHIRE

It is essential to park above the village, for there is little if any room for cars at the foot of the steep road that descends to the water's edge. From the car park a sign, 'To the beach', directs you to the start of a footpath that zigzags down past a jumble of quaint cottages perched precariously, layer upon layer, on the side of the steeply sloping hill. A network of narrow cobbled streets and alleyways twist between houses of every shape, size and hue.

Bluff headlands tower above each end of the harbour; and a sturdy sea wall acts as a protection to the front line of houses. Nevertheless the attractive **Cod and Lobster Inn** is said to have been washed away by the high seas on at least three occasions. Near to the inn is a small house, once a grocer's shop, where the explorer James Cook was apprenticed before running away to Whitby and signing on as a cabin boy.

As in *Robin Hood's Bay*, a somewhat similar coastal village, a number of cottages have now been taken over by 'weekenders' — some of them artists, following in the footsteps of the celebrated Dame Laura Knight who lived and painted here over a period of 18yrs. Two miles to the S of Staithes is **Boulby Cliff**, which at 666ft is the highest coastal point in England.

Pubs: **Captain Cook Inn** |**A**|**Bs**| *Tel*. (0947) 840200.
  Cod and Lobster Inn |**Bs**|

The charming little harbour at Staithes. On several occasions over the past 100yrs high seas have been responsible for the destruction of many of the waterfront buildings.

GREAT AYTON, NORTH YORKSHIRE

The first sight of this large, sprawling village on the A173 is not impressive. However, it is well worthwhile following the signs to the village centre for here is a placid scene full of historic interest. There is a large, semi-circular village green and the little River Lever flows benignly beside the main street.

The **Royal Oak**, an old coaching inn, faces the green with a 1771 sundial over the porch. On the green is a noticeboard depicting a Heritage Trail, linking places associated with Captain James Cook (1723–79) over 80 miles of surrounding countryside. Great Ayton has many associations with the explorer. It was here that his family moved in 1736 when he was eight, and that he was educated, in the little brown school-house near the green, now a **Cook museum** with an inscription telling that the boys' fees were paid for by the employer of his father, a farm labourer.

Not far away, in Bridge Street, is a **monument** hewn out of stone from Hicks Point, the explorer's first sighting of Australia, which was named after one of his officers, Lieutenant Zachary Hicks. The monument stands on the spot where the Cook family's red-brick cottage was located before being dismantled and shipped to Australia. The cottage now stands proudly in Melbourne.

In the graveyard of the parish church is the tomb of Cook's mother and his many sisters. Finally, high above the village on Easby Moor, is Cook's own memorial, erected in 1827, 48yrs after the explorer was killed at Owkyee.

Pub: **Royal Oak** |**Bs**|

HUTTON-LE-HOLE, NORTH YORKSHIRE

This village lies just within the southern boundary of the North Yorkshire Moors Park in the most peaceful of settings. The village cottages fan out in a V shape, the two prongs divided by Hutton Beck which cascades swiftly down from Spaunton Moor to the north. Several little footbridges span the beck, on either side of which large expanses of green entice sheep to graze among the village buildings. Wooded hills shelter stone-built cottages, roofed with red tiles or slate.

Although mentioned in the Domesday Book, the village only really developed when it grew into a Quaker settlement. **Quaker Cottage**, near the **Crown Inn**, is the village's oldest building, dating from 1695, and was once the home of John Richardson, who emigrated to America with William Penn (1644–1718), the founder of Pennsylvania. Another building of interest close to the inn is the **Ryedale Folk Museum**, filled with local agricultural and domestic implements used over centuries and standing in a folk park displaying period buildings, vehicles and machinery.

Pub: **Crown Inn** |**Bs**|

EGTON BRIDGE, NORTH YORKSHIRE

High on the windswept North Yorkshire Moors lies the little village of Egton, noted for its Gooseberry Fair held each August, when prizes are given for the best gooseberries. From Egton the road drops sharply into the leafy hollow of Egton Bridge where the River Esk, famous for salmon fishing, flows. The existing bridge replaced an old stone bridge that was swept away during the floods of 1930; near to it is the site of a small stone building known as **Kirkdale House**, the birthplace in 1599 of the last of the English martyrs, Father Nicholas Postgate.

A little above the river is the **Postgate Inn** and near to it the beautiful Roman Catholic **Church of St Hedda**. It is thought that Nicholas Postgate's early youth was spent as a strolling player, performing in plays with a local group which was unfavourable to non-Catholics.

Between 1630 and 1679 Father Postgate ministered in Yorkshire, sometimes as chaplain to a leading Catholic family and at others taking on the duties of an itinerant priest. In 1678 Titus Oates revealed details of the alleged Popish Plot, and during the 'witch hunts' that followed Postgate stood trial for baptising a baby. On 7 August 1679 the 83-year-old priest was dragged on a hurdle to the Knavesmire at York, where the top joints of his thumbs and forefingers, which had held the Sacred Host at Mass, were cut off. He then suffered the barbarous fate of being hung, drawn and quartered. John Reeves, his accuser, was struck with remorse and drowned himself at Devil's Dump, a deep, dark pool off the Esk.

Many items connected with Father Postgate, including the model of his Egton Mass-house, can be seen at the **Postgate Centre** in St Hedda's Church. The two chalices used by him are preserved at nearby St Anne's, Ugthorpe. Perhaps his finest memorial, however, is the hymn composed by him in prison while awaiting execution that concludes:

My wearied wings, sweet Jesu, mark,
And when Thou thinkest best,
Stretch forth Thy hand out of the ark,
And take me to Thy rest.

Pubs: Horseshoe |**A**|**R**|**Bs**|**Ra**| *Tel.* (0947) 85245.
     Postgate Inn |**A**|**R**|**Bs**|**Ra**| *Tel.* (0947) 85241.

GOATHLAND, NORTH YORKSHIRE |✝|

Goathland lies in a remote part of the North Yorkshire Moors. Hotels, inns, stone-built farmhouses and cottages are dotted around a huge moorland green in a haphazard fashion. The **Church of St Mary**, built in 1890 by a respected York architect, W. H. Brierley, although comparatively modern, fits harmoniously into the scene. Sheep wander unconcernedly around the grey-stone village buildings, nibbling at the rough grassland as if they were the real masters of the place. Minor roads and footpaths hive off from the village in almost every direction, making Goathland a popular centre for motorists or ramblers who want to explore the many interesting natural features in the surrounding countryside.

Waterfalls, often called fosses, abound in the area. Immediately to the S of the village is the 70ft **Mallyan Spout** with **Nelly Ayre Foss** beyond it. Other strange named falls include **Water Ark Foss**, **Thomason Foss** and **Falling Foss**. A road to the NW drops into a beautiful wooded valley hamlet, **Beck Hole**, where there is a small inn.

The Goathland Hunt has been established since 1750 and a village tradition that began even earlier and takes place annually in January is known as Plough Monday. On this occasion dancers take on the role of ploughmen, dressed appropriately, and cavort around the village collecting donations for their various activities.

The North Yorkshire Moors Railway, originally planned by George Stephenson but closed by Beeching, was reopened by a voluntary society in 1973. Now, once again, steam trains ply their way from Goathland across the rugged moors to Grosmont a few miles to the north.

Pub: **Mallyan Spout Hotel** |**A**|**R**|**Bs**| *Tel.* (094 786) 206.

THORNTON DALE, NORTH YORKSHIRE |❖|✝|

This large village must certainly be included among Yorkshire's loveliest villages. A footpath leads from the spacious car park through a copse, crossing the river to reach the central part of the village. Thornton Beck, a clear sparkling stream, runs through the village, almost forming an S shape, and following the banks of the stream is sheer delight.

From the car park footbridge, the minor road southeastward follows the course of Thornton Beck. The picturesque stone cottages and bright flower gardens are approached across little stone footbridges.

In the other direction, to the N, the main road is lined by a row of terraced dark-stone bungalows built in 1656 as almshouses by the Lumley family. A little further N, and very much tucked away, is the most delightful part of Thornton Dale, where a footpath, on the left, leads past a thatched cottage and gracious Georgian houses with lawns and gardens, the beck in constant attendance and spanned by white painted bridges.

Close to the main road bridge is **Thornton Hall**, originally a Tudor building and now a hotel. The adjacent **All Saints' Church**, rebuilt in the 14thC, has a large 19thC chancel.

Pub: **Hall Hotel** |**A**|**R**|**Bs**| *Tel.* **(075 14) 789.**

ROBIN HOOD'S BAY, NORTH YORKSHIRE

Tier upon tier of closely packed shops and houses, linked by narrow passages and steps, cling in topsy-turvy fashion to the steep cliff which overhangs what was once an important fishing bay. It seems scarcely surprising that over the years a number of houses have fallen from their precarious sites — victims of the raging seas below. On one occasion, it is said, the bowsprit of a drifting ship shattered the windows of a village inn.

Today the jutting, brightly painted houses, with window boxes full of flowers, are holiday homes or the retreats of artists and writers. Yet little more than a century ago this was one of Yorkshire's thriving fishing communities with no less than 174 registered ships. Smuggling, too, was then a popular occupation, and in the early 1800s the entire village traded in contraband.

There are numerous theories regarding the origin of the village name. One is that Robin Hood was offered a pardon if he agreed to protect the coast from pirates. Another contradictory belief is that Robin Hood came here to find a boat in which to make his escape.

A tragic reminder of the way the seas once took their toll of the fishing community here can be seen in the form of an epitaph in the churchyard of the early 19thC **church**:

> *By storms at sea two sons I lost*
> *Which sore distresses me*
> *Because I could not have their bones*
> *To anchor here with me.*

Pub: **Victoria Hotel** |**A**|**R**|**Bs**|**Ra**| *Tel.* **(0947) 880205.**

The path leading down to the sea at Robin Hood's Bay. Once a thriving fishing community, the village, with its pretty colourwashed houses, is now a haven for writers and artists.

AREA TWELVE

Durham and Northumberland

NORTHUMBERLAND

52

51

DURHAM

Touring centres
50 Barnard Castle
51 Hexham
52 Berwick upon Tweed

50

Some of the most beautiful countryside in England can be seen in the counties of Durham and Northumberland. Although the eastern coastal area of Durham is heavily industrialized, to the W the land rises towards the crest of the Pennines and the magnificent scenery of Teesdale and Weardale.

Northumberland is bordered on the S by the county of Durham, and separated from the lowlands of Scotland by the Cheviot Hills and the Tweed. The coastline is as beautiful as any in the country; here, for example, is *Holy Island*, inaccessible from the mainland at high tide; the huge cliff fortress, *Bamburgh* Castle; and the tiny picturesque harbour of *Craster*. The flat country in the E of Northumberland rises to the central moorland area, and in the NW the mountainous region is crowned by the Cheviot (2,676ft). Hadrian's Wall, built in AD122 to define the northern boundary of Roman Britain, stretches from E to W for a distance of 73 miles across the S of the county. Parts of this ancient fortification can still be seen.

Stone is the basic building material found in Northumberland; typical examples being the grey-stone cottages of *Bamburgh* and those of brown stone seen at *Whalton*. In common with its neighbouring border county, Cumbria, Northumberland is notable for its fortified towers; an impressive example being the pele tower at *Elsdon*. Stone, too, is the fabric of many Durham villages, among them *Staindrop* and *Romaldkirk*.

Tour 50 from Barnard Castle takes the motorist on a 46-mile trip through Teesdale and back via *Staindrop*, with its typical stone houses; one day will allow enough time to complete this tour. Further N, **Tour 51** from Hexham traces a 112-mile route across rugged, heather-clad moorland, linking three remote villages; this journey can easily be accomplished in one day. **Tour 52** (123 miles), centred on Berwick-upon-Tweed, leads S through four picturesque Northumberland villages, then N along the A1 with diversions to *Craster*, *Bamburgh* and *Holy Island Village*. The inaccessibility of Holy Island around high tide can affect the length of this tour considerably, and it is wise to time your arrival carefully. The tour takes at least one and a half days.

Touring centre

Barnard Castle, Durham

Hotels: **Kings Head, Market Place,** *Tel.* **(0833) 38356❸**
Montalbo, Montalbo Road, *Tel.* **(0833) 37342❷**

ROMALDKIRK, DURHAM |✝|

Grey-stone houses and cottages are scattered around the three well-tended greens of this lovely village in the heart of Teesdale; a village that is cupped in a small valley and sheltered from the surrounding fells and moors. The area is sometimes called the Alpine district of Yorkshire, although boundary changes mean that Romaldkirk is no longer part of Yorkshire and now lies within the fringe of Durham.

Part of the old village stocks can be seen on the green that fronts the 18thC **Rose and Crown**, once a flourishing coaching inn served by the village brewery that catered for five inns. Now only two remain. Near to the inn is the gracious **Church of St Romald**, with a nave and N aisle built *c.*1155, and a 15thC tower. Traces of its Saxon origin can also still be seen.

St Romald was the infant son of a Northumbrian princess, born at Buckingham after his mother had fled there to escape a local war. Legend tells that immediately after his birth the infant exclaimed in a loud voice, 'I am a Christian', and then, 'he made a noble sermon with marvellous good eloquence'. Three days later he died and is now a patron saint of Buckingham.

Pub: **Rose and Crown** |A|R|Bs|Ra| *Tel.* (0833) 50213.

MIDDLETON IN TEESDALE, DURHAM |✝|◆◦|

Known as the capital of Upper Teesdale, Middleton would once have been styled a town rather than the village it is today. In the mid-18thC the Quaker-run London Lead Company arrived here; employers with a deep social conscience who set up solid stone houses and cottages for the miners who lived here and in the surrounding villages. The headquarters of the company was at **Middleton House**, which is now used as a shooting lodge, for mining activities ceased in the early 20thC.

Today Middleton is little more than a village, the houses built in terraces and standing placidly above the wooded valley of the River Tees. Outside the **Church of St Mary**, which was rebuilt in 1876, a cross marks the spot where the stocks once stood. In the churchyard, a 13thC window has been retained, one of few relics from the older church. Within easy reach of the village are several of Teesdale's outstanding beauty spots that include the famous **High Force** with its spectacular 70ft fall of water, **Gibsons Cave** and **Waterfall**, **Wynch**

Bridge, Low Force and **Cauldron Snout**.

Teesdale has been acclaimed in the poetry of Sir Walter Scott and William Wordsworth, but Teesdale's own poet is Richard Watson (1833–91). Watson was born in Middleton, started work in the lead mines at the tender age of ten and now lies in the village churchyard. This lesser known poet, many of whose verses can be found in the village bookshop, sums up the beauty of the country he knew so well with the lines:

> *Let minstrels sing till they are hoarse,*
> *Of Scotia's woods and dells,*
> *And winding streams and mountains steep,*
> *Where bloom sweet heather bells.*
> *Their strains still fail to touch my heart,*
> *My fav'rite ones shall be*
> *Those that remind me of my home,*
> *The Teesdale hills for me.*

Pub: **Teesdale Hotel** |**A**|**R**|**Bs**| *Tel.* (083 34) 264.

STAINDROP, DURHAM |△|†|

Stone houses, many dating from the 17thC and 18thC stand well back from Staindrop's single street which is graced by a very long village green. **St Mary's Church** contains many monuments to the Neville family, original owners of nearby Raby Castle. Among these is an alabaster tomb-chest of 1425, inscribed with the figures of Ralph Neville and his two wives. A church stood on this site as early as the 8thC and traces of the original Saxon work remain. The W tower is Norman and much of the additional structure was completed between the 13thC and 15thC.

Raby Castle stands a mile outside the village on the Bishop Auckland road (A686), and is open to the public on specified occasions. It is a huge medieval stronghold with nine imposing towers each bearing a distinctive name — the highest of the towers (80ft) being known as Clifford Tower. Standing in a superb 270-acre deer park with two lakes, the castle is built around a courtyard and guarded by a moat. A feature is the Neville gateway, an entrance through which carriages once passed in order to allow their passengers to alight at the foot of the castle stairway.

Pub: **Black Swan** |**Bs**|**Ra**|

GAINFORD, DURHAM |†|

This village lies half-way between Darlington and Barnard Castle on the A67. Motorists hurrying along this busy main road are unlikely to note anything of particular architectural interest, perhaps not appreciating that by turning S down the narrow lane from the **Cross Keys Inn** they are due for a reward.

The River Test runs parallel with the main road; and the land between the river and road is where the beauty of Gainford lies. Here is a huge, sloping green, an undulation that once made an ideal strategic area for an enclosed pen where cattle could be herded and protected from invading Scots. This green, appropriately named Low Green, is overlooked by spacious Georgian houses on High Green to the north.

The houses that line the southern edge of Low Green overlook the river, as does the **Church of St Mary**, tucked away to the extreme SW corner of the green. The church, mainly 13thC with late 18thC extensions, lies on the site of a former Saxon stone church. On a lighter note there are records that tell how, on three successive days, the vicar married a Pigg, christened a Lamb, and buried a Hogg.

Returning to High Green and running westwards from the Cross Keys Inn is **High Row**, a curved raised terrace of delightful Georgian houses and cottages, beneath which, on the other side of the row, are well-tended flower and vegetable gardens. High Row culminates at **Gainford Hall**, a huge structure built in 1603 by the vicar and now a farmhouse with gables, mullioned windows and crowned by no less than 11 chimneys.

Pub: **Cross Keys Inn** |**Bs**|

TOUR FIFTY-ONE
Touring centre
Hexham, Northumberland
Hotels: **Beaumont, Beaumont Street,** *Tel.* **(0434) 602331 ❸**
County, Priestpopple, *Tel.* **(0434) 602030 ❷**

ELSDON, NORTHUMBERLAND |✝|

Set amid rugged moorland in the heart of the Northumberland National Park, Elsdon has a spacious, sloping village green that once served as a pen where cattle were herded to protect them from border raids. Nearby flows Elsdon Burn where mounds are all that remain of a Norman castle. The mainly 14thC **St Cuthbert's Church** stands beside the green, and during its restoration in the 19thC more than 100 skulls were unearthed here; they are believed to be those of the fallen at the Battle of Otterburn in 1388.

An interesting relic of the green is the stone slab that was once part of the bull baiting ring. Flanking the upper part of the green is a battlemented tower, built *c.* 1400, one of the many pele towers needed for defence in this border country.

Two miles to the SE is **Steng Cross**, originally a landmark to guide travellers, and in 1791 the site of the execution of one William Winter, who, with two female pedlars, murdered an old woman for her stock of drapery. There was once a superstition that chips from Winter's gibbet if rubbed on the gums would cure toothache. Today a replica of the gibbet marks the site.

The celebrated historian George Macaulay Trevelyan (1876–1962) pays his tribute to Elsdon, in *English Social History* (1944), by describing it as

> the spiritual capital of the Middle Marches, the yet unviolated shrine of the tradition of the English border.... It lies low in a green hollow, visible from many surrounding heights; and one glance at it from afar recalls the life of innumerable generations... the stone houses scattered round the broad village green mark the civilising progress of the 18th century.

WHALTON, NORTHUMBERLAND |✝|

A spacious village where the bulk of the houses and cottages are of brown stone and lie along a broad, tree-lined street. Many buildings date from the 17thC and 18thC, a group on the N side of the street being raised on a grassy terrace. Among this group is the pleasant inn, the **Beresford Arms**. At one end of the street is the manor house (not open to the public), a combination of four small houses designed by the celebrated architect Sir Edwin Lutyens (1869–1944).

The parish **Church of St Mary** lies off the main street next to the village school. It is mostly 13thC, although parts of the tower date from the 12thC. A notable feature is the Norman dogtooth decoration in the N chapel.

Whalton has the unique distinction of preserving the Bale festival every 4 July. 'Bale' is from an Anglo Saxon word, meaning 'great fire', and the bonfire lit on the village green on Bale night stems from the custom of driving cattle through the fire to rid them of vermin. Today this bonfire ceremony is an occasion when folk-dancing takes place accompanied by the music of Northumbrian pipers.
Pub: **Beresford Arms** |**Bs**|

BLANCHLAND, NORTHUMBERLAND |△|✝|

Tucked away in the midst of heather-clad moors which stretch for miles in every direction, Blanchland lies in a wooded glen of the River Derwent — a picturesque oasis in the wild surrounding countryside, and considered by many to be Northumberland's loveliest village.

Grey-stone buildings fringe the little square that was once the outer court of Blanchland Abbey, founded in 1165 and subsequently burned down by the Scots. The only substantial remains of the vandalized abbey are the gatehouse that marks the northern entrance to the village and the abbey church, which was restored in the 19thC.

Most of Blanchland's houses were built some 200yrs ago out of the estate of Lord Crewe, a former Bishop of Durham, for the miners who then worked on the moors. The **Lord Crewe Arms** stands on the site of what was originally the abbey guesthouse, retaining some of the walls of that building with a cellar bar said to have once been the crypt. Before this building became a hotel it was the home of the Forster family, Jacobite sympathisers at the time of the Rebellion who forfeited the property in 1715. The priest's hole, a hiding place used by them, can still be seen in the hotel and some of the scenes of Walter Besant's historical novel, *Dorothy Forster*, are set here.
Pub: **Lord Crewe Arms** |**A**|**R**|**Bs**| *Tel.* (043 475) 251.

Touring centre
Berwick upon Tweed, Northumberland

Hotels: **Kings Arms**, Hide Hill, *Tel.* (0289) 7454❸
Queens Head, Sandgate, *Tel.* (0289) 7852❶

NORHAM, NORTHUMBERLAND |△|✝|◆◆|

Day set on Norham's castle steep
And Tweed's fair river, broad and deep
And Cheviot's mountain lone:
The battled towers, the donjon keep
The loop-holed walls where captives weep
In yellow lustre shone.

The immense rose-coloured ruins of **Norham Castle** stand proudly above the River Tweed, immortalized in the words of Sir Walter Scott's epic poem, 'Marmion', in a setting very much as he described it.

This border stronghold was first built as a wooden structure in the early 12thC, a flimsy object to confront the invading Scots who found little difficulty in capturing it. In 1160, however, Bishop Pudsy of Durham rebuilt the castle with its massive walls, gateway and keep, and today the impressive ruins stand among spacious lawns, and are encircled by beech trees.

The castle dominates the village of stone houses that cluster around a number of greens; among them a triangular green graced by a market cross with a 13thC base surmounted by a weathervane in the form of a fish, a symbol of the importance of fishing here in the River Tweed.

The **Church of St Cuthbert** was built at the same time as the castle. In 1320, some 160yrs after the church's construction, it was occupied by Robert Bruce who fortified it when he laid siege to Norham Castle. On the S wall of the church is a model of a coble (a flat-bottomed fishing boat) complete with fishing nets and inscribed

'God Bless the Tweed Fisheries' — yet another reminder that fishing plays an important part in the life of this historic village.

Pubs: **Masons Arms** |**A**|**Bs**|**Ra**| *Tel.* (0377) 86644.

    Victoria |**A**|**Bs**|**Ra**| *Tel.* (0289) 82237.

ETAL, NORTHUMBERLAND |△|✝|

This picturesque estate village lies on either side of a single road that runs above and parallel with an entrancing section of the River Till. At one end of the street is the 18thC **manor house**; at the other are the ruins of Etal Castle. Within the grounds of the manor house (not open to the public) is **St Mary's Church**, built in 1858, and presented by Lady Augusta Fitzclarence in memory of her husband, Lord Frederick Fitzclarence, one of the ten children of William IV and Mrs Jordan, whose monument can be seen in the church.

    Etal Castle, one of several local strongholds against the Scots,

Norham's 19thC market cross on a 13thC base, the main feature of the triangular green. The weathervane on top of the cross in the shape of a fish emphasizes the significance of the local fishing industry.

217

eventually fell to James IV of Scotland in 1496, 17yrs before his defeat by the English at Flodden. The tall four-storied keep still stands, as does the gatehouse with the coat of arms of the original owners, the Manners family, above the entrance.

These impressive ruins stand on a mound from where there is a spectacular view of a salmon leap on the river. The village houses that link the castle and manor are graced by lawns, well-tended flower gardens and trim hedges. Thatched buildings are not often found in Northumberland, so it is of interest that among the handful of houses that make up the village several are thatched, among them the attractive white washed **Black Bull Inn**.

Pub: Black Bull Inn |**Bs**|**Ra**|

FORD, NORTHUMBERLAND |★|†|

This model village was built by Louisa, Marchioness of Waterford, as a memorial to her husband who died after a riding accident in 1859. The village street is broad and lined with gracious stone houses fronted by lawns and well-kept gardens. At one end of the street, near an entry to the gardens of **Ford Castle**, is a tall column with the figure of an angel, another memorial to the Marquis of Waterford.

The **Lady Waterford Hall**, once the school and now open to the public, has walls covered with watercolours painted by Lady Waterford over a 22-yr period following her husband's death. The paintings depict Biblical scenes in which the villagers served as models, the artist paying her child sitters sixpence and a 'gilly piece' (bread and jelly).

A glimpse of **Ford Castle** can be seen from the main road above the village. In common with the castles of *Norham* and *Etal*, Ford Castle originally served as a defensive stronghold, all three castles suffered extensive damage by the Scots before their eventual defeat at Flodden in 1513. Ford Castle was restored in the 18thC and 19thC, and is a massive building with four corner towers now in use as an Adult Education Centre and not open to the public. No visit to Ford would be complete without taking in the spectacular view from the lofty churchyard of **St Michael's Church**. From here is a magnificent panorama that includes the distant Cheviot Hills and Flodden Field, scene of the memorable battle. In a field close to the church are the remains of a **pele tower**, once the priest's fortified house.

Pub: White Hart |**A**|**R**|**Bs**|**Ra**| *Tel.* (0249) 782213.

CHILLINGHAM, NORTHUMBERLAND |△|†|

The church and a handful of cottages nestle outside the walls of **Chillingham Castle** (not open to the public), ancestral home of the Earl of Tankerville. The principal reason for visiting this remote hamlet is to see the Wild White Cattle of Chillingham, descendants of prehistoric wild oxen, which roam in the 300-acre wooded park of Chillingham Castle.

The herd is maintained by a voluntary organization, the Chillingham Wild Cattle Association, which employs a warden, from whom tickets can be bought for a conducted tour of the park. This tour involves a stiff 10-minute climb up the steep, wooded hillside before crossing fields which lead to the entrance gate of the parkland enclosure. From here the warden identifies the position of the free-roaming herd, leading his party to within a few hundred yards of them. They are rarely dangerous, he explains, but they have been known to stampede with dire consequences to bystanders.

The Eighth Earl of Tankerton, F.Z.S., has written an excellent pamphlet describing the white cattle and their history. It is certain that this existing herd has been at Chillingham for the past 700yrs, probably contained in the 13thC, when a park wall was built. They have crescent-shaped horns and are the only herd of white cattle that breed true to type, never having produced a coloured or even partially coloured calf. The fittest and strongest bull in the herd assumes the mantle of 'King', permitting no other bull to mate with the cows unless successfully defeated in combat.

The statistics of the herd are of interest. In 1692 they numbered 28 and in 1838 had reached their highest total, 80. From that time there was a general decline in numbers until, by the early 1950s they averaged around 15. Since then, however, breeding has increased and in June 1982, the herd of bulls, cows and calves totalled 62, a similar figure to that recorded in 1875.

The herd graze through the idyllic surroundings of this lovely park, sheltering in copses when the weather is bad and overlooked to the NE by a steep conical hill known as **Ros Castle** (owned by the National Trust), the site of an Iron Age Fort. From this point there are superb views across the Cheviots into Scotland and of the castles that line the Northumbrian coast.

Before leaving Chillingham it is worth looking in on the little **Church of St Peter** if only to see the splendid tomb of Sir Ralph Grey (*died* 1443), engraved on all sides with a great variety of saintly figures.

CRASTER, NORTHUMBERLAND |△|

Craster must number among the most compact and picturesque villages to be seen along the entire English coastline. Cars can be parked in a spacious area immediately above the village, and the first view of Craster is a line of brown-stone cottages bedecked with climbing plants and fronted by splendid flower gardens. The tiny harbour which next comes into view was built in 1906 by the Craster family, owners of **Craster Tower** over the past 700yrs, in memory of a relative who died in Tibet.

Whitewashed terraced cottages face the sea, encircling the harbour. The area between the cottages and the harbour is enriched by pretty sunken flower gardens. A small fishing fleet still operates from Craster.

From the harbour walls there is a good view of the ruins of **Dunstanburgh Castle**, built in the early 14thC and the largest of all Northumbrian castle ruins. It can be reached by a coastal footpath of about 1 mile.

Close to the harbour, on the shore's edge, is the attractive **Jolly Fisherman Inn**. Opposite the inn are the kippering sheds where the famous Craster kippers are produced.

Pub: **Jolly Fisherman Inn** |**Bs**|

BAMBURGH, NORTHUMBERLAND |❖|△|★ |✝|

This unspoilt coastal resort, made up largely of grey-stone cottages and shops, is dominated by its imposing **castle**, an enormous structure of red sandstone that stretches for almost a quarter of a mile along cliffs that tower above the village and the shore 150ft below. The first **Bamburgh Castle**, a wooden structure, was built by King Ida in AD547. It was rebuilt and enlarged to its present size in Norman times, was restored in the 18thC, and then underwent more extensive restoration by the first Lord Armstrong who bought it in 1894. The castle is open to the public. The only significant remains of the

Norman building are the massive keep, with walls some 10ft thick in places, and a well sunk from the basement through 150ft of solid rock. Among other notable features of the castle are the stone-roofed armoury that contains a great variety of weapons; and the King's Hall with fine displays of carved teak brought by Lord Armstrong from Siam.

The street beneath the castle, lined with mainly 19thC houses, leads to the tree-shaded triangular village green where pleasant hotels, shops and houses are grouped, unmarred by amusement arcades and the type of cafe so often prevalent even in smaller resorts.

Bamburgh is crowded with memories of its heroine Grace Darling, who together with her father battled through the stormy sea off this coast in 1838 to rescue survivors from a stricken steamer, 'The Forfarshire'. Grace was born here in 1826 and a plaque on an antique shop in the main street tells that this was the house where she died when only 27. Her canopied monument above the family tomb stands to the N of the churchyard. Close to the church is the **Grace Darling Museum** where, among many relics associated with the Darling family, are paintings, verbal tributes, and the boat, 21ft long and 6ft wide, used in the famous rescue.

Pubs: **Victoria Hotel** |**A**|**R**|**Bs**| *Tel.* **(066 84) 236.**

    Castle Hotel |**A**|**R**|**Bs**| *Tel.* **(066 84) 351.**

HOLY ISLAND VILLAGE, NORTHUMBERLAND |❖|△|★|†|

The island, famed as the birthplace of English Christianity, and before the 11thC known an Lindisfarne, lies a few hundred yards off the Northumbrian coast and can now be reached by a metalled causeway across the sand dunes. At high tide this causeway becomes submerged, and before crossing, motorists are advised to heed the tidal warning posted at either end of the causeway.

The island, 1½ miles from N to S and 1 mile from E to W covers some 1,350 acres. The population, roughly 200, depends on inshore fishing, farming and the tourist trade. In AD635 St Aidan made his pilgrimage across the sand dunes to this remote sanctuary, bidden by King Oswald from Iona to teach Christianity to the Angles of Northumbria. St Aidan was followed by St Cuthbert, but in 875 a Danish invasion virtually destroyed all traces of this early Christian period, although, happily, the Lindisfarne Gospels survived and are now kept in the British Museum.

Today the greater part of Holy Island Village is composed of closely grouped houses and cottages — many of the older buildings constructed of rough-cut Northumbrian stone — with a pleasant village green and market cross. Near to the centre of the village are the magnificent red and grey sandstone ruins of the Benedictine **priory** that rose like a phoenix in 1093 on the site of several earlier structures. Close to the priory ruins are the **Priory Museum** and the parish **Church of St Mary**, which was begun in 1140, and has a carpet that is a replica of a page from the Lindisfarne Gospels.

To the SE of the island, perched 100ft above the sea on a conical rock, is a fort built in 1550 as a bulwark against invading Scots. **Lindisfarne Castle**, as it is called, was converted in 1902 into a private house by the celebrated architect, Sir Edwin Lutyens. In 1944 it was given to the National Trust and the comfortable rooms, furnished with Flemish and English 17thC oak are open to the public. More than 250 species of wild birds have been observed on or around Holy Island, among them the eider duck, locally called St Cuthbert.

Pubs: **Castle View Hotel** |**A**|**R**|**Bs**| *Tel.* **(0289) 89272.**

    Crown and Anchor |**Bs**|**Ra**|

INDEX

Picture credits
Photobank pp. 19, 32–3; S & O Matthews
pp. 20, 45, 70–1, 85; Tony Stone Associates
Ltd p. 25; Trevor Wood Picture Library
pp. 38–9, 103, 122–3, 136; J. Allan Cash
pp. 50, 57, 98–9, 178, 188; A. F.
Kersting p. 79; Derek Widdicombe p. 200;
Brian Shuel pp. 128–9, 145, 152; Colin
Molyneux pp. 170–1.